D0205989

THE GROWTH OF AMERICAN GOVERNMENT

INTERDISCIPLINARY STUDIES IN HISTORY
Harvey J. Graff, editor

THE
GROWTH OF
AMERICAN
GOVERNMENT

Governance from the Cleveland Era to the Present

BALLARD C. CAMPBELL

Revised and Updated Edition

INDIANA UNIVERSITY PRESS

Bloomington & Indianapolis

This book is a publication of

Indiana University Press
Office of Scholarly Publishing
Herman B Wells Library 350
1320 E. 10th St.
Bloomington, IN 47405 USA

iupress.indiana.edu

Telephone   800-842-6796
Fax   812-855-7931

Library of Congress Cataloging-in-Publication Data

Campbell, Ballard C.
    The growth of American government : governance from the Cleveland era to the present / Ballard C Campbell. — Revised and Updated Edition
        pages cm
ISBN 978-0-253-01418-4 (paperback) — ISBN 978-0-253-01427-6 (ebook) 1. United States—Politics and government—1885–1889. 2. United States—Politics and government—1889–1893. 3. United States—Politics and government—1893–1897. 4. United States—Politics and government—1897–1901. 5. United States—Politics and government—20th century. I. Title.
    JK421.C23 2014
    320.973—dc23
                                                                    2014011873

1 2 3 4 5 19 18 17 16 15

TO

Allan G. Bogue and John D. Post

TEACHERS,

COLLEAGUES,

FRIENDS

CONTENTS

FIGURES

TABLES

PREFACE

This updated edition of *The Growth of American Government* has two principal objectives. The first is to review the course of governance over recent decades, picking up the story from where the initial version of the book ended. My orienting question during this survey was: has the scope and power of government grown? Answering this query requires the inspection of evidence on several dimensions of governance, particularly legislative actions concerning public functions, public finance, administrative capacity, and legal rulings. This objective continues the primary mission of the first edition, which has undergone some rewriting and updating. The new chapter on "The Debate Over 'Big' Government" examines key elements of governance over recent decades, but especially since 1992, covering the presidential administrations of Bill Clinton, George W. Bush, and Barack Obama.

The second objective is to address an omission in the first edition. With some exceptions, principally the Great Debate during the transition era (1880s–1920s) and my review of the Reagan years, I had said little about the argument over expansion of government. My original purpose of the book was to trace the course of the governing process over a hundred years, focusing on the accumulation of functions, the evolution of administrative capacity, the restructuring of public finance, and shifts in civic ideology. Although the expansion of government elicited ongoing criticism, I had not emphasized the point. The updated edition gives more attention to this side of the story. Chapter 11 identifies critics of "big" government, reviews their complaints, and suggests reasons for the remarkable resurgence of the Republican Party. As with the first edition, my goal is describe and explain these developments, without taking sides in political disputes. *The Growth of American Government* is a history book, not an editorial polemic.

Although not an objective per se, a third consideration has influenced my approach to the updated edition. I have kept the concept of *state building* more firmly in mind than I did for the first edition. The term originated with political scientists. Few historians explicitly used "state building" as a theoretic construct when I began outlining this book twenty-five years ago. Now the concept has penetrated historical studies. A more explicit concern with the state as a semiautonomous entity facilitates my synthesis of the debate over government during the past quarter century, for the power and the reach of government (some would say "intrusiveness") is a central irritant to conservatives, and certainly a concern to many liberals. While I do not explicitly address the literature of state building in this book, works in this genre have influenced my thinking about contemporary governance, as well as my research on the American state during the long nineteenth century.

On the other hand, I have not changed my position concerning historical explanations of the growth of government. Some reviewers of the first edition called for a more explicit theoretical model that accounts for state expansion. All I can say is that I see things differently. My study of state building suggests that a historically contingent path works best as an explanatory orientation. From this perspective determinants of outcomes varied with time, subject, and circumstance. I have tried to demonstrate these historically contingent interactions in chapters 3 through 8 on the late nineteenth and early twentieth centuries (the "transitional" polity), New Deal, economic controls, income security, rights and nondiscrimination policy, and taxation. Chapter 2 offers a longer essay on the generic features of these processes. If there is a single magic bullet that accounts for the evolution of American governance I have not found it. But there were several reoccurring motifs.

When I considered writing an updated chapter I thought I had a pretty good idea about what had happened in recent American politics based on years of observing and teaching about it. But once I began the new edition I realized my need to dig deeper into the literature. I can't say that I have fully mastered this large body of writing, but I have sampled much of it. Fortunately, my determination to keep this book short allowed me to skip most extraneous details and focus on the larger contours of recent governance. Here, as before, my goal is to sketch patterns and synthesize trends, not to compile a compendium of political details. The works in the bibliography recommend references for further study. Besides making suggestions for exploration of governmental history, the footnotes and the bibliography acknowledge my debt to other scholars. The first order of business for the historian, indeed for all social scientists, is to get the facts straight. This is no easy task. I am grateful for the work of many able scholars whose concepts of analysis and synthesis of evidence has made my job easier. The bibliography in the original edition and its short supplement, and that for chapter 11, represents my cherry-picking from this rich field of scholarship. Largely because of indexing and definitional changes in data sources, I have placed recent financial information in chapter 11 rather than revise the tables in the original edition.

Observers have lamented in recent decades that political history has fallen out of favor with historians. This is unfortunate and unwarranted. In my opinion the history of public life gets to the heart of the United States of America.

Many thanks to Charles W. Calhoun, Eugenie B. Campbell, Richard J. Jensen, Anthony N. Penna, Michael C. Tolley, Philip R. VanderMeer, and John Wilson for their helpful suggestions on chapter 11.

Ballard C. Campbell
Portland, Maine
September 2013

ACKNOWLEDGMENTS

I take great pleasure in thanking my family, friends, and associates for their help with this book. Clay McShane, Marge Murphy, John Post, and Michael Tolley read portions of the manuscript and offered me sound advice about it. My parents, Ruth B. Mathias and Ballard C. Campbell Sr., put their understanding of contemporary government at my disposal. Like a good son, I took the suggestions I liked and ignored the rest. Samuel McSeveney applied his vast knowledge of the American political system and his sharp editorial eye to the entire manuscript. Epitomizing how historians excel in their insistence on clear writing and factual accuracy, Sam left his mark on every chapter of the book. Ken Goodall tidied up numerous loose ends in the writing with a deft editorial pencil. Bob Sloan of Indiana University Press was a source of many helpful ideas. Harvey Graff kept faith in the project during its long gestation period and suggested ways of improving the finished product.

I was blessed to have four dedicated graduate assistants help me with the research and writing. My thanks to Carl Hoar, Perry Tapper, Nathan Martin, and Brian Carr. Ray Robinson, formerly chair of the Department of History at Northeastern University, lightened my teaching responsibilities, as did Suzann Thomas-Buckle and Leonard Buckle, codirectors of the Law, Policy, and Society Program, during the years that I worked on the volume. I am grateful to the American Council of Learned Societies for an award that permitted time off from teaching for research, and to the American Philosophical Society and the Research Fund of Northeastern University for defraying research costs. A history that reviews more than a century of governance at several levels of the federal system naturally makes one a heavy library user. I am happy to have the opportunity to thank the many librarians who helped me on the project, and especially the staffs at Northeastern University Library and Arlington Public Library. My wife, Genie Benoit Campbell, was a constant source of support as I worked on the manuscript.

Writing a book that is based upon research in documentary sources, scholarship from several different disciplines, and arrays of numeric information prompted me to reflect on my intellectual roots. This introspection led naturally to two individuals who helped to shape my thinking as a historian. Allan G. Bogue introduced me to the logic of systematic empiricism and the importance of literary clarity. Both goals strike me as sensible now as when I first encountered them many years ago. John D. Post urged me to evaluate hypotheses in light of cross-national and interdisciplinary criteria, two references that form a powerful methodological blend. In addition to these explicit lessons, their scholarship has served as a model for me. I feel lucky to count such fine teachers as good friends.

THE GROWTH OF AMERICAN GOVERNMENT

Introduction

GOVERNMENT IN THE UNITED STATES underwent a major transformation in the years after 1887. Before the 1880s government performed a limited range of functions and rarely intruded into everyday life. In our own time the public sector manages an immense array of programs that affect all aspects of society. The manifestations of this new civic agenda are so common that we take them for granted. We expect roads to be paved, plowed, and policed. We are annoyed when potholes sit unfilled. We take as a matter of course that our children can go to high school without charge, that someone will automatically collect our garbage, and that the water flowing from our faucets is pure and clean. We expect government to help people who fall on hard times and to prevent the elderly from living in destitution. Announcement of a new disease triggers our presumption that public health officials have already begun their search for a cure.

Americans before 1887 might have dreamed of such assistance, but they did not expect it. They lived in a different political time, when public officials attended to comparatively few civic tasks. Government did not guarantee the security of their bank deposits or ban hazardous substances from their workplaces. It did not say that denial of a job because an applicant was black or female was illegal. It did not even print a uniform dollar bill. Life was riskier before the expansion of the modern state. In prior generations individuals were forced to rely more on themselves and private organizations than is now the case. Today we are shielded from many of life's uncertainties because government has applied collective solutions to common problems. The majority of

Americans appeared to have agreed that most of these interventions were jus-
tifiable responses to contemporary problems. Yet they tend to remain ideological adverse to the expansion of government and to complain about its cost.

This book is about these changes in government. There are several things to
learn from such a study. Examining the circumstances that transformed public
life helps us to understand our society as well as our government. Actions in
the public sector reflect more than is usually conveyed in the word "politics."
Public life is a window to our culture because civic affairs are a focal point of
the traditions and aspirations of a people and their patterns of behavior. Sooner
or later their hopes and fears get played out in the political process. Politicians
respond to these concerns in various ways, and their decisions affect social and
economic life. Public policy is both the product of society's social and political
makeup and an influence on its subsequent evolution.

Government did not take on its modern form overnight, but it has added
new functions incrementally starting in the latter half of the nineteenth century. The growth of government represents the accumulation of decisions made
at numerous points in the American past. The story of this transformation is,
therefore, an exercise in history. I have viewed this evolution from the perspective of a wide-angle lens, which allowed my gaze to pan the entire political system over a long sweep of time. The desire to understand broad, system-
wide changes recommends this macroscopic approach. American government
is composed of numerous parts, and its actions concern many kinds of issues.
The farther the observer stands back from these developments, the easier it is
to discern patterns in the mass of political detail. The underlying rationale for
a panoramic orientation to history rests on the quest to identify underlying
currents within the sea of human activity.

A long-run view of American history suggests the existence of four broad
stages of civic activity from the 1780s to the twenty-first century (see table 0.1).
These political eras, each of which I have called a distinctive polity (a governing
arrangement and the society it served), provide conceptual reference points for
the review of policy development in this book. Although commonalities existed between adjacent polities, each of these four political periods possessed
a characteristic style of governance.

The republican polity refers to civic patterns prevalent from the American
Revolution through the 1870s. During its reign, governmental institutions
remained small and extremely decentralized; the objectives of government
underwent minimal expansion. Non-career politicians dominated most as-

Table o.1. Stages of American Civic Expansion

	Republican Polity	Transitional Polity	Claimant Polity	Restrained Polity
Era	1780–1870s	1880s–1920s	1930s–1970s	mid-1970s–
Suberas	Civil War 1860s	Progressive 1900–1916	New Deal 1930s Great Society 1960s	Reagan admin. 1981–1989 Gingrich 1990s
Policy innovation	Limited Civil War policies	Regulations Services	Economic & global stabilization Social standards	Privatization Deregulation Rights expansion
Fiscal pattern	Low costs Indirect taxation	Increasing costs Higher property & new taxes	High costs Direct taxes	Stable costs Tax cuts Large deficits
National-state relations	Noncentralized Dual federalism	Emergent cooperation & centralization	From cooperative to national regulations	Limits on mandates on states
Economy	Preindustrial Emergent Industrialization	Industrializing	Mature industrial Rising affluence	Slower growth Postindustrial Recessions
National politics	Modern parties Part-time government	High voter turnout Partisan, declined after 1896	Administrative state Presidential leadership	Highly partisan Gridlock Antistatist critique

pects of government, which relied on patronage appointments more than professional administrators. Government placed comparatively small demands on the public purse. But above all, apprehension of political power gave the republican polity its distinctive signature. Allegiance to this principle was reiterated time and again in public pronouncements and was embedded in constitutional limitations on authority.

Because Americans of the republican period believed that governmental power threatened their liberty, they stressed the moral imperatives of limiting the prerogatives of public officials. Nonetheless, government during this formative era was not powerless. It did maintain order, distribute economic resources, and regulate some social and commercial matters.[1] Local governments saw for care of indigent citizens. The national government built a huge territorial state by 1848 that stretched from coast to coast. During the Civil War the federal government adopted several important economic policies and mobilized a large military force to crush the southern challenge to national unity. But this burst of innovation during the 1860s is notable because it was exceptional. Washington did not sustain this pace of growth during the next several decades.

Departures from the classical ways of governing are clearly discernible in the Gilded Age, which marks the dawning of the transitional polity. By the middle of the 1880s state governments had formulated laws concerning public health, education, cultural mores, private enterprise (including railroads), and the conditions of workers in the factories and mines. The Interstate Commerce Act, the national government's first regulation of an industrial business, and the Agricultural Experiment Station Act, the first continuous federal financial contribution to a state-run program, were enacted in 1887, symbolizing the birth of a new policy regime in Washington. These early signs of change blossomed during the Progressive Era, when an array of economic, social, and political regulations was adopted, new public services were offered, and the management of national resources expanded. Officials spent greater sums of money than formerly, improved the administrative abilities of government, and began to manage programs cooperatively between the states and Washington. In addition to Theodore Roosevelt's innovative use of the presidency, executives at every level displayed new levels of policy leadership. During these years a great debate raged about the role of the public sector. The positions articulated in this dialogue laid the philosophic cornerstones of modern political liberalism and conservatism. Measured by its ideas and actions, the transitional polity embodied the first significant stage in the growth of American government.

As a general rule, power was used sparingly during the republican polity. This hesitancy waned during the transitional polity, which bridged the period between early American politics and the claimant polity. A permissiveness toward the use of public power defines the heart and soul of the claimant polity, which assumed coherent form during the New Deal in the 1930s and matured in the middle decades of the twentieth century. Whereas members of the republican polity warned about government's inherent capacity for harm, the mentality of the claimant era saw power as a practical tool to remedy problems in society and reduce personal risk. Constituents of this new regime expected public officials to ameliorate ills at home and stem threats from abroad. Most citizens were only secondarily concerned about the consequences of endowing the civic sector with the power necessary to satisfy their practical goals. In responding to a growing list of "needs," policy makers expanded the functions of government during the New Deal, World War II, early Cold War, and Great Society years. Public costs rose dramatically, funded by taxes levied directly on individual and corporate income. This transformation increasingly centralized power in the presidency and in the nation's capital, where professional politicians and administrators, many of whom were ambivalent about the moral rationale that once dictated scrupulous adherence to constitutional limitations, managed national affairs. Power was no longer feared. It had been refashioned into an instrument to shield people from risk and insecurity.

The new uses of power generated a groundswell of resentment about big government after the mid-1970s. In subsequent years a new regime emerged, which I have labeled the "restrained polity." Its defining attributes are resistance to the expansion of government, the reduction of economic regulations, and opposition to spending and tax increases. Tax cuts early in Ronald Reagan's presidency added fuel to a debate over public spending and budget deficits. The politics of the 1980s were instrumental in initiating a campaign against "big" government in the 1990s and afterward. This resurgence of antistatism and the partisan gridlock it fostered blocked most proposals to create new public programs and advanced portions of its cultural agenda. But the conservative movement failed to repeal much of the civic functions that had become commonplace in the claimant polity.

This book represents my interpretation of the history of government since the 1880s. The conceptual footing for this narrative rests on several elementary ideas about the nature of government. First among these orienting references is the fundamental relevance of political power to the conduct of public affairs. Inherent in every government, power is the capacity of individuals to make decisions that affect people and society. Holders of political power frequently are officials of government. The rules they adopt customarily have some authorizing foundation, such as exists in constitutions in the United States. But political power is also wielded by people who are not formally part of government, as in the case of voters and influential pressure groups. Political power is an elastic and allusive idea that defies neat definition. It has, political scientist Robert Dahl writes, "many faces."[2] But surely power exists. It is what we mean when we say that some people have the ability to shape how others live and act. In essence, the growth of American government is about the expansion of political power.

The goal of tracking the history of political power naturally leads to public policy, which refers to the ways that authority and influence were used. Policy encompasses all the choices that power holders make. The act of a legislature constitutes policy; so do the rulings of courts and the decisions of administrators. Specific instances of rulemaking by a legislature produce programs. The adoption of the Social Security Act in 1935 is a case in point. This statute established mechanisms designed to achieve several goals, such as the reduction of poverty among retired workers and dependent children. The welfare and retirement benefit programs in the Social Security Act extended direct income assistance to individuals. Other laws offered similar kinds of help. Clustering programs of related purpose into larger categories of policy creates general civic objectives called "functions" in this book.[3] Programs that provide direct subsistence benefits to individuals, for example, collectively represent an income assistance function, which is the subject of chapter 6. Other chapters examine the regulation of commercial activities and social behavior, economic stabilization, taxation and fiscal policy, defense policy, and the protection of civil rights. Chapter 11 focuses on the battle between conservatives and liberals over the role and size of government that raged in the 1990s and later.

Sometimes policies fell short of fulfilling their goals. Occasionally they failed altogether. Critics who point out these imperfections do not necessarily object to the broad aim of a policy but find fault with its design and implementation. Policy evaluation is the art of assessing the success of a program in fulfilling its objective. The analysis of the growth of government requires attention to this issue because the way a policy is designed bears upon its political acceptance and its impact. In an ideal world one would formulate policy according to rational criteria whereby efficiency and fairness are equally maximized. In reality, public policy is made in a political world where different interests battle for control. Signs that competitive struggles affected the policymaking process often are detectable in the form and composition of a program. The passage of a law represents an intermediate stage, not the end, in the process of program formation. Because administrators have discretion in managing their program, the way in which they implemented a policy can have as great a bearing on its effect as the provisions of the program's authorizing legislation. The expansion and performance of bureaucracy, consequently, figures in the growth of government.

Every policy affects society in some manner, but sometimes particular outcomes were not anticipated, or at least the result was not emphasized among the program's publicly announced objectives. A classic case in point was Lyndon

Johnson's War on Poverty, which helped to expand the welfare rolls rather than reduce them, as planners had sought. These unintended consequences occur because people cannot accurately predict the future and because of the complex circumstances that gave birth to most programs; yet, unintended consequences of political decisions play a major role in American political history.[4] A long-run perspective aids in visualizing how numerous separate policy decisions added up to an unplanned revision of the governing system.

Policy makers act within a set of constraints known as "structure," which comprises formal and informal rules that specify how the game of politics should be played. Informal instructions are contained in political ideology, which embodies the accepted principles of a civic culture. A reflection of deep-seated and predisposed values, ideology is resistant to rapid change.[5] "Public opinion," by comparison, refers to attitudes about specific issues that sometimes evoke passionate disagreement; it can rise and fall rapidly on the horizon of politics. Americans are famous for embedding their ideological axioms in constitutions, which are written statements of a polity's fundamental law. These documents created units of government, assigned them power to act, and outlined rules to guide officials in exercising authority. Legislative, judicial, and executive action take place within the constitutional structure of American government. Although scholars frequently cite the impact of public opinion and ideology on policy, there is less acknowledgment of the effect of legal structure on the evolution of American governance.

The existence of many governments—state and local governments as well as the one headquartered in Washington, D.C.—constitutes one of the most important structural features of American politics. One implication of this federal arrangement of governance is that the states and local government have always played a major role in the conduct of public affairs in America. The initial expansion of civic functions in the United States occurred largely at the subnational (that is, state and local) level of policy making. Thereafter the states and localities served as the workhorses of the polity in the delivery of public services. Preoccupation with affairs in Washington misrepresents the nation's governmental tradition. Exclusive concentration on the national level leads to an underreporting of the volume and character of civic activity and obscures much of the dynamism in the political system. A comprehensive history of American government must integrate all parts of the polity into the story.

Power, policy, and structure serve as conceptual benchmarks for the examination of governance in this book. "Governance" refers to the patterns of civic life formed from the interplay of structure and the process of politics. "Process" refers to the actions through which people seek to exercise power. The election of individuals to governmental posts is a part of process. So are lobbying tactics of pressure groups, the ways candidates appeal to the predispositions of voters, and the strategies used to form coalitions in legislatures. Policy designates the substance of civic decisions. Structure comprises the ideological and legal standards that limit the range of policy options available to decision makers. Process concerns the sequence of events and interactions that produces policy.

Thinking about politics as a process of unfolding events that are conditioned by the past and that interact with the culture of a society helps us to envision the dynamics in the history of government. The notion of a continuous flow and interplay of behavior in the political arena implies that diverse influences shaped public decisions. Elections and political parties constitute an important set of these determinants but are not the only ones. Because the popular side of American democracy has its own voluminous literature, I have de-emphasized this aspect of the story. When elections and parties had a marked impact on policy making, their role is acknowledged. This history shows that major shifts in partisan control of government have overlapped with significant changes in governance.

1

~

Governing the Cleveland Era

AMERICANS FACED A PERIL, Grover Cleveland warned in his annual message of 1887. This danger, the president continued, threatened widespread disaster and a "brood of evil consequences." Phrased in such foreboding terms, the peril must have seemed formidable. The modern mind envisions horrors on the scale of a 9/11 attack or the unchecked spread of a virulent flu. But those were not the kind of hazards that Cleveland saw. His menace was surplus revenue, and the source of the problem was a tariff, which the president repudiated as a "vicious, inequitable, and illogical source of unnecessary taxation."[1]

Viewed from our own time, Cleveland's alarm seems quaint and a bit puzzling. Chronic deficits have been government's normal way of operating since the 1930s. Modern critics complain about excessive spending and mounting debt. Cleveland fretted about government having a surplus of cash. He recognized that government had to collect some revenue, for no public regime can survive without a reliable income. Benjamin Franklin captured the essence of this truism long ago in his observation that "nothing is certain but death and taxes."

Cleveland may have overdramatized government's affluence, but he wasn't an impulsive alarmist. His reputation rests solidly on his caution and integrity. These qualities appealed to Democratic politicians, who nominated him for president on three successive occasions, and to voters, who elected him to the White House in 1884 and 1892. Assumptions about government in those years contrasted markedly with attitudes prevalent in our time. Examination of these older ideas helps to make sense of Cleveland's apprehension of surplus revenue. A good place to begin is with the president's own analysis.

The abundance of dollars in the Treasury, Cleveland argued in his 1887 annual message, tempted "unnecessary and extravagant appropriations" and stimulated "a habit of reckless improvidence not in the least consistent with the mission of . . . our Government." To this the president added a more specific objection. The surplus subtracted from private flows of funds in the "channels of trade." Turning the Treasury into a "hoarding place" also increased pressures to deposit public funds in commercial banks. Both uses of money were bad because they promoted "too extensive a commingling" of private and public interests. "The functions of our National Treasury," Cleveland explained, "should be few and simple."

The president also disliked the method by which the tariff raised public funds. Tariffs were taxes on goods imported from other countries. These levies applied to some four thousand different items at the time that Cleveland denounced tariff policy as a "perversion of governmental powers." According to the president, these duties overcharged consumers for the "necessaries of life" under the guise of protecting American producers from foreign competition. Cleveland did not oppose private enterprise or even tariffs per se. He objected to using the tariff to favor special interests. The tariff, he explained, tempted local and selfish groups to devise schemes of "public plunder that were . . . reckless of the welfare of the entire country" and rewarded them with immense profit. The charge that uses of public power bestowed special favoritism was not new in 1887. The criticism was a staple of America's traditional political philosophy.

Cleveland ended his annual message, unique in its exclusive focus on a single issue, with a plea to Congress for lower tariff rates. If they put patriotic duty before partisanship, lawmakers could reform the tariff, he predicted. Congress did not sidestep the subject. The House of Representatives heard 151 speeches strung over fifty-one days on the Mills bill, which contained the Democrats' version of tariff reform. Leading Republicans, including future president William McKinley, took turns ridiculing the president's "free trade" position. Protective tariffs, they trumpeted, created national wealth, raised American wages, transformed potential foreign profits into Treasury receipts, and thus promoted the glory of the nation.[2] Yet in the end the debate may not have changed a single vote. Democrats marshaled all but two of their slender majority in the House to pass the Mills bill over united Republican opposition.

Returning to work after the 1888 election, senators took up the tariff issue with as much partisan ardor as their colleagues in the House had exhibited. The clerk called the roll of senators 112 times for recorded votes on tariff questions, most of which were amendments on specific items, ranging from duties on brooms, bricks, and bibles to taxes on macaroni, matches, and marble. Repeatedly, Republicans united against a solid phalanx of Democrats. Even the motion to put Bibles on the "free" list engendered a straight party-line vote. Eventually, Senate Republicans enacted their own bill, which the House ignored as the 50th Congress closed. The president had suffered a double defeat, both by razor-thin margins. He failed to win tariff reform and he saw the presidency slip away to a Republican. His successor, Benjamin Harrison (1889–1893), went on to approve record-high tariff duties.

A thousand miles west of Washington, where cows and corn dominated the Midwestern landscape, another political storm brewed. There, Republicans had thrown down a challenge: "Iowa has no compromise with the saloon," they stated flatly in their 1887 state platform. The Grand Old Party had labored through the 1880s to rid the Hawkeye state of Demon Rum, yet increasingly stiffer prohibition (antiliquor) laws had failed to board up the saloons. Many Iowans continued to visit illicit holes-in-the wall for a glass of beer or harder spirits. Enforcement of the state antiliquor rules hinged on local support. Where Germans and Irish abounded and the Democrats had strongholds, county sheriffs winked at violations of the law. Republicans expressed outrage at these transgressions. "True Americans are law-abiding," the Republican governor thundered, implying that Democrats were not. Democrats refused to concede the point. The problem, they retorted, lay with fanatical prohibitionists who sought to impose their own code of values on others and had pressured Republicans into serving as their political front. The American way, Democrats said, was personal liberty and local self-rule.

These charges and countercharges reverberated in the state capitol at Des Moines throughout the 1880s. Prohibition had the state on edge, yet neither political party wavered in its position on the issue. Republicans argued that standards of community decency justified uniform social regulation. In the absence of comprehensive control the saloon would fester as the incubator of anarchy and harlotry. Democrats rejected statewide codes of morality, which they said trampled the principle of local self-determination. Although the sustained intensity of Iowa's struggle over liquor was rarely matched elsewhere, the question divided policy makers in most states during the Cleveland years.[3] And it percolated down to the very foundation of the American political order—the cities, towns, and villages.

Arlington, Massachusetts, was one of these communities. Situated seven miles northwest of Boston, Arlington was a small rural town about to blossom into a bedroom suburb. The catalyst of this metamorphosis was the electric trolley, which first went into commercial operation the year that Cleveland attacked the tariff. Two years later the machine came to Arlington, laying a convenient transportation link to Boston via the intervening city of Cambridge. The trolley unleashed a building boom in Arlington, as developers turned vacant land into affordable homes for buyers and renters. The lure of living in quiet spaciousness within commuting distance of jobs in the city caused the town's population to triple to 15,000 by 1915. The new suburbanites flooded into a community that had taken its stand against the saloon. Massachusetts law allowed localities to decide the fate of alcoholic beverages, and Arlington voted by a two-to-one margin in 1887 to keep the dramshops out of town. Arlingtonians stuck with their decision for over a century.

The tracks that cut through the heart of Arlington traversed unpaved and often muddy streets. Most roads in America of the Cleveland era were in similar or worse condition. As Congress debated the tariff in the spring of 1888, farmers in Wisconsin were leveling ruts left by fall rains, winter ice, and narrow-gauged wagon wheels. Under state law each of Wisconsin's 1,300 towns (the smallest unit of general-purpose government) was divided into road districts under the supervision of a locally elected overseer. Towns levied a road tax on residents, but the law allowed them to satisfy this obligation with a day or so of labor. This latter option was the most popular by far, in Wisconsin as in most of rural America. The working-out system not only allowed farmers to avoid paying road taxes in money, but also afforded an opportunity to catch up on local gossip when neighbors gathered for this spring ritual. It was silly to take this work too seriously, for summer rains and the knifing effects of wagon wheels soon returned the roads to their usual condition.[4]

City streets were in only slightly better shape. American law allowed municipal residents whose property abutted a thoroughfare to petition city hall if they desired street improvements (such as gravel paving). City officials contracted the job to private firms and billed abutters for the work. Many city dwellers preferred to keep their streets in a pristine state. Besides the financial saving, some urbanites opposed paving for social reasons. Improved streets induced heavier traffic, which was a hazard to children and neighbors who used their thoroughfare for play and socializing.[5]

Birmingham, Alabama, had a ready supply of workers to keep its streets clean and in repair. City officials bound jail inmates in chains and set them to labor ten hours a day on the streets. Southern justice provided endless candidates for this "free" labor. The police preyed upon the city's black population and made arrests for petty offenses, such as violation of the city's vagrancy laws. A vagrant, according to the 1891 ordinance, was a person "who habitually walks and rambles upon the streets at unreasonable hours of the night, or who habitually loafs and loiters about disreputable places." If this provision seemed vague, the law contained other criteria that translated into the same offense.[6]

The county sheriff had a personal stake in enforcing justice, Birmingham style. Instead of receiving a salary, sheriffs derived their income from fees for making arrests and fines levied on the guilty. People unable to pay were sentenced to hard labor; convictions for gambling drew a hundred days. The sheriff could lease convicts to coal and iron companies in the county, a practice that the Birmingham police also followed. To keep up with industrialists' steady demand for cheap labor, the sheriff hired deputies by private arrangement. The chief duty of these assistants was to conduct dragnets among the idle class, as the black community was stereotyped. In Birmingham as elsewhere in Dixie, law was an instrument of oppression of the underclasses.

Chain gangs in Birmingham, the rites of road work in Wisconsin, the spat over liquor in Arlington and Iowa, and the wrangling over tariffs in Washington are remnants of America's governmental past. These episodes may seem to lack a common thread, but they were manifested facets of the classical pattern of governance in the United States. The political design laid at the country's founding unfolded around a fundamental idea—that government threatened liberty. Keeping government local and divided was a key to protecting this freedom. Restrictions on uses of civic power was the hallmark of the republican polity.

A republic is a government whose power derives from the consent of the governed. The rationale for locating ultimate political authority in the people arose from the fear of placing all sovereignty in a single ruler, such as a king. Most adherents of republican government believed that vesting power in the hands of self-perpetuating officials inevitably threatened people's most precious possession, their "unalienable rights." The axiom that liberty could not survive in an absolute monarchy was conventional wisdom in America when Thomas Jefferson summarized the principles of republicanism in the Declaration of Independence. To document the point, Jefferson listed twenty-seven instances of tyranny by the king of Great Britain. These charges reflected keystones of republican thinking. The Crown had disallowed colonial laws necessary for the public good. He had withdrawn the right of representation in the legislature. He sent "swarms of officers to harass our people," and he imposed "taxes on us without our consent." The monarch had denied Americans trial by jury. These transgressions, Jefferson concluded, deprived Americans of "life, liberty, and the pursuit of happiness."

Americans of the Revolutionary Era believed that rulers were innately inclined to misuse their authority. This proclivity was rooted in human nature, they said, because self-interest tempted governors to appropriate power for personal purposes at the expense of the general good. Government, not private concentrations of power, was believed to be the prime threat to liberty. American independence from English control did not remove this danger. Liberty was at risk in colonial empires as well as in monarchies because the temptation to pervert power was inherent in human behavior. Yet the survival of freedom also required that the government maintain order. Herein lay the dilemma inherent in republicanism: governmental power was both necessary and dangerous.

One solution to this impasse was cultivation of a virtuous citizenry whose civic responsibility was to monitor closely the official exercise of power. But Jefferson and like-minded statesmen counseled an additional safeguard. Republics had to construct their government in such form as would minimize harm to the public good. Three objectives guided their thinking. First, power holders should be made accountable to citizens, principally through the mechanism of regular elections. Second, political power should be divided among several units of government. And third, these arrangements must be anchored in formally written compacts. The process of composing these fundamental charters began in 1776 when Americans transformed their colonies into state governments by adopting constitutions. After a few years of experimentation these first republican governments assumed features that Americans intuitively recognize as parts of democracy: separate branches that allowed checks and balances between power holders, a legislature of two bodies composed of elected representatives, and specific prohibition on uses of power, such as those contained in bills of rights.

These early state constitutions reflected republican insistence on explicit limitations on political power. This principle produced a second equally momentous decision: to divide power among many governments. This dispersion of authority was manifested in the semiautonomous status of each of the original states. The addition of a strong central government in 1787 carried the idea a step further. The authors of the Constitution of the United States, which established the Federal government, sought to create an independent authority that would temper the purported excesses of the state governments and simultaneously guarantee their existence.[7] The new national constitution, said James Madison, a major architect of its construction, established a governmental system of mixed nature that contained "many coequal sovereignties."[8] From the start, the American plan of politics provided for two official locations of authority: the states and the general government.

In establishing two tiers of government, the Constitution of the United States offered, in Madison's opinion, a double security for the rights of the people.[9] This federal scheme (or "federalism" for short) did not eclipse the authority of the states, but it did limit it through selective prohibitions. The states were integrated into a jurisdictional arrangement that awarded predominant authority over certain subjects to the central government. This dual allocation of power, which recognized the existence of two centers of political authority and divided civic responsibilities among them, became the structural arch of the republican constitutional order.

Leaders paid homage to the link between federalism and liberty throughout the republican era. "The essential principles of our Government," Thomas Jefferson said in his 1801 presidential inaugural address, balanced "the support of the State Governments in all their rights, as the . . . surest bulwarks against anti-republican tendencies" with "the preservation of the General Government in its whole constitutional vigor." Jefferson's successors in the White House, from Madison through Cleveland, reiterated the interdependence of a confederated republic and liberty. President Abraham Lincoln, even as he was poised to break the Southern siege of Fort Sumter at the onset of the Civil War, reaffirmed the rights of the states to control their local institutions, slavery included. The Civil War confirmed the supremacy of the national government in its sphere of activity. But the sectional conflict did not repudiate federalism as the legal cradle of liberty. James Garfield reaffirmed the connection in his presidential inaugural address in 1881. He used the occasion, as had his predecessors, to venerate the foundation of liberty and law that the Founding Fathers had laid. America's dual constitutional system, the new president observed, had secured "the manifold blessings of local self-government." Grover Cleveland repeated the homily with only a slight change in wording at his inaugural four years later.

The respect paid to constitutional federalism was a shorthand expression for a larger set of revered principles. At the center of this ideological matrix was the axiom that government was empowered to act only for the general good. Special-interest favoritism was condemned as subversive of republicanism. The conduct of public business should scrupulously conform to the letter and spirit of constitutional law in order to prevent the perversion of the general welfare. Because of the ever-present temptation to exercise authority for illegitimate purposes, officials were implored to use power judiciously. This warning was redoubled for government's most potent power, the authority to tax.

The protection of private property was central to the republican conception of individual rights. Because taxation permitted official expropriation of wealth, government had the potential to abuse the rights of property and thus deny a fundamental liberty. The way to minimize misuses of taxation was to keep government's costs low. For this reason presidents from Jefferson through Cleveland pledged economical government. Benjamin Harrison coupled this fiscal principle to the republican condemnation of special-interest government. "Favoritism in public expenditure," he stated in his inaugural address in 1889, "is criminal." Cleveland called unnecessary taxation "ruthless extortion."

These ideas formed the core of republican civic ideology. An ideology is a system of fundamental beliefs that specifies appropriate and inappropriate political conduct. These ideas reflect the way individuals understand their world and assign value to their social arrangements. People may not always act consistently with their philosophy, but the standards by which they judge government tend to be based on broad ideological criteria. Ideology is thus like religion. Both begin with premises that are accepted as given axioms and rarely challenged. The civic religion of the republican polity warned citizens of inevitable attempts to abuse public power. Most agreed in general that this risk could be minimized by limiting the activities of government. Henry David Thoreau summed up the presumption in the maxim "That government is best which governs least."

Republican ideology provided an intellectual rationale for restricting the use of power. Yet republicans recognized that good intentions alone could not prevent the seduction of authority; legal reinforcement of civic virtue was needed. Hence republicans constructed a constitutional framework designed to impede the capricious use of power. Unlike the malleable quality of ideology, constitutions offered specific and durable restraints on authority. Many of these legal constraints lingered in existence long after revolutionary ardor had faded from republican ideology.

Constitutional structure and civic ideology worked together to keep government small through 1887. The social and economic conditions of nineteenth-century America complemented these political constraints. For most of its history the republican polity was rural, agrarian, and localized among thousands of comparatively isolated communities. The high degree of individual self-reliance, social fragmentation, and economic simplicity in this society generated little enthusiasm for governmental intervention. The limited technological capability of the preindustrial era was not conducive to adopting policies that required complex administration. Still, conditions did not remain static in the nineteenth century. By the 1880s Americans stood on the threshold of a new economic and technological era.

Federalism anchored the constitutional framework of the republican polity. The federal system has two defining characteristics: spatial boundaries that delineate the territorial scope of a government's authority, and allocation of powers between a central and subnational (state) governments. The geographic range of national (Federal) power extended to all parts of the nation, while the territorial extent of a state's authority was confined within its borders. A version of this territorial principle existed within the states, which were partitioned into counties and other political subdivisions. Counties in half of the states contained smaller units, called "towns" in New England and "townships" in the Midwest. Densely populated localities were granted status as cities or villages, which gave them additional prerogatives. Over 30,000 of these general-purpose local governments existed in 1890. The nation also supported 100,000 special-purpose bodies, primarily school districts. The power to tax is a key test of the existence of a governmental body. Lawmakers counted 18,000 such units in Illinois in the 1930s.

In addition to its spatial dimension, federalism also distributed civic jurisdiction between governments. Citizens of the republican polity supported the principle of creating a dual structure of governance that gave certain powers to the central government and left the remainder of public activities to the states. Article I, section 8, of the Constitution of the United States, which enumerated the powers of Congress, listed the largest collection of authority granted to the Federal government. Congress was empowered to collect taxes and duties, regulate commerce with foreign nations and among the several states, coin money, establish post offices, declare war, maintain an army and navy, and "make all laws which shall be necessary and proper" for carrying out these functions. In addition, the national government conducted foreign relations, could admit new states to the Union, and administered Federal lands (the public domain).

The Constitution also prohibited the states from doing certain things. Forbidding a state from impairing the obligation of contracts was the best known of these restrictions. Aside from its guarantee of a republican form of government to the states, the Constitution did not grant specific powers to states. State lawmakers made these determinations, beginning with their own constitutions, which vested broad policy-making prerogatives in the legislature. In effect, states could undertake any task not prohibited by their own charters or by the national Constitution, or not reserved exclusively to the Federal government. State legislatures, in turn, decided what local governments could do. The most conspicuous feature of nineteenth-century state constitutions was an emphasis on procedural and substantive restrictions concerning how states went about using their powers.

The negative cast to the character of American constitutions reflected republican insistence on the explicit delineation of permissible power. This philosophic requirement resulted in the division of authority among distinct branches of a government (such as legislatures and courts, which provided the structural foundation for the so-called checks and balances among policy-making institutions), outlined procedural rules for their operation (such as electing a president every four years), and listed things officeholders could not do (such as impair the obligation of contracts). Constitutions did not say which policies officials should or would adopt. Answers to these questions lay with lawmakers in the various governments. The record of their actions shows that the Federal government undertook relatively few tasks in the republican era. Its chief duties centered on the conduct of diplomatic relations, the maintenance of a military, the distribution of the public lands, the operation of a rudimentary postal system, the collection of certain taxes, the regulation of a handful of commercial activities, and the support of a small administrative establishment. With a few exceptions, such as national security and the admission of new states, Federal functions concerned a narrow band of activities that affected the nation's preindustrial economy. At the same time, however, the national government used its limited authority to build a territorial state that stretched from the Atlantic to the Pacific coasts by the middle of the nineteenth century.

The state and local governments were the workhorses of the republican polity. Their authority extended over a wide range of affairs. Laws concerning social issues, such as marriage and divorce, the education of children, the care of the poor, and the specification of moral misconduct, were state prerogatives. So too was most policy on gender and race, including the legality of slavery until its national abolition in 1865. The protection of people and property (through the criminal law) lay largely with the states, which delegated most administration of these matters to local government. Responsibility for police, fire, public health, and the transfer of property illustrates important localized activities. States also exercised wide discretion in the economic arena. Their officials authorized individuals to form business firms (via incorporation laws), licensed practitioners of certain trades and professions, and regulated business and labor (although more in statutory theory than administrative practice). They developed a body of law concerning commercial transactions, which affected business contracts and rates of interest on loans. Most rules concerning the political process, such as specification of who could vote and the formation of new units of government, lay in the hands of state legislators. And both state and local officials possessed the power to tax.

Iowa's ban on liquor, Wisconsin's amateur road crews, and Birmingham's vagrancy laws were manifestations of dual federalism. "Dual federalism" refers to a feature of the republican polity in which a relatively sharp delineation of responsibilities between the states and the national government existed. Not only did each political level in fact handle separate functions, but republicans believed that the system *ought* to operate this way. The idea had evolved during the revolutionary era out of the fear of concentrating too much power in a single government. The essential form of dual federalism remained in place for a century after its creation in 1787. Agreement over principle, however, did not eliminate debate over its implementation. Controversies erupted over the points at which state power stopped and Federal power began, or in other words, at the legal seams of America's division of civic authority. Customarily these disputes were settled amicably, usually by lawmakers but sometimes by judges. On rare occasions, most notably during the Civil War, power holders turned to military force to resolve a conflict between the states and the general government.

The shadow of dual federalism was only dimly visible in the debate over the tariff in the 50th Congress. The power of Congress to levy a tariff was not an issue, for the Constitution explicitly granted this authority to the Federal government. Legislative disagreement arose over how to compose tariffs and its connection to the public finance and the economy. The taxation of imports was one of the few significant powers that Washington exercised in the republican era. Tariffs were Washington's primary source of revenue in the nineteenth century. Custom duties accounted for 58 percent of Federal income when Grover Cleveland denounced "this vicious, inequitable, and illogical source of unnecessary taxation." And the tariff was one of the major tools for stimulating economic growth available to national lawmakers (that is, the Congress and the president).

Republican ideology preached "economy" and frugality in government. To spend, government had to tax. Yet the exercise of this power could also abuse the rights of property. By common consent, therefore, tax policy had to be framed with temperance and justice. Disagreement flared over what was the appropriate level of taxation and how best to raise public moneys. Critics of high tariffs charged that these levies were unjust taxation. They saw tax discrimination against specific products as special legislation that enriched some producers at the expense of consumers and other businesses. Moreover, the larger the amount of tariff revenues, the more lawmakers were tempted into unnecessary expenditures. Low tariffs comported with the view that public budgets should be lean and tax policies should avoid favoritism.

Nonsense, retorted supporters of a high tariff. The protection of American producers by customs duties promoted the welfare of the whole nation. Since everybody benefited, tariffs hardly qualified as class (special-interest) favors. The assertion was debatable, but the defense of protective tariffs must be considered in light of the realities of governance at the time. Whatever their motives, Federal policy makers who wish to nurture the economy had few tools other than the tariff. And, in an era without income taxes, customs were the primary mechanism for funding the Federal government. Members of the Republican Party understood this reality when they made protective tariffs a centerpiece of their national policy, a stance they equated with patriotism. Electoral considerations reinforced this commitment. Tariff barriers rewarded numerous manufacturers, and Federal dollars financed the pensions of Civil War veterans in the North. Both groups were key Republican constituents.[10]

Yet tariff fights were as much about symbolism issues as they were about material effects. The growth of American industrialism was not dependent on tariffs; nor was Federal taxation excessive, at least by modern standards. Most taxation and spending in the Cleveland era, in fact, was controlled by local, not national, officials. The nation's first comprehensive report on public finance, covering the year 1902, makes this point. Local governments spent a little more than one-half of all public funds that year (see table 1.1). The Federal government accounted for a third. Slightly more than a dime on every public dollar was credited to state spending. Of the sixteen major categories of expenditure listed in the 1902 report, Washington paid all of the bill for four activities. Defense, veterans' benefits, and the post office consumed the lion's share of the Federal budget. Local government shouldered the costs of most domestic functions, such as schools, roads, police, fire and sanitation, care of the poor, and the general maintenance of government.

This summary of national accounts points up the policy of self-reliance that characterized governments under dual federalism. Each of the most expensive functions was financed separately by a single level of government, as in the instance of federally run post offices and locally funded schools and roads. Local government, not Washington, was the senior financial partner in this decentralized arrangement. Cleveland's government spent $2.81 per person for nondefense goods and services in 1887. Close to half ($1.25) of this amount went to one group—Union Civil War veterans. That same year, Arlingtonians in Massachusetts voted a budget of $18.44 per person. Figures varied with locale, yet it was in the Arlingtons of America, not in the nation's capital, that the largest share of the public purse resided in the republican age.

The congressional deadlock over the Mills bill stymied Grover Cleveland's quest for tax reform. Classical republicans could, nonetheless, console the president; representative democracy was operating as theory had intended. The founders of the Republic had fashioned legislatures in ways that disadvan-

Table 1.1. Government Expenditures, 1902 (in Millions of Dollars)

	All	U.S.	State	Local
Defense	165	165	0	0
Veterans	141	141	0	0
Post office	126	126	0	0
Education	258	3	17	238
Government operations	175	34	23	118
Highways	175	0	4	171
Interest	97	29	10	58
Police and fire	90	0	0	90
Utilities (mainly water)	82	0	2	80
Hospitals and health	63	3	32	28
Sanitation.	51	0	0	51
Public welfare	41	4	10	27
Parks and recreation	29	0	0	29
Water transportation	22	22	0	0
Natural resources	17	8	9	0
Corrections	14	0	14	0
Miscellaneous	121	37	15	69
*Total (%)	1,710 (100)	565 (33)	186 (11)	959 (56)

Source: U.S. Bureau of the Census, Historical Statistics on Governmental Finances and Employment (Washington, D.C., 1985), vol. 6 of 1982 Census of Governments, tables 10–14. Note: *Totals may not match details because unclassified expenditures are included in the totals.

taged transitory whims and slender majorities. Americans of the revolutionary era agreed that legislatures offered the safest forum to which to entrust public business. But like any officeholder, John Adams wrote in 1776, legislators were susceptible to all sorts of "vices, follies, and frailties." James Madison saw "a powerful tendency in the Legislature to absorb all power in its vortex," which enhanced the potential of factions to incite political mischief and compromise liberty. Both men had urged the creation of structural safeguards to deter abuses of legislative power.[11] Bicameralism, whereby representative assemblies were split into two coequal bodies, was one device intended to counter ill-tempered politics. The Mills bill tripped over this bit of republicanism.

The revolutionary generation's infatuation with legislatures waned with the passage of decades. Criticism mounted that assemblies abused the public trust and that lawmakers enacted too much legislation (as opposed to too little). Accusations pilloried legislators as pawns of private interests, cavalierly voting class legislation and recklessly misusing public funds. Popular stereotypes in the late nineteenth century, in elite circles at least, portrayed state legislators caving in to the cunning schemes of business and marching in lockstep to the commands of political party bosses. At best, most representatives were hacks. At worst, they were crooks. Americans who accepted the latter verdict could point to what became known as the Black Horse Cavalry in the New York Assembly. The members of this legislative troop were said to supplement their three-dollar-a-day pay by proposing bills designed to elicit corporate payoffs for burying the offensive legislation.[12]

Lobbyists, especially agents of corporations, came in for particular rebuke. Appearing regularly at capitols by midcentury, these emissaries of "selfishness" purportedly worked in secret to shortcut the link between citizens and elected representatives. Hired agents of the Standard Oil Company, one detractor charged, had "done everything in the Pennsylvania legislature except to refine it." Such allegations of wrongdoing reinforced the conviction that the fundamental principles of moderation and justice had become polluted by a cesspool of legislative "venality." Bottomless corruption and "vicious" special-interest legislation had prostituted the republican ideal of public virtue.

Americans did more than complain about their legislatures; they changed them, drawing on the lessons of 1776 for inspiration. Then, as later in the republican polity, the solution to abuses of power lay in improving constitutions. Nineteenth-century reformers strengthened the state chief executives by granting them the power to veto legislation. Courts were given greater independence, and voters were allowed to vote directly on policy questions (referendums) as well as for numerous executive posts (state constitutional officers). Legislatures were stripped of certain powers, such as authority to enact private and special local legislation. The list of prohibitions grew long in some state constitutions. But the most popular remedy to tame overactive legislatures was to prevent them from assembling at all.

Americans of 1776 believed that frequent elections and legislative sessions complemented republicanism. The original thirteen states convened their assemblies annually, some even twice a year. New states followed this practice until the 1840s, when a stampede toward biennial meetings swept the nation.

By 1900 all but eight states put their legislative meetings on an alternate-year schedule. The citizens of Alabama and Mississippi took this restrictiveness a step further by convening their session but once every four years. Reformers also inserted into state constitutions limits on the length of time that lawmakers could remain in sessions. At the turn of the century the typical state legislator stayed at the capitol sixty days or less and received $300 on average per term.[13] Congress, by contrast, met annually and remained in session as long as it wished, which averaged about twelve months during each two-year congressional cycle in the Cleveland era. The Constitution mandated annual meetings for national lawmakers and permitted them to set their own salaries. Congressmen of Cleveland's time pocketed $5,000 a year. Most state lawmakers were beholden to voters to authorize a change in state constitutions to get a raise.

Poorly paid, lacking permanent staffs, and buffeted by criticism, most state representatives did not remain on the job for long. The vast majority served one term and retired, partially on their own volition and partially on account of the custom that dictated rotation of office holding. The membership of legislative councils in big cities turned over equally often. Reelection rates to Congress were somewhat higher, yet most national lawmakers saw their work in Washington as a temporary diversion from private pursuits.[14] Part-time citizen policy makers conducted America's legislative business at all levels of government during the waning decades of the republican polity. Arlington staffed its twenty-five administrative units with seventy-five persons, virtually all of whom served without pay. These part-time posts included fence viewer, field driver, measurer of wood, fish preserver, sexton, trustee of the public library, and sealer of leather. They were appointed at Arlington's annual town meeting, which epitomized citizen-based government in New England. This was as close to popular, hands-on lawmaking as America got.

Administration of higher levels of government differed only in degree from the way Arlington ran its affairs. The governor's office staff in Wisconsin, to cite one example, totaled five workers if we count the lieutenant governor and the janitor. A budget-conscious Congress made presidents get by with an executive staff of a few clerks and messengers. President Cleveland personally answered the White House telephone and sometimes the doorbell. State legislators deliberately avoided the creation of large bureaucracies. Instead, they placed most administrative responsibilities in assorted boards and commissions that acted independently of the governor. Oregon counted sixty-two such units in 1900.

Illinois had a hundred by 1914. Most board members served part time without salary, although some pocketed fees collected by the board. Patronage appointments filled most of these positions. Elected officials were besieged with job requests that far exceeded available positions in the nation's small administrative establishment. Although merit-based hiring had begun with national civil service in 1883, Grover Cleveland called patronage a personal nightmare. But he had to approach appointments with care, because behind a supplicant for a government post might be an influential sponsor, such as a Democratic member of Congress. The post office offered the largest number of places to employ faithful party foot soldiers.

Exceptions existed in America's citizen-style administration. Some of the large cities turned to experts to direct technical affairs, such as waterworks, sewage disposal, parks, and public health offices. Some among this nascent group of professionals remained at their posts for twenty or thirty years. The appointment of specialists as city engineer indicates that urban officials valued expertise in coping with the technical problems that accompanied the rapid expansion of city populations. The secretary of the U.S. Department of Agriculture hired PhDs and other technically competent people to direct its scientific work.[15]

The courts were another office where a kind of professionalism reigned. Justice in a republic required independence from political pressures. One way to implement this theory was to give judges long terms. The U.S. Constitution allowed the president to nominate Federal judges who served for life if confirmed by the Senate. The nine members of the U.S. Supreme Court averaged twelve years on the high bench at the time Cleveland attacked the tariff. Two of these judges went on to serve a third of a century. Most state supreme court jurists were elected, yet many held their positions for long periods. Republicans wanted incorruptible legal wisdom to anchor their constitutional system. For this reason they violated the principle of rotation in office for judges.

Officeholders in the republican polity were expected to walk a fine line between promoting the public good and protecting private property. Government's power to tax, spend, and borrow bore directly on these two responsibilities, because the arrangements made to fund civic activities rested on government's authority to expropriate wealth. By the middle of the nineteenth century a body of opinion concluded that lawmakers abused this financial prerogative too frequently and recommended revisions of state constitutions as a way of reducing fiscal mischief. From the 1840s onward, reformers grafted a battery of financial restrictions onto these documents. Authority to borrow money was limited in virtually every state, either by outright prohibition or by regulation of amounts and method. New York's requirement that each bond issue be approved by voters in a referendum was replicated by other states. Also common were limitations of state and local debt to a percentage of the assessed value of property (5 percent was typical), provisions that reflected state and local reliance on property taxes for the bulk of the revenue. Some constitutions mandated that public borrowing be coupled with a special tax dedicated to paying off the debt in a timely fashion.

Restrictions on taxation, such as capping the rate of property taxes, crept into constitutions. One common rule prohibited officials from extending fiscal favors to particular groups. Illinois's version of this sentiment stated that taxes could be imposed only "by general law, uniform as to the class upon which it operates." Some constitutions delegated the job of restraining local finance to the state legislature. The prohibition of certain kinds of expenditures indirectly constrained taxation, as in the case of Wisconsin, which barred any state investment in roads (under blanket restrictions concerning internal improvements). By combining such prohibitions with stringent procedures for amending constitutions, republicans hoped they had placed ironclad yokes on fiscal capriciousness.

Full compliance with republican fiscal principles required the sustained vigilance of the citizenry over public accounts. Observance of this axiom explains why Arlington itemized every single expenditure in its annual town reports. Thus Arlingtonians knew that the town paid eight cents to Matt. Rowe for oil and that Bastine and Gates billed the treasurer thirty cents for a bottle of ammonia delivered to Crosby school in 1887. Explicit financial disclosure reinforced the goal of fiscal parsimony, which became the watchword of Republicans and Democrats in San Francisco. There, leaders of both parties pledged (and observed in office) a one-dollar limit (per $1,000 of assessed property) on the tax rate throughout the 1880s.[16] Grover Cleveland was a devotee of strict economy, a reputation he earned with repeated vetoes of special pension bills for Civil War veterans and other spending measures. Each rejected bill caused some grumbling, yet Americans agreed in principle with the norm of fiscal restraint.

Cleveland's pension vetoes threw fuel on the fire of debate over Federal finances. The tariff held center stage in this fight because it was the chief means by which the Federal government paid its bills. Cleveland's insistence on economy is understandable in the abstract, but his application of it is puzzling if we gauge his actions solely by financial standards. The revenue raised by customs in 1887 averaged $3.62 for every person, not a burdensome amount, and importers, not individuals, actually paid the levy. Arlington taxed its citizens directly. The town's property tax in 1887, levied on homes, farms, and businesses, worked out to $17.41 per person. In compliance with the norm of citizen watchfulness, the town report named each individual who paid and the amount of the tax. Cleveland's discomfort with the tariff and Federal spending grew out of his vision of the ideal polity, whose fundamental principles were fiscal frugality, avoidance of special-interest favors, and opposition to centralization of power in Washington. He knew that a substantial tax burden already lay on the shoulders of property owners, but he also recognized that the president had no authority to adjust them. That power lay at the underside of the federal system.

Where constitutions served as legal blueprints and legislators as policy contractors, judges acted as building inspectors of the republican structural design. Upon complaint, they reviewed what lawmakers did; and where the work deviated from the constitutional plan in their opinion, they refused to certify it. This process of disallowing a statute, known as judicial review, gave judges authority to decide whether an exercise of governmental power violated the terms of the political compact between rulers and the ruled. Complaints that lawmakers had exceeded their authority entered courtrooms with increased frequency in the Cleveland era, when judges declared more laws unconstitutional than had their predecessors.[17]

The nine members of the Supreme Court of the United States are the most visible judges in America, and their decisions, along with the Constitution and Federal acts, form the supreme law of the land. Each state also had its own supreme court, which sat atop a system of lesser judicial bodies similar to the hierarchical arrangement of Federal courts. These subnational courts did the largest share of the nation's legal business, including judicial review. In a sense a state was a mini republic, with its own constitution serving as its primary standard to guide its civic conduct. The number of state governments in America and the diversity of their legal systems complicates the tracking of judicial rulings at the subnational level. State courts did not need to copy each other and didn't. Moreover, these courts were confronted with increased challenges to legislative action, which had branched into new ground in the late nineteenth century. Many of these laws encountered the legal minefields embedded in state constitutions.

The Iowa Supreme Court triggered one of these devices in 1883. Foes of saloons in the Hawkeye State sought a constitutional prohibition on the manufacture and sale of liquor. Following the procedure for altering Iowa's constitution, two successive legislatures passed an amendment designed to dry up the state. The electorate fulfilled the second step in the process by approving a referendum on the proposed change. Dramshops in Iowa had been padlocked—or so it appeared until the court reviewed the process. The state's high court disallowed the amendment on the grounds that a slight change in the wording had occurred between the first and the second legislative approval. Iowa's six top justices defied a popular majority by clinging to the strict letter of the state's constitution.

Just across the Mississippi, seven judges cited another republican rule to impede policy making. Illinois's constitution specified that taxes must be uniform in application, levied equally upon property without favoritism or special exception. The state supreme court struck down several tax laws by a literal reading of this rule, including sales and income taxes adopted in the twentieth century. The republican remedy for dealing with constitutional bottlenecks was to amend the fundamental rules, but this was easier said than done in Illinois, for the process was purposefully strewn with obstacles. Nonetheless, proposals to discard the uniformity clause had cleared the legislature on several occasions and received voter approval in 1916. But not really, ruled the high court, which blocked the amendment on a procedural technicality. Tax uniformity stayed until Illinois got a whole new constitution in 1970.

Illinois's top jurists earned a reputation for legislative obstruction. Their rejection of laws to protect workers, such as a limitation on the hours of female labor, prompted charges that the court served as the handmaiden of employers. Whether the court purposely acted in the interest of managers is unclear, but the rationale for its actions rested on republican reasoning for limiting legislative prerogatives. Between 1870 and 1947 the Illinois top court struck down 308 statutes, which ranged across numerous areas of policy and ran afoul of various constitutional checkpoints. Yet most state courts did not put government in a straitjacket; they upheld the vast majority of laws that litigants put to a constitutional challenge. Laws to protect the health and safety of workers, for example, generally survived judicial review.[18]

What state courts permitted, the Federal courts might disallow. That there could be two legal tests of constitutionality fit comfortably with republican insistence on vigilance against misuses of power. The federal system permitted contradictory rulings, and this happened in the litigation of an Illinois law. The state's constitution instructed the legislature to regulate railroad charges. One such statute prohibited a railroad from charging more for a short haul than a long haul. The Wabash, St. Louis, and Pacific Railway Company challenged the enactment in a state court, which held that the rule was a legitimate exercise of Illinois's "police power." The term referred to the authority of a state to protect the health, safety, morals, and general welfare of its people. The railroad appealed its conviction to the Federal courts, arguing that since the company did business in several states the Illinois law interfered with the flow of interstate commerce, which was beyond the state's jurisdiction. The U.S. Supreme Court agreed. It ruled in the *Wabash* case (1886) that Illinois intruded on Federal power to regulate interstate commerce.[19]

The *Wabash* decision underscored the fact that the Supreme Court was the umpire of last resort over disputes concerning the allocation of powers in the federal system. Federal justices possessed the authority to rule on the constitutionality of both state and national legislation. And they found the states, not the central government, the most frequent trespassers of constitutional prohibitions. This tendency did not mean that federal justices had an inherent dislike of states, for they repeatedly reaffirmed the broad reach of state police power. They certainly subscribed to the philosophic rationale of dual federalism. But in the Cleveland era the states enacted far more laws than did Congress, and many of these statutes embodied innovative uses of power.

Moreover, in the 1880s the court found a new standard for evaluating the legality of state actions in the Fourteenth Amendment to the Constitution, which provided that "no State shall . . . deprive any person of life, liberty, or property without due process of law; nor deny to any person within its jurisdiction the equal protection of the laws."

The sentiment was classic republicanism, but the remedy was innovative. The amendment gave the Federal government broad authority to hold the states accountable to standards of fair conduct regarding individual rights.

The intent of the provision was the protection of the rights of former slaves. In theory the federal balance of power had been tilted toward Washington, yet in practice the amendment conveyed no more actual authority than Congress chose to exercise or the courts would accept. African Americans received virtually no assistance from the amendment in the Cleveland era. In the words "person" and "property," however, the court saw legal sanctuaries for private enterprise.

A ruling on a dispute between the Chicago, Milwaukee, and St. Paul Railway Company and the state of Minnesota in 1890 inaugurated this unintended application of the Fourteenth Amendment. The Minnesota legislature had created a commission with authority to regulate railroad rates. By interpreting "person" to include a corporation, magistrates gave the company a hearing in a Federal court concerning the charge that a state had deprived the railroad of property without due process of law. Then the justices declared that both the commission's procedure for determining fares and the particular rate it established violated the Fourteenth Amendment. Critics of the decision claimed that the court had exceeded its jurisdiction and had ruled on the content of policy in addition to the procedure of policy making.

The court relied on an analogous substantive interpretation of due process in its decision concerning a New York law that limited employment in bakeries to sixty hours a week. Conceding that the sovereignty of each state allowed broad discretionary application of its police power, the court observed that such authority did not give states a blank check. Limits on state power existed, and the justices suggested some. State regulation to protect the public good could intrude on the right to make a contract in the course of running a business. In the opinion of the court, Mr. Lochner, the proprietor of a bakery in New York, had been so victimized. New York had convicted Lochner of requiring an employee to work more than sixty hours a week. Lochner complained that the state restricted the use of his property in violation of his liberty. The court agreed in *Lochner v. New York* (1905). Bakery work in the justices' view did not present special health hazards. Regulation of employment in this industry, therefore, was an "unreasonable, unnecessary, and arbitrary interference with the right of the individual to his personal liberty." *Lochner* presented a clash between two republican tenets. At one pole stood the obligation of government to promote the general good. At the other was the responsibility to prevent government from infringing the fundamental rights of individuals. Usually the court upheld state action when forced to choose between these two standards. Yet well into the twentieth century the justices reiterated the maxim that government inherently threatened liberty and disallowed numerous "unreasonable" state laws on these grounds.

Congress also could violate freedom of contract. The court determined this to be the case in a congressional statute that prohibited railroads (engaged in interstate commerce) from firing workers because they joined a labor union (*Adair v. U.S.*, 1908). Both workers and owners, the court held, have "equality of right" to enter into contracts, and in this instance a regulation impinged on corporate freedom. In the court's words, the law "arbitrarily sanctions an illegal invasion of personal liberty as well as the right of property." Judicial regard for dual federalism also limited the reach of Federal power. The court relied on this principle to overturn a Federal conviction of a sugar manufacturer charged with violation of the 1890 U.S. antimonopoly law (*U.S. v. E. C. Knight*, 1895). The justices distinguished between commerce among the states, over which the central government had clear constitutional jurisdiction, and manufacturing, which was deemed a localized activity and thus beyond the supervisory reach of Congress. It was vital that this distinction be observed, Chief Justice Melville Fuller wrote, lest the urge to remedy "acknowledged evils" run the greater risk of undermining republican constitutionalism. Local regulatory prerogatives were "essential to the preservation of the autonomy of the States as required by our dual form of government." The language was classic republicanism.

Time changed the court's personnel but not judicial respect for dual federalism. The philosophical resiliency of this tenet was clear in the decision concerning a national law that prohibited child labor (*Hammer v. Dagenhart*, 1918). Congress could neither coerce states to equalize the conditions of labor with uniform laws nor do the job for them, the court ruled. If Congress exceeded its enumerated powers by assuming control over production, the progression of such infractions would "practically destroy" the American system.

The court's defense of dual federalism was so dogmatic that it gave the tenet priority over blatant violations of human freedom. This was manifest when the court overturned a Federal conviction of a Louisiana white man accused of murdering two citizens of African descent (*U.S. v. Cruikshank*, 1875). Charges had been brought under an 1870 Federal law aimed at curtailing the Ku Klux Klan and other night riders from depriving Southern blacks of basic rights.

Chief Justice Waite acknowledged that the American idea of justice demanded reverence for individual liberties. The right of citizens to assemble for the redress of grievances, he wrote, was embodied in "the very idea of government republican in form." And "the equality of the rights of citizens is a principle of republicanism. Every republican government is duty bound to protect all its citizens in the enjoyment of this principle, if within its power."

Since blacks were citizens and republican principles presumably applied to all citizens, how could all nine justices agree to set the murderer free? The key lay in the words "within its power." The remedy to the wrongs documented in *Cruikshank* did not lie with the Federal government. Its powers, the chief justice argued, were "enumerated and defined." National authority "was erected for special purposes," which did not include the protection of the rights of one citizen from deprivation by another. "That duty," he held, "was originally assumed by the States; and it still remains there."[20] In other words, neither the 1870 act nor the Fourteenth Amendment authorized the Federal government to restrain individuals (who acted as private citizens and not in a "state" capacity) from depriving the liberty of others. The court took the same position on a Federal civil rights statute that made it illegal for proprietors of private facilities to deny access to blacks. Unless state action was involved, Federal officials were powerless under the Fourteenth Amendment to prevent racial discrimination.

But what if a state explicitly denied rights? The court considered this question in *Plessy v. Ferguson* in 1896. The case involved a Louisiana law that prohibited blacks from traveling in the same railway cars as whites. The Fourteenth Amendment plainly stated that no state could deny the equal protection of the law to any person. Louisiana legislators just as plainly enacted a law requiring unequal treatment of African Americans. But the court let Louisiana dilute the meaning of "equal protection" by holding that the Fourteenth Amendment did not outlaw "reasonable" regulations based on "the established usages, customs, and traditions of the people." Subordination of blacks was the custom in the South, and the Constitution could not change this social fact. All the Constitution required was "separate but equal" accommodations for each race.

But the railway cars, the schools, and similar facilities available to blacks were not equal to the ones whites enjoyed. Southern law confined African Americans to second-class citizenship. Modern interpretation of *Plessy* correctly sees racial prejudice behind the court's opinion. Yet the 1896 ruling also was consistent with the norms of governance in the republican polity. *Plessy* tapped a political philosophy that reached back to the American Revolution. This ideological tradition saw the power of government as inherently dangerous to liberty. Constitutions were designed to restrain the inevitable tendency of officials to abuse power, but legal constraints worked only if the strict letter of the law was observed. The maintenance of explicit limits on national power within the confines of dual federalism was part of this understanding. In *Plessy* the court elevated the principle of dual federalism above the denial of equality. Until policy makers revised their priorities concerning the reach of national power and the importance of equal protection of the law, racism remained legal in America.

2

The Course and Causes of Growth

EIGHTEEN EIGHTY-SEVEN symbolizes the dawn of modern governance, when older ways of transacting civic affairs came into conflict with new demands on the uses of power. Grover Cleveland's attack on the tariff in his 1887 address demonstrates the continued vitality of traditional axioms about good government. Wrapped in the rhetoric of republicanism, the president's denunciation of public favoritism and high taxation showed his devotion to classical American ideals of limited government, fiscal parsimony, and strict dual federalism. These principles underlay his vetoes of spending bills and his passive reaction to the economic depression of the middle 1890s. To many contemporaries then and most historians later, Cleveland has been typed as a conservative whose style of leadership embodied "laissez-faire" government.

Yet the twenty-second president showed another side to his political personality, one that anticipated tendencies exhibited by later chief executives. Signs of this modern style appear in Cleveland's State of the Union message in 1886. The president's constitutional responsibility in the annual address includes the recommendation of measures that the chief executive deemed necessary and expedient. Cleveland drew up a long list of suggestions for Congress's consideration. He urged better fortification of coastal and Great Lakes cities, modernization of the navy, extension of postal service, construction of the first Federal prison, reorganization of the Federal courts, and a policy that would induce American Indians to abandon tribal living. The president wanted legislation that would stop fraudulent acquisition of public lands, enlarge the Labor Bureau and authorize it to arbitrate worker grievances, arrest an infectious disease afflicting cattle, and fill the void created by the Supreme Court's rejection of state regulation of railroads engaged in interstate commerce. He defended his vetoes of individualized pension bills for Civil War veterans by advocating a generalized program where "relief may be claimed as a right." And he recommended Federal compensation for depositors in the Freedman's Bank, a private institution whose financial collapse had stripped thousands of former slaves of their hard-earned savings.

Cleveland was not an activist president in the manner of later chief executives. But his legislative wish list has a modern ring to it. Like his counterparts in the twentieth century, Cleveland identified specific problems that government should address. It was this practical posture, together with the range of issues and Congress's action on them, that gives the Cleveland administration a modern coloration. In 1887 Congress authorized free mail delivery to homes in small cities, allotted funds to the Department of Agriculture to eradicate diseased cattle, created a plan to move Indians off reservations and make them land-owning citizens, and began a program of annual Federal grants-in-aid to agricultural scientists. The lawmakers' most innovative action was the enactment of the Interstate Commerce Act., which authorized Federal regulation of railroads and created a special unit, the Interstate Commerce Commission, to administer the law. This last step inaugurated the national government's modern regulation of business activity. The Federal government had embarked on a new role in American society.

Many state and city governments had already pursued an expanded agenda. Laws that regulated personal social behavior, such as the consumption of alcoholic beverages, gambling, and sex, and private economic activity, such as railroads, insurance companies, and drug stores, appeared in the 1860s and 1870s, and proliferated in the 1880s. The states, often acting through local governments, took steps to protect the health and safety of citizens and workers and expanded numerous services, especially public schooling. The statutes that authorized state and municipal action in these areas did not create a modern administrative regime immediately, but officeholders at all levels did turn to government as a remedy for societal problems with increased frequency during the late nineteenth century. This activism gained speed over the life span of the transitional polity, which experienced a major economic slump during the mid-1890s, an outpouring of progressive reforms early in the new century, and a major military campaign during World War I (1917–1918). By the 1920s contemporary observers emphasized the enlarged scope and role of government when reviewing the previous fifty years of public sector activities. Political scientist Charles Beard called the trend "one of the outstanding facts of modern civilization." He and other observers attributed the expansion of government to "a thousand forces in modern civilization," which they predicted would cause further growth of the public sector.[1]

These pundits were right. Public expansion continued during the Great Depression of the 1930s, World War II, and subsequent decades. Only a remarkable visionary in 1880 could have imagined the scope of government a hundred years later. By the 1980s nearly one of every two households were receiving financial assistance from government. One of every six employees worked for government, and this figure does not count military personnel. A myriad of national, state, and local agencies regulated hundreds of social, economic, and political activities. Keeping up with these rules produced a flood of paperwork and a mountain of documentary records. Complying with national reporting requirements cost private business an estimated $100 billion in 1980.[2]

Printing, processing, and preserving records and performing all the other things government did in 1985 cost $8,000 per person. These dollars provided 37 million individuals with Social Security assistance, 170,000 schools for 50 million kids, four million miles of roads and one million bridges, 5,500 military installations, 29,500 post offices, and over half the cost of treating patients in the nation's 6,800 hospitals. Some Federal dollars were invested in office buildings, which contained four times the square footage of private companies in the country's ten largest cities. The Federal government owned 17,000 computers, 400,000 nonmilitary vehicles, and one-third of the nation's land mass. Its total assets were valued at $1.26 trillion. The holdings of state and local government were worth twice this amount.

These facts suggest the size of the public sector in the 1980s, yet anecdotal information cannot illuminate the full development of modern governance. This history requires systematic analysis. The first step in this task is to summarize the historical evolution of the public sector. With this descriptive sketch in hand, the discussion can turn to the causes of expansion and its effects.

Three criteria will help us to track the growth of government. First, our view should encompass a period of sufficient duration to allow us to delineate the broad trend of civic activity from short-term anomalies. A perspective of a hundred years satisfies this requirement. Second, our survey must embrace all levels of government, because governance in America has always been decentralized. Unfortunately, gaps in records and scholarly studies of state and local government make this criterion easier to honor in theory than in practice. And third, it is critical to recognize the difficulties of analyzing political power. Varied in its manifestations, power is an elusive concept that defies neat measurement. We must be content to use surrogate indicators of government's capacity to marshal influence and authority. This chapter will concentrate on three such indicators—the adoption of policy functions, public expenditures, and the development of administrative capacity.

Tracing the accumulation of civic functions is a reasonable way to begin this history. A policy function is a cluster of programs that address a similar general objective. For the moment our summary will emphasize the functions of the Federal government. A survey of state and local functions, some of which paralleled Washington's uses of power, is presented in later chapters.

Table 2.1 lists eight major Federal functions in the chronological order of their creation (left-hand column). These general categories are subdivided into more specialized policy topics, each of which is illustrated in the right-hand column by an action that symbolized the government's entry into the field. Notice that a steady accretion of Federal functions has occurred since 1887. Moreover, the list is cumulative, because each policy topic became a permanent part of Washington's workload. Congress occasionally killed particular programs, but it never jettisoned an entire function or subfunction listed in the table.

The Interstate Commerce Act of 1887 initiated the modern era of national commercial regulation. Congress extended its control over economic activity during the next quarter century by enlarging Federal authority to manage natural resources, provide assistance to certain producers (such as farmers), and construct public works (such as roads). During these years Congress inaugurated Washington's modern interest in social control. This policy thrust included the social classification of people (e.g., designating unacceptable immigrants) and the specification of illicit moral behavior (e.g., prohibiting prostitution). Social services were extended to individuals on a mass basis (e.g., rural free delivery of mail). Early in the twentieth century the Federal government demonstrated a wider involvement in civil liberties. On the one hand Washington restricted forms of political speech and created a national police agency, the Federal Bureau of Investigation, to combat subversive and criminal activity. On the other hand, the Supreme Court imposed standards of conduct on the states concerning limitations of free speech and criminal prosecutions ("fair trial" standards). These were dramatic additions to the Federal role, yet the states pushed more vigorously into commercial regulation, social control, and social services during the transition era. Better schools and public-health facilities (such as sewer systems) illustrate the last category of policy innova-

Table 2.1. Evolution of Federal Functions since 1887

Function name and formative period	Symbolic entry action
Commercial regulation 1887–1916	
Sector regulation	Interstate Commerce Act 1887
Resource management	Forest reserves 1891
Sector assistance	Loans for farmers 1916
Infrastructure promotion	Federal aid for roads 1916
Social control and services 1891–1910s	
Inspection of individuals	Ellis Island opened 1892
Social services	Rural mail delivery 1896
Vice control	Anti-prostitution Act 1910
Regulate civil liberties 1918–1935	
Restrict political speech	Sedition Act 1918
Control crime and subversive activity	Modern FBI 1924–1935
Limit state restrictions on speech	*Stromberg v. California* 1931
Fair trial standards in states	*Powell v. Alabama* 1932
Economic stabilization 1933–1946	
Commercial management	National Recovery Admin. 1933
Compensatory spending	Emergency relief 1933
Producer subsidy	Agricultural Act 1933
Fiscal control	Modern income tax 1943
Income Assistance 1933–1965	
Employment assistance	Employment offices 1933
In-kind assistance	FHA mortgages 1934
Income "insurance" and "welfare"	Social Security Act 1935
Medical care	Medicare and Medicaid 1965
Global stability 1940–1949	
Military capability	Atom bomb project 1940
Foreign aid	Lend Lease program 1941
Foreign intelligence	Central Intelligence Agency 1947
Military alliance	NATO 1949
Nondiscrimination 1954–1960s	
Equal protection of law	*Brown v. Bd. of Education* 1954
Gender equality	Equal Pay Act 1963
Equal opportunity and desegregation	Civil Rights Act 1964
Social and consumer protection 1962–1970s	
Environmental protection	Motor Vehicle Control Act 1965
Consumer protection	Fair Packaging Act 1966
Worker protection	OSHA 1970
Electoral regulation	Campaign funding 1974

tion. The states also imposed closer control over elections and reformed their administrative organization.

National lawmakers took unprecedented steps to stimulate recovery of the economy during the Great Depression of the 1930s. Temporary measures designed to revitalize industry, agriculture, and finance (e.g., the National Recovery Administration, the Agricultural Act of 1933) evolved into continuous economic stabilization efforts that sought "maximum employment, production, and purchasing power," as the Employment Act of 1946 stated the function. Similarly, Congress turned temporary relief of employed workers during the early 1930s into an ongoing program of income assistance (e.g., the Social Security Act of 1935). Lawmakers greatly expanded income-assistance programs in kind and cost after 1945 (e.g., adoption of Medicare and Medicaid in 1965). By first extending military aid on a massive scale to allied countries (Lend Lease), then by officially entering World War II (1941), the United States initiated a new chapter in its international role. After 1945 national policy makers continued their quest for global stability, an objective that led to unprecedented expenditure on the military, participation in defense pacts, and creation of national security agencies, as well as military interventions in Asia and the Middle East.

These developments were a turning point for American federalism. Between 1887 and 1932, Washington and the states tended to adopt programs in similar functional areas without upsetting their traditional relationship. After 1933 the central government took on functions that had no state equivalent (economic stabilization and global stability) or that required compliance or cooperation from the states (income assistance, nondiscrimination, and social and consumer protection policy).

The Supreme Court's ruling in *Brown v. Board of Education* (1954), the landmark case that held racial segregation in public schools unconstitutional, elevated nondiscrimination policy to a prominent spot on the national agenda. It took years of the civil rights movement, however, to coax Congress into enacting enforcement mechanisms (e.g. the Civil Rights Act of 1964). The 1960s also marked the emergence of a new regulatory impulse in Congress, which passed a battery of laws to protect workers, consumers, the environment, and the election process. Most commercial regulations of the pre–World War II variety had applied to competitive practices between business firms in individual sectors of the economy. The new social and consumer regulations sought to improve the quality of life for individuals in their capacities as consumers, employees, and citizens. Federal sponsorship of nondiscrimination and social protection policy took the national government into areas once reserved to the states and brought considerably more complexity to relations between the levels of government.

Government became more costly as it assumed new tasks. Like a business or household, modern government pays for goods it purchases and services it provides. Expenditures, therefore, are handy data with which to track certain aspects of public-sector growth. We must make two technical adjustments in order to make sense of historical finances. First, the data must be expressed on a per-person basis to account for the growth of the country's population. And second, the fiscal indicator has to be converted into constant dollars in order to control for changes (usually, declines) in the purchasing power of money over time. The financial time series in table 2.2 uses 1958 for the reference price. This table also relates public spending to the GNP (gross national product), which measures the total dollar amount of activity in the economy.

The cost of government has risen enormously over the past one hundred years (see table 2.2). This increase began early in the transition period, when spending by government nearly doubled (from $56 in 1890 to $109 per person, constant dollars, in 1913). State and local expenditures slightly outpaced Federal outlays during these years, as can be seen in the breakdown of spending by level of government in table 2.2. Each level of government increased its spending during the later transition years (1913–1927), so that public-sector costs were three times greater on the eve of the Great Depression than during Cleveland's first term in the White House. Outlays doubled during the 1930s, with Washington leading the way in this surge. Public costs rose even faster during World War II (1941–1945) and continued to mount during the immediate postwar years (1946–1962) and the 1960s and 1970s, although at reduced rates of increase. On the basis of constant dollars, government spent eight times more in 1980 than it had in 1927. By midcentury the Federal government became the dominant player in a new federalized system of public finance.

Government had become twenty-eight times more expensive in one hundred years since Grover Cleveland took up residency in the White House. This expansion can be tracked from a different angle, whereby spending is set as a proportion of the GNP (see table 2.2). This percentage grew moderately during the transition era (from 7 percent to 12 percent), leapt higher during the Depression, the war, and the immediate postwar period (from 12 percent to 31 percent), and settled into a slower-paced rise through the 1960s and 1970s. Keep in mind that the economy itself grew in real (constant-dollar) terms during these

Table 2.2. Public Spending, 1890–1990

	Percent of GNP	Expenditures per person in 1958 dollars			
		All government	Federal	State-Local	Federal social welfare
1890	7%	$56	$20	$36	$7
1913	8	109	33	76	7
1927	12	188	59	129	10*
1940	20	352	173	179	59
1962	31	893	575	318	155
1980	36	1,584	1,020	564	500
1990	40	2,025	1,271	754	623

Sources: U.S. Bureau of the Census, Eleventh Census of the United States: Report on Wealth, Debt, and Taxation (Washington, D.C., 1895), 406, 409, 411; U.S. Bureau of the Census, Historical Statistics on Governmental Finances and Employment (Washington, D.C., 1985; vol. 6 of 1982 Census of Governments), tables 10–12; updated with U.S. Bureau of the Census, Statistical Abstract of the United States: 1993 (Washington, D.C., 1993), various tables; and author calculations based on U.S. Bureau of the Census, Historical Statistics of the United States (Washington, D.C., 1975), series F 1, 4, H 1.
Note: *For 1929.

years and that government purchases of goods and services are included in the GNP. Clearly, government in general and Washington in particular assumed a greater and greater role in the nation's economy as the twentieth century advanced. Public spending equaled 36 percent of the GNP when Ronald Reagan won the presidency in 1980, and it crept up several points more by 1990. (See chapter 11 for trends since 1990.)

In his election campaign Reagan criticized the level of spending on social welfare, which is shorthand for programs such as education, health, housing, veterans, welfare, and Social Security. These activities consumed roughly a third of all government expenditures at the beginning of the twentieth century, when state and local government shouldered 80 percent of the bill. Led by the rise in Social Security benefits, social welfare costs accounted for half of all public outlays in 1980, and Washington paid 60 percent of the tab.[3] These two trends—a growing investment in human resources and services and greater national responsibility for these functions—explain why Federal spending on social welfare ballooned from $7 to $623 (constant dollars) per person in a little over three generations. By the end of the twentieth century Federal spending for social welfare approached the entire budget of state and local government.

Led by social spending in recent decades, public outlays rose substantially in the twentieth century. The enlarged Federal role in this fiscal growth represents a form of *centralization,* which refers to Washington's increased share of all governing activity. Centralization itself does not measure the size or power of government but rather a greater concentration of political authority in a particular government. There is, however, a connection between the growth of government and increased centralization, both in the United States and in other countries.[4] These trends are visible in public finance, although we must exercise caution in relying on statistics about spending and taxing to represent the totality of what government does. In the first place, all dollars are not equal in what they tell about public activities. Some expenditures support labor-intensive services, such as teaching and police work. The purchase of military weaponry, on the other hand, is a capital-intensive outlay, while Social Security payments to retired workers represent a financial "transfer" payment. Some uses of governmental power, such as the regulation of commercial or individual conduct, cost much less than programs such as Social Security or defense weapon procurement.

The capacity of public administration presents a third index of government's evolution. Administrative capacity expanded as statues conveyed authority and responsibilities to agencies charged with implementing public policy. Human institutions tend to become more specialized as they perform a wider array of functions. In the public sector this division of labor usually was accompanied by an increase of bureaus and agencies, each responsible for managing a distinct area of government's work. Complexity results from the multiplication of these units, the increase in administrative activities, and the regulations they implement. Further permutations arise as contacts between agencies multiply. One agency, for example, may find it necessary to coordinate its operations with several others located at different levels of the federal system.

Administrative capacity is easier to envision in the abstract than to document factually, because much desired information is not available. No firm historical count of state and local administrative units exists, for example. The tendency of state governments to consolidate small boards and bureaus into larger cabinet-like departments since 1917 complicates a historical tracking of their administrative agencies. Scholars have provided ballpark estimates of the number of Federal organizations. One estimate found 68 in 1880, 170 in 1932, and 394 in 1973. Another study identified 6 Federal regulatory agencies in 1900 and 56 in 1980. President Jimmy Carter placed the number at 90.[5] Government also has put more people on the public payroll over the years. From an estimated half-million civilian workers in 1880, public employment rose to over 3 million in 1930, 16 million in 1980, and 22 million in 2009. Measuring these figures in relation to the size of the workforce, one in every thirty-three employed persons in 1880 was a public servant. Fifty years later the ratio dropped to one in sixteen; between 1980 and 2009 government hired one of every six workers.

The growth of public employees reflects an increase in programs and regulations. One tally of major national regulations counted 6 in 1900 and 310 in 1980. Most of them had been enacted in the 1960s and 1970s.[6] The *Code of Federal Regulations,* which publishes administrative directives, grew four and a half times longer between 1950 and 1980. But the real complexity of public business lies in the transactions themselves. Consider the Department of Defense, whose 14,766,545 separate procurement (purchase) contracts in 1984 were subject to 16,000 pages of regulations. The 117 congressional hearings held to review the DOD's request for funds covered 22,000 pages of printed testimony.

Federal grant-in-aid programs produced administrative complexity of a different sort. Federal grants are financial subsidies to state and local governments. These moneys are usually earmarked for specific activities and are subject to various conditions. Because grant programs have proliferated over the years and because they require interactions among administrative specialists at two or more levels of government, grants symbolize the evolution of complexity in modem governance. Grover Cleveland signed the first permanent Federal grant-in-aid program into law in 1887. Over the next sixty years the number of grant programs grew at a moderate rate, totaling 34 by the end of World War II. Then the pace of adoptions quickened, reaching 132 by 1962 and mushrooming to 539 by 1981, the year Reagan entered the White House. Like barnacles on the hull of a ship, regulations piled up on grant programs. Most of the thousand or so conditions that governed the use of subsidies were adopted in the 1970s.[7] These developments transformed the comparative simplicity of nineteenth-century federalism into networks of interconnections called intergovernmental relations in the late twentieth century.

Between the presidencies of Grover Cleveland and Ronald Reagan, policy makers in city halls, state capitals, and Washington added one task after another to government's workload. Eventually few fields of endeavor were beyond the reach of public policy. Public expenditures multiplied manifold as civic functions accumulated. A proliferation of rules and regulations, administrative authorities, and intergovernmental programs created a governmental complex unknown to members of the republican polity. The sum of these developments bestowed immense power on public officials to influence society and individual behavior. Government, in short, had become bigger and more powerful.

What caused this transformation? Why did government grow? This intriguing puzzle has sparked numerous speculations. One view posits industrialization as the primary cause of public-sector growth. This hypothesis contends that social and economic changes created dislocations and imbalances in society that required the collective power of government to solve. Another line of thinking argues that interest groups, such as private corporations, professionals, and labor unions, pressured policy makers to act in their favor. In his 1887 annual message Grover Cleveland pointed to an organized combination that induced Congress to design tariff policy for its selfish advantage. The democratic system that allowed interest groups to compete over policy also permitted voters and political parties to influence government through elections. Some observers argue that voters have demanded more of government over the years and that political parties abetted this desire by catering to voters' whims as a way of winning electoral support. Still another interpretation locates the critical dynamic of growth in government itself, whereby legislators, administrators, and other public officials manipulated public power for their own personal interest.

Each of these ideas has some validity, yet none is sufficient by itself. The historical transformation of government is too complex to be explained by one or two factors. A more plausible case can be made that numerous influences combined and interacted to cause government to grow. The real analytic challenge lies in determining the relative importance of each factor. Because no foolproof method exists to calibrate the contribution of individual factors across time, space, and policy functions, or even to ensure that all relevant factors have been identified, explanation of the growth of government continues to provoke debate.[8]

Given the absence of a single widely accepted explanation, a reasonable approach to the problem is to begin with an analytic framework that identifies key elements in governing and suggests their likely influences on the growth of government. The scheme laid out in figure 2.1 offers no definitive causal ex-

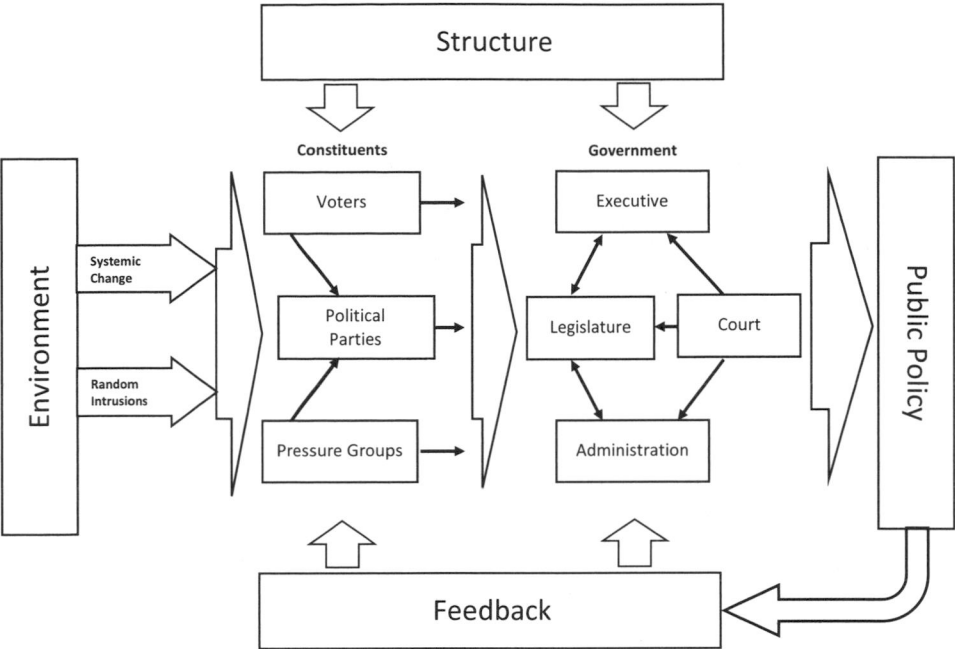

FIGURE 2.1. The Process of Growth in American Government

planation; rather, it is a device for organizing pertinent factors for discussion in this chapter.

Figure 2.1 identifies three broad dynamics of growth—the environment, constituents, and government. *Environment* refers to general social and economic conditions of society. One set of environmental influences comprises broad, long-term processes, labeled *systemic change,* that radiate widely but gradually through society. A second set, called *random intrusions,* points to abrupt and irregular events whose timing and impact are highly unpredictable. *Constituents* are politically relevant groups of voters, political parties, and pressure groups that inhabit political spaces outside government. *Government* refers to persons in official positions of authority—legislators, elected executives, administrators, and court officials—who constitute the third major source of policy-making energy. These three clusters of factors exist within the boundaries of structure, which denotes the ideological principles and constitutional frameworks that shaped the playing field of politics. A fifth element depicted in the figure is *feedback,* which is placed in the model to acknowledge that governmental decisions themselves can stimulate demands for further policy change.

Environment, constituents, and government interacted within a historically specific structure to produce *policy,* which represents the decisions or outputs of the policy-making process.

The arrows and brackets in the diagram denote principal paths of influence in the policy-making process. The model's layout implies that the origins of policy emanate from the environment and work their way through constituents, who pressure or entreat government to adopt policy. This textbook version of how laws are made in America seldom occurs in such an idealized fashion, although policy proposals have become law by this route. Many actions of government, however, have remote if any overt connection with the general social and economic conditions of society. Sometimes the most conspicuous force for policy innovation comes from individuals in government, such as the president, who may exhort voters to urge members of Congress to adopt a policy proposal. Various paths of influences among the components of politics, in other words, have occurred historically, although the figure does not diagram all of them. Nor does the model show how the causal factors themselves changed over time. It is reasonable to suppose that each cluster of factors varied in its contribution to the growth of government at different stages of history. The history of policy making reviewed in the chapters ahead shows that the mix of causes varied from one era to another. The impact of industrial change relative to the importance of other factors, for example, probably was greatest during the transitional polity.

Few students of government doubt that industrialization reshaped the environment of politics of the United States. The preindustrial community that defeated Britain in the American Revolution clearly was a very different place from the country that placed a man on the moon. Yet the social and economic transformation of America does not prove that every policy had its immediate origin in some environmental condition. What the socioeconomic thesis does say is that a sweeping process of change after the eighteenth century created new problems for the polity and altered contexts in which individuals viewed their society and government. The United States as well as other industrialized nations underwent a series of evolutionary changes that turned rural, agrarian, tradition-bound, and locally oriented communities into an urban, industrial, interconnected nation in which aspirations for individual advancement and economic progress became dominant values. Referred to as *modernization* when discussed in a multinational context, socioeconomic changes created not only new forms of social and economic organization and greater wealth but also new ways of understanding the natural world and human behavior.[9] Modernization, in other words, entailed changes in attitudes that rested on advances in science, education, and technology. Some scholars see an organizational revolution emerging from these developments, in which technologically driven corporations, middle-class professions, and bureaucratic institutions in both the private and public sectors came to wield dominant influence in American society.[10] These industrial and scientific revolutions nurtured the idea that people could ordain their own progress by controlling elements of their environment.

A correspondence exists between stages of economic development in the United States and the sequence of governmental regimes. The republican polity flourished during the preindustrial period of American history and survived the early decades of industrialism during the mid-nineteenth century. The main thrust of the industrial transformation of the economy occurred between the 1870s and the 1910s, when iron, steel, and steam came of age and large business enterprises were formed. The transitional polity, which broke with many of the nation's older governing practices, overlapped this stage of economic history. A period of mature industrialism, lasting roughly from the 1920s to the 1970s, ushered in a consumer-based society in which mass-marketed goods, credit purchases, and expanded service industries characterized the economy. This new commercial regime, in which the quest for personal economic security became pronounced, corresponds to the emergence of the claimant polity. Economic growth has slowed in the years since the mid-1970s, as globalization of commerce and increased inequality in wealth etch contrasts with prior decades. The slow-growth economy has tracked closely with the restrained polity, which is characterized by a hesitancy to expand government. This synopsis of economic stages and political eras does not assert that policy flowed automatically from economics. But it does suggest that the material conditions of life altered the way that people looked at their society and its government.

Three aspects of socioeconomic change had particularly potent political ramifications: the emergence of a wage-labor market economy, the appearance of new threats to personal and community well-being, and the growth of affluence, symbolized by the rise of the urban-suburban middle class. We can begin to get a sense of the scope of these changes by looking at how Americans earned a living over the years. Two-thirds of the workforce toiled on farms, in the forests, or as fishermen when Grover Cleveland was a boy. This proportion dropped steadily over the decades, from roughly one-half in 1870 to one-

Table 2.3. Socioeconomic Changes, 1870–1990

	1870	1920	1950	1970	1990
Workforce (%)*					
agriculture	52	27	12	4	3
industry	29	44	36	34	33
services	20	27	52	62	64
% female	17**	20	29	38	45
Urban (%)	25	51	64	73	75
Suburban (%)	6**	9	23	38	46
Autos (millions)	0	8	40	89	144
(per 1,000 people)	0	76	350	438	578
Residential electric (KW per person)	0	30	476	2,297	3,701
GNP per person (1972 $)	852	2,012	3,517	5,248	7,509
Median family income (1990 $)	—	—	17,986	33,238	35,353
Life expectancy at birth (years)	41	54	68	71	75
Infant deaths (per 1000 births)	158 (Mass.)	85	29	20	9
Elderly: % over 64	3.0	4.7	8.2	10	12.5

*Agriculture includes fishing and forestry; industry includes transportation, mining, and construction; services includes trade, finance, and public administration.
**1890.
Sources: U.S. Bureau of the Census, *Historical Statistics of the United* States (Washington, D.C., 1975), various tables; updated with U.S. Bureau of the Census, *Statistical Abstract of the United* States, various issues.

quarter in 1920 and 12 percent in 1950 (see table 2.3). Farmers were a rarity by the late twentieth century, when most people worked at service jobs, in wholesale or retail sales, in finance or insurance, or in government. Employment in industry, which includes manufacturing, transportation, mining, and construction, overtook agriculture in 1920 but slipped to second place behind service positions in 1950. This shift away from agriculture reduced the number of self-employed Americans and increased the number of persons who worked as employees for a wage or a salary. Industrial and service jobs tended to be located in or near cities and suburbs, whose growth was another sign of socioeconomic change. Urban places contained one of every four persons in 1870, one of every two in 1920, and three of every four in 1980 (see table 2.3). As they grew in population, urban areas tended to spread out geographically in wider metropolitan configurations, with suburbs proliferating beyond city borders. The twelve largest such metropolitan regions were home to nearly a third of all Americans when Ronald Reagan was president.

Industrialization created new forms of work and upset traditional relationships between business enterprises and the community. Managing a large industrial corporation was not the same as running an eighty-acre farm. In response to the competitive pressures of a commercial market, industrial firms developed sophisticated business strategies, hired more employees, and devised complex organizations. Some businesses used sharp—and, in the view of critics, unfair—practices in an attempt to dominate their field of enterprise. The epithets *monopoly* and *trust* flowed freely in political commentary during the transition era, when the battle between corporate titans was raw and the power they commanded new and alarming to many people. In the more dispassionate language of economists, unchecked competition could create artificial barriers to trade that resulted in "market failure."

Early industry tended to rely on skilled artisans, many of whom organized trade unions. With the rise of mass-production industries, employers turned increasingly to less-skilled workers. Seen by managers as anonymous inputs of labor on the corporate balance sheet, industrial workers were highly vulnerable to the uncertainties of the business cycle and the whims of shop foremen. These changes in the nature of work stimulated the formation of labor unions in the mass-production industries, which employed many thousands of semiskilled and unskilled workers. Negotiations between labor and employers over recognition of the union as a bargaining agent for workers, working conditions, and pay produced repeated disputes, many costly strikes, and, occasionally, deadly confrontations. Labor strife, dangerous working conditions, the ability of corporations to wield vast financial and political power, and breakdowns in business competition were derivatives of the new industrial economy. The economic foundation of the republican polity, which rested heavily on the shoulders of small, independent farmers, artisans, and merchants, steadily disappeared between the 1840s and 1920s. In its place rose an interconnected commercial regime that relied on bureaucratic institutions, hired managers, and impersonal relationships.

Technology drove many of these changes. In the latter half of the nineteenth century railroads and telegraphs forged new links across state lines and between regions of the country. The telephone, typewriter, adding machine, punch card, and vertical file cabinet had begun to revolutionize office work at the time Grover Cleveland served as a public official. This technological revolution overlapped with the transformation in industry whereby standardized goods were mass-produced for widespread distribution. The automobile symbolizes this marriage between technology and a mass-consuming public. Beginning commercial production in the 1890s, auto manufacturers accelerated output in the 1920s when cars became affordable for the middle class. Following a slump during the Great Depression and World War II, auto sales sped forward when less troubled times returned. Auto registrations rose from 40 million in 1950 to 144 million in 1990, which translated into more than one car for every two persons in the United States (see table 2.3). At this point half of all American households had at least two cars. In the second decade of the twenty-first century drivers had to negotiate a quarter of a billion motor vehicles on the roads.

The proliferation of motor vehicles had an enormous impact on public policy. Government laid out and paved highways, constructed bridges, installed traffic controls, licensed drivers, registered vehicles, required auto insurance, and formed highway patrols to police the behavior of motorists. Traffic accidents forced revisions in the laws covering property damage and personal injury. Specialized policies for companies that located, extracted, and refined petroleum were adopted; taxes were levied on the sale of vehicles and motor fuels and, in some states, on motor vehicle ownership. In recent decades policy makers have wrestled with issues such as air pollution from engine emissions, the improvement of fuel efficiency, traffic snarls in urban areas, the safety of auto design, drunk drivers, and the share of the vehicle market captured by foreign manufacturers. In one way or another and at all levels of government, the car touched large segments of policy. The automobile story dramatizes the impact of industrialism on policy. All of the actions just enumerated followed in the wake of the automobile; with some minor exceptions, all were illogical prior to 1900.

Americans were able to buy more cars because they became more affluent. Industrial development increased economic productivity, which translated into higher incomes for most people. Table 2.3 traces the growth of this affluence, which is measured as GNP per person and expressed in 1972 dollars (to hold price changes constant). Average wealth in America more than doubled during the transition era (from $852 in 1870 to $2,012 in 1920) and nearly doubled again by 1950. Twenty years later GNP per person registered another sizable gain (up to $5,248), and it rose again in the next twenty years, although median family income only nudged up slowly after 1973. The purchasing power of the average household expanded by a factor of six in the one hundred years between 1870 and 1970.

The mass consumption of durable goods like autos was not the only way rising affluence altered lifestyles. A wealthier society was a healthier one, a fact reflected in lengthening life expectancy and the growing proportion of seniors in relation to younger citizens. There were twice as many elderly people relative to the entire population in 1950 compared to 1870, and this proportion doubled again by 1990, when one out of every eight individuals had celebrated his or her sixty-fourth birthday. Industrial life and the desire for a higher standard of living also dampened the rate of births as modern couples opted for smaller families. These demographic trends, along with the emergence of a wage and salaried workforce and urban-suburban lifestyles, anchor the socioeconomic background of modern income-assistance policies. It is impossible to imagine the adoption of a Social Security program, for instance, in the preindustrial era.

Rising affluence also appears to have been instrumental in stimulating increased investment in public goods. Since the late nineteenth century government has devoted larger shares of the national wealth to collective amenities such as roads and airports, garbage collection and public health, free schools and subsidized colleges, clean water and air, national defense and help for the disabled and aged. There is no irrefutable proof that an increase in national income induced policy makers to offer more goods and services. Yet numerous studies have found a correlation between increases in GNP and public expenditures, both in the United States and in other economically developing nations.[11] These findings breed a strong presumption that these phenomena are linked causally. Yet factors other than wealth are involved in the expansion of the state, which helps to explain why the formation of the welfare state in the United States lagged behind its development in Europe by several generations.[12] Greater expenditure on public goods and services generated a need for more revenue, so it is not surprising that government took a much bigger bite out of individual pocketbooks in 1980 than in 1880. Yet economic growth softened the impact of higher taxation, leaving people better off financially even with steeper levies. Rising affluence, so it appears, made it easier for citizens to accept the diversion of more of their income for public goods. By the same token the slow growth economy since the early 1990s was joined by elevated complaints about public spending.

Industrialism reshaped the environment of politics, but the link between social change and public policy is clearer from a distance than up close when particular governmental decisions are the focus. At this microscopic level, politically active groups, such as political parties and pressure groups, are more visible instruments of policy making. Constituent and socioeconomic factors, however, can work together, a union that can be triggered by an unexpected event. Unlike the slow pace of systemic change, *random intrusions* are irregular shocks that can jar the polity into action.[13] Wars and economic depressions are the most potent of these disturbances because they have prolonged nationwide impact. The most profound modern disruptions of this variety, the Great Depression of the 1930s and World War II (1941–1945), had enormous influence on the expansion of the Federal role.[14] Washington inaugurated three of the eight major Federal functions during these two national emergencies. The depression of the middle 1890s and World War I (1917–1919) had lesser although important political reverberations as well.

A second type of random intrusion is a distinct event of a dramatic nature whose effect is short-lived and usually confined to a single issue. The Haymarket Square riot of 1886, a rally of factory workers in Chicago that led to the death of several policemen, was an event of this kind. The Illinois state legislature responded to the affair by enacting a conspiracy law in 1887 that imposed new penalties on "fomenters and inciters" of riots. This pattern of a specific stimulus and an associated policy response has occurred repeatedly in American history. Disasters such as the fire at the Triangle Shirtwaist factory in New York City (1911) that killed 146 female garment workers and the oil spill from an offshore drilling rig that fouled the beaches of Santa Barbara (1969) form one category of politically potent events. Major political demonstrations such as the civil rights march in Birmingham, Alabama, in 1963, which galvanized support for an effective civil rights act, and the violent urban riots in the 1960s, which resulted in stronger police controls, illustrate a second type. Sensationalized crimes such as the kidnapping and murder of Charles Lindbergh's young son (1932), spectacular technological breakthroughs such as the successful launch of the Russian space satellite (Sputnik, 1957), and unexpected shortages of vital commodities, as occurred in the Arab oil embargo (1973), represent other types of events that had direct political repercussions. Random intrusions seldom are solely responsible for putting a new law in the statute books. The potency of dramatic events comes from the way they interact with other factors, including structural constraints on governmental action. The American political system is littered with devices designed to impede the use of power. An unpredictable but highly newsworthy disaster that shocked the public could rally the nation behind a proposal that otherwise would have failed. The 9/11 attacks are exhibit A of this pattern.

The classical model of American democracy holds that citizens exercise control over government by selecting officials who will represent the policy preferences of their constituents. In theory at least, elections are the central mechanism that forges a link between constituents in society and policy makers in government (see figure 2.1, above). We know, of course, that the United States has had a representative political system since the birth of the nation. Therefore, if the electorate was a cause of civic expansion, some aspects of participatory politics must have changed in the nineteenth and twentieth centuries.

The popular basis of politics did undergo several structural changes after the American Revolution. The eligible electorate was substantially enlarged, first by the elimination of property requirements to vote, then with the enfranchisement of women during the transition era and of blacks and eighteen-to twenty-one-year-olds during the 1960s. These additions more than doubled the relative size of the electorate, thereby adding complexity to the job of election campaigners. The representational basis of legislatures also has changed as district boundaries were redrawn, the number of lawmakers increased and decreased, and seats were reapportioned in line with population shifts. The socioeconomic composition of legislative constituencies evolved as well. The growth of cities between the mid-nineteenth century and 1940 created big city districts populated with foreign-born voters and their American-born children, industrial workers, and white-collar employees of varying income levels and occupational pursuits. Generally speaking, voters in the central cities have given more support to the regulation of business, the protection of workers, and income-assistance programs than have rural residents.[15] Internal migrations within the United States since 1940 have shifted workers from the midsection of the country to the Pacific Coast states, blacks out of the South and into northern cities, retirees from the North to southern Sunbelt states, and much of the middle class out of cities and into the suburbs. These relocations have had impacts on electoral outcomes, most noticeably in the selection of African Americans to represent many central-city districts.

One line of argument holds that voters whose incomes were below the median in the country had a rational interest in supporting governmental policies that increased their economic well-being.[16] In addition, political writers have noted that voters have expected more from government as the twentieth century unfolded.[17] Generalization about the behavior of the public before the advent of opinion polling is speculative at best, but the available evidence suggests that attitudes began to gravitate toward support of collective solutions for many problems during the transition era. Voter surveys, available since the mid-1930s, show consistent public support for the regulation of commerce, the provision of income assistance for the aged and the deserving poor, good public schools, a strong national defense, and protection of the environment, consumer rights, and civil rights.[18] Although voters habitually have complained about the cost and bureaucratization of government, the majority have not demanded the rollback of any major public function. On the contrary, they have been highly protective of the public benefits they receive.

Other observers of the American scene are skeptical that voters exert much direct input to public policy making. This view argues that citizens pay little attention to the details of governing and have only a limited understanding of the construction of most policies.[19] Fuzziness about what government does and how it actually does it no doubt has increased with the expansion of the public sector, as programs have multiplied and become exceedingly complex. The long-term decline in voter turnout in elections that has taken place since the 1880s is consistent with the hypothesis that voters are content to let elites such as community leaders and political officials take the lead in policy making. The electorate, in other words, appears to act more as consumers of public goods than as initiators of new policies. This line of thinking sees voters as assuming a reactive posture, in which their most important role is to reassert traditional ideological limits on the options available to policy makers every so often.

Political parties have historically endeavored to mobilize popular support for particular courses of public action. By campaigning on behalf of their candidates, defending their records in office, and attacking their opponents when out of power, political parties educated voters and made them feel a part of the policy-making system. Partisan activity also transmitted policy cues from the grass roots to lawmakers, thus forging a dynamic link between constituents and representatives. With some conspicuous exceptions, such as the dominance of Democrats in the South, these activities have been competitive, intensely so during the Gilded Age, the classic period of partisan mobilization of the electorate. To the victors went the emotional satisfaction of siding with a winning team and the possible reward of a patronage job in government. Some scholars contend that in the republican era the parties had enough things of value to distribute, such as cheap public lands and privileges for businesses, to permit the parties to barter for votes.[20] How much distributional policy actually existed and its connection to partisan politicking before 1900 is up for debate. But the expansion of the public sector in the twentieth century certainly offered a greater range of options, such as higher Social Security payments and lower income taxes, with which Democrats and Republicans could bid for votes.

Has partisan competition led to an enlargement of government? To some degree, yes, but how much is a matter of continuing speculation. Some major changes in the direction of governance, such as the crusade against slavery in the 1850s and 1860s and the attempt to stabilize the economy during the Great Depression, had unmistakable partisan sponsorship. These famous policy shifts and alternating sequences of Republican and Democratic electoral dominance are the primary ingredients in the party realignment thesis. This hypothesis holds that critical elections periodically break through the political stalemates that tend to envelop the polity; and when they do, they realign the underlying patterns of voter support for the parties, producing new partisan majorities in government.[21] These rare realignments afford an opportunity for the newly empowered party to redirect the course of government. By controlling the legislature and the executive offices and by manifesting high cohesion on the issues that had provoked the electoral upheaval, the dominant political party was able to enact major policy changes.

The most persuasive case of a policy realignment occurred during the Great Depression when Franklin Roosevelt and the Democrats replaced Herbert Hoover and the Republicans and legislated the New Deal. The New Deal voter alignment survived for most of the life of the claimant polity, during which the Democrats advocated a broader role for government than did the Republicans. On balance, a vote for a Democrat for national office during the New Deal party system increased the odds of getting a higher level of public spending, more regulation of business, more generous income-assistance benefits, more aggressive enforcement of nondiscrimination policy, and a greater chance of going to war. Some scholars believe similar sequences of partisan replacements and subsequent policy upheavals occurred in the 1860s, in the years following William McKinley's victory over William Jennings Bryan in 1896, and in the 1990s when the Republicans won control of the House of Representatives.

The party realignment thesis has considerable innate appeal. In the first place, its rhythmic periodicity fits comfortably with our sense that some things seem to reoccur in patterns: business cycles and depressions, the succession of generations, severe climatic swings. Some of these long-term oscillations may

have induced or abetted party turnovers.[22] Second, political parties have occupied a conspicuous place in American politics. They have been the primary
mechanism of organizing state and national election campaigns for most of
American history in most regions. Political leaders sometimes have paid lip
service to the model of responsible parties, whereby a party is urged to stake
out a distinct policy position in an election, coordinate the campaigning of
party nominees, and muster unified support of their legislative delegation behind the party program. But a wide gap between this theory and political practice usually prevails, in good measure because leaders have few ways of controlling the rank and file of their party. Yet research on lawmakers' responses
to policy questions has identified party affiliation as the most common factor
that describes voting conflicts when the two major legislative parties held a sizable number of legislative seats.[23]

On the other hand, a convincing case can be made that party has packed
less of a policy punch than is commonly alleged. There are two parts to this argument. The first raises questions about the confirmation of the party realignment thesis on its own terms. A clear and consistent correspondence between
cycles of party dominance and policy changes has not been demonstrated for
state and local government, where a significant expansion of the public sector
occurred, especially during the transitional polity. Many states have lacked
vigorous two-party competition for long stretches of their history. This pattern was so pervasive in the states below the Mason-Dixon Line that the region was known until recent decades as the solid Democratic South. Much
of New England was solidly Republican for generations. The adoption of primary elections to select candidates and other changes in electoral mechanics
introduced at the turn of the century in most states have undercut the ability of
party leaders to pick nominees and manage campaigns. Many cities instituted
nonpartisan elections as a matter of law. Some scholars contend that these legal changes and the popular revolt against party government during the progressive era (circa 1895–1920) were instrumental in causing the decline of intense partisan competition, voter loyalty to a particular party, and turnout at
the polls. The collapse of nineteenth-century-style partisanship, according to
this view, fed the rise of administrative government and executive leadership,
at the expense of partisan influence over governance.[24]

An additional challenge to the party realignment hypothesis lies in the ex-
tensiveness of nonpartisan policy making. Much of the output of American legislatures did not evoke partisan conflict, even in settings where each party had
sizable representation. Neither the Interstate Commerce Act nor the Agricul-

tural Experiment Station grant-in-aid law, both 1887 enactments, provoked partisan dissension. Divided party control of Congress and the executive branch after 1945 has not prevented the Federal government from producing a regular harvest of important enactments through the 1970s.[25] The rate of voting disagreement between congressional parties has declined over most of the twentieth century, yet the Federal role expanded during these years.[26] For every partisan dispute over a bill in Congress there are as many if not more instances of bipartisan support for innovative legislation. The ratio is higher in the states. We can only guess at the role of parties in urban policy making in the past.[27]

Even when party differences over policy are observable, one can raise the question about their meaning and significance. Did parties actually serve as a rudder that steered the ship of state, or have they functioned more like sails that were propelled by stronger winds? Some scholars argue the latter, that parties served primarily as conduits for impulses arising elsewhere in the polity.[28] The necessity of building coalitions has forced party activists to seek a wide spectrum of voter support. Advancing innovative proposals to controversial issues may alienate key groups in the party's electoral coalition and thus jeopardize its chance to gain or retain power. To minimize risk, therefore, party officials customarily stay in the middle of the road on sensitive questions and exhibit a willingness to compromise when faced with contradictory pressures. Rather than being purposeful builders of the state, the argument runs, parties are facilitators and brokers of demands placed upon them. Politics since 1994, on the other hand, has exhibited a new rejection of compromise.

Pressure groups, by contrast, faced fewer restraints in setting forth policy positions. Their objective was to advance the interests of a specific collection of people rather than to balance the demands of an entire nation. Members of interest groups share concerns by virtue of common experiences or objectives. The organization of individuals around such particularized interests has multiplied since the 1880s as specialization among commercial, worker, professional, administrative, and social networks developed. Public administrative officials began organizing as early as the 1870s, and elected officeholders, such as mayors and governors, followed suit in the early twentieth century.[29] Officials used these public interest organizations as platforms to lobby other lawmakers, as governors now do with Congress. A proliferation of interest groups set up shop in Washington after 1920, especially after 1965.[30]

Historically, Americans saw special-interest lobbying, especially on behalf of large concentrations of economic power, as contrary to the general good. Grover Cleveland expressed this view in his 1887 denunciation of "an organized combination" that imposed its "selfish claims" on tariff policy. The platform on which Franklin Roosevelt won the presidency in 1932 condemned paid lobbyists who buttonholed members of Congress. These complaints can be understood as acknowledgments that pressure groups had become fixtures on the policy-making circuit in the transition era.[31] Because they commanded resources and expertise, lobbyists for well-heeled organizations possessed considerably more power than ordinary voters. In the claimant era large associations such as the United States Chamber of Commerce, the American Farm Bureau, the American Medical Association, the American Association of Retired Persons, and labor's AFL-CIO maintained full-time employees who cultivated first-name associations with key legislative and administrative figures. It was not uncommon for lobbyists to confer with legislators and administrators in areas of mutual interests (such as Social Security and agriculture) over the composition of policy. The sheer proliferation of public business has tended to shield these negotiations from close public scrutiny. The full story of this private-public collaboration often received little if any coverage in the news media.

Yet enough special-interest legislation reached public attention to convince many citizens that policy makers were putty in the hands of the big pressure groups. One line of scholarship maintains that special interests have in effect captured many governmental agencies, which is reflected in their favorable treatment of private groups.[32] But the public perception that lobbyists controlled all aspects of government tends to get exaggerated. In all likelihood pressure groups had greater success in lobbying defensively to stave off a reduction of benefits than in inducing lawmakers to enact new programs. How effective these groups have been in achieving either goal is a matter of continuing debate. That private groups have focused formidable resources on the quest for governmental assistance is beyond dispute.

Lobbyists focused their attention on the individuals who held the official instruments of power. Legislators, city councilors, presidents, governors, and mayors usually come to mind when we think of lawmakers. But appointed administrators and judges also played instrumental roles in the expansion of the public sector. The American way, as we know, was to divide up power in government among separate legislative, executive, and judicial branches. Since this structure was established long before the modern expansion of the public sector began, we must look beyond the formal layout of government for clues regarding how institutional features contributed to policy expansion.

Several possibilities warrant consideration, including ideas about the nature of representation. Democratic theory suggests that lawmakers should act in accordance with the wishes of their constituents. But there is no law that they must do so. When they do seek guidance from the grass roots, information about popular policy preferences may not exist or may show divided opinions. Public officials are also free to assess the needs of society and initiate policy solutions to them on their own. The notion that legislators serve as trustees for their constituents and exercise their own judgment regarding the directions of government is not incompatible with democratic thinking. Certainly politicians can assume both roles at various times. One constancy to their behavior, some have said, is to put their own personal interest ahead of the public good. This charge is as old as the republic, and it intensified during the Gilded Age, when critics saw corruption rampant in politics, particularly in urban government. The modern version of this indictment holds that the retention of power is the first priority of public servants, who use the prerogatives of office to achieve their goal. On this point the literature tends to finger Congress, especially members of the House and officials of many agencies.[33]

A critical difference between the republican, transitional, and claimant polities regarding self-interested politics is the length of time that officials remained in office. Tenure was short during the republican era, when few officeholders made a career out of government and the norm of rotation was widely observed. This pattern declined rapidly during the transitional polity, and by the claimant era length of service had grown markedly for both elected and appointed officials, many of whom made government a long-term commitment. As the pay, prestige, and power of public service rose, so did the inducement for officials to adopt strategies for political survival. One pathway to success was to draw upon the resources of government to develop a base of political support. The reputation of a legislator or an administrator could be enhanced, for example, by promoting a specialized policy objective, such as clean air or occupational safety. The public-choice theorists add a twist to these theories based on economic assumptions about rational behavior. They argue that politicians in a democracy will select spending and taxing options that maximize current benefits and delay their costs. The theory predicts that when faced with a choice between higher taxes and deficit financing, officials will side with more debt, which defers costs into the future.[34] Considered on their own merits, programs that are created partially out of political or professional self-interest do not necessarily result in poor policy. Yet the collective result of many individuals pushing their own legislative initiatives is the proliferation of programs that tend to lack effective coordination or overall limits.

Defenders of lengthy tenure have replied that government benefited from the skills and experience gained in the course of public service. The development of science, technology, and organizational efficiencies in the private sector, some reformers contended, had a parallel in civic affairs, where there was a growing need for experts to manage the complex tasks of modern governance. Specialized expertise could be acquired by learning on the job, as in the instance of members of Congress who sat on the same committee for decades, and by providing administrative agencies with adequate resources and qualified staff.[35] Some scholars locate the seeds of public-sector expansion in the emergence of professional administration. This view holds that nineteenth-century governance was handicapped by its dependence on locally based political parties, whose activities were oriented around distributional policy, and by heavy reliance on courts for administration. Reformers consciously set about to create a competent national bureaucracy, which they saw as critical to the development of a coherent capacity to govern. Most members of the state-building school, as this perspective is called, tend to date the emergence of an American administrative state in the first decades of the twentieth century.[36] Like Pandora's box, modern administration took on a life of its own, some students of government hold, as bureaucrats endeavored to maximize the size and power of their agencies as a way of furthering their personal interests.[37]

Despite the cynicism about their motivations, politicians have not been entirely free to do their own thing. They were obliged to work within a framework of ideological principles and legal rules, which I have labeled "structure" (see figure 2.1). A set of commonly accepted standards about the proper conduct of politics had evolved during the republican polity. Axioms central to this thinking included a commitment to the personal ownership of property, a market-base economic system, representative political institutions (such as legislatures), freedom of speech and religion, and a criminal justice process based on fair procedures and citizen juries. These common tenets also disapproved of unfair taxation, centralized authority, bureaucracy, and special-interest lobbyists. Most of these ideas survived in one fashion or another into the twentieth century. The penetration of these axioms through all strata of society and their influence in reducing conflicts between economic classes in the United States, at least in comparison to Europe, constitute the essentials of the consensus thesis of American political history.[38]

Constitutions helped to preserve the longevity of republican axioms. The arrangement of government into separate branches, the division of authority between a central government and states, and the prohibition of certain actions as a device to protect individual liberties represent long-standing constitutional principles. Within this framework existed specific guidelines for political conduct. Some well-known examples, such as the limitation of the president to four-year terms (and, since 1951, no more than two terms), are found in the national Constitution. Statutory law set many more. Lawmakers might wink at ideological norms and they could amend statutory rules, but they were less able to ignore the restrictions embedded in constitutions.

Structure did not cause the growth of government, yet it had an immensely important impact on how this process evolved. Structure's potency lay in its ability to channel power. Federalism offers a prime illustration of this effect, one that scholars have not adequately incorporated into American governmental history. In dividing power between two centers of authority, federalism placed considerable governing responsibility in the states and localities, both in the past and in our own time. The tendency of Congress to rely on the states to manage many aspects of national policy, from agricultural experiment stations in 1887 to President Obama's health-care reform (2010), reflect the tradition of decentralized governance under American federalism. Moreover, the semi-sovereign status of the states within the federal system has permitted, perhaps encouraged, these individual centers of policy-making initiative to adopt dissimilar policies in many functional areas. These local policy actions were accepted in the republican era as a fulfillment of federalism's democratic design. But as industrialization promoted a national view of society, new justifications arose for adopting national policy standards. The patchwork of policy actions across America, in other words, became a contextual reason for greater centralization of power at the Federal level. As later chapters illustrate, the division of authority between the states and Washington had numerous repercussions on the selection, financing, and administration of the nation's expanding policy agenda.

The interaction of the environment, constituents, and governmental officials within the nation's political structure produced new public policies. But

analysis of the causes of growth does not end here, because government's decisions carried consequences, called *feedback*. Inherently part of change and
growth, feedback is an acknowledgment that governance was a process that
unfolded over time. The idea holds that policy outputs at one point affect the
performance of the political system in the future. Feedback travels through
microscopic and macroscopic channels. At the microscopic level the design of
a program can leverage further growth. A tax law whose provisions maximize
revenue gains by capturing economic growth and inflation or a benefit program whose costs rise with the longevity of recipients illustrates program design that is inherently expansionary.

Macroscopic feedback reflects the fact that individuals learn to adapt to
their environment. Change can be unsettling. People tend to be apprehensive
about the unknown consequences of civic innovations, similar to their anxieties about major changes in their personal lives. Time has a way of reducing
these insecurities as people adjust to new circumstances. Over the years since
1887 Americans have adapted to the growing propensity of government to use
power. Innovative policy proposals initially generated apprehension and controversy. The enactment of a program, perhaps after years of struggle, marked
an important political milestone. Once the major policy threshold had been
breached, subsequent policy making on the subject tended to settle around pe-
ripheral concerns. Additions to the original program and adoption of similar
programs became easier. As time passed and young adults matured into political consciousness, memories about older political controversies faded. Genera-
tional cycling and the process of adjustment to new circumstances disposed
people at specific stages of our political history to see the policy landscape
about them as the normal state of affairs.[39] Admittedly, politics since 1992 has
challenged much of this complacency.

The modulating effect of accommodation to policy change underscores the
historical dimension of feedback. The growth of government was an evolutionary process that engaged interactions among all parts of a political system.
The comprehensive nature of this development foils the attempt to isolate a
single spark that ignited civic expansion. Elmer Schattschneider put the challenge succinctly: "The theoretical problem involved in the search for a single
cause is that all power relations in a democracy are reciprocal. Trying to find
the original cause is like trying to find the first wave of the ocean."[40] In other
words, it is futile to look for a magic bullet that explains a phenomenon as com-

plex as the transformation of government. Its growth followed an evolutionary path, with many side trails that meandered with time, place, and issue.

Feedback's historical dimension implies that the growth of government was both incremental and cumulative. The incremental model of policy making holds that present policy decisions are influenced by past practices. Unlike innovative proposals that broke with precedent and usually were controversial, the incremental process of policy making followed the course of least political resistance. It built on existent policy.[41] Yet many small steps accumulated over time into more fundamental alterations. Schattschneider captured the significance of these policy drifts. "Change is possible," he wrote, "in part because it is often imperceptible, because it is usually done in the name of preserving the status quo."[42] A series of small, relatively minor additions to Social Security over the years demonstrated, Martha Derthick concluded, "the radical potential of incremental changes."[43] Her observation applies to numerous areas of policy.

Each round of policy development expanded people's expectations about the purpose of civic action, reestablishing the context in which subsequent decisions were made. This process gradually undermined the foundations of the republican polity and crystallized into a claimant outlook. Americans allotted government-wide latitude to manage human affairs in this new style of politics. Older fears that officeholders would reward their friends and deny liberty to their rivals diminished. Republican suspicions gravitated toward an instrumental outlook that accepted public authority as a pragmatic tool to solve problems. The 1880s through the 1930s, when clashes among old and new ideologies peaked, dates the transition from classical conceptions of government to its modern substitute. The mentality of the claimant polity, wherein power was viewed as a solvent rather than a toxin, took on distinct form in the 1930s and matured into the dominant civic philosophy in the 1960s.

Claimant politics has two fundamental components. At the system level, Americans saw government as a mechanism to reduce the risks of an unpredictable and sometimes harsh world. They did not always agree on the priority of problems that government should tackle or on the means of handling them. But by the middle twentieth century, wide agreement prevailed that public officials should regulate many aspects of commercial activity; stimulate the economy to ensure profits and full employment; provide a range of services such as schools, highways, clean water, and fire protection; help the neediest and underwrite the income of the elderly; maintain the basic contours of a peaceful world order; protect consumers, workers, and the environment from severe hazards; and uphold standards of equal political and economic opportunity for minorities and women. The guarantee of universal access to health care perhaps can be added to this list. Older ideas about fairness survived, but traditional fears about placing power in the hands of officeholders faded. Americans increasingly judged government by how effectively it handled the agenda of the claimant polity.

The second meaning of claimant politics was its capacity to provide benefits to individuals. Since the mid-nineteenth century government had distributed more and more things of value, many of which it had created. These services, subsidies, and permissions ranged from free schools, cash stipends for the elderly and farmers, and tax breaks for homeowners, slumlords, and cigarette manufacturers to sweetheart contracts for weapons makers, restricted competition for taxicab drivers and doctors, and government investment in private businesses and university research. In the language of the republican polity, claimant-era politicians produced a long list of "class legislation." Americans have complained about the size and cost of government over the years, but they showed little willingness to give up their personal benefits. Whatever their partisan leanings, special interests sprang into action when their own benefits were targeted for reduction or extinction. Such a "me-first" attitude is apparently what John Kennedy attempted to counteract in his inaugural address in 1961. "Ask not what your country can do for you," the president appealed, but "ask what you can do for your country." JFK's call for renewed dedication to the common good lured some young idealists into the Peace Corps but did not reduce government benefits. Neither did the resurgence of conservative criticism of "big" government since the 1980s.

Although the performance of government inherently elicits judgmental opinions, the question of whether modern governance is constructive, inevitable, or counterproductive is not the purpose of this book. This chapter has sought to explain the growth of government by abstracting the leading speculations about the process. This review demonstrated that the dynamics of growth are exceedingly complex, largely because history is complex. The mix of causes shifted as policy making moved from one subject area to another and as the polity proceeded from one historical era to the next.

3

The Transition Era

JULIAN WEST GAZED in amazement at his native Boston. It was not the city he remembered. Marvelous public structures adorned an immaculate landscape where hovels once stood. Doors were left unlocked because burglars no longer prowled the night; with "care and crime" abolished, thieves had vanished. The reconstruction of society had closed the chasm between the "wanton luxury" of the rich and the "general misery" of the masses. Now all members of a classless community shared equally in the nation's expanded bounty. Who managed this utopia, Julian West asked? Government, his host replied. "The nation guarantees the nurture, education and comfortable maintenance of every citizen from the cradle to the grave."[1]

This was Boston in the year 2000, more than a century after Julian West had fallen into a "mesmerized" sleep. The America he remembered had been torn by economic warfare, in which greedy entrepreneurs battled for financial survival. The winners of these wars had accumulated fortunes befitting royalty, but the cost of their victories was high. Economic titans had swallowed up competitors, allowing the control of industry to fall into "a few powerful hands." In this "era of corporate tyranny," many businesses transformed themselves into trusts and monopolies by forming syndicates and fixing prices. In this drive to crush rivals, corporate cutthroat competition had caused the "maim and slaughter" of workers and the waste of talent and resources. Capitalism of the Cleveland era thrived on the "brutal side of human nature."

This brutish picture of America flowed from the pen of Edward Bellamy in his book *Looking Backward, 2000–1887,* the country's most famous utopian novel, written in 1887. Julian West's long sleep was the author's literary device for envisioning a better world than the one the hero had remembered. *Looking Backward* depicts a society of the future in which material comfort and the collective interest of the nation had replaced inequality between the classes and ruthless commercial competition. Individuals found their place in the new economic structure according to their personal preference and natural aptitude. The fruits of an individual's labor were available equally by virtue of a person's humanity. Economic security had become a birthright. Selfish advancement and monetary privilege had been programmed out of the new social order.

Eradicated too was the "corruption of our public men" that Bellamy saw rampant in the 1880s. Economic equality had eliminated the temptation for lawmakers "to misuse their power for the private profit of themselves or others." Now officials served "a single syndicate representing the people . . . in the common interest." Allocating the assignment of workers in accordance with popular tastes for goods had become the primary task for civil servants. The system ran like clockwork because decisions were based on meticulous record keeping of consumption and sophisticated estimates of needed production. Statisticians, not ward-heeling politicians, ran its administration, headquartered in Washington. Efficiency of scale and scientific management was in; state governments and political profiteers were out. A nationalized democracy of workers, not federalism, secured liberty in Bellamy's utopia.[2]

"Absurd," scoffed William Graham Sumner, America's most famous sociologist in Bellamy's day. It was the height of folly "to sit down . . . and pencil out a new social world." Property was the "bulwark against want and distress" and the accumulation of capital provided "the fortification of existence." Deprive individuals of the right to acquire property and to use it in enterprise, Sumner postulated, and watch poverty flourish. One could not "make the world over" by the schemes of dreamers. Immutable laws of nature, such as the ambition to gain wealth, drove an economic system. And the result was positive, not negative as Bellamy held. Out of the private pursuit of property came collective benefits for society. Competition, the invisible regulator of the marketplace, balanced supply to demand and lowered prices through more efficient business practices. Private self-interest, in other words, could promote the general welfare.

Sumner's response to Bellamy drew on the theories of Adam Smith, the philosophic godfather of a free-market economy. Sumner embellished these ideas by joining them to social Darwinism, a social theory that rested on primitive thinking about biological evolution. And he coupled his defense of property with a reworking of America's historic ideology—republican political liberty. Governmental meddling in the marketplace, Sumner held, stymied economic progress by impeding competition. Laissez-faire—where individuals, not government, "mind your own business"—was the appropriate environment for capitalism. Disregard of this maxim portended danger because government had the capacity to reward a few at the expense of others. The holders of wealth had the motives and a history of ruthlessness to abuse power in the political arena for their own advantage. The more that the captains of industry gained a foothold in government, the more that politicians would cooperate to "surrender public to private interests." Left unchecked, this process promised plutocracy, a political regime where wealth ruled and the middle class bore most of the costs of overlegislation. This mishap could be avoided, however, if government confined its activity to its two legitimate concerns: protection of the property of men and the honor of women. Sumner, like Bellamy, saw economic changes propelling the polity toward domination by the rich. But unlike the novelist, Sumner came to a strikingly different conclusion about how government should respond to this outcome.[3]

Sumner and Bellamy charted the outer boundaries of the Great Debate about government that flourished during the transition era (1880s–1920s). From church, labor, and government leaders to journalists, academicians, and industrialists, most segments of society joined the dialogue. The debaters began with a common premise: life as the generation of 1787 had known it was gone. Industrialization was reshaping the social and economic face of America. In place of a smaller and simpler social arrangement appeared big business, big labor, technological wonders and mechanical hazards, mushrooming cities, millions of immigrants, and bastions of wealth amid a sea of poverty. While specific aspects of these transformations proved distressing to particular groups, individuals from a wide range of backgrounds worried about a common denominator in many of these changes: the growth of private power. This development was most visible in the rise of large business corporations, whose accounts grew to hundreds of millions of dollars and whose managers employed small armies of wage earners. But the unionization of workers was equally ominous to some. Millions of words in print and in speeches were devoted to these transformations and how to cope with them.

Traditional ideology had depicted government as the greatest danger to freedom. But as private groups came to possess resources that rivaled public authority, government no longer monopolized power. This was the critical fact to many observers in the transition era. The rise of private power constituted a new threat to liberty. The Great Debate turned on whether the older republican view of the relationship between citizens and their government retained validity. Should the polity revise its historic antipathy to public power in the face of social and economic dislocations? Did the new age, in other words, require more active government in order to protect the welfare of individuals from the dangers of private aggregations of power?

Bellamy answered yes. His solution to the problems of his time transposed the old relationship between government and liberty. Whereas republican ideology had emphasized the penchant of rulers to restrict freedom, Bellamy believed that government should protect individuals against oppression. Because corporations had replaced kings as the source of tyranny, the state was obliged to tame the economic barons in order to free workers from "wage slavery." That the expansion of the public sector itself could create new abuses of power was a minor concern to Bellamy.

Bellamy's ideas represent the statist position in the Great Debate. Today we would say that his outlook is situated near the left end of the political spectrum. Bellamy's plan actually added up to an Americanized version of socialism, although he did not call it that. Various groups in the transition era offered recommendations that sounded much like Bellamy's. The most doctrinaire anticapitalists, the Socialist Labor Party and the Industrial Workers of the World (IWW), saw class struggle as inherent in industrial capitalism and advocated public ownership of the means of production. The Populists, a largely rural-based political party with whom Bellamy's fans flirted in the early 1890s, supported more limited public control. Their statism went no further than government ownership of transportation and communication facilities. Distinctions between partial and complete socialism were too fine for people who sided with Sumner. To them, all shades of statism were radical.

Sumner took the antistatist position in the Great Debate. This outlook held that private property was sacred, natural forces ran the economy, and government should not interfere with commercial activity. Public intervention not only distorted the regulatory magic of private competition, but it also would produce a bureaucracy dominated by the rich. Few antistatists went as far as Sumner in seeking to constrict the functions of government. But strains of his free-market dogma ran through the ideas of other political thinkers of the era. Cleveland's denunciation of protective tariffs and the courts' defense of entrepreneurial liberty contained antistatist sentiments. So did the explanations of the "gold" Democrats for their opposition to the party's nomination of William Jennings Bryan for president in 1896. Bryan's election, predicted these Cleveland diehards, would lead to paternalism and class legislation. The gold Democrats claimed to uphold orthodox republicanism, including its monetary standards. Today we would label them "conservatives." Adherents of Sumner's doctrinaire brand of laissez-faire, then and now, are situated toward the right pole of America's political spectrum.

Conservative thinking experienced a resurgence in the 1920s. Presidents Warren Harding (1921–1923) and Calvin Coolidge (1923–1929) revived traditional ideas about the preservation of liberty, which in their view required restraints on the use of power, respect for traditional (dual) federalism, and the supremacy of representative bodies. Harding advised the members of Congress in his inaugural address to reflect upon "the inexorable laws of nature" before contemplating legislative action. This admonition coincided with Coolidge's philosophy that "the coercive powers of Government" should not be used to burden taxpayers with unnecessary expenses and "a great array of public employees." Coolidge justified his veto of an act to raise farm prices on classic republican grounds: the special tax to finance the measure rewarded a few at the expense of most farmers. The president also thought that the plan ran "counter to our traditions" in granting arbitrary power to administrators. Herbert Hoover, the last of the three Republican presidents during the 1920s, agreed that large bureaucracies threatened individual liberty. Cognizant of the need for coordination in the industrial age, Hoover urged the formation of private trade associations as a compromise between government intervention into business and destructive competition among private interests.

Between the extremes of the Sumner and Bellamy prescriptions lay a broad middle ground where most debaters rested their case. Most of these middle-of-the-roaders agreed that changes in their society required selective applications of government power. Moderates quarreled about precise remedies, but they concurred that industrialization had produced new needs in society and that government offered a practical instrument with which to restore justice. We can call this intermediate position on power the instrumentalist outlook. Its hallmark was moderate reform designed to rectify inequities in a changing environment while preserving the existing institutional structures of American society. This willingness to use power conditionally, in a selective and practical way, to address specific problems, was termed "progressive" in the early twentieth century. The progressives were instrumentalists whose pragmatic brand of statism contained the philosophical seeds of liberalism that blossomed after 1933.

Theodore Roosevelt was an archetypical instrumentalist. Born in 1858, he served as a state legislator, a city and Federal administrator, governor of New York State (1899–1900), and vice president of the United States before William McKinley's assassination elevated him to the presidency (1901–1909). "TR" saw American institutions as fundamentally sound. Like Sumner, he believed that capitalism was an engine of economic progress. But unlike Sumner, Roosevelt believed that the social effects of industrialization necessitated compensatory responses from government. "We must face accomplished facts," he argued, pointing to issues such as the rise of giant corporations and the increase of women in the workforce. If government didn't act, rule by a plutocracy or by a mob would fill the void. The best strategy to counteract corporate abuses and to protect the weaker wage earner from oppression was cautious, case-by-case applications of power.[4]

Roosevelt's progressive approach downplayed old republican homilies and relied instead on lengthy agendas for public action. His 1905 annual message, fifty pages long, urged Congress to look into matters big and small, from air pollution in the nation's capital, the slaughter of the buffalo in the West, and the installation of automatic signals on railroad lines to the method of promoting army officers and the addition of submarines to the navy. Modern industrial conditions required "affirmative action" from all levels of government, he observed. Because he gave responsiveness to society's "needs" higher priority than deference to old dogmas, Roosevelt saw no reason to defend dual federalism.[5]

TR's prescription for good government also addressed the moral decline of politics that many Americans had lamented for decades. The Independent Republicans, who deserted James Blaine in favor of Grover Cleveland during the 1884 presidential election, used the occasion to underscore this critique, which blossomed into conventional thinking by the early twentieth century. Public officials, these renegade Republicans said in their campaign "Address," had strayed from pure republicanism and allowed an "insidious political corruption" to prostitute the public welfare. Politics had become dishonest because politicians put their personal interest and party patronage ahead of the public good. The Independent Republicans saw Grover Cleveland as the best hope for elevating Federal administration above "mere partisan and personal advantage."

Proposals to rid the political process of its most distasteful faults were restorationist in character. Adherents of this outlook did not urge expansion of the public sector or any sweeping reconstruction of the political order, but rather emphasized the need to restore virtue to the public arena. They urged destruction of the alliance between party politicians and businessmen that was widely believed to form a secret, invisible government. Journalists who wrote for the mass-circulation magazines that emerged in the early twentieth century played on this conspiratorial theme. Titles of their muckraking exposés— "The Treason of the Senate," "The Shame of Minneapolis"—popularized the belief that politics had become perverted and foul. This motif crept into fictional accounts of the day's politics. Railroad domination of state government in New Hampshire was so complete, the novelist Winston Churchill had a lawmaker proclaim, that it was "a sheer waste of money for the State to pay a Legislature. They might as well run things from the New York office."[6] Support for tax reform drew on similar displeasure with party politics. Property owners in the cities blamed their rising tax bills on wasteful politicians, whose financial schemes were presumably aimed at buying votes.[7]

The statute books and constitutions of the states swelled with new provisions designed to clamp down on partisan evils. Civil-service laws, which sought to base government appointments on merit rather than party patronage, began this legal strategy in 1883, with enactments in New York and Congress (the Pendleton Act). In the next decade emphasis shifted to ballot reform, whereby government rather than political parties printed election ballots, registered eligible voters, and supervised voting in secret (the Australian ballot). Primaries, in which voters (not the party bosses) selected party nominees for elective offices, proliferated after 1900. Numerous states allowed voters a voice in statute making through procedures called initiatives and referenda. A battery of state and national laws sought to regulate financial contributions to candidates and required the registration of lobbyists.

A common denominator in these actions was the presumption that changes in the formal rules of politics would reduce partisan venality and restore a citizen-based polity. Two of the four additions to the U.S. Constitution in the transition era—popular election of U.S. senators (Seventeenth Amendment, 1913) and female suffrage (Nineteenth Amendment, 1920)—grew out of this conviction. Ironically, the turnout of voters at the polls declined in subsequent decades, in part due to the new political regulations. Registration made voting more difficult, ballot laws handicapped third parties and independent candidates, and reformers disenfranchised some people, notably blacks and unnaturalized immigrants.[8] A second irony of the good-government reforms was the expansion of public authority. In the name of restoring honesty and integrity to government, antiparty critics granted more power to public officials to regulate the political process. The modern analogue to this progressive-era crusade is the creation of the Federal Election Commission (1974), which allocates public financial assistance to presidential nominees.

The political restorationists had soul mates of a sort in the social preservationists. People who exhibited this ideological disposition lamented the breakdown of cultural and community homogeneity in American society. They perceived the nation's moral fiber to be unraveling owing to liquor peddlers and saloon dwellers such as gamblers and prostitutes, immigrants from southern and eastern Europe and Asia, and assorted "un-American" political radicals, who were often lumped together as "anarchists." To eradicate these malevolent influences on society the social preservationists campaigned to padlock the breweries and taverns, ban undesirable immigrants, and muzzle the political radicals, even if it meant deporting them. The transition era enacted a battery of these efforts at social control, which were part of a broader trend of public intervention that sought to protect the public health, safety, and morality of the community. Many of these restrictions, such as penalizing drunk drivers and restricting the number of immigrants, can stand on their own objective merits. In the transition era many reformers advocated social controls out of the fear that the foundation of the Republic was imperiled by undesirable groups. Inflated claims about these dangers influenced many lawmakers to overcome their apprehensions about power and legislate controls on the unworthy classes.

There was another voice heard in the Great Debate, one whose pitch was more academic than the other lines of discourse. Claiming disinterest in the substance of policies, these professional types centered their concern on the administration of government. Traditional methods of public management, they held, produced corruption and waste. The achievement of more honest and effective government required the separation of administration from politics and the transformation of executive management into a science. These organizationally minded reformers were apostles of civic efficiency. They shared many of the prejudices about conventional politics common to the transition era, but their solutions were different. Drawing ideas from organizational and technical developments in society, the apostles of civic efficiency created a code of professional public administration. In the large corporations they saw models for businesslike civic management, whose operations would be organized into units according to their function and whose activities would be monitored by cost accounting. Breakthroughs in science suggested how systematic investigation, quantitative analysis in particular, could be applied to civic problem solving. And the emergence of scholarly disciplines (such as economics and political science) produced experts whose specialized talents could guide the process of reforming administration.

The organization of professional and civic associations, under way in the last third of the nineteenth century, created forums where the new possibilities in civic management were discussed. Some groups, such as medical doctors, engineers, and accountants, represented the private side of professionalization. A second type brought together government officials who were engaged in the public tasks invented or expanded during the transition era. State bureaus of labor statistics and municipal boards of public health were among the first of the public groups to form national associations. This process accelerated in the twentieth century as civil servants organized trade groups around their policy specialty. Municipal electricians, inspectors of weights and measures, seed analysts, and sewage works officers suggest the range of functional interests among the organizers. Their annual meetings and newsletters provided vehicles for disseminating ideas, building a sense of professionalism among members, and planning strategy. While professional networks tended to operate within specific occupational specialties, lines of communication opened up between different associations.[9] The National Municipal League, formed in 1894, offered a common meeting ground for persons of diverse professional backgrounds. The urban focus of the league's administrative reform reflected the reality of governance at the time: local officials managed the largest body of public tasks and supervised the largest number of public employees.

The apostles of civic efficiency, who were found in the universities, in government, and in private industry, developed a recognizable structure of ideas just after the turn of the century. The titles of their publications suggest their message: "The Budget as an Instrument of Financial Control" (1908), "Training for Efficient Public Service" (1916), "The Application of Scientific Management to the Activities of State and Municipal Government" (1912). Effective administration, the apostles preached, required the appointment of experts who had training in civic administration or a policy specialty. Administrative decisions should be based on objective analysis, which could be achieved by reliance on quantitative data. Managerial productivity necessitated careful cost accounting of financial transactions and the preparation of a budget under executive (not legislative) direction. The fragmented array of boards and commissions that handled most administrative chores had to be grouped into general departments whose heads were responsible to a single chief executive. President William Howard Taft's appointment of a Commission on Economy and Efficiency in 1910 signaled the spreading appeal of these propositions. In promising impartial oversight of government's growing workload, the apostles of civic efficiency parented modern administration in America.[10]

As these proposals gained popular support, politicians took note and merchandised some of them as partisan ideas. The major political parties were more interested in placing their nominees in office than in crusading for administrative innovation, for they measured success by the number of their candidates that won election. Experience had taught politicos that berating their opponents for misdeeds and appealing to traditional voter prejudices and loyalties offered less risk than advocating new policy proposals. Yet politicians could not ignore important developments in society or major currents of thinking among the public if they wished to be competitive at the polls.

The platforms of the parties reflected these changes in appeals to the electorate. Axioms of republican ideology permeated these campaign statements in the 1880s. The Republican Party still looked back to the Civil War in its 1884 platform, claiming credit for the preservation of liberty by saving the Union. By the 1920s an instrumental conception of government had gained a foothold in election copy. Herbert Hoover campaigned in 1928 on a platform that asked voters to judge the GOP by tangible economic results and pointed to the success of Harding-Coolidge policies in promoting prosperity. Republican platforms of the 1920s ran four times longer than their statements of the 1880s. Democrats similarly lengthened their documents. The added length of the platforms paralleled the expansion of the public agenda during the transition era. Yet the new campaign documents did not dismiss all the old ideas, which produced some strange contradictions. In 1928, for example, the Democrats condemned bureaucracy in one plank and urged a liberal retirement law for Federal employees in another.

The changing standards of good government undermined stability in the electoral arena. The minor "third" parties were barometers of the new cross-currents that buffeted traditional partisan politics. A variety of smaller parties, from worker- and farmer-based groups in the late nineteenth century to socialists and assorted reformers in the 1920s, challenged the two major parties by advocating greater public intervention in society.[11] Their prescriptions for better government contrasted sharply with those of the Democrats in the Cleveland years and of the Republicans in the 1920s, the partisan groups most closely associated with antistatist outlooks. But neither major party was philosophically homogeneous, especially by the early twentieth century, when progressive and nonprogressive factions coexisted in each organization.

The election of 1912 showcased this disharmony. Three major presidential contestants, not the customary two, ran that year. Democrats backed Woodrow Wilson, an academic political scientist turned politician who was governor of New Jersey. Republicans stood by William Howard Taft, the incumbent who had succeeded Theodore Roosevelt as president. A coterie of instrumentalists, mainly disgruntled Republicans, formed a Progressive party and nominated Roosevelt, who sought to reclaim the White House. Eugene Debs headed the Socialist ticket, which scored its best showing (6 percent of the popular vote) since it first fielded a presidential ticket in 1900. After the Socialists completed their obligatory attack on corporate plutocracy and the Prohibitionists, the other sizable third party on the ballot, unleashed their invective on the "drink traffic," the platforms of each group went on to support a long list of conventional progressive reforms.

The split among Republicans elevated Wilson to the White House. His two terms in the presidency (1913–1921) interrupted the GOP's control of the Oval Office between Cleveland's retirement in 1897 and Franklin Roosevelt's inauguration in 1933. Wilson was a transitional figure in his party's history. Cleveland loyalists clung to the axioms of classical republicanism, especially concerning the role of the Federal government. After 1932 Democrats in national office supported a major expansion of national power. Wilson contributed to this transformation by advocating a program of national economic controls and by expanding the dimensions of presidential leadership. Possessing a logician's knack of blending new ideas with old principles, he appealed to restorationist sentiments with pledges to cleanse evils from society. At the same time he drew back from embracing strict dual federalism. His messages to Congress, in which he urged public redress of "the consequences of great industrial and social processes," epitomized the instrumental concept of government that blossomed in the Progressive Era.[12] According to this outlook, the public good required government, including officials at the national level, to address modern problems. Experts with a nose for efficiency should oversee the implementation of government's new agenda. This last recommendation came straight out of the textbook on administration, a new field that Woodrow Wilson, the former political scientist, had helped to launch.[13]

The Great Debate represented an extraordinary period of reassessment of American government, perhaps the most comprehensive reappraisal since the American Revolution. This discourse reflected attempts of Americans to reconcile older libertarian fears about government power with an emerging sense that the public community had a responsibility to control the manifestations of social change. Out of this exchange of opinion came the rationale to build the modern governmental regime. Virtually all the essential ideas of political liberalism were aired during the years of this dialogue. But the Great Debate was more than an exchange of opinions about the future direction of government. It was also a response to the actual growth of the public sector. This fact was the critical cue for antistatists, who saw the republican model of limited government under attack.

Public expenditures documented the expansion of civic activity. In terms of unadjusted ("current") dollars, government was fourteen times costlier when Hoover entered the White House in 1929 than when Cleveland first served as president. The population and the economy had increased during these years, and inflation had reduced the purchasing power of the dollar. Yet even with adjustment for these factors, "real" (per-capita constant dollars) public expenditures quadrupled between the 1880s and the late 1920s. As America grew richer during the transition era, lawmakers diverted a greater share of the nation's wealth to public goods. All levels of government participated in this fiscal growth, although state budgets outpaced the rate of increase in the others. By the end of the 1920s state spending accounted for three and a half times more of the GNP than in 1890. The rate of public outlays accelerated at all levels of government after 1913 as Washington kept pace with the pack. Federal spending ballooned during World War I (a twenty-five-fold increase between 1916 and

1919) and never returned to prewar levels, despite Harding's and Coolidge's efforts to roll back war-born taxes.[14] National outlays consumed 50 percent more of the GNP in 1927 than they had in 1913 (from 2.4 to 3.7 percent). Defense-related functions claimed nearly two-thirds of the Federal budget in the 1920s; congressional appropriations for interest charges on the debt and for veterans' benefits (a type of "fixed costs") alone exceeded outlays for all national purposes before the Great War.

Despite enlarged Federal budgets in the 1920s, Washington's share of public expenses remained equivalent to the ratio that had prevailed in the Cleveland era. The cities, counties, and school districts still outspent the state and national governments combined. Arlington, Massachusetts, for example, spent seventy-five dollars per person in 1927 compared with the national government's thirty dollars, sixteen dollars of which was defense related. Arlington was more generous with its money than many localities, a contrast attributable in part to the town's rapid growth and relative affluence. Local budgets must be seen in conjunction with state finances, because this relationship varied from place to place. Massachusetts, which relied heavily on its local communities for the financing of programs, especially education, spent less than most other state governments (roughly twelve dollars compared to seventeen dollars per person in 1927). Yet the combined state and local government outlays in the commonwealth were higher than in most other states.

The affluence of localities had a lot to do with how much money a state and local government spent. Generally speaking, richer communities purchased more public goods and services than did poorer localities.[15] These variations flowed from the reliance on local governance that prevailed during the republican era. During the transitional and claimant eras the states increased their fiscal involvement with local governments by providing grants-in-aid to cities and towns and by monitoring their financial management. One rationale used on behalf of a larger fiscal role for states was the need to compensate for the low levels of taxable wealth in some communities. Efforts to equalize educational expenditures among school districts throughout the twentieth century rested on differences in local ability to raise tax revenue. In some matters the states extended financial assistance to local government, which managed functions such as primary education and local roads, subject to state guidelines. In other policy areas, such as state colleges and public welfare, they eventually assumed direct fiscal and administrative responsibility.

The growing cost of government sparked interest in improving techniques of fiscal management. Efficiency reformers ridiculed the lack of legislative co-ordination between appropriations and taxation and the loose, sometimes non-existent, oversight of administrative purchases and payments. Steps to rectify these holdovers from the republican era were under way by 1900, as numerous cities and states required accountants to audit transactions. Better record keeping of financial activity was linked to proposals to have an integrated financial plan prepared under the direction of a budget office, preferably supervised by the chief executive. The idea caught fire around 1910, and by 1930 all the states and most large cites had some form of "executive budget."[16] The fiscal consequences of World War I prompted Congress to stop its foot-dragging on the issue and enact the Bureau of the Budget Act of 1921, which directed the executive branch to prepare a fiscal plan each year. The law also created a General Accounting Office under Congress to monitor Federal fiscal transactions.

Truly efficient management, reformers argued, depended on a sweeping overhaul of administration, not just an improvement in fiscal control. With their haphazard arrangements for implementing policy and their expanded programs and employees, state governments were prime candidates for reorganization. Between 1917 and 1929 a third of the states streamlined their administrative structures. One model for this restructuring existed in the national cabinet-style executive departments, which housed (in theory) functionally related subunits whose heads were appointed by the president. Constitutional rules and legislators' fears that reorganization would lessen their influence and inflate the costs of government, however, slowed movement in this direction. Political opposition also blunted efforts to authorize stronger mayors in the big cities and appoint city managers in the smaller ones.

Administrative reorganization went on in Washington too. Cabinet-level departments were created for agriculture (1889) and for commerce and labor (1903), which were separated into independent units in 1913. But managerial restructuring in Washington occurred mainly within existing departments, where new bureaus were added and existing units consolidated or divided. As Federal activities grew, so did the number of Federal employees and the range of their occupational specialties. Closer attention to the classification of personnel for salary and related purposes followed in the wake of these changes. And as more employees made a career out of Federal service, pressure mounted on lawmakers to provide retirement pensions for government workers. Congress and the president complied in 1920.

Industrialism had profound effects on life in Arlington, Massachusetts. One vehicle of change was the automobile, which accelerated the process of suburbanization that the trolley had initiated. The flexibility of auto travel allowed contractors to build houses beyond walking distance of the trolley lines. Buyers snatched up these single-family units, causing Arlington's population to double in the 1920s, from 18,000 to 36,000. Here as elsewhere on the fringes of Boston and other large cities, the rise in personal affluence and the spread of auto ownership among the middle class after World War I fed suburban growth. With middle-class life came rising expectations about how government should manage the local community. Most newcomers to Arlington were upwardly mobile sons and daughters of immigrants. They wanted homes with garages, a clean and green environment, and above all, good schools.

Officials in Arlington responded to demands for public services, beginning with actions taken in the 1890s during the trolley phase of suburbanization. The town constructed four schools including a high school, built a library, began garbage collection, established a board of public health, inaugurated a park system, electrified its streetlights, joined the metropolitan area water system, and added miles of paved streets and sewer lines. As population grew and technology advanced, town services proliferated, as the items on the agenda of the town meeting in 1927 attest. The police chief recommended the purchase of automatic stop-and-go signals to relieve auto congestion on the main drag. The town meeting approved his request, voted funds to study pollution of the local lake, and agreed that a third junior high school was necessary. The committee charged to review the school situation observed that quality education was a major reason people eagerly sought to settle in their "delightful town." In the eyes of suburban partisans, a good and wholesome community life required a well-managed town government.[17]

New and improved services, however, required more money. Education, streets, police and fire, health and water, and debt payments consumed the lion's share of the town budget in 1927, as they had in 1887. But the scope of these functions had grown, driving up their cost faster than the population. The fire department had phased out its volunteer "call men" and now relied on a hired force. The firemen had motorized their equipment and wanted a new truck in 1927. The police asked for an ambulance. These vehicles and the thousands of cars Arlingtonians owned performed better on "high-type" paving than on the old gravel surfaces. But hard pavement cost more. The town payroll in 1927 contained numerous positions created since 1887. The enlarged list of public employees included an accountant; an engineer (and staff); inspectors of milk, plumbing, and wires; a full-time fire chief; and a public welfare nurse. An insurance plan, which partially offset wage losses of employees injured on the job (workmen's compensation), had been put in place. Retired workers had begun to receive town-subsidized pensions. And Arlingtonians invested in their schools, spending twice as much per person on education ($26) than Washington did on all national domestic programs.

"Happy are we to live in an Arlington free of slums, of belching smokestacks and noisome factories, of towering structures to darken our thoroughfares." That was how a local savings and loan institution, which financed many of the new homes in town, boasted about their community. The bank's managers went on to congratulate local officials for keeping "our town beautiful."[18] That goal was achieved in part by using a new legal tool called zoning, which authorized restrictions on the uses of land. Zoning evolved from older law that allowed localities to abate nuisances and from a city planning movement that gained ground after 1900. Building contractors saw zoning as a way to increase profits. Arlingtonians saw it as a way to preserve the suburban ideal, which increasingly meant a landscape dominated by single-family homes. The two- and three-family houses of the trolley period contradicted this revised community image. Further construction of multifamily structures was virtually halted in 1924 by the town's first comprehensive zoning ordinance. By setting the height and type of buildings permitted in various zones, the law dictated where new houses, apartments, and retail outlets could be built. These restrictions formed a legal wall to insulate the community from undesirable influences, which for many suburbanites meant factories, poor people, racial minorities, and the problems of the city.

All Americans did not live in places like Arlington, of course. But the town was typical in two fundamental ways. The United States was a collage of local communities and separate governmental jurisdictions. Half of the nation's population in 1920 lived in urban places, most of which were small cities more like Arlington than Boston. Arlingtonians clung tenaciously to their town-meeting form of government as they entered the urban age, even though the size of the population qualified the community for city status in most states. And Arlington's history synchronized nicely with the expansion of municipal governance in the nation. The timing and details of this growth varied from place to place, yet local government in the transition era grew and continued to provide Americans with most of their direct public services. Birmingham, Alabama, although poorer than Arlington and home to powerful business interests, fell in with the general pattern. In addition to levying new taxes on merchants and the parents of public school children during the depression of the 1890s, the city regulated a host of activities from labor agents and railroad crossings to building codes and the quality of milk.

The decentralized character of American governance explains why reformers concentrated so much attention on the municipal level. Many in their ranks saw a conflict between the expanding scale of city governance and the way local officials managed these tasks. Out of these administrative critiques came a movement to modernize municipal administration in cities large and small. Arlington created a finance committee (1899) to formulate the budget and hired an accountant (1903) to review fiscal transactions. A planning board followed, and in the 1930s town employees were placed under civil service. In the interim Arlington modified its town meeting. Attendance in the old forum, open to all citizens, had declined, and the enfranchisement of women in 1920 doubled its potential membership. Adoption of a mayor-council form of government was out of the question because it smacked of big-city politics. So the suburbanites compromised and created a representative town meeting of elected members (1922). Eventually the accumulation of administrative chores led town officials to a classic Progressive Era reform: they hired a professional manager to serve as their chief executive (1953).

Despite America's tradition of reliance on local government, Arlington and other towns were not the sole masters of their political fate. Lawmakers at the state capitol in Boston enacted legislation that granted Arlington permission to switch to an elected form of town meeting and to zone its land. Massachusetts statutes required state inspection of local finances, school buildings, and sewer plans. The town's board of health enforced rules set by the state. Massachusetts instructed communities to maintain high schools, although Arlington had established one before the size of its school population made compliance mandatory. Even the town's battle with gypsy moths followed guidelines set by state legislators on Beacon Hill. Most of Arlington's policy actions, in other words, were authorized, recommended, or mandated by officials in state government.

Massachusetts's supervision of local affairs was part of a national trend toward state centralization. Signs of this expansion of state government are found in the accumulation of new laws, the proliferation of administrative boards and commissions, and rising expenditures. "The statute books swelled like balloons," one legal historian wrote in reference to the increased number of state regulations in the late nineteenth century.[19] New policy adoptions continued during the Progressive Era and through the 1920s as well, despite the notion that antigovernment advocates dominated this decade. In its early phase, state centralization focused on the regulation of business, the protection of workers, and public health. Massachusetts, for instance, a pioneer in industrial-era legislation, regulated banks, insurance companies, railroads, gas and electric utilities, and the hours of work for women, children, and public employees; it also commenced an ambitious public health program that included standards of water purity and factory safety before 1900. Services, especially schools and roads, became leading objects of state attention in the early twentieth century. An enormous number of issues gained access to state legislative agendas, especially during the Progressive Era. One recurrent concern was tax reform, long a goal of critics who lamented archaic revenue mechanisms and undertaxed corporations. The expansion of state functions boosted the case for the reorganization of administrative agencies and for greater authority for governors.

The full effect of many of these laws was blunted by penny-pinching lawmakers, who underfunded their administration. But the traditional distaste for bureaucracy should be weighed against the marked growth in the number of state employees. Their increase signified that states were assuming more direct oversight of public affairs. The expansion of state policy making also proceeded along traditional lines, as states assigned local communities broader responsibilities. Some state oversight of local governance can be found throughout the nineteenth century, but it became more pervasive in the transitional polity.

American law always obligated businesses to operate in the public interest. This concept was never widely doubted, even though lawmakers battled over how to apply the maxim in practice. By the beginning of the 1880s states had already placed banks, insurance companies, and railroads under some regulation. Demands to tame the "greed and rapacity" of the railroads spread in the 1870s as the nation confronted the first major concentration of private commercial power of the industrial age. Railroads were large, heavily capitalized businesses, requiring substantial investment in construction and rolling stock before realizing a dollar in return. Their high fixed costs induced railroad managers to reduce destructive competition by avoiding duplicate service (usually on short hauls within a state) and by proposing cooperative agreements (pooling) with other lines (usually on long hauls between states). These economic differentials meant that rates for short hauls tended to be higher than (and to compensate for lower) rates on long hauls. Moreover, some roads offered special rates (rebates) to favored customers as a way of securing steady traffic where competitive lines existed. Losses from such deals could be recouped by charging higher rates on runs where the road had a monopoly. Most consumers, such as small businesses and farmers, cared little about the economics of operating a railroad and a lot about price discriminations they faced for a crucial service. Sentiment to regulate the railroads also arose from hostility to the power that corporate heads had amassed.

Half of the states established commissions to monitor the railroads by 1890. Some bodies, as in Illinois (1873), could adjust rates, but most commissions, such as the one in Massachusetts (1869), were largely investigatory in nature and relied on publicity to elicit cooperation from railroad owners. Assigning these tasks to a commission blended political practices of the republican era with prejudices of the late nineteenth century. The choice of creating quasi-independent bodies, which maintained loose ties to the legislature, reflected lawmakers' aversion to bureaucrats who owed their loyalty to governors. Delegating a regulatory function to a relatively autonomous commission staffed with experts was seen as a way of eliminating blatant political influences on decisions. To increase accountability to the public, many states allowed voters to elect commissioners.[20]

Increasingly the public came to see railroads not simply as businesses run for private profit but also as a public utility with some specific responsibilities to the community. This new designation included certain commercial services (as distinct from the sale of durable goods) that tended to have a single local provider (so-called natural monopolies) and that sold a service which everyone in a community used. Water, natural gas, telegraph, package delivery services (express companies), telephones, electricity, and urban rapid transit lines were placed in this classification. In the Progressive Era, lawmakers transformed many of the railroad agencies into public service commissions that were delegated regulatory jurisdiction over several types of utilities. Some states went a step further and directly operated a service. Massachusetts, for example, acquired the trolley system in the Boston region when the private transit companies went bankrupt. Belmont, a community adjacent to Arlington, established its own town-run electric company.

Regulation also spread to the learned professions and the trades. Increasing reliance on specialized practitioners such as doctors, engineers, and accountants fed pressure for public certification of professional competency. For this job lawmakers created licensing boards vested with authority to admit qualified individuals to a practice. The licensing movement accelerated after 1900, branching into everyday commercial activities that bore some connection to public health, such as beauty parlors, barbers shops, and bakeries. These controls usually were not controversial, because entrance standards worked in the economic interest of qualified and established professionals. Even when they hadn't lobbied for their creation, practitioners tended to control the boards that regulated their livelihood.[21]

The licensing movement developed in the context of occupational specialization, which was a derivative of industrialization. During this economic transformation the source of people's livelihood shifted away from agriculture and self-employment toward wage and salaried jobs in manufacturing, transportation, finance, retail, and services. Farmers declined to half of the workforce by 1880, and in the next fifty years they shrank to less than a quarter of all workers. In the long run, technological innovation, factory production, and systematic management increased the standard of living. In the short run, however, the industrial transformation created new hazards for workers. Few railroad linemen (who uncoupled the cars) retired with all their limbs intact. Mining was an even riskier business. Employee fatigue brought on by six-day workweeks of fifty and sixty hours contributed to the dangers of the workplace. As the size of industrial firms expanded and as modernized production systems substituted unskilled workers for skilled craftsmen, employees became impersonal factors of corporate cost accounting. Formalized labor relations replaced the personal interaction between employee and employer that had existed in the shops of the republican era.

Changes in the conditions of work generated demands for public protection of workers. States imposed safety precautions on factory and mine operations, and they limited the hours of labor for children and females and for males in certain occupations. Employers were forbidden to pay workers in scrip, redeemable only at the company store. Some states set minimum wages for women. Statutes and court decisions narrowed the legal defenses that employers could use to avoid responsibility for injuries to their workers. Because it was uncommon for employees to take their company to court, regardless of prevailing legal doctrines concerning the responsibility of injuries, states enacted workmen's compensation laws in the 1910s and 1920s. These plans compelled employers to purchase accident insurance that provided financial aid to injured workers or paid a death benefit to a widow. The sentiment was compassionate, but early policies offered meager stipends and spotty coverage.

There was a greater political consensus behind efforts to protect the health and safety of workers than there was for intervention into employer-employee relations over wages. Some states did create boards of labor arbitration to mediate strikes, but that was the limit of their interference in bargaining matters. States also had a duty to preserve the public peace, and they devised new means of ensuring order in the transition era, as law enforcement agencies became larger, better trained, and more organized. Police remained predominantly local, but states developed their own security agencies by revitalizing the militia (a citizen-based army, now called the National Guard) and by creating state police forces. On occasion states used their new coercive capacity to break up workers' strikes against employers.

State lawmakers favored the schoolbook over the picket line as a way to advance the well-being of the community. Americans placed enormous faith in education as a springboard to economic success and as the incubator of proper civic values. This sentiment and the crusades of educators built a groundswell of support to expand schooling. Public investment in education rose faster than most objects of spending and remained the largest category of outlays in the transition era. Education became more costly, largely because youngsters spent more time in school, as the result of a lengthening of the school year and an increase in the number of years spent in school. Compulsory education laws (in the North, 1870–1890s, in the South, 1900–1918) made mandatory what many parents already imposed on their children. The most dramatic expansion of education in the period was the growth of public high schools. Arlington started its high school in 1869, and Birmingham opened one (for whites only) in 1883, although the city charged tuition until 1910. Only 3 percent of teenagers attended high school in 1880, compared with more than half in 1930.

The states enacted a battery of rules that regulated local school administration. Besides compulsory education, which made some high school mandatory, states required localities to provide free textbooks, teach certain subjects, observe building codes, hire only state-certified teachers, and contribute funds to teacher retirement plans. They permitted two or more communities to merge one-room schools into consolidated districts and to operate countywide high schools. States upgraded teacher training by phasing out normal schools in favor of state teacher's colleges and education programs in expanded state universities. Cities and towns still operated the public schools, but increasingly officials in state departments of education held them accountable to general standards.[22]

State officials also centralized another traditionally local activity, road construction. A good-roads campaign gained headway in northeastern states by 1890, spearheaded by clubs of adult bicyclists, who took up cycling with a passion in the nineties. The spread of automobiles after 1910 and of trucks and buses after World War I pushed the movement further and faster. Many governors in the 1920s made hard roads, suitable for motorized traffic, the centerpiece of their administration. While few people opposed the idea of good roads, the questions of who would pay for them and who would control highway policy were controversial. Most good-roads advocates urged the coordination of highway routes (first within counties and later across the entire state), trained engineers to supervise construction, and elimination of the traditional system of paying road taxes in labor rather than money. The states gradually adopted these reforms, including the creation of highway commissions (1893–1917), usually headed by an engineer.

Wisconsin illustrates the incremental pace of this reform. In the initial phase of its highway movement, state legislators restricted local ability to avoid paying road taxes in money, then authorized the Geological and Natural History Survey, formed in 1897, to study road-building materials, and later (1907) formed a highway division within the survey. In 1911 the legislature established an autonomous highway commission in an act that authorized the state to subsidize counties for one-third of their road-building costs, contingent upon local compliance with state standards of construction. This statute was the culmination of a fifteen-year campaign to remove the prohibition of state investment in "internal improvements" from Wisconsin's constitution. Officials employed by the Geological Survey took an active role in the campaign to persuade voters to support this constitutional amendment.[23]

Wisconsin improved its ability to finance highways and other functions in 1911 by adoption of an income tax. Over the next eighteen years, nineteen other states followed Wisconsin's lead by enacting similar levies on individual or corporate income, or both. But income taxes were not the principal source of funds for highway construction, which boomed in the 1920s. Most of the money came from fees imposed on motorists. All states charged fees in conjunction with their requirement that owners register their vehicles and that drivers obtain operator's licenses (1901–1914). This revenue stream was greatly enhanced by the adoption of taxes on the sale of motor fuel (1919–1929). The gasoline tax proved a boon to lawmakers, who were hesitant to increase general taxation yet were under pressure to pave more miles of road. Fuel taxes were painless to collect (service stations did it), and their exclusive dedication to highways fashioned a powerful constituency behind them. Members of the highway lobby fought to establish and earmark these funds for road construction.[24] Staked with a guaranteed stream of dedicated moneys, which underwrote multimillion-dollar loans (bond issues), the states moved rapidly to accommodate the auto age.

Given Americans' traditionally decentralized approach to civic affairs, the states were logical candidates to shoulder much of the new agenda of the transition era. The system of localized government that Americans found ideologically appealing, however, also had certain practical drawbacks. One nettlesome tendency was the habit of the states to enact dissimilar laws on similar subjects. The absence of uniform state law troubled many observers, despite their support of state action over Federal intervention. But if the states persisted in going their separate ways or failed to act at all, some warned, the people would look to Washington for satisfaction. To prevent such "regrettable" centralization, some reformers urged coordinated adoption of uniform state laws. Beginning in 1889, committees formed at the recommendation of the American Bar Association, an organization of lawyers, wrote model laws for state consideration. The campaign won some skirmishes but lost the war, because the logic of uniformity could not overcome the independence of state politics. National convocations of governors (beginning in 1908) and of state legislators (from 1933 onward) failed to offer effective leadership on the subject, which left a void for Washington to fill.[25]

Since the late 1880s Congress had steadily added new items to the national government's agenda. Grover Cleveland's 1887 approval of the Interstate Commerce Act and grants to states for agricultural research symbolized the inauguration of this expansion. Over the next several decades the Federal government initiated regulation of numerous commercial enterprises, commenced a range of service and assistance programs, and began active management of natural resources. By 1916 these policy innovations added up to considerable national intervention into the private economy. World War I occasioned a marked enhancement of these controls, although most emergency powers lapsed when peace returned. No one individual, group, or event dominated policy making during this transformation. Rather, the Federal role expanded in response to numerous pressures, unfolded incrementally, and grew cumulatively. Railroad regulation followed this evolutionary track. Congress entertained proposals on the subject for years but did not authorize national oversight until the court disallowed state regulation of interstate rail commerce in 1886 (the *Wabash* case). The national Interstate Commerce Act of the following year prohibited special rates for favored customers, certain short haul–long haul price discriminations, and collusive arrangements (pooling) among railroads. A five-member commission (the ICC) was appointed by the president to administer the law. Companies had to publish their rates, which the ICC could investigate. Initially the ICC approached its job in a reactive fashion, whereby it investigated complaints, issued cease-and-desist orders to offenders, and referred persistent violations to Justice Department prosecutors. The commission lacked power to fix rates, which the act said should be reasonable and just. In 1887 Congress had followed the Massachusetts example by creating a "sunshine" commission that relied heavily on investigation and publicity.[26]

The ICC remained a toothless tiger until Congress granted it power to fix maximum rates, first after hearing complaints (1906) and then on its own initiative (1910). Three years later the commission was permitted to appraise the value of railroad property as a guide to rate making. With these jurisdictional hurdles crossed, attention shifted to ICC hearing rooms, where deliberations on a case-by-case basis sought to determine reasonable rates. In 1915 the commission had 2,000 employees who received 7,500 complaints, took 200,000 pages of testimony, referred 161 safety violations to the courts, and found defects in half of the 77,000 locomotives inspected. The ICC's exercise of its new regulatory muscle passed court scrutiny, including a case in which the commissioners had overruled a state whose rates concerned intrastate traffic. The Supreme Court agreed with the commission that the state regulations affected interstate commerce, over which the national government had jurisdiction (the *Shreveport* cases, 1914).

World War I spawned further Federal control of rail lines. The inability of the railroads to untangle freight bottlenecks in 1917 prompted President Wilson to place rail companies under government management. Owners were paid "rents" set by national officials. In 1920 Congress returned the lines to private operation but also expanded ICC powers by granting the commission authority to set not only maximum but also minimum rates for railroads within various territories. Because this new rate-fixing arrangement threatened the financial survival of some railroads, the ICC withheld profits above 6 percent (the recapture clause), half of which could be loaned to financially weak lines. The design of the 1920 law indicated that Federal rail policy had evolved from the idea of maintaining reasonable rates in order to protect shippers and consumers to a goal of promoting adequate service nationwide. This new mandate instructed the ICC to plan a network of consolidated railroads, a challenge never fulfilled. But the commission did gain supervisory authority over all phases of rail operations and finances, including the appointment of directors on company boards. By 1920 rail transportation had become a full-fledged public utility.

The rise of big business and its tendency to dominate some markets induced Congress to adopt rules regarding the monopolization of trade. The landmark Sherman Antitrust Act of 1890 provided that "every . . . combination . . . or conspiracy in restraint of trade or commerce among the several states" and "attempt to monopolize" was illegal. Enforcement rested with Federal attorneys, who could initiate criminal prosecutions. Private citizens could file civil suits to recover triple damages from a firm that had illicitly harmed competitors. The spirit of the law squared nicely with republican sentiment that the right to engage in commercial enterprise did not allow purposeful elimination of competition. But despite the prosecution of some businesses for unfair practices and the dissolution of a few large companies, the United States never launched a vigorous antitrust campaign. The crusade against monopoly posed a dilemma for policy makers. The growth of firm size was believed to represent a rational strategy for increasing efficiency and competing successfully. In fact, the courts had held that corporate size alone was neither a measure of monopoly nor evidence of "conspiracy in restraint of trade." And the dividing line between fair and unfair practices in the rough-and-tumble world of private business was hardly clear, especially as industries continually altered their strategies to stay competitive.[27]

The Clayton Act (1914) sought to add clarity to this uncertainty by prohibiting forms of price discrimination (such as rebates), corporate acquisitions that lessened competition, and interlocking directorates, where the same individual served on the boards of several large firms. The act's restriction on multiple board memberships placed special attention on large national banks, trust companies, and railroads. A Federal Trade Commission (1914) was created with instructions to prevent "unfair methods of competition in commerce" and authority to issue cease-and-desist orders to violators. But the commission lacked strong enforcement powers, a weakness that arose from the political cross-pressures that swirled around antitrust policy. Lawmakers wanted to affirm their commitment to economic opportunity and fair play publicly, but they did not want to be labeled antibusiness in the process. Thus they settled for laws that were as much symbolic as significant in regulatory effect. Congress frequently lamented the growth of corporate size but never stopped it.

The dilemma inherent in applying general antitrust rules to all types of businesses was more pronounced than regulations designed for specific economic sectors (specific kinds of commercial activity). Congress authored numerous laws, particularly during Woodrow Wilson's administration, that extended controls to particular industries, such as grain and cotton wholesalers, warehouses of agricultural commodities, and meatpackers. The Federal Reserve System (1913) created a uniform currency (paper dollars) for the country and provided for a more reliable flow of commercial loans. The plan revolved around twelve district reserve banks, which were owned and largely controlled by member banks, some of which (nationally chartered ones) were compelled to join the system. Federal policy makers began professional management of forest lands, brought long-distance gas and oil pipelines under ICC jurisdiction, licensed electrical power production on navigable rivers, licensed airplane pilots and radio broadcasters, and set standards for food processing. National lawmakers established eight hours as the basic workday for employees engaged in interstate transportation.

Growth of the Federal role was visible too in service activities, which offered citizens new forms of assistance. Rural residents were the most favored beneficiaries of Federal services in the transition era. Delivery of the mail to rural homes, authorized on a trial basis in 1896, eventually served millions of country dwellers. By the mid-1920s rural mail carriers plied 45,000 separate routes. Rural free delivery was a subsidy to rural residents because delivery costs were higher in sparsely settled communities than in densely populated places but the same stamp sent a letter anywhere in the United States. Mail-order houses (such as Sears, Roebuck, and Company) benefited from cheaper rates for commercial mailings and from parcel post (1913), which forwarded their goods directly to consumers in the countryside.

The creation of programs that distributed public goods stimulated the formation of new interest group communities. Recipients of a governmental benefit often worked in tandem with its public administrators to become the program's chief champions. The Department of Agriculture (USDA), the largest provider of Federal services, fit this pattern. Created in 1862, the USDA underwent a coral-like growth as it acquired new programs and expanded existing ones. No two-year congressional cycle passed without additions to its activities. Elevation to cabinet status in 1889 signified the department's enhanced role. Despite disavowals by its administrators, the USDA was generally regarded as a client-oriented agency, dedicated to the interests of farmers and the improvement of rural life.[28]

Research was one of the four main ways the USDA pursued this mission. The department was Washington's scientific showcase. Thousands of professionals in agricultural and biological sciences, the physical sciences, engineering, and economics worked on hundreds of separate investigations by the 1920s. Twenty of the Bureau of Plant Industry's twenty-four subdivisions alone conducted research, both in the lab and in the field, and this bureau was just one of eighteen major units in the department, most of which sponsored technical inquiries. These studies ranged wider and grew more specialized over time. By the 1920s projects in home nutrition, farm income, and rural engineering had been added, for example, to more conventional agricultural investigations, such as the habits of queen bees, the microbiology of hides and skins, and the eradication of the European corn borer.

Getting this information to patrons was the second major USDA task. The department sponsored numerous outreach programs to disseminate its research and recommendations to farmers, their families, and allied professionals. Leading mechanisms for these purposes were agricultural experiment stations (1887), demonstration projects conducted by county agents (1914), and subsidy of agricultural education in rural high schools (1917). These programs were linked to the state agricultural colleges and received their largest funding from non-Federal sources. Virtually every rural county had at least one county agent by 1930, and many had female agents who advised farmwives. That year 34 million scientific and popular publications poured from USDA units, making it the government's most prolific publisher. The department took to the airwaves when radio arrived, broadcasting weather and crop reports, frost warnings to fruit growers, and a daily homemakers' program.

The USDA also was a regulatory body. It oversaw dozens of rules concerning products and their producers that Congress had approved between the 1880s and 1920s. These assignments, distributed among various USDA subunits, ran from enforcing the food and drug laws and licensing processors to quarantining infected fruit, grading agricultural commodities, and monitoring cotton futures traders. The secretary of agriculture could issue cease-and-desist orders for certain violations and recommend the prosecution of unrepentant offenders. The general rationale for this police work was the goal of maintaining safe and uniform commodities marketed in a fair economic environment.

Congress went beyond forms of indirect assistance and voted more direct benefits toward the end of the transition era. Agricultural land banks were instituted to underwrite loans for farmers. Arranged along the lines of the public-private mix in the Federal Reserve System, these credit institutions had the right to sell tax-exempt bonds, the critical lever in their ability to raise capital. Absolving agricultural cooperatives from antitrust restrictions encouraged farmers to market their products collectively. In a groundbreaking although futile effort to bolster sagging farm prices, the Federal government began the purchase of surplus commodities in 1929. A few years later the USDA owned a quarter-billion bushels of wheat and 12,000 farms.

Federal highway policy intersected with several of the USDA's functions. As its administrative location in the department suggests, Washington's early road work favored rural America. The evolution of national road policy, moreover, epitomizes the growth pattern of several USDA activities. The highway story began in 1892 when Roy Stone, an engineer and lobbyist for the nation's major association of bicyclists, asked Congress to appropriate ten thousand dollars for the study of roads. Lawmakers' rejection of the request stimulated Stone to organize the National League for Good Roads for the purpose of broadening constituent support for road reform. Stone got Federal funding in 1893, persuaded the USDA to create an Office of Road Inquiry, and parlayed his way into its directorship. Once installed in office, Stone and his single assistant devoted much of their time to campaigning for good roads—and the idea that Washington should help pay for them. Stone's successors in the road office continued this crusade, drawing upon the burgeoning resources of their agency. By 1915 the Federal road unit had a quarter-million-dollar budget and 450 employees, most of whom worked on promotional activities.

The campaign for Federal roads achieved a milestone in 1916, when Congress inaugurated a grant-in-aid program to assist highway construction. Actual control of building roads still resided with state and local government, but now Washington helped to finance them, provided that states accepted Federal conditions. Advocates of the Federal grant approach included private and commercial interests, as well as the directors of state highway departments, who had an interest in maintaining control over local road work. These highway administrators worked with Logan Page, Washington's top road man, to draft the Federal aid bill. Page, in fact, had spearheaded the formation of the American Association of State Highway Officials (AASHO), which represented the interests of these professionals. Page's replacement as Federal highway chief in 1919, Thomas MacDonald, had been one of the group's organizers. A graduate of the state agricultural and mechanical college in Iowa with a degree in engineering, MacDonald had served as the Hawkeye state's highway commissioner since the commission's inception (1904). As Federal road director, he reinforced his ties with the AASHO and got it to carry the case for increased aid for rural roads to Congress. In 1921 legislators authorized substantial new funding, which was subject to the proviso that the money be spent in a coordinated way so as to create a national network of highways. The national and state highway administrators worked in tandem to hammer out the details of the measure. This cooperative alliance between state and national road administrators produced the numbering system of Federal highways and its familiar shield logo.[29]

Farmers were the primary beneficiaries of the good roads campaign and other Federal aid programs adopted during the transition era, which explains why most grants operated under USDA tutelage. Financial assistance was one way the department fulfilled its larger purpose of serving rural America. This orientation appealed to national lawmakers, most of whom represented country districts. But the department helped to propagate its expanding mandate by portraying itself as an organization of impartial professionals who sought technical, not political, solutions to common problems. This flattering self-image helped to vest more functions in the department, which in turn opened up more career opportunities for specialists. In 1890 the USDA employed 2,000 people on a budget of $2 million. State government in New York, by comparison, spent $13 million at that time. Forty years later USDA operations cost $177 million, exclusive of special accounts, and engaged 25,000 employees. Roughly half as many more people staffed federally assisted outreach programs that technically were run by the states. The department had grown into a massive quasi-independent public corporation that rivaled New York, the largest of the state governments, in size and expenditures.

America's entrance into the Great War in 1917 should be seen in the context of the Progressive Era's enchantment with the new possibilities of power. The extent to which the war in Europe threatened American security and subjected the country's vital interests to clear and present danger is still debated. Perhaps to deflect criticism of his course of action, Woodrow Wilson developed the case for war against the "autocratic" German government in unequivocal terms in his war message to Congress. The president stated that the nation had a duty to restrain "this natural foe to liberty" and that the fate of "civilization depended upon restoration of the rights of all mankind." Wilson's war message was instrumentalism applied to the international arena. Federal power would be unleashed to fix a problem, in this instance, Germany's blatant disregard of international law. The notion that America could exorcise wrongs by military might had taken root in the late nineteenth century and had sprouted into war against Spain (1898) over its suppression of revolution in Cuba and against indigenous guerrillas in the Philippines (1899–1902), where the United States replaced Spain as the colonial power. Wilson's goal was grander. "The world must be made safe for democracy," he trumpeted, implying that America would be its protector.

Congress grumbled about White House requests for expansive new authority to mobilize the military but could hardly deny administration requests after having voted for war. The president was empowered to regulate production, fix prices, seize and operate factories, mines, and transportation facilities, open people's mail, and raise an army of draftees. Skyrocketing military costs forced the first extensive use of the Federal income tax, which the Sixteenth Amendment to the Constitution (1913) had authorized. Most of these war-born powers expired with the armistice (1918), but precedents for future presidentially centered governance had been established. But in 1918 and 1919 it was too much executive centralization too fast and too erratically managed for many people. The resounding Democratic defeats in the elections of 1918 and 1920 suggested that this was the public's verdict.

The war affected social policy at home by helping to generate a critical mass of sentiment for restriction of immigration, liquor, and political dissent. The seeds of these developments had been sown decades earlier. Washington had begun the exclusion of certain categories of persons (e.g., Chinese laborers, lunatics, paupers) in the 1870s and 1880s and took over the admission of immigrants from the states in 1891. The following year it opened a large immigration inspection facility on Ellis Island in New York harbor. Twelve million newcomers eventually passed through this landmark reception center, all scrutinized by immigration officials who gradually acquired a long list of grounds on which to deny admission to newcomers. The law of 1917 added new criteria for exclusion, such as illiteracy and Asian origin, and broadened the basis for deportation of people already admitted into the United States. In 1921 and 1924 (the National Origin Act), Congress supplemented these qualitative criteria with numeric quotas on admissions, which favored northern Europeans, the largest ethnic bloc in America.

Two categories on the immigration exclusion list, prostitutes and anarchists, reflected the proclivity of the transitional polity to outlaw personal behaviors that contradicted traditional standards of social and political propriety. The states had piled up a battery of prohibitions since the 1880s concerning matters such as impermissible activities on Sundays, gambling, prostitution, drugs and tobacco, and obscene literature. At the top of this list was liquor, the object of the era's greatest moral crusade. Half of the states had banned the manufacture and sale of alcoholic beverages by 1916, when prohibition advocates turned their attention to the national level. In keeping with the dictates of dual federalism, the republican polity had lodged policy-making authority over social behavior primarily in the states. The Eighteenth Amendment to the Constitution (passed by Congress in 1917, ratified in 1919), which enabled the Federal government to restrict the distribution of liquor, was a radical break with tradition. It was the only constitutional provision that conveyed explicit power to Congress over social conduct. Once empowered, national lawmakers criminalized the manufacture and sale (but not personal possession) of alcoholic beverages. The 1929 enforcement act could put bootleggers in prison for five years and fine them $10,000. Police at all levels had authority to search and seize banned substances. This experiment in the national control of liquor ended in 1933 with the adoption of the Twenty-first Amendment, but precedents for future national control of personal behavior had been laid.

An attempt to muzzle political radicals constituted the war's third contribution to social control. Drawing on state and Federal precedents dating to 1887, the Sedition Act of 1918 criminalized forms of political expression by making it illegal "to utter, print, or publish disloyal, profane, scurrilous, or abusive language" about the American form of government and its war effort. Socialist Eugene Debs' criticism of the country's participation in the war earned him a sentence in a Federal penitentiary. The states joined the antiradical crusade by enacting criminal syndicalist and sedition acts, which were vague restrictions on political speech and association aimed in good part at curtailing labor activities. Armed with the national sedition and other antiradical laws, the U.S. Army harassed and disrupted the Industrial Workers of the World (the Wobblies), a militant labor organization popular with western miners and lumberjacks. Wartime fears of disloyal behavior at home had provided cover for employers and their allies in government to manipulate public power for private ends.[30]

Federal social controls invented a new form of crime—Federal crime. With it arose a Federal police force that consisted of prohibition agents, immigration officials, postal inspectors, Justice Department investigators, Treasury agents, and military intelligence officers. The modern FBI was born in the hysteria over anarchists in America following the Communist revolution in Russia (1917). New Federal crimes led to a mushrooming of prosecutions. In 1928 alone there were 75,000 arrests and 21,000 seizures under prohibition laws, and 11,000 aliens were deported. Between 1915 and 1930 the number of Federal prisoners, half of whom were incarcerated for prohibition violations, swelled eightfold.[31] Crimes defined by Federal law and arrests by Federal police officers were sure signs that the republican polity had expired.

Government underwent extensive reform and expansion between 1887 and 1929. Five distinguishing features of this transition stand out and bear restatement.

First, the Great Debate produced a philosophic alternative to republican ideology about the nature of government. Contrary to the classical belief that public power should be carefully limited as a precaution against its abuse, a new view held that government had an obligation to correct problems in society. In essence, a radically redefined conception of well-being had emerged whereby the liberty of individuals was protected by (and not from) government.

Second, an intellectual and institutional foundation for implementing the new tasks of government was laid. During the transition era, reformers developed a philosophy of rationally based public management and took the first steps toward creating organizations that practiced the new art of administration.

Third, the public sector adopted several new policy functions. Government initiated the regulation of a wide variety of commercial activities and personal behaviors, and it extended new public services and benefits to millions of individuals. The states and localities offered free kindergartens, compelled all children to attend school, built high schools, and expanded higher education. States required individuals to register their cars and obtain driver's licenses, made them obey traffic rules on publicly paved highways, and hired police to enforce these laws. Public officials set rates that people paid for gas, electricity, trolley fares, and other public services and supposedly ensured that food was safe to eat. Federal workers delivered the mail to all residences in the country, processed millions of newcomers to America, fed, clothed, and trained millions of young men for military service during the First World War, and attempted to suppress alcoholic beverages in an unprecedented nationwide crusade. These new contacts between government and citizens brought the state into the lives of average people on a much greater scale than had occurred in earlier eras. As individuals came to take these new functions for granted their historic suspicion of power probably lessened and their expectations about the problem-solving capacity of government probably rose.

Fourth, both the states and the national government assumed greater responsibility for governance. As centralization proceeded, the autonomy of local government decreased relative to the other governments even though the scope and cost of local services grew. The expansion of Washington's role brought millions of people into contact with national policy for the first time and opened up new administrative links with officials in other governments. Federal grants-in-aid, for example, encouraged all the states to adopt certain programs, such as agricultural experiment stations, the construction of coordinated roads, and vocational education. In other areas, such as railroad regulation, national intervention preempted state control. In several instances, such as the enforcement of food and drug standards and antiliquor laws, the two governments administered regulations cooperatively. Dual federalism wasn't dead in 1929. The idea that the states had sovereign rights still retained vitality. Yet the assumptions that had sustained classical federalism gradually dissolved as national state building proceeded. As people's concerns turned toward finding solutions to contemporary problems, their attachment to traditional political formulas waned.

Finally, most additions to the civic agenda occurred incrementally. Small and often uncoordinated policy innovations at each level of government accumulated over the years. Once initiated, most programs tended to survive and expand. Moreover, the creation of one new line of activity bred a rationale for action in adjacent areas. The growth of rural mail delivery, for example, bolstered the case for road improvement. The construction of paved highways and the increased use of motor vehicles facilitated the consolidation of schools. Highway police, first formed to regulate motorists, were assigned additional functions, such as criminal investigations and security details during strikes and civil disturbances. Few if any members of Congress voted to go to war against Germany as a way of shutting down the breweries in the United States, but America's entrance into World War I helped to bring on national prohibition. Numerous policy developments followed this progression, where the operation of existing programs had the unanticipated consequence of stimulating other policy innovations.

4

The Great Depression and Economic Policy

PHOTOGRAPHS CAPTURED THE tragedy of the Great Depression. Bleak expressions of men slouched on park benches, small groups huddled around ashcan fires near closed factories, lines queued for blocks outside food kitchens, families with their belongings bundled onto ancient autos, shacks in the shadow of city skyscrapers. These poignant images are unmistakable signs of hard times in the 1930s. Yet the pictorial record only hints at the wounds the Depression caused. Survivors of these years remembered the frustration, humiliation, and despair. The trauma of joblessness immobilized some, who became recluses; others got on by stealing food and clothes and by adopting, one recounted, "a coyote mentality." A few could not face the personal failure of unemployment or financial ruin and found a way out by suicide. Most Americans, however, chose less extreme remedies. They coped with hard times, as people generally do, by becoming cautious, tightening their belts financially, and postponing major decisions such as marriage and children. Many dreams of becoming a doctor, a scientist, a writer evaporated in the struggle to earn a living.[1]

The unparalleled depth and duration of the economic decline made this the Great Depression. From an unemployment rate of 3 percent in 1929, the last year of prosperity, joblessness increased to a quarter of the workforce in 1933. Idleness was greater in the industrial states and in the big cities, reaching estimates of 40 percent of the workforce in New York and Chicago and even higher in locations with a greater concentration of manufacturing workers. Arlington, Massachusetts, fared better than many places, if one can call 19.6 percent unemployment in 1934 good news. Shortened hours, smaller paychecks, and fear of the pink slip stalked people still on the payroll. The headlines in 1933 explained their apprehension: 4,000 banks closed, 70,000 factories shut down, stock prices tumbled to two-thirds their earlier value, sales of new cars dropped to a fourth of the volume in 1929, and housing starts were off 90 percent from their best year in the 1920s. Nor did the economy bounce back quickly. Unemployment stayed above 14 percent for ten straight years, through 1940. In no other year in twentieth-century America has joblessness gone that high.

The Great Depression did not spare rural America. In the country, however, the price of agricultural products in the marketplace, rather than the jobless rate, charted families' economic fate, and here the news went from bad to worse. Income per farm plummeted from $900 in 1929 to $300 in 1932 and remained depressed for the remainder of the decade. Public protests, such as dumping milk onto highways, and demonstrations at sheriff's sales of farms, which were farmers' homes as well as their workplaces, registered signs of hard times in the countryside. Some rural residents were forced off the land forever.

The gross national product (GNP) is an economist's measuring rod of the general health of the economy. The index dropped by nearly one-half between 1929 and 1933. Disposable personal income, a close approximation of the money that consumers have to spend, fell by an equal magnitude. If there was a saving grace in these depressed times it was that prices also declined. Cheaper goods helped families get by with less earnings. But deflation also caused caution among corporations, which curtailed production and investment. The resulting layoffs of workers meant less take-home pay and hence dwindling sales for shopkeepers, some of whom were forced out of business. The decline of agricultural prices turned some farm owners into tenants and some tenant farmers into migrant workers. Conditions improved somewhat later in the decade, but national income did not return to its pre-Depression level until 1941.

The Depression posed two overriding questions for policy makers. What should government do to help individuals who were unemployed? And what should it do to revive the faltering economy? The thirties named these twin challenges "relief" and "recovery." Although these objectives were easily defined, the methods of achieving them were not, largely because the polity lacked precedents for mounting a coordinated response to depression. The nation did not have a philosophy that legitimized massive public intervention to stabilize the fluctuations of the business cycle or to care for the victims of industrial downturn. Nor were policy mechanisms in place that could have addressed these problems swiftly. Yet the sheer magnitude of the economic collapse moved policy makers to do something.

The heritage of dual federalism guided the initial responses to the faltering economy. According to traditional thinking about the assignments of government, public assistance for the poor was seen as a local responsibility, or more accurately, a local option. Many jurisdictions, especially in rural areas and in the South, offered no help for the indigent early in the Depression. In other locations, particularly in northern cities, governments distributed unprecedented amounts of relief funds when the mounting unemployment swamped the resources of private charity by 1931. But the combination of local private and public relief was not enough.[2]

Municipal and county officials were caught in an untenable dilemma in the early thirties. On one hand, the deteriorating economic conditions rapidly built up the caseload of people in need; on the other hand, local revenues dwindled. The property tax provided most of local government's funds, but idle workers, unpaid merchants, and bankrupt farmers could not pay these annual levies. Oregon illustrates the dimensions of this economic pinch: county welfare expenditures tripled while revenues fell by one-half between 1929 and 1933, mainly because one-third of the property taxes were delinquent. And local officials in Oregon and elsewhere lacked independent authority to impose alternative taxes. Many communities turned to borrowing, but municipal defaults on loans and a massive number of delinquencies among property taxpayers made private bankers leery about extending further credit. Although some communities were in better shape than others, it is only a slight exaggeration to say that local government was broke in 1932.[3]

The logical sources of help were state governments. Many of them passed laws that delayed bank foreclosures on home mortgages and arranged generous terms for the payment of back property taxes. They approved new borrowing and tax authority for local government. New York went one step further in 1931 by voting a grant of money as a supplement to local relief funds. Ten states provided similar aid, but the majority offered no relief funds during the Hoover years. Nor did the states do much to reverse the economic decline, largely because there was little they could do. Each state, empowered to act only within its jurisdiction, had little independent influence over an economic slump whose causes and effects were national and international in scope.

President Herbert Hoover (1929–1933) was unwilling to challenge the premises of dual federalism or dramatically alter the traditional Federal role. He concentrated his efforts on encouraging coordination among state and local relief activities and exhorting businessmen to remain optimistic about recovery. Along with the majority of Congress through 1931, he opposed Federal spending to assist unemployed individuals. The president relented a bit in the face of further economic deterioration, approving for example a purchase by the Federal Farm Board (created in 1929) of wheat and cotton in an attempt to bolster agricultural prices. To reduce the deficit brought on by declining revenues, Congress raised income taxes and levied the first Federal excise on gasoline sales. The most innovative initiative of the Hoover administration was creation of the Reconstruction Finance Corporation (RFC) in 1932. Its principal task was the extension of loans to faltering banks and railroads and to state and local governments for public works projects. The offer looked better on paper than it worked in practice. Red tape prevented the release of much RFC credit during the agency's first year of life.

Pictured as callous toward the unemployed and wedded to outdated laissez-faire attitudes, Hoover has become a symbol of modern conservatism. His party, which controlled most major offices outside the South in the 1920s and early 1930s, was pilloried by critics for its do-nothing philosophy. According to the detractors, the Republican Party's primary interest was protecting the rich and corporations. When state officials are added to this scenario, a political trinity is formed that purportedly put government in a straitjacket through 1932. State lawmakers turned their backs on people in desperate need, so accusations went, because Republicans, corporations, and parochial small-town politicos dominated most state legislatures. Grains of truth exist in these indictments, but they are stereotypes, distorted by partisan rhetoric and historical misperception. Critics in the 1930s and later either purposefully downplayed or overlooked the extent to which America was a victim of its own political heritage.

The chronology of the Depression plays a role in the real story. The stock market crash of October 1929, which sent the price of corporate securities through the floor, may seem to imply that the economy immediately ground to a halt. In fact, the economy declined in stages, year by year, and hit its low point in 1933. But officials whose perspective was shaped by week-to-week and month-to-month reports had no way of foreseeing this progressive decline from the vantage point of 1930, 1931, or 1932. Furthermore, economic and employment information available to them was spotty and imperfect. Yet the existence of modern-day economic indicators probably would not have changed thinking about the likely course of the Depression. History showed that hard times eventually self-corrected. Only from hindsight do we know that these hopeful prognoses proved wrong in this depression.

The grip of political tradition worked in tandem with this confidence in the recuperative capacity of private enterprise. Classical American ideology discouraged public spending to assist the unemployed and encouraged retrenchment as the appropriate response to dwindling public revenues. From the president on down to mayors, leaders believed that government, like families who had to do with less in hard times, should tighten its belt when the money was tight. Considerable apprehension also lingered about placing more power in Washington. President Hoover, for example, clung to the model of a decentralized polity. He feared that expansion of the Federal role would enlarge the bureaucracy, which would then become the captive of private special interests. A different problem existed at the underside of federalism. The reach of each state stopped at its border, and coordinate cooperation among the states was absent.

Lawmakers who did want greater initiatives from their state encountered formidable obstacles. American fears about the abuse of power left numerous legal impediments on the exercise of authority. The condition of state legislatures, for example, had changed little since the late nineteenth century. Virtually all of them convened in biennial short sessions. Special meetings required the call of governors, who usually were obligated to specify the agenda of these extraordinary sessions. Over half of the state legislatures did not meet at all in 1932, when the economy hit bottom. The absence of permanent professional staff and the high turnover of lawmakers hampered the ability to apply policy expertise to rapidly altered circumstances. Many legislators placed a high premium on serving the interests of their own district. Most states had not redrawn their district lines in accordance with urban growth in the twentieth century, which left cities underrepresented at the statehouses. This *malapportionment* cost Democrats more seats than it did Republicans.[4]

Regardless of where they were elected, state lawmakers faced the battery of constitutional restrictions on financial powers. Most devastating in light of the fiscal crisis were limitations on the ability of states to borrow funds. Tax authority was also hampered, and balanced budgets were nearly universally required, by either constitutional fiat or statute and custom.[5] The politics of tax legislation led lawmakers to dedicate a sizable part of state revenue to particular programs. These *earmarked* funds, which explicitly linked a particular tax to a specific function, reduced flexibility in state budgeting. On occasion legislators bent these rules to raise new moneys, but such circumventions ran the risk of court rejection. In theory, constitutions could be changed. In practice, their alteration was difficult. Amendments in most states first had to receive the approval of a large (extraordinary) majority of legislators or of two successive sessions, then win popular consent in a referendum. Even if successful this process took a year or longer. Thus the states entered the Great Depression burdened with fiscal and structural handicaps inherited from the republican era.

The election of 1932 broke the nation's political logjam. Voters replaced the discredited Hoover with the effervescent Franklin D. Roosevelt, governor of New York. Roosevelt brought to the presidency a rare combination of charismatic appeal and political dexterity, qualities that complemented his pragmatic attitude toward governmental power. FDR was no radical. Many of his ideas about government stood squarely within orthodox politics. But more than previous presidents, Roosevelt was willing to experiment with Federal solutions to social and economic problems. And he used the presidency in new ways to push his New Deal into law.

Roosevelt's leadership owed much to the changed partisan balance in Washington. The election of 1932 filled Congress with a large majority of Democrats, who outnumbered Republicans in both the Senate and the House for the remainder of the decade. Virtually all Democratic gains were won in congressional districts outside the South, for Republicans were rare in Dixie. The enlarged contingent of northern Democrats was extremely important to the success of presidential proposals. Each Democratic victory in a northern state removed a Republican and thus the most consistent source of opposition to the New Deal in Congress. Democrats did not always stand together on legislation, but they maintained sufficient unity to place an unmistakable partisan signature on the New Deal.

Democratic support for the president was dramatically revealed soon after Roosevelt's installation into office. The president pledged in his inaugural address to act on the public cry for "action, and action now." The economic collapse created conditions, he said, equivalent to "the emergency of war." The gravity of the situation warranted remedies suitable to the crisis, of which joblessness was the first challenge. The president called a special session of Congress to tackle these issues. During their ninety-nine days of deliberation (later nicknamed the first Hundred Days) lawmakers gave the president most of what he requested.

The Hundred Days marked a turning point in the history of federalism. In three months Congress and the president vastly extended the reach of the national government into the economy. They wrote new rules for banks and launched an adventurous experiment in monetary policy. Initial steps were taken to curb speculation in corporate stocks. Public jobs were created for young men in forestry and conservation projects. Half a billion dollars was appropriated for relief of the jobless, and another $3 billion was authorized for large-scale public works. Measured against the $1.9 billion of revenue that the Treasury received in 1932, these figures were enormous. Congress approved mortgage refinancing and debtor relief measures to stem foreclosures on homes and farms. Eventually a fifth of all urban residencies and farm properties received New Deal mortgage assistance.

Special programs sought to revitalize industry and agriculture. The National Recovery Act authorized cooperation among businesses in hopes of stabilizing employment, wages, and production. The Agricultural Adjustment Act launched an ambitious quest to increase farm prices. A plan of regional flood control and electrical production was entrusted to a new agency called the Tennessee Valley Authority. Another law sought solutions for the depressed railroad industry. And to permit spirited celebration of these accomplishments (or numb the outrage of critics), Congress legalized the sale of near beer (3.2 percent alcoholic content) in anticipation of the state ratification of the Twenty-first Amendment, which repealed Prohibition.

The Hundred Days symbolized Washington's new approach to governance. Part of the New Deal's innovativeness was the sheer volume and range of congressional enactments and administrative orders. By the standards of the past, these actions were extraordinary exercises of Federal power. But just as significant was the birth of a new conception of governmental responsibility toward the economy. The Great Depression had demonstrated that reliance on self-correcting mechanisms within the private market place had failed. To many politicians this experience bred the conclusion that the Federal government was the logical instrument to counteract the periodic fluctuations that appeared to be inherent in an industrial economy. This new civic outlook included a public obligation to assist individual victims of hard times.

The emergence of the new public economics during the 1930s requires an important qualification. No broad public agreement emerged during the decade about the degree to which officials should control private enterprise nor about the techniques that would effectively achieve economic recovery. These questions were vigorously debated inside Roosevelt's circle of advisers and among members of the Congress and the general public. Policy makers of the Depression era did not embrace all the premises later associated with liberal economics. Traditional ideas about the importance of entrepreneurial liberty, the impropriety of national centralization, and the wisdom of balanced budgets were entrenched too deeply to be cast aside casually. The old republican conviction that special interests could manipulate government for personal gain at the expense of the general good still had adherents. The Democrats concluded their 1932 party platform with this very axiom: "Equal rights to all; special privilege to none."

Largely because of the weight of this ideological tradition and because of the lack of tested theories about economic stabilization policy, the New Deal unfolded by a series of pragmatic actions and practical political compromises. No integrated master plan charted the course of anti-Depression policy. In a sense, the New Deal acted first and acquired a justifying ideology later. Many programs were reputed to be temporary expedients that would expire with the end of the emergency. These and other actions poured forth in a piecemeal fashion, born more out of experimentation and a rare combination of political and economic circumstances than the deliberate extensions of a comprehensive economic theory. Nor did most people foresee how the result of these policy innovations would transform the Federal role. Widespread acceptance of the new public economics came after subsequent political developments turned New Deal experiments into permanent assignments.

The new political economy of the 1930s assumed the tasks of relief and recovery, terms that were the product of the period. The modern equivalents of the economic objectives initiated during the New Deal are now called economic stabilization and income assistance policy. Incorporation of both the old and the new terminology in table 4.1 helps to summarize the directions of New Deal economics. The older policy designations appear on the left side of the table; the modern functional terms are listed at the top. Economic stabilization is divided into policies that affected the economy as a whole (system-wide policy) and measures aimed at a particular part of the economy (economic sector). The scheme is intended as a rough guide to the character of economic policy in the 1930s and does not list all New Deal actions. Nor are the classifications rigid or mutually exclusive. Some programs served several purposes simultaneously. Control of agricultural production, for instance, was

Table 4.1. New Deal Economic Policy

| | Economic Stabilization | | |
	System-wide	Economic Sector	Income Assistance
Relief	Income assistance		Emergency relief Public employment Mortgage refinancing
Recovery	Monetary policy Loans and purchases	Banking regulation and assistance	
	Fiscal policy: deficit spending	Agricultural commodity controls	
	Public works		
	Cooperative business agreements (National Recovery Act)		
Reform	Pricing regulation	Stock market	Social Security Act
	Unemployment compensation	Labor	Resettlement of poor farmers
		Trucking	
		Coal, natural gas	Public housing
		Power production	Minimum wage

designed principally to increase the price of farm products, but also functioned as a form of relief for individual farmers. This duality is captured by the term *reform,* which New Dealers used as a catchall characterization for permanent policy solutions to various long-standing problems.

The New Deal's attempt to revive the economy began with banking reform and adjustments to the money supply. Two days after his inauguration Roosevelt ordered a suspension of all banking activity. Three days later Congress enacted legislation that permitted the reopening of banks under Treasury supervision and with an infusion of Federal credit. Later measures established stricter rules by which national banks operated and provided more flexible means by which the Federal Reserve System made credit available to them. The regional Federal Reserve banks were placed under the more centralized control of a Board of Governors, appointed by the president. And to restore public confidence in an industry bordering on collapse, a federally supervised insurance fund, the Federal Deposit Insurance Corporation, was created to protect the bank deposits of individuals.

The administration hoped that a stable banking industry would encourage private investment, which in turn would regenerate economic activity and raise prices. A companion strategy created a more flexible and plentiful supply of money. Some of the new rules for banks, whose loan and reserve regulations affected the currency supply, sought this expansionary objective. The administration also reduced the tie between the stock of dollars and gold. By this and other monetary actions, some forced on Roosevelt by Congress, policy makers gambled that currency inflation would boost prices at home and orders for American goods from abroad. When the economy proved unresponsive to this stimulus, the administration abandoned a policy of monetary inflation.

Roosevelt believed that sound Federal finance was critical to restoration of confidence among businessmen and therefore sought to bring spending in line with available revenue. Since raising taxes to reduce the gap between receipts and outlays had little support, the alternative was a reduction of expenses. Following the lead of state and local officials, the president took this latter path and cut Federal salaries, as well as veterans' pensions, in 1933. The retrenchment program was short-lived, but Roosevelt clung to the goal of a balanced budget, which he regularly promised or predicted through 1937. Public opinion polls, which appeared regularly by 1935, showed clear majorities in favor of this goal, even if it meant reducing expenditures for relief. What significance Roosevelt attached to these voter surveys is conjectural, but orthodox political thinking abhorred deficit spending during peacetime. The president strained to contain Federal spending throughout the New Deal, yet he never presided over a balanced budget during any of his twelve years as president (1933–1945).[6]

Peacetime budget deficits were largely due to the weakened economy, which produced deep cuts in Federal revenue collections. Receipts in 1933 were half the 1930 level, and improvement was slow over the next five years. FDR's response to this dismal news marked a sharp break with past budgeting practice. Rather than reduce spending to the level of revenue, he announced that recovery would eventually bring the budget into alignment. In the meantime the Federal government should spend to alleviate the worst symptoms of the Depression. The economy proved fickle and did not rebound as swiftly as the president hoped, yet Roosevelt and his congressional allies stuck to their choice of placing greater value on responsiveness to need (i.e., by spending) than on balancing the budget. These decisions produced unprecedented deficits during peacetime and record levels of Federal expenditure and borrowing. Real Federal outlays (in constant dollars) by the end of 1940 were twice the most generous year of the Hoover presidency. The borrowing required to fund these outlays expanded the Treasury's role as a manager of the Federal debt, which grew from 16 percent of the gross national product in 1929 to 46 percent in 1939.

Roosevelt defended deficit spending as a temporary stopgap, designed to counter an extraordinary social emergency.[7] With the arrival of the New Deal, Congress appropriated funds for the direct relief of unemployed workers and others in financial hardship, created several public employment programs (such as the Civilian Conservation Corps, 1933–1942, and the Works Progress Administration, 1935–1943) and sponsored the refinancing of home and farm mortgages. The goal of providing financial help to individuals (in their capacity of consumers) explains the classification of these measures in table 4.1 as income assistance rather than economic stabilization policy. As the Depression lingered, temporary relief programs were transformed into permanent income assistance policies through the Social Security Act (1935), the Public Housing Act (1937), federally prescribed minimum wages (1938), and other laws.

Only unemployment compensation among these economic security plans was conceived as an anti-Depression measure, whereby assistance was triggered by slumps in the economy. Contained in the Social Security Act, this program provided payments to full-time workers who had been laid off their jobs. States actually paid the benefits, contingent upon their adoption of the plan. Since the process of enacting state enabling legislation for unemployment compensation took several years, the program was not effective nationwide until the end of the 1930s. Although the permanent income assistance programs had a limited effect in generating economic recovery, they represented a giant step in the expansion of the Federal role. From its initial emergency relief spending in 1932 through RFC loans, Washington made personal economic security a fixed obligation of American government by the end of the decade.

Political pressure as well as humanitarian concerns pushed these initiatives into law. Roosevelt and many Democrats in Congress probably saw greater political risk in not extending assistance than in the conservative criticism that economic security measures would (and did) incur. Random acts of violence had occurred in 1932 and 1933, including the U.S. Army's attack on WWI veterans who had come to Washington to lobby for full payment of promised bonuses. Whispered rumors of more serious and radical actions to come circulated in Washington. With hindsight we know that the chances of a full-scale revolution were slight in 1933, but New Dealers considered it a possibility. More conventional partisan concerns, however, offered a greater stimulus to the adoption of relief and income-assistance measures. Numerous schemes to aid the unemployed, the poor, and the elderly surfaced during the Depression. Champions of these plans posed electoral threats to Democrats in Congress and the White House. Roosevelt's economic security legislation blocked these political interlopers and endeared the Democratic Party to millions of working people.[8]

Economic recovery was not a major consideration behind Federal spending during the first five years of the New Deal. Roosevelt repeatedly refrained from drawing a connection between public expenditures and stimulation of the economy, although he acknowledged that Federal programs provided employment. Some members of Congress and economists went further, contending that public expenditures would prime the pump of the stalled economy. They urged much larger construction programs than Roosevelt assigned to the Public Works Administration (1933–1942) and to states through highway grant-in-aid moneys. By the late 1930s, thinking about the leverage that deficit spending could have on business slumps assumed more developed form. Influenced by the ideas of John Maynard Keynes, the English economist, some fiscal experts reasoned that public expenditures during low points in the business cycle would offer a stimulus for recovery. This theory held that compensatory fiscal policy produced a ripple effect in business, whereby each dollar of public spending generated several dollars of activity in the private sector.

Whether or not Roosevelt fully understood the complex technicalities of Keynes's theory, he remained ambivalent about it. But a major downturn in the economy late in 1937 led the president to adopt a Keynesian response. Stung by charges of a Roosevelt recession and out of new ideas for reversing the economic slide, Roosevelt authorized a new round of spending and loans. His budget message of 1939 revealed the shift in his thinking about public finance. The "policy of expanding capital outlays to compensate for variation in private capital expenditures," FDR stated, had helped "to check a recession and increase national income." Contrary to his previous defensiveness about unbalanced budgets, the president now claimed that budgetary deficits contributed to national wealth. And his former reservation about the macroeconomic effect of spending gave way to the claim that "wise fiscal policies and other acts of government" stimulated recovery.[9]

More than the conscious application of economic theorems, hard practical choices made in the context of ten years of Depression led Roosevelt to lay the foundation of a compensatory fiscal policy. Symbolic of this new macroeconomic role for public finance, Congress in 1939 permitted the relocation of the Bureau of the Budget from the Treasury Department to the newly created Executive Office of the President. The executive order that completed this transfer directed the bureau to assist the president in formulating a fiscal program. Because this task required specialized expertise, the bureau's enlarged staff took on professional economists.

Government compensation for the contraction of private investment and credit in fact had begun in 1932 through the Reconstruction Finance Corporation. Mainly a lending agency, the RFC had its authority and capital expanded greatly under Roosevelt. By 1939 it had loaned $10 billion, aiding banks, savings and loan institutions, railroads, insurance companies, and farmers. Not only did Washington act as a banker to private industry, but the government also bought stock in banks and other enterprises. The RFC was the largest of various public credit authorities born or enlarged during the New Deal. The public housing program launched in 1937 utilized credit arrangements rather than direct expenditures. Farmers, exporters, and ship owners received loan assistance. By 1939 over $11 billion of Federal loans were outstanding, compared to $2 billion in 1929.

Before the possibilities of fiscal policy had crystallized among policy makers, New Dealers had experimented with a plan for the industrial and commercial sectors of the economy. Many policy makers believed that unrestrained competition and unreasonable business practices stood in the way of expanded industrial production. To control this problem they sought to coordinate business activities through trade agreements among owners and workers in particular industries. The National Recovery Act (1933) delegated authority to the executive department to oversee the drafting of codes of fair practice that were to embody these ideas. Under the supervision of the National Recovery Administration (NRA), over five hundred codes were signed by early 1934. Each agreement sought to stabilize production (or a service), prices, and employment and to eliminate unfair business practices. Codes also acknowledged the right of workers to organize unions and use them as bargaining agents with management. Roosevelt called the plan "the most important and far-reaching legislation ever enacted by the American Congress."[10]

The justices on the Supreme Court also saw the new power vested in the executive branch as "without precedent" and unanimously ruled the National Recovery Act unconstitutional (*Schechter v. United States,* 1935). The court rejected the executive's contention that the Depression justified this extraordinary expansion of Federal authority and explained its position with reasoning inspired by classical republicanism. The code in question, which regulated slaughterhouses in New York City, did not have a direct effect on interstate commerce and thus regulated an activity outside Washington's legal reach. In giving the president wide discretion to implement the codes, the law also breached the separation of legislative and executive functions. In the robing room following the decision, Justice Louis Brandeis hinted at the jurists' objection to Federal collusion with private enterprise. "This is the end of this business of centralization," he told Thomas Corcoran, one of the young lawyers attracted to the New Deal. Instruct "your young men" to leave Washington, Brandeis advised. "Tell them to go home, back to the states. That is where they must do their work."[11]

The court won this battle against the breakdown of traditional federalism, but it lost the war. The New Deal continued to bring public officials into closer working relationship with business. Most of these steps represented sector policies (see table 4.1), wherein regulatory measures were fitted to particular lines of commercial activity. The diversification of the economy into specialized components, each with a comparatively unique set of characteristics, provided a general economic rationale for this particularistic approach. The National Recovery Administration in effect had adopted this strategy, in that each code was tailored to the circumstances of the industry it covered. Justifications of Federal intervention into the marketplace drew on arguments that originated in the transition era. The essence of this analysis held that the domination of industries by a few large firms, coupled with unfair business practices, restricted competition and impeded the operation of market forces. A corollary to this diagnosis stated that a modern industrial economy would become more productive through centralized coordination and rational planning. The prime candidates for governmental supervision were sectors where conspicuous failures in the private market occurred and where businesses were deemed to have special public interest.

Armed with these justifications, New Dealers extended public control of private enterprise considerably beyond the ranges established during the transition era. Many entrepreneurs understood the challenges that public power posed to their economic interests and repeatedly denounced New Deal moves as detrimental to economic liberty. Labor policy provoked especially bitter outcries from employers. Some members of the business community stood steadfastly by the philosophy that the condition of labor was the exclusive prerogative of employers. Government interference with labor-management relations was destructive of this principle. Numerous lawmakers, however, saw the public interest at stake in these matters and sought to harmonize the interests of entrepreneurs and workers by means of labor arbitration, which was seen as conducive to industrial expansion. This thinking was reflected in the collective bargaining provisions of NRA codes and in the creation of a National Labor Relations Board (NLRB) in 1934. Given minimal authority, the NLRB had little success in ameliorating industrial turmoil in 1934 and 1935. The board's chief contribution was advocacy of a stronger labor law.[12]

The National Labor Relations Act (1935) established protections and obligations for both workers and owners. Employees were guaranteed the right to elect representatives to bargain on their behalf with employers. Managers were prohibited from engaging in unfair practices that undercut collective bargaining, such as dismissing workers for joining a union. Workers had to abide by similar rules, such as avoidance of illegal coercion of employers over matters of employment and labor negotiations. Enforcement of these provisions and control over the critical question of determining the appropriate bargaining unit to represent workers in a plant were placed in the three-member NLRB. This panel had authority to issue cease-and-desist orders regarding violations and to petition the court for an injunction (court order to stop a particular practice) when NLRB orders were ineffective. The public correctly saw the law as representing new Federal protection for workers, who joined unions in record numbers during the remainder of the 1930s. Less generally understood was the extent to which government now set the conditions of labor for factory hands as well as members of the corporate board.

The labor act was more broadly conceived than most New Deal sector policies. By the end of the 1930s a host of industries had been folded into the expanded Federal supervisory regime. The list included agriculture, trucks and buses, airlines, stock markets, natural gas, coal, banks, oceanic shipping, radio broadcasting, electric utilities, and the cosmetics industry. In acts of 1936 and

1937 Congress regulated price agreements between suppliers and retailers in an effort to reduce predatory pricing and cut-rate schemes that hurt small local merchants. Although the common ingredient in these actions was the expansion of public regulation of private enterprise, sector policies varied widely one from another. In many instances the policy designs differed markedly within subdivisions of a particular industry. Regulatory complexity and administrative fragmentation became generic to Federal economic policy, characteristics that appear in the New Deal's approach to agriculture, trucking, and the stock market, discussed in the next sections.

The Depression hit farm country especially hard. Farmers' net income in 1932 plummeted to a third of its 1929 amount. Although agriculture accounted for a comparatively small part of the nation's earning (about 9 percent), a fourth of all Americans lived on farms. Moreover, many villagers and city dwellers were dependent on hauling, selling, and processing farm goods for their livelihood. Even before the Depression hit, many farmers knew hard times. Tenant farmers and sharecroppers (people who worked lands owned by others), a system that thrived in the South, tended to live on the economic edge. In its Black Belt region, which ran through the heart of cotton country from South Carolina to Mississippi, nearly nine of every ten blacks and half of the white farmers worked under some tenancy arrangement. The rate was higher in the counties situated along the lower Mississippi River. There and throughout the rural South, homes without electricity and running water were customary. African Americans occupied the bottom rung of the region's impoverished economy, and most lived in perpetual poverty.[13]

It was not income inequality in rural America but the commercial structure of agriculture that guided the New Deal's approach to the farm problem. Although the nation's six million farm operators shared a nominal occupation, in fact they were economically diverse. Differences in land and capital requirements, techniques of production, and the structure of markets for agricultural goods created innumerable variations among farmers. The routines of dairy farmers bore little resemblance to the practices of orange growers. The demand for wheat was not the same as for tobacco. Cotton could be stored indefinitely; fresh eggs and milk had to be marketed within days of production. Regional characteristics further differentiated farmers. Southern cotton and tobacco, Iowa corn, Kansas wheat, Wisconsin cheese, Massachusetts cranberries, Washington apples, California grapes, and Florida oranges are familiar symbols of this pattern. Most operators sold one or two of the hundred items that formed distinct commodity markets for agricultural products. Politicians from farm country understood the connection between the well-being of their constituents and the price of commodities produced in their districts. And if a public official failed to grasp this fact, a trade association for the pertinent commodity drove the point home.

A calamitous drop in commodity prices brought the Depression to rural America. Its most immediate cause was the decline of demand for farm products due to the squeeze on consumers' pocketbooks, but behind this crisis loomed a problem of longer duration. Agricultural output had increased since the late nineteenth century in response to the spread of farms and improvements in techniques of production. Although the full impact of scientific farming lay in the future, the productivity of agriculture had increased in prior decades. Experts in the U.S. Department of Agriculture (USDA), the state agricultural colleges, and the experiment stations (all federally subsidized) took an active role in promoting more efficient farming. The rising bounty of agricultural commodities was a boon for urban consumers, but it put downward pressure on the prices that farmers received.

Unlike an automobile manufacturer, individual farmers lacked the ability to adjust the total supply of a product to fit anticipated demand for it. A million and a half farmers planted cotton in 1930; 600,000 others earned their living from dairying. A farmer's normal response to a drop in the prices of a commodity was to produce more in the hope of maintaining his income by selling greater volume. But the cumulative result of these individual decisions was disastrous if most farmers followed this strategy, because the mounting supply drove prices down further. The marketing of products added still more headaches for farmers, who sold their goods to wholesalers and commodity dealers. These intermediaries were in a position to balance supply to demand, and thus gained considerable influence over the prices farmers received for their products.

An elite within the world of farm politics and economics, not farmers with manure on their boots, had the largest hand in designing Federal agricultural policy. Most of these influential individuals had ties with the USDA, the state agricultural colleges, the farm newspapers, or a commodity trade association. Many also were connected with the American Farm Bureau Federation, a powerful lobby. In addition to the power wielded by these groups, ideological perceptions of farm life affected agricultural policy. Preservation of the family farm, a virile symbol of American virtue, comprised one influential premise. Retention of local political control and maintenance of entrepreneurial freedom for farmers constituted two others. Working within these assumptions, farm planners sought to find ways of increasing the prices of agricultural commodities. The problems of income inequality in the countryside and southern racism were scarcely considered.[14]

Three techniques were used to stabilize agricultural prices during the 1930s. First, farmers were paid to reduce the number of acres planted. For selected field crops such as cotton, tobacco, wheat, and corn, state committees assigned acreage quotas to individual farmers in accordance with production targets for certain basic commodities established by the secretary of agriculture. Usually the plan was contingent upon a two-thirds vote of the producers of a commodity. In some programs penalties (usually taxes) were assessed on farmers who violated their quota. Second, the Federal government offered an insurance program for the prices of certain commodities. The primary instrument for this job was the Commodity Credit Corporation (CCC), created in 1933. An adjunct of the USDA, the CCC had powers similar to a private corporation's, with authority to buy, sell, and store commodities and to borrow money. Through a procedure called commodity loans, the CCC guaranteed a price floor to producers of designated (selected) commodities. Farmers (by contractual prearrangement) in effect sold their crop to the Federal government if the price on the open market was below the target figure set by agricultural officials. In good times the farmer sold the crop on the open market and paid off the loan from his receipts. And third, the Federal government supervised marketing agreements between producers and dealers that placed a floor under the price farmers received for their commodity.

The Agricultural Act of 1933 empowered the secretary of agriculture to apply these techniques in combinations of his choosing. Advocates of this administrative discretion claimed that this authority was a temporary expedient. The preface of the statute stated that the intent of the law was "to relieve the existing national economic emergency" in agriculture, implying that agricultural controls terminated with the return of normal times. Public regulation of agriculture in fact outlived the Depression, although the future of Federal assistance to farmers looked uncertain in 1936, when *United States v. Butler* declared the 1933 law unconstitutional. The legal issue before the Supreme Court was a tax on processors of agricultural products (cotton in this case), which raised the funds used to pay farmers for acreage reduction. Justice Owen Roberts's opinion for the court ruled that the Constitution restricted Federal authority to specific delegated powers, which did not include the regulation of agricultural production. To permit exemption from this rule under the guise of emergency would subvert the "entire plan of our government" and threatened to convey "uncontrolled police power" on Washington. Unchecked centralization would obliterate the independence of the states. The issue as Roberts saw it did not hinge on the economic merits of the policy but on the philosophic propriety of observing strict dual federalism. Justice Roberts added another complaint reminiscent of earlier republicanism: the payment of "benefits" bestowed special-interest favoritism.

New Dealers denounced the *Butler* decision as outdated constitutional theory that ignored modern economic reality. Prodded by the powerful farm lobbies, Congress maneuvered around the court's technical objections and restored the powers previously granted to the secretary of agriculture in three laws enacted between 1936 and 1938. In a historic about-face, the court accepted Federal controls on agricultural production in 1942 (*Wickard v. Filburn*). The outbreak of World War II and the continuing arrival of Roosevelt appointees to the court produced a new reading of the Constitution. The justices scrapped the old, narrow conception of interstate commerce and substituted a flexible test of Congress's power to regulate entrepreneurial activity. Writing for the court, Justice Robert Jackson said that agricultural production (wheat in this case) was not a local matter, even if part of the crop was consumed on the owner's farm. The legality of Federal economic controls turned on whether an activity "exerts a substantial economic effect on interstate commerce." In Jackson's opinion, wheat production did. Regardless of where any stalk was grown or consumed, each bushel contributed to the total volume in the national marketplace. The implication of this reasoning was that the production of virtually any good fell within the scope of interstate commerce.

The *Butler* decision turned out to be the Supreme Court's last stand against Federal breaches of commercial dual federalism. A revolution in constitutional interpretation began the following year, and in the next decade virtually all New Deal economic policy adopted after 1934, as well as numerous uses of state regulatory power, passed constitutional muster. The *Wickard* decision was part of this constitutional revolution, in which the court came to accept the proposition that the interconnectedness of the modern economy justified extensive government intervention, even if it was achieved by broad delegation of authority to executives. After generations of service as the constitutional watchdog of commercial dual federalism, the court in effect removed itself as an impediment to Federal economic policy.

The new judicial permissiveness affected Washington's regulation of the milk business under the Marketing Agreement Act of 1937. Milk and its derivative products constituted an important part of farm income, especially in northern states such as Wisconsin and New York. Similar to other sectors of agriculture, a large number of dairy farmers sold their commodity to a few dealers who processed and marketed it, and who exercised considerable influence on prices. Dairying also had some unique aspects. Cows produced different amounts of milk from season to season, and farmers delivered fluid milk to dealers on a daily basis. Although consumer demand for drinking milk was relatively constant, dairymen worked to prop up interest in their product. To hear dairy farmers tell it, drinking milk was in the national interest. The cow was portrayed as "the foster mother of the race," which made dairymen surrogate fathers to American babies.

Many dairy farmers had organized business associations (cooperatives) that acted as their marketing agent with milk wholesalers, such as the Borden Company. Individual dairymen were paid on a formula basis from the pooled receipts of their cooperative. Milk used for drinking commanded a higher price than surplus milk, which could be manufactured into storable products such as cheese and ice cream. Workable at times and in some milk sheds (the area that supplied a metropolitan market), marketing arrangements were plagued by three problems: fierce competition among dealers, individualistic dairymen who operated outside of cooperatives, and numerous complaints about the financial management of dairy cooperatives. The price collapse and heightened competition brought on by the Depression hastened government intervention into an industry already ripe for public supervision.[15] Federal intervention added a second layer of control over dairying. Dealers were required to secure licenses to operate from a state milk board or the USDA.

The Marketing Agreement Act of 1937 became the statutory foundation for permanent Federal supervision of the dairy industry. This institutionalization of Depression-era experimentation with milk regulation represented control only in the sense that Washington enforced price agreements reached through negotiation between cooperatives and dealers. Each Federal marketing order applied to a particular milk shed; not all milk sheds were regulated. Pricing schemes, whose complexity only the experts could fathom, varied from market to market and were conditional upon a two-thirds vote of affected dairymen.[16] Largely at the request of dairymen, the milk business became a three-way collaborative between producers, dealers, and government.

Whereas the cow was the emblem of American farms, trucks symbolized the modern transportation industry. Truck ownership mushroomed after World War I owing to the vehicle's versatility on the farm, in metropolitan deliveries, and in intercity freight transportation as a network of paved roads connected metropolitan areas in the 1920s. Railroads watched apprehensively as trucking firms cut into traditional rail business. When the number of registered trucks surpassed rail freight cars in service in 1925, a new competitive battle in intercity transportation was in progress. The following year, legislation that authorized national regulation of the trucking industry appeared in Congress. When Federal supervision of motor carriers won approval ten years later, four million trucks were on the roads.

The states preceded the Federal government's entry into the field. In the 1920s states required truck owners to secure permission to operate (certificates of public convenience and necessity) from licensing bodies, which required operators to observe safety, financial, reporting, and scheduling requirements. Customarily the state railroad or public service commission, which administered these rules and collected license fees, was given authority to fix reasonable rates. Choruses of complaints, centering on two issues, pointed to imperfections in these laws. The first concerned the classification of types of motor carriers, which fell into three rather ill-defined legal categories of usage. Common carriers accepted all forms of business, whereas contract carriers operated under more permanent agreements with specific shippers. Private carriers were owned and operated by firms engaged in nontransportation business (such as Sears). Entrepreneurs jockeyed to fit these distinctions to their own economic interests. The second problem grew out of the jurisdictional peculiarities of state government. States had established a collection of dissimilar rules, especially concerning safety and loads, much to the annoyance of truckers who made interstate runs.

The faltering economy during the early years of the Depression unleashed cutthroat competition in trucking as small-time "gypsy" operators proliferated and underbid more established firms. The New Deal's NRA code (1933) sought to stabilize this chaos, but it proved ineffective. Before the collapse of the code, however, its administrators insisted that rival groups of truckers form a common new trade organization, which emerged as the American Trucking Association (ATA). The ATA became an active advocate of Federal regulation and worked closely with Joseph Eastman, a former interstate commerce commissioner whom Roosevelt had appointed as coordinator of transportation in 1933. Eastman's objective of reducing the oversupply of transportation facilities and destructive competition complemented the aspirations of established trucking firms to stabilize their competitive position. State transportation regulators, the railroads, and the president played minor roles in formulating a new policy. And other than giving his blessing to some form of national supervision, Roosevelt took no active part in designing trucking regulation.[17] The new statute (Motor Carriers Act of 1935) instructed the Interstate Commerce Commission to license common carriers and issue permits to contract carriers. The ICC was to set both minimum and maximum rates for common carriers but minimum rates only for contract trucking. The commission also wrote requirements concerning financial reporting, schedules and loads, vehicle safety and insurance, and practices of employment.

At first blush the 1935 act appeared to transfer the management of trucking from private to public hands, yet nothing so draconian happened. Only a small proportion of trucking actually was subject to Federal regulation. National controls applied primarily to common carriers engaged in interstate traffic, and they comprised about 2 percent of all trucking activity. Most motor carriers remained under exclusive state jurisdiction. The statute was pockmarked with exemptions, such as the exclusion of unprocessed agricultural commodities and newspapers. Nor did ICC price setting prove heavy-handed. The law permitted firms to form rate-making bureaus, which were exempted from antimonopoly prosecution. The ICC customarily ratified the price proposals requested by these associations of truckers.[18] The possibilities under this model of business-government cooperation, which thwarted entry to newcomers under the rubric of preserving competition and providing reliable service and virtually guaranteed a profit to firms favored with an ICC certificate, was not lost on the airlines. In 1938 the handful of trunk (interstate) air carriers received similar national regulatory protection.[19]

The stock market crash in 1929 burst a bubble of investment speculation. The collapse shook public confidence in the securities industry and in the financial soundness of American corporations. Securities consist of stocks (shares of ownership in a business corporation) and bonds, which are used to raise capital for the issuer. Investment banks acted as underwriters for these instruments and offered stocks for sale in stock exchanges. Of the twenty-nine organized securities markets in 1929, the New York Stock Exchange was the oldest, largest, and most prestigious. Securities were also sold by thousands of individual dealers and brokers in over-the-counter transactions throughout the country.

Behind the glamour of high finance lay pitfalls in the fast lane of securities trading. An inherent instability existed in the industry because of the tendency of individuals and firms to engage in stock trading, wherein investors hoped to profit by buying cheap and selling dear. It was a risky business, somewhat like legalized gambling. The value of a stock could be influenced by investor psychology and rumors as well as objective evidence about a firm's prospects. The uncertainties innate to investment in the stock market were compounded by lax practices of its management prior to the 1930s. Companies were not required to disclose financial information about their stock issues or to have independent auditors appraise them. Moreover, stocks were frequently purchased with borrowed money, with the stock itself serving as collateral for the loan. This gambit worked as long as stock values continued to rise. Some commercial banks speculated with their depositors' funds. Further instability in the market resulted from insider trading, where investors capitalized on secret information about a stock or manipulated rumors to rig the market. Weak state laws and an elitist air among the leaders of big-time finance worked to obscure the shady side of the securities business from public view.

Roosevelt put reform of the "naked speculation" of the securities industry high on his agenda in 1933. For help he called on Felix Frankfurter, a professor at Harvard Law School, who sent three of his brightest former students—Thomas Corcoran, Benjamin Cohen, and James Landis—to Washington. This trio symbolized the new prominence of lawyers in the national administration. Young attorneys, many fresh out of law school, flocked to Washington in 1933 and later to tackle complex policy issues. The Harvard law school, FDR's alma mater, was the largest feeder in this legal pipeline, followed by Yale and Columbia.[20] James Landis was a professor at Harvard when summoned to Washington in 1933, and he returned to the law school as dean four years later, after helping to shape Federal securities policy.

Analogous to agricultural and transportation policy, securities regulation sought to reform a troubled sector of the economy. But unlike the controls on farmers and truckers, securities policy neither set production goals nor fixed prices. Because of the nature of securities transactions and vociferous opposition by New York financiers to federal intrusion, policy toward stocks utilized two alternative strategies. First, the industry was required (acts of 1933 and 1934) to furnish adequate and independently audited information about stocks and bonds, which Federal regulators had to approve. And second, security traders were obligated to abide by rules designed to eliminate unsound and unfair practices. Congress created a new agency, the Securities and Exchange Commission (SEC) in 1934 to formulate and administer these standards of conduct.

Under the commission's first chair, Joseph Kennedy (a Harvard alumnus and a former Wall Street trader), and its second, James Landis, SEC regulation relied heavily on self-policing by the managers of the exchanges. The financiers became convinced that it was in their interest to cooperate with the commission after the conviction and sentencing of the president of the New York Stock Exchange for financial irregularities.[21] SEC officials and industry representatives took self-regulation a step further in 1938 with a law that placed the over-the-counter market under national supervision. The act required trade associations to fine, suspend, or expel members that violated industry rules, which were written according to SEC standards.

Instead of adopting a confrontational posture, the SEC worked to persuade the securities industry that it was in the interest of traders to keep their own house in order. This approach relieved the commission from direct oversight of numerous firms and countless transactions, a decision that saved money and litigation. This regulatory design was made possible by extensive discretion that Congress granted to SEC officials, who in turn negotiated with industry leaders to find a mutually agreeable form of public supervision. The result clothed private citizens with quasi-official authority to protect the public interest.

If one took FDR's conservative critics at face value, the president had put the nation on a course toward socialism or worse. The republic withstood the New Deal, of course, but the role of the Federal government did grow substantially during the 1930s. While few experts called the new political regime "socialist," the political landscape had been altered. Three changes are especially noteworthy: the increased influence of the president, a shift in the balance of power in the federal system toward Washington, and the birth of modern liberalism.

To Franklin Roosevelt goes much of the credit for rewriting the president's job description. FDR assumed active leadership of the New Deal (although not of every proposal) and made his agenda the reference point for policy discussions. Congress still proposed legislation and modified bills sent to it from the White House, but the momentum of policy initiative had shifted to the executive branch. Roosevelt did not personally draft New Deal laws or even rough out their policy designs. His primary role in policy formation was the identification of issues that he believed required public attention. Roosevelt's greatest legacy for the modern presidency was elevation of this agenda-setting function to the top of the chief executive's list of tasks.[22] While legislators and the public looked to the president for answers, Roosevelt turned to appointed assistants for solutions. Congress facilitated this reliance on the executive branch by delegating considerable authority to administrative units. The enhancement of executive power during the 1930s therefore included not only the growth of presidential influence but also the expansion of the role of administrators as formulators and implementers of policy. The commodity sections within the USDA, the Motor Carrier's Bureau of the ICC, the Securities and Exchange Commission, and the revamped Bureau of the Budget (which later evolved into the nerve center of federal fiscal policy) are tangible signs of the spread of bureaucratic government.

The rise of the national executive establishment contributed to a shift of power in the federal system toward Washington. Initiative from the White House and the Congress had created economic stabilization and income assistance policy as major new civic functions during the 1930s. After some judicial soul-searching the Supreme Court dropped its constitutional objections to these new Federal responsibilities. This change of heart removed most aspects of Federal economic policy from the court's docket. By the mid-1940s old economic dual federalism was legally dead.

The court also relaxed its constitutional vigilance over state economic actions, which poured forth in profusion during the 1930s. The states adopted an unprecedented number of new taxes, which helped to double their revenue collections between 1932 and 1940.[23] These new moneys allowed states to increase their contribution to programs formerly wholly or largely under local management, such as public works and welfare. The states also expanded their regulation of business and public utilities, agriculture, labor unions, trucking companies, "resale" and other retail pricing practices, and criminal activity. There were variations among the states, of course, but some compiled records that observers dubbed "little New Deals."[24] How much these state policy innovations were due to the economic impact of the Depression as opposed to pressures applied by national officials remains an unanswered question. The Democratic Party provided one avenue of cooperation between New Dealers and state policy makers. Democrats wrested control of the majority of states from Republicans in the years around 1935, with some victors riding the coattails of FDR's popularity into office. The accomplishments of the first Hundred Days and later probably put pressure on state-level Democrats to emulate the activism of their colleagues in Washington. Yet despite Roosevelt's popularity, shown in his landslide reelection in 1936, the New Deal did not infect all local Democrats. Some exhibited more conservatism than Republicans.[25]

Such resistance to change, whether by Democrats or Republicans, motivated New Dealers to urge action from state officials through formal and informal stimulants. Many federal programs, especially ones that offered national subsidies, required formal state legislative acceptance. Loans and grants channeled through the Reconstruction Finance Corporation and the Public Works Administration contained this requirement, as did Federal mortgage and lending ventures. In other cases state cooperation was desired but not mandatory. Federal officials urged state lawmakers, for instance, to enact intrastate NRA business codes. Most states did not, despite delivery of model bills from Washington. On the other hand, the states did consent to enforce truck safety regulations that the ICC's Bureau of Motor Carriers proposed. Intrastate NRA codes and the ICC highway safety plan represent two of many instances in which national administrators shipped drafts of legislation to state capitols.[26]

These gestures, virtually unheard of in earlier eras, opened new lines of communication between the levels of government. Washington launched an unprecedented, though poorly coordinated, intervention into state policy making and in some cases bypassed state lawmakers altogether to work directly with municipal officers. On the surface, most new cooperative programs seemed to offer states the opportunity to join in partnership with the federal government on a voluntary basis. In reality these programs allowed less discretion because the failure to participate in a program usually meant a loss of money for the state. The design of the unemployment compensation plan was predicated on this principle. If a state failed to levy a tax on employers to fund the plan, the federal government did so but without assisting the jobless in the recalcitrant jurisdiction.

These breaches in the boundaries of traditional federalism were a consequence of lawmakers acting according to the premises of liberalism. The New Deal embedded the term *liberalism* permanently in the vocabulary of American politics. Despite its constant use over the succeeding decades, the idea lacked a distinct and coherent meaning. Liberalism's vagaries lay in the nature of its content, which in fact was constantly evolving. America's old political philosophy had keyed on power, which was viewed as inherently dangerous because it threatened liberty. As the objectives of governance turned increasingly toward solving problems, abstract apprehensions about potential abuses of power receded, although they did not vanish. Most citizens appeared to accept the enhanced capacity of government to ensure a new and broader meaning of liberty.

In this reconceptualized view of the public good, Americans expected government to focus on the problems facing modern society. This expectation reinforced decisions of policy makers in the emergent claimant polity to use public power to solve socioeconomic and global challenges and to provide for the economic security of individuals. In essence, liberalism represented the polity's demand to use the collective authority of government to reduce risks and ensure security. Historic preoccupations with potential abuses of power faded as this instrumental conception of government's purpose took hold. Liberalism, in short, became anything Americans identified as an issue worthy of civic redress.

5

The Managed Economy since the New Deal

"MAN, IT WAS the war time. There was jobs all over." That's how Muddy Waters remembered Chicago in 1943. On the day he arrived in the Windy City, Muddy found work at a box factory.[1] The prospect of a steady job at decent wages had lured him out of Mississippi and the poverty that enveloped black farmhands in the river delta region. What Muddy Waters really wanted, however, was a paying audience to hear him play the blues. So he followed tens of thousands of blacks who quit the cotton fields along the lower reaches of the Mississippi River and went north in search of a better life.

Success to Muddy Waters was snaring a gig in a west side tavern at five dollars a night. Economists saw the mass migration of blacks out of the South as the tendency of labor to flow from low- to high-wage areas. World War II magnified the economic imbalances between regions, which in turn spawned internal migration. Government orders for military goods opened up new positions for men and women in the factories of the East and Midwest, in the shipyards of coastal cities, and in the aircraft plants of California. The creation of well-paying jobs induced a massive relocation of blacks and whites. This reshuffling of people across America was one of several momentous changes caused by the war.

If a successful economic policy means full employment, the New Deal was a failure. Seventeen percent of the labor force remained out of work as late as 1939, the year war erupted in Europe. Two years later, following the Japanese attack on Pearl Harbor, the United States was officially in the fight and defense mobilization sprang into high gear. Service in the military grew to a peak of 11.5

million by 1944. The civilian workforce expanded by a fifth, with women new to the job market comprising half of this increase. The insatiable hunger for workers during the early forties virtually eliminated joblessness. At the peak of the war the employment rate dropped to 1 percent, its lowest level on record. With idle able-bodied men as scarce as hen's teeth and with overtime pay plentiful, incomes rose. The real GNP increased 50 percent in the five years after 1939. The Second World War caused hardships and heartbreaks, but it also left Americans richer.[2]

The Federal government orchestrated this economic surge. War may not seem to be public policy in the ordinary sense, yet in setting military strategy in motion, raising armed forces, and organizing the society for defense production, governmental officials had an immense impact on the economy. Under the rules of American federalism the responsibility for protecting national security lay with the central government. Historically its power had expanded during periods of active hostilities, which were viewed as times of national emergency. World War II was the most profound of these international crises. Neither the Korean War (1950–1953) nor the Vietnam War (1962–1973) nor conflicts in the Middle East produced as sweeping Federal presence in the economy as occurred during the early 1940s. There were four major dimensions of this intervention. First, Washington became a mammoth employer. Second, Federal officials decided which goods should be produced. Third, government curtailed civilian purchases. And fourth, Congress and the president spent huge sums of money to fight the war. On this last score alone, wartime Washington dwarfed the scale of earlier governance.

In their most generous year (1939) New Dealers paid out $9 billion, which constituted 10 percent of the GNP. In 1944 national officials pumped $100 billion into the economy, a sum equal to nearly one-half of the GNP. Most of these funds went to private producers of war-related goods. Such massive outlays required a bold renovation of Federal revenue policy. One major change greatly expanded the reach of personal income taxes. By 1943 most full-time employees were liable for this levy, compared to less than 5 percent of the workforce before Pearl Harbor.[3] Yet even with this expansion taxes paid only one-half of the war bill. Because borrowing was the only acceptable way to cover the shortfall, the Roosevelt Treasury floated loans on an unprecedented scale. Americans' determination to win the war muted criticism of these unbalanced budgets and the ballooning national debt. The Federal government's huge wartime payroll consumed much of this new revenue. Most of Washington's enlarged workforce comprised personnel in the military, which grew by a factor of thirty-six after 1939. Federal civilian workers quadrupled, an expansion that exceeded the growth of administration during the New Deal. Besides the employees who reported directly to a Federal official, several million more worked in plants under contract to Washington, which in effect paid the labor costs for privately managed defense production. Altogether about a third of the labor force was directly or indirectly employed by the national government at the peak of the war.[4]

Federal administrators coordinated the nation's war production effort. Officials established manufacturing and agricultural priorities, allocated supplies and resources, financed the construction of manufacturing facilities, enticed people into the workforce, and kept transportation unsnarled. Congress delegated sweeping authority to the president for these purposes, and Roosevelt then created a jumble of temporary agencies to supervise defense mobilizations. The War Production Board (WPB) was one of the most powerful of these ad hoc bodies. Roosevelt created it by executive order in 1942 to coordinate the procurement of military goods. The scope of the WPB's power was evident at its very first meeting when board members forbade the manufacture of autos for private sale. Most of the board's work lay in negotiating contracts with private firms, usually on a cost-plus basis that included automatic profits for producers. Large corporations received the lion's share of this business. The WPB also invested billions of dollars in the construction of factories, airports, and other facilities. The board turned to the business world for its executives because they were viewed as the most available source of managerial expertise.

The wartime economy put Americans back to work, but their extra earnings caused unwanted inflation. The scarcity of consumer goods (due to manufacturers' switching from civilian items like autos to military equipment like Jeeps), coupled with workers' increased purchasing power, pushed prices up. Policy makers countered this inflationary pressure with three strategies. First, Washington skimmed off a substantial portion of wartime earnings with higher taxes and sales of savings bonds. Even schoolchildren were encouraged to invest their dimes in weekly U.S. savings stamps. Second, Congress allowed Federal administrators to regulate prices, wages, and rents. And third, certain goods, such as gasoline, sugar, and coffee, were rationed to consumers. Seven hundred local boards staffed by volunteers distributed the coupon books that entitled individuals to purchase their allotment of rationed goods. All three steps were extraordinary in view of America's free-market and low-tax traditions.

Congress delegated sweeping, open-ended, though ostensibly temporary, authority to the executive branch to regulate the home front during the war. These actions, which were a radical departure from conventional American governance, are explicable only in terms of a crisis forged by all-out war. Franklin Roosevelt had called the Great Depression an emergency too. But history is written more by actions than words. Measured by the actual application of Federal power, the early 1940s brought a greater emergency than the 1930s. War-born programs forged contacts between individuals and the national government on an enlarged scale. Federal income taxes now took a bite out of the paycheck of nearly every full-time worker. Sixteen million Americans had donned military uniforms, and many had been compelled to do so as draftees. Price controls and rationing forced civilians to observe an equality of sacrifice on the home front while their men risked their lives on the battlefield. In contrast to New Deal programs, many of which had been administered by local government, national officials dominated the supervision of the war effort.

These extensions of Federal power elicited little dissent. No constitutional impasse hamstrung lawmakers during the war. Few people quibbled about legalities when the survival of the nation appeared to be on the line. This was a "good" war whose goals and rationale went unquestioned. And if this argument failed to convince the few skeptics, defenders of centralized power cited two further arguments. The prerogatives of the president, they said, were greater during war than during peacetime because the chief executive also commanded the armed forces. Furthermore, the expansion of executive power was temporary. Peace, so the argument went, would bring a contraction of the Federal establishment.[5]

This last prediction seemed destined for fulfillment in the immediate aftermath of the war, in 1946 and 1947. The WPB and other wartime agencies closed shop, price controls ceased, millions were mustered out of the armed services, and taxes edged downward. But complete demobilization of wartime powers did not occur. The war established a new plateau in the scale of Federal operations. The maintenance of the mass-based income tax and a large military establishment illustrates this continuity between the war and later governance. Yet a tally of discrete policies will not capture the war's full effect on American politics. The war also contributed to a metamorphosis in political outlooks. Admittedly it is hard to be precise about the scope of this change because the further in time one is from an event, the more difficult it is to determine how a prior occurrence affected later developments. Numerous factors played a role in shaping public opinion in the postwar decades.

A plausible case can be made, nonetheless, that the war accelerated public acceptance of a broadly based public effort to achieve economic stability and a wider role for the Federal government in fulfilling this goal. The victories over Germany and Japan reinforced the consensus that the struggle had been a "good" war. The central government had defeated powerful adversaries and at the same time cured the country's worst economic setback. Americans' position in the world in 1945 had never been stronger. At home they were prosperous, compared to the remainder of the industrialized world, which lay in shambles.[6] The war demonstrated that centralized controls could promote economic growth and raise incomes while still preserving most elements of private enterprise. The monopoly of the atomic bomb (until 1949) anchored a feeling of military invincibility in the world at large. America's new might and the lessons extracted from Hitler's treachery convinced leaders that the nation should play a leading role in shaping the postwar international order. Thus the war offered a model of how Federal power could be effectively applied at home and abroad. Lip service to traditional political goals persisted but increasingly these principles were overwhelmed by actions. The reality was a continued expansion of the public sector, of governmental intervention into the private marketplace, generously leavened with favoritism for special interests.

The Employment Act of 1946 formally announced Washington's promise to maintain a healthy economy. This law stated that "it is the continuing policy and responsibility of the Federal Government . . . to promote maximum employment, production, and purchasing power." In a purposefully vague grant of authority, Federal policy makers were instructed to use "all practical means" consistent with "free competitive enterprise" to reach these goals. The job of proposing a specific economic program was assigned to the president, who was given technical advice from a Council of Economic Advisers. The language that created this three-member panel virtually ensured that each councilor would be a professional economist.

The promotion of stable economic growth was not a new public objective. Washington had pursued this goal during the 1930s, but Federal efforts to end the Great Depression had been seen largely as temporary expedients. In 1946 policy makers moved beyond a crisis rationale and made the economic health of the nation an ongoing commitment. Two factors played instrumental roles in this decision. First, lawmakers feared the country would slip back into depression with the return of peace, which would terminate Washington's massive defense purchases and wartime controls.[7] And second, the actions of the 1930s and early 1940s conditioned the public to expect that Washington could and should produce prosperity. Franklin Roosevelt alluded to this thinking in an economic bill of rights that he incorporated into his annual message of 1944. First among the economic truths that have become accepted as self-evident, the president said, was "the right to a useful and remunerative job." Thomas Dewey, the Republican challenger for the Oval Office in 1944, agreed. "Never again must Americans face the specter of unemployment," he said. If free enterprise could not put people back to work, government itself "must create additional jobs."[8] Republican presidents later balked at proposals that had government hire individuals as a way of combating unemployment. But all of Roosevelt's successors took for granted that the president served as the nation's chief economist.

Agreement in the abstract that government should promote prosperity was easier than devising ways to achieve the goal. Two major complications existed. First, the technical know-how for stabilizing the economy had to exist. Economists became increasingly confident about their ability to supply these ideas after World War II. Yet their craft remained as much an art as a science. And second, any proposal to manage prosperity had to win over lawmakers, many of whom were skeptical about modern economics. Even when the professionals were in agreement, which was rare, lawmakers haggled over the politics of economic policy. Washington's economic strategies, therefore, were political compromises. This outcome held for other fields of legislation too, yet the jargon of the economists influenced the public to see economic policy as rational solutions to technical problems and tended to obscure the political character of these decisions.

The common ground that emerged between economists and politicians settled on fiscal and monetary policies as the basic tools for stabilizing the economy. Fiscal policy encompasses Federal spending, taxing, and borrowing.

As the level of these transactions increased and recognition of their economic repercussions crystallized, the Federal budget took on added prominence. Because spending became increasingly central to the business of governance and because Washington's share of public finance expanded, the Federal budget evolved into the closest approximation of a policy master plan that existed in the United States. The perennial disputes that flared between the president and Congress over spending and taxing was a sign that budget debates were also about making substantive policy choices.

Monetary policy concerns the creation of funds available in the economy (the money supply) and the rates of interest charged to borrow them. Public management of this realm rested largely with the Federal Reserve Board, a body that functioned as an independent regulatory commission for banks. The president appointed board members, but neither the executive nor Congress directly controlled the Fed's policy. If board members felt that inflation ran too high, they could raise short-term interest rates in an endeavor to cool off the pace of commercial activity. Conversely, the Fed could (but was not required to) counter rising unemployment by lowering interest rates and expanding the money supply in an attempt to stimulate new business investment. Monetary and fiscal policy appealed to lawmakers' political instincts because it held out the promise of promoting economic growth and full employment with minimal interference with private enterprise. Politicians, in other words, could claim credit both for creating prosperity and for respecting the fundamentals of capitalism.

World War II had demonstrated the clout of fiscal policy. Government spending put the nation back to work, and Federal taxation restrained inflation. Besides giving credence to Keynesian theory about the utility of government compensatory spending, Federal management of the wartime economy left another legacy for policy makers: piles of data. As part of its mobilization effort Washington expanded its compilation of statistical indicators of national income.[9] This development was important because numbers were the raw material with which modern economists worked. Better data not only contributed to improvements in economic theory but also signaled the rising influence of economists on government. Increasingly they became part of government. By 1946 people trained as economists were mainstays in various Federal agencies, such as the Treasury, the Department of Commerce, the Bureau of the Budget, the Federal Reserve Board, and various regulatory agencies. The Joint Economic Committee, which Congress created in 1946 as a counterweight to the president's economists, hired them too. Establishment of the Congressional Budget Office (1974) increased the legislature's pool of experts. Constitutional lawyers once were the intellectual gurus of the U.S. government. Economists took over this position in several areas of the claimant polity. The new experts did not offer counsel about the legality of using power, for this question lost most of its relevance. Rather, they provided practical advice on how to solve economic problems.

The new counselors developed two pivotal ideas about fiscal policy and prosperity between 1945 and 1960. One was the concept of a full-employment economy. This notion provided a model with which to judge actual conditions, expressed in objective terms such as GNP (now GDP). The smaller the gap between the theoretically possible GDP, or the economy at full employment, and its actual level of activity, the better the economy was performing. The job of economic policy makers was to close the gap. The second intellectual breakthrough elevated taxation to a status equal to expenditures in its ability to draw current conditions closer to the optimum level. According to this reasoning, demand could be stimulated and thus output and employment increased by either increasing expenditures or reducing taxes.[10] The latter approach might incur a budget deficit in the short run but supposedly would generate greater revenue in the long run as the economy expanded. The critical parameter in this scenario was that rates had to be high enough so a tax cut would produce the desired effect. World War II gave the nation such a levy and the postwar polity preserved them through the 1970s (see chapter 8).

As experts refined these ideas during the 1950s, politicians viewed inflation, not unemployment, as the nation's most pressing economic problem. Tax reduction threatened to create unbalanced budgets, which would fuel inflation. Besides, cutting revenues without an equal reduction in expenditures in the absence of war or depression violated the ideological axioms of most policy makers, including President Dwight Eisenhower (1953–1961). President John F. Kennedy (1961–1963) brought a less conventional outlook on this issue to the White House. More impressed with the possibilities of the new economics than Eisenhower officials had been, Kennedy's Council of Economic Advisers preached the wonders of a tax cut. First they educated the president about the new public economics, arguing that the existing tax structure exerted a fiscal drag on the economy. Then they recommended that he act on this theory in order to prevent a "Kennedy recession." No president, especially in the years after the adoption of the Employment Act, wanted to be blamed for rising unemployment. JFK took the economists' advice and presented a revenue reduction plan to Congress. "The largest single barrier to full employment . . . and to a higher rate of economic growth," Kennedy announced, "is the unrealistically heavy drag of Federal income taxes on private purchasing power, initiative and incentive."[11]

Congress remained skeptical. Unemployment in 1963 was nowhere near Depression levels and had actually declined since 1961. The Kennedy budgets were already unbalanced, and establishment politicians abhorred deficits. Success depended on winning over influential lawmakers. The Kennedy administration targeted Wilbur Mills as their point man for this job. As chairman of the Ways and Means Committee in the House of Representatives, this influential Democrat and fiscal conservative from Arkansas presided over Congress's chief tax-writing body. Mills was converted to a tax-cut believer and then led the legislation through the House, presenting it as an alternative to "more and more" spending. Mills told his colleagues that tax reduction avoided further drift toward "big central Government" and relied on the private sector to spearhead economic expansion.[12]

An assassin's bullet cut down the president before the bill reached the Senate. Lyndon Johnson inherited the Oval Office (1963–1969) and leadership of the plan to reduce revenue. Tax reduction, Johnson predicted, would send $11 billion "coursing through the arteries of the private economy," causing the GNP to rise, profits to mount, and unemployment to fall, while achieving a balanced budget in the process.[13] It sounded almost too good, like having your cake and eating it too. How many senators understood or believed the theory behind this fiscal magic is unknown. But in 1964 most of them voted for it.

Tax cuts had a seductive appeal because they stimulated the economy and saved people money at the same time. Increased expenditures can accomplish the same macroeconomic objective, but they have the political liability of registering on the cost side of the budget. Before the 1930s America's ideology of fiscal parsimony dominated national budget making and thus limited the use of spending as a macroeconomic lever. Federal expenditures accounted for 3.7 percent of the GNP in 1929 (see table 5.1). This was 50 percent greater than in 1902 but still very small by later standards. The Depression and wartime economic policy dealt a one-two knockout punch to the traditional Federal budget. National spending per capita was five times higher (in constant dollars) in 1948 than in 1929. Real outlays tripled again during the next third of a

Table 5.1. U.S. Government Expenditures, 1929–1990

	1929	1940	1948	1960	1980	1990
Per capita (1958 $)						
Total	62	173	304	521	1,020	1,271
Defense	11	27	137	262	246	304
Social Welfare	10	59	81	133	500	623
Percent of GNP						
Total	3.7	10.1	13.8	19.3	23.4	22.7
Defense	.7	1.6	6.2	9.7	5.7	5.4
Social Welfare	.6	3.4	3.7	4.9	11.5	11.1

Sources: U.S. Bureau of the Census, *Historical Statistics on Governmental Finances and Employment* (Washington, D.C., 1985), vol. 6 of 1982 Census of Governments, table 11; updated with U.S. Bureau of the Census, *Statistical Abstract of the United States: 1993* (Washington, D.C., 1993), various tables; and author calculations based on U.S. Bureau of the Census, *Historical Statistics of the United States* (Washington, D.C., 1975), series F1, F4.

century. By 1980 Federal expenditures accounted for nearly one-quarter of the GNP, a proportion six times greater than in 1929. But the pain of this larger tax bite on personal pocketbooks was eased by an economy that grew more affluent during these five decades.

Americans who came of age in the postwar era inherited a fiscal regime vastly different from the one their parents and grandparents knew. It is true that the rate of spending increases slowed down after 1948 when compared with the New Deal and wartime periods. But these postwar increments were added to budgets that had ballooned during times of economic and international emergencies. Policy makers did not undo these earlier crisis budgets. Instead they built on them incrementally. Defense and social welfare, the two main lines of modern Federal spending, illustrate postwar fiscal tendencies. World War II was a permanent watershed in the cost of U.S. national security. The tensions of the Cold War (late 1940s to the mid-1980s) prompted policy makers to invest much greater sums in military procurement than occurred before Pearl Harbor (see table 5.1). Defense took about one out of every two Federal dollars in 1960. National security spending contracted, both as a percentage of the GNP and in per capita terms, after the Vietnam War in the 1970s.

Ronald Reagan made much of this slippage when he ran for president in 1980. Yet defense cost Americans nine times more in 1980 than it had in 1940, and twenty times more than before the Great Depression.

These military expenditures reflect an extraordinary transformation, yet the growth of social welfare costs surpassed it. National expenditure for income assistance and social services increased modestly after the war until 1960, then rose rapidly. Social welfare expenses quadrupled in the next twenty years, overtook defense spending, and commanded half of Washington's outlays in 1980. Most of these dollars were transfer payments paid directly to individuals through programs such as Social Security, welfare, and veterans' benefits. These plans became nicknamed "entitlements," because the law gave an individual a statutory claim to an assistance payment. By 1980 they consumed roughly 60 percent of Federal expenditures.[14]

Because entitlement programs are viewed as Federal guarantees to the people, they are virtually never terminated and rarely scaled down. Dubbed relatively uncontrollable costs, these expenses represented ongoing, fixed obligations that have a low probability of change in the short run. Federal contracts with civilian producers of goods and services (such as manufacturers of defense equipment), assistance payments to farmers, and interest on the national debt also are debited in the uncontrollable area of the budget. They accounted for three-quarters of U.S. outlays in 1980. These expenditures do not include the salaries of the five million civilian and military personnel on the Federal payroll. Federal credit programs comprised another uncontrollable fiscal commitment. The largest volume of these activities involved Federal guarantees of privately issued loans (such as home mortgages) and government-sponsored corporations that bought and sold Federal bonds. Federal insurance schemes expanded rapidly during the 1970s. Critics charged that these authorizations constituted back-door or hidden financing because these obligations were not recorded in the Federal budget.[15]

The expanded size and complexity of Federal fiscal activities elevated the importance of the Bureau of the Budget. The agency had a staff of forty-five when it was placed in the president's office in 1939 and six hundred people by the end of the war. The bureau's size stayed constant over the next few decades, but its mission expanded. By the time of its reorganization into the Office of Management and Budget (OMB) in 1970 the agency had become a policy as well as a fiscal nerve center of the Federal establishment. Its staff participated in the formulation of new policy for the administration and assessed the operation of existing programs. But the composition of the annual budget remained the centerpiece of its work. Presidents turned increasingly to OMB directors for advice on how to allocate available resources to a growing array of programs.[16]

Compared with the 1930s, Federal macroeconomic policy was a relative success through the early 1970s. Real GNP nearly doubled between 1945 and 1980, and unemployment remained far below Depression levels. But fiscal and monetary policy did not eliminate all joblessness or provide every worker with an adequate income. Unemployment hovered between 4 and 5 percent in the fifties and sixties and crept up to 6 percent in the seventies. Joblessness among blacks was double the rate among whites. Economically depressed areas, such as the coalfields of Appalachia and the textile mill cities of New England, contained local reservoirs of idleness. This was structural unemployment, caused by declining industries, workers who lacked marketable skills, and social discrimination rather than by general stagnation of the economy. Poverty was partially a consequence of structural flaws in the economy.

Policy makers were surprised to learn in the early 1960s that one-sixth of all families received income below a newly invented measure of poverty.[17] This discovery resurrected a policy question raised a generation earlier: would government guarantee work for everyone who wanted a job? The majority of policy makers answered no. The 1946 Employment Act, in their view, did not assure universal employment. Massive WPA-like jobs programs received little serious consideration, and Republican presidents from Dwight Eisenhower to George Bush derisively denounced them. Even more modest proposals to provide loans to businesses in depressed areas and to grant Federal financial aid to states for training workers failed in the 1950s. Area redevelopment and manpower training programs were begun during the Kennedy administration and expanded in the middle 1960s and later, when they overlapped with the antipoverty and nondiscrimination efforts of the Johnson administration. The numerous, narrowly drawn job training programs that had evolved by 1973 were consolidated into a more flexible block grant approach as part of the Comprehensive Employment and Training Act (CETA). This package targeted aid to localities with numerous minority and unemployed workers. A year later Congress added public-service jobs in government for workers with long-term unemployment. By the late 1970s CETA provided 600,000 short-term positions at a cost of $8 billion a year.[18] Always controversial, the Federal jobs program was terminated in the early 1980s.

CETA's demise still left Washington with a jobs program. It was called "defense." National security policy during the Cold War (1945–1986) and afterward resulted in massive Federal investment in the private economy at home. In 1980 Washington spent $155 billion, or nearly 6 percent of the GNP, on defense and security functions, including benefits for military veterans. Defense expenditures maintained between 2 and 3.5 million individuals in uniform and operated four thousand bases in the United States through the 1980s. National security policy also hired several million civilians who were employed by private businesses under contract to the Department of Defense and other security agencies. These workers, plus uniformed personnel, totaled roughly 9 percent of the labor force in 1970. Between a third and a fifth of all scientists and engineers in the country and up to a tenth of the manufacturing labor force worked directly or indirectly for Uncle Sam during the Cold War era.[19] Measured by the size of this payroll, defense policy in the Cold War era doubled as a huge public employment program.

The scale of these investments in effect made the Pentagon, the nerve-center of defense management, a command post for American business. The fortunes of many corporations hinged on decisions made at the Pentagon, especially for electronics, aircraft, and shipping industries. Ten companies each did more than one billion dollars' worth of business with the Pentagon in 1978. The nature of negotiations over research and production of defense materials forged a close working relationship between Pentagon officials and corporate executives. High-level managers on both sides regularly traded places. It became commonplace for high-ranking military officers to go to work for the contractor with whom they had been conducting public business. Some observers criticized this practice as unethical collusion between the public and private sectors. As he exited the presidency in 1961, Dwight Eisenhower, an old soldier himself, warned Americans about the dangers of the "military-industrial complex." The influence exerted by "a permanent armaments industry of vast proportions," he said, had "the potential for the disastrous rise of misplaced power" which could "endanger our liberties." Ike included the nation's universities, which did defense-related research, in his apprehension that military policy would become "the captive of a scientific-technological elite."[20]

A fundamental change in the U.S. military establishment had provoked Eisenhower's worry. During Grover Cleveland's years in the White House fewer than 40,000 men were in military uniform and expenditures for national security purposes totaled only 1 percent of the GNP. Except for the Spanish-American and First World Wars, important exceptions but still anomalies, subsequent administrations did not exceed this proportion until 1940, when war in Europe had erupted. The nation's penny-pinching approach to national security was a staple of republican thinking, which saw standing armies and large public expenditures as inimical to liberty. America's geographic isolation from Europe reinforced this outlook. In times before intercontinental air travel, technology limited the capacity of adversaries to pose an immediate military threat to the United States. A very different national security outlook existed after World War II, when defense consumed between 6 and 10 percent of the GNP (see table 5.1) and placed extensive authority in national security officials, who projected American power throughout the world.

What caused lawmakers to abandon the republican aversion to a war-ready military after WWII? The most important factor can be summed in a single word: communism. With concerns chiefly centered in the Soviet Union but reinforced by China after 1949, policy makers claimed that U.S. security was threatened by a single-minded, ambitious foe. The danger became elevated in the 1950s when Russia obtained nuclear weapons. As President Eisenhower put the challenge, the danger to American security was imminent and "of indefinite duration." "We face a hostile ideology," he explained, "global in scope, atheistic in character, ruthless in purpose, and insidious in method." To combat this threat to Western civilization, Ike stated that "our arms must be mighty, ready for instant action, so that no potential aggressor may be tempted to risk his own destruction." Presidents from Truman through Reagan all reiterated this policy. Justification for keeping a large, combat-ready military force during peacetime invariably pointed to the Red threat. After the Soviets launched Sputnik, the first space satellite, in 1957, U.S. technological superiority in weaponry became an added requirement for keeping the country safe.

Scholars debate whether the responsibility for the Cold War was as one-sided as American presidents have asserted. Regardless of the causes of this diplomatic confrontation, America's response to it exhibited an instrumentalist mindset. Policy makers justified the expansion of the defense state with explanations that were analogous to reasons for greater spending on domestic affairs—there was an imminent need that demanded public action. The Red Threat thus joined the list of other problems, such as unemployment, muddy roads, and market failures, that government was obliged to fix. Unlike republicans who distrusted the power of government, defense policy makers in the claimant era dwelled on dangers arising from a *lack* of action. As with other eras of policy growth, the rise of America's military might reflects an attitudinal transformation concerning the legitimate uses of civic authority.

Foreign and domestic policy had parallels also in that they both conveyed things of value to certain beneficiaries. In defense the process worked through the procurement of military goods. The way Washington purchased these items helped to sustain a large industry. The top brass in the Pentagon drew up the list of hardware that the military wanted. Congress invariably deferred to the expertise of the generals and admirals, granting most of their requests. The criteria for selecting particular weapon systems and designs were primarily strategic and technological (and sometimes reflected interservice competition), not primarily economic. Only the most modern state-of-the-art weaponry satisfied these objectives. Ronald Reagan's "Star Wars" antimissile defense plan of the 1980s followed a Cold War pattern of enhancing the technological capability of U.S. armaments. With the emphasis on increasingly complex electronics and state-of-the-art performance rather than price, each round of weapons development increased the per-unit cost of an armament system, such as a variety of aircraft or missile.[21] Military procurement policy built in cost escalation.

Private corporations filled the Pentagon's orders. A handful of large firms that served as prime contractors were the giants in this business. They coordinated weapons research and production, while much of the actual manufacturing was done by thousands of smaller subcontractors, who were located in most congressional districts. Despite their modest profit margins, the large prime contractors liked doing business with the government. For one thing, they were allowed to use the results of military research (done at public expense) in their private-sector business. Once a deal was struck with the Pentagon, moreover, Washington kept a steady flow of payments coming to corporate coffers, even when production lagged behind schedule. Washington was a good business partner. It handed out most of these contracts without competitive bidding, because design features and production capabilities outweighed cost as criteria for picking suppliers. The trick to landing a contract was to convince the Pentagon of the technical feasibility of your company's weapon design and give it an unrealistically low price tag. Once production was under way the corporation submitted bills for design changes (sometimes requested by the Pentagon) and other unforeseen costs. The result of this procurement system was repeated cost overruns.[22]

The relationship between the Pentagon and defense contractors did not operate according to free-market conditions. Government was the sole buyer of products built according to official specifications, often by a single supplier. Unlike the downward pressure on prices that technology exerted on products developed for private sale, the continuous technical upgrading of the government's defense purchases pushed their per-unit cost upward. Because of the special circumstances of the defense business, Congress enacted innumerable guidelines that made military contractors one of the most regulated industries in America. An avalanche of paperwork accompanied government orders, which was especially burdensome for smaller contractors. Many quit the business rather than face the frustration of this regulatory gauntlet. But not the prime contractors. They had made friends in key places in Congress and the Pentagon who could bend the rules when necessary. Moreover, the defense giants settled for a tradeoff made possible by claimant economic policy. They accepted government control and narrow profit margins in exchange for assurance of a guaranteed return on investment.

Cars with tailfins and drive-in restaurants, Dr. Spock's *Book of Baby and Child Care,* parent-teacher association meetings, and TV's *I Love Lucy* and *Howdy Doody,* Levittown tract housing, and the birth of Barbie the doll. These flashbacks to the 1950s reflect the start of a new era in the United States. The changes that sprouted in this decade and blossomed during the next twenty years profoundly affected the way Americans lived, worked, shopped, and played. The critical dynamic behind this evolving lifestyle was greater wealth. Real personal income nearly doubled during the postwar era (1946–1980), a gain reflected in the quadrupling of automobiles. The car become a standard fixture of middle-class life, and so, increasingly, did home ownership. Houses cost a lot more than cars, yet some 40 million families were able to make the American dream come true by purchasing a home. Between 1940 and 1980 dwellings owned by their residents rose from 41 to 64 percent of all housing stock. The most desired property was a detached, single-family house, which increasingly was found in the suburbs, where land was cheaper than in the city. By the 1950s a massive exodus from urban neighborhoods was under way as their more affluent residents relocated to the metropolitan locales that surrounded urban hubs. In 1970 more people lived in suburbs than in central cities, many of which actually declined in population.

The shopping mall was the monument to the suburbs and the expanding middle class. Surrounded by parking lots, malls became the marketplaces for auto-dependent suburbanites. A curiosity in 1946, integrated shopping centers had multiplied to 20,000 by 1980, when they did half of the nation's retail business. Many of the sales occurred in franchised outlets (such as Radio Shack), which were evidence of basic changes in retailing practices. But regardless of the kind of store where shoppers made their purchases, buying at the mall became the lifeblood of an economy whose vitality depended upon sustained consumer expenditures.

Something else would have caught the eye of a visitor to the malls of the 1950s and 1960s. They swarmed with small children and teenagers. These youngsters were the baby boomers, the result of an extraordinary upsurge in births between the mid-1940s and the early 1960s. The increase reversed the slide in the birthrate, which had declined for more than a century. Births dropped further during the fifteen-year period that began with the 1930s, a decade of scarcity, and extended to the emergency of World War II. But far more newborns entered the world in the fifteen years between 1950 and 1965.

The postwar surge of fertility sent ripple effects throughout society. Hospital maternity wards were the first to reel under the impact of the rising numbers. Next were the schools, which sprouted like mushrooms, especially in the expanding suburbs. The elementary school population of Arlington, Massachusetts, for example, jumped 50 percent between 1950 and 1969. The town responded by building four schools and enlarging most of the eight existing ones. By the 1970s baby boomers crowded college campuses and swelled the ranks of job seekers and house hunters. And they represented a massive future cost to Social Security. Because they would always outnumber the Depression (1930–1945) and baby bust (1965–1980) generations, baby boomers strained the capacity of public and private institutions throughout their life cycle.

Increased births and postwar suburbanization both rode the crest of rising affluence. Good times were conducive to having kids and buying a house. But decisions to move to the suburbs were not just the result of marketplace conditions. Government played a significant role in the redistribution of population. The Federal government laid groundwork for this shift during World War II when it invested billions of dollars in new manufacturing facilities, which were disproportionately located outside the central city. The siting of plants and jobs in suburbs continued during the postwar decades, spurred in part by defense procurement practices, which invested heavily in the electronics and aircraft industries.[23] Washington assisted the training of many of the young men and women who went to work for a defense contractor. The program was nicknamed the GI Bill, which Congress enacted in 1944 to help military veterans readjust to civilian life. Eight million service men and women received Federal financial aid toward their vocational and university education. College enrollment rose sharply as a result. During the 1947–1948 academic year the Veteran's Administration (VA) contributed to the costs of nearly half of the male student body enrolled in higher education. The program also extended loans to veterans to start their own businesses and gave them preferential treatment in Federal hiring.

The GI Bill also helped veterans of the Second World War and Korean War buy houses. Because the cost of real estate was so great relative to their income, most Americans borrowed money to finance their home purchases. This demand for large loans with long payback periods (mortgages) put banks in a pivotal position in the housing market. Lenders could, for instance, deny mortgages to applicants who appeared to be poor credit risks. The GI Bill made it easier for veterans to get a home loan by guaranteeing that the VA would reimburse the lender in the event that the borrower defaulted on the mortgage. The law allowed veterans to buy VA-approved houses with very little down payment. Veterans' mortgage insurance covered a quarter of all new home sales in the 1950s, a decade of booming home construction.[24]

Federal insurance for home loans began in 1934, when Congress created the Federal Housing Authority (FHA) to stimulate recovery in the construction industry. The agency came to have a decisive impact on the way houses were purchased. Before the Depression home buyers took out short-term loans (three to five years) for up to half of the purchase price of a house and paid the balance in cash. Loan payments to the bank were for the interest only, however, which meant that the borrower still owed the principal (the amount borrowed) when the loan period expired. This arrangement contributed heavily to the massive defaults of mortgages and the subsequent loss of homes during the Depression. Many people simply had no savings left to pay off the principal when it came due. And banks refused to refinance many mortgages.

The FHA replaced these nonliquidating mortgages with a plan that retired the principal over a long payback period. The FHA did not lend money to home buyers. Rather, it insured privately issued mortgages against borrower default in a fashion similar to VA housing assistance. But in exchange for this Federal guarantee, the FHA required that its mortgages have low down payments, lengthy payback periods (up to thirty years by 1954), and a ceiling on rates of interest that banks could charge. Borrowers paid a monthly fee to the FHA for this benefit. Although FHA mortgages were designed to aid buyers at the lower end of the income scale, the agency's standards were adopted by private lenders for most home loans.[25] The Housing Act of 1934 helped home buyers in another way. The law established a mechanism that made mortgage funds more plentiful to lenders. Fannie Mae, as this federally chartered institution was nicknamed, bought FHA mortgages from lending institutions and sold them to investors in the secondary mortgage market. Washington created other such mortgage investment organizations in later years. And the government lowered the real cost of home ownership by exempting interest payments on mortgages from Federal income taxes. As mortgage debt rose after the war (from 14 to 42 percent of the GNP), this tax deduction grew increasingly valuable to the middle class.

Because suburban homeowners were dependent on their cars, roads played a vital role in America's housing expansion. People born into the auto age tend to take roads for granted. But the construction of every street and highway represented a distinct policy decision whose costs collectively summed to a hefty total. America invested over a quarter of a trillion dollars in roads in the postwar era. The availability of faster cars and the desire for more spacious homes and yards generated demands for thoroughfares that would allow traffic to flow more swiftly and safely. Transportation planners, who were primarily engineers in state and Federal highway departments during the 1930s, 1940s, and 1950s, invariably recommended more and better roads as the solution to metropolitan transportation problems. Their designs emphasized freeways that led from the central city to urban outskirts, a scheme the planners trumpeted would reduce urban traffic congestion by dispersing people into suburbs. It was an arrangement that favored the middle class and commercial interests, such as road builders and trucking firms. The planners gave far less consideration to improvements in rapid (rail) transit, which would have benefited lower-income residents.[26]

Following experimentation during the 1930s, states in the eastern part of the country began construction of limited-access highways in earnest in the 1940s. The Boston area's Route 128 (now part of I95), sections of which were opened in 1947 and which was completed in 1960, was the first limited-access, multilane circumferential route around and outside of a major U.S. city. Seven major superhighways eventually radiated out from this metropolitan beltway to more distant tiers of suburbs, while a lesser number of arteries fed autos into the downtown area. Although burgeoning traffic sometimes overwhelmed its capacity, Route 128 was a boon to suburbanites, who customarily drove substantial distances to work and shop. The beltway also accommodated the redistribution of businesses in the metropolitan region, as new plants and wholesale outlets sprang up along its route and its outer spokes. The Massachusetts Turnpike, a state-operated toll road that ran from the state's western border eastward to Route 128 (initially, in 1957, before the turnpike was extended into Boston in 1965), similarly encouraged commercial and residential decentralization.

The residents of Arlington felt the effects of the new highways. Although integrated (in theory) into one of the nation's best public transit systems (a bus and rail network), most Arlingtonians drove their cars to work. Many commuted to new high-tech firms that sprouted up along Route 128.[27] This pattern of private commuting helps to explain why the town's voters overwhelmingly rejected a plan in 1977 to extend the rapid-transit subway from Boston and Cambridge into their suburb. Despite their trolley heritage, Arlingtonians stopped the subway dead in its tracks at the town's border with Cambridge.

The popularity of limited-access expressways moved Congress in 1956 to authorize a national network of "free" (nontoll) interstate highways. Because the price of the projects exceeded the fiscal capacity of most states, Congress upped its contribution for road projects from 50 percent to 90 percent for the interstates. Washington's share of funds came from additional levies on gasoline, truck, and bus purchases. Taking a page from the book of the states, which routinely prevented the diversion of gas taxes to nonhighway uses (Massachusetts did so in 1948), the new Federal road taxes were deposited in a trust fund dedicated to the interstate system. Road builders spent $70 billion over the next twenty-five years on the 42,000 miles planned for the road system, whose eventual cost was pegged at $114 billion. Because Washington supplied most of these funds, the Federal fiscal role in transportation and roads expanded. By 1980 the national government paid for most highway construction and spent as much as local government on road work of all types.

Most interstates ran between cities, but an eighth of the mileage (and nearly half of system expenditures) lay within metropolitan areas. Most large cities had at least one circumferential beltway and a network of arterial spokes that linked the downtown with the outlying suburbs, much like the pattern in Boston. These rings of concrete around the city were monuments to postwar transportation policy. Initially the superhighways linked city and suburb, but they became increasingly important as connectors between suburbs. The result of this evolution in Boston and elsewhere in the nation left the central city progressively isolated from the affluent homeowners, as well as the new industry that mushroomed in the suburban hinterland. This relocation of economic power drained enthusiasm for investing in public transportation within the central city. More commonly, plans for freeways bulldozed into the heart of the city, leveling thousands of homes in poorer neighborhoods, until public outcries ended the practice. Playing to a middle-class audiences, road builders tended to overlook the low-income people they uprooted.[28]

"It is harder and harder to live the good life in American cities today," President Lyndon Johnson observed in 1964. He neglected to mention that the good life had migrated to the suburbs, leaving numerous problems behind in the cities. The metropolitan centers had more poor, more renters, fewer homeowners, and lower property values than most of the communities on their fringes. Industries declined in city after city in the Northeast and Midwest. Despite this economic sag, uprooted minorities with meager education and few marketable skills continued to flow into the older urban centers. These changes discouraged private investment in downtown businesses and moderately priced housing. The result was the spread of blight, areas of high unemployment and deteriorating construction, in the urban core.

The distance between the cities and the suburbs in postwar America increasingly was measured by income as much as by geography. This economic disparity was clearly visible to the casual observer, as a drive from the neighborhoods of the decaying urban core to the tidy spaciousness of suburban homes vividly demonstrated. The political consequences of this social geography might have canceled out in a highly centralized polity. But America's political heritage had bestowed considerable power on local government, which meant that the social and economic conditions in a community affected its governance. Cities had higher public costs than suburbs because urban centers served both a large community of low-income residents and a transient workforce of commuters who lived outside the city. But the cities had less wealth to tax than did suburbs. Ironically, affluent suburbanites might pay less property tax per person than the poorer inhabitants of the big city. This was the case for Arlingtonians, who were richer on average than Bostonians but had a smaller property tax bill. Budgetary mismatches such as this help to explain why a fiscal crisis enveloped the nation's cities as postwar suburbanization proceeded.[29]

America's fragmented structure of government influenced the way policy makers responded to these problems. The first priority of rural and suburban residents was to manage affairs within their own community. Their representatives in the state legislature were more interested in assisting the voters and officials in their own districts than in diverting resources to needy residents in the central cities. The boundaries that enclosed each suburb thus doubled as political barriers that isolated suburbanites from local difficulties. This structural impediment to action at the state level was one pretext for the entrance of the Federal government into the fight against urban blight.[30]

Congress had been cognizant of urban decay for years, evidenced by its adoption of a public-housing program for low-income individuals in 1937. The national government did not build homes for the poor; rather, Washington offered loans and subsidies to public-housing agencies created and controlled by local governments. These authorities initiated and sited housing projects, applied for Federal money, and assigned tenants to completed dwellings. The program was always controversial and poorly funded, in part because all forms of welfare provoked spirited resistance. Members of the real estate industry (such as realtors and mortgage bankers) attacked the program. As a result, the one million dwelling units constructed through 1962 housed only 6 percent of the population that lived in poverty.

According to its statutory purpose, public housing had to replace slums. In the postwar city this requirement focused reconstruction efforts on places where blacks and other poor persons tended to reside. Commercial groups had little interest in building homes for the poor, but some did see economic possibilities in redeveloping blighted central business districts. The urban-renewal provision of the 1949 amendments to the Housing Act made it profitable to do so. Based on urban renewal's ostensible goal of replacing slums with low-cost housing, thousands of dwellings and small business structures were razed. Yet little affordable housing rose in its place because of a loophole in the law. Federal housing subsidies were given to locally run redevelopment agencies for the acquisition of property in blighted areas. These agencies then sold the land to private interests at prices below market value as a way of inducing development of the site. Finally, commercial developers frequently built complexes that contained a mixture of moderate and high-priced apartments, office buildings, and public arenas, sometimes to the exclusion of low-cost housing. The combination of vaguely worded statutes and compliant public officials permitted private entrepreneurs and downtown elites to profit handsomely from Federal urban policy.[31]

Combined city and Federal efforts did rebuild the central business districts of many older cities. But a coordinated attack on urban problems failed to materialize. The reason for this shortcoming lay partly in the conflict between scarce resources and competing policy objectives. Federalism interfered too, in that control of urban planning was divided among policy makers at several levels of government. Even after the marked expansion of the Federal role during the 1960s, local officials retained considerable discretion in implementing national programs. Finally, urban policy making was a battleground between groups that sought to place the rebuilding of the nation's cities in the hands of private developers and others who favored publicly managed programs.[32] All of these considerations influenced the revision of urban policy during the administration of President Richard Nixon (1969–1974).

The Housing Act of 1974 included a multipurpose program of financial aid for community development in urban areas. The Community Development Block Grants (CDBG) program folded ten existing special-purpose grants (such as urban renewal) into a package of spending options from which recipients could choose. Officials of local governments could spend funds on thirteen different activities, such as land acquisition, the construction of certain facilities, and eligible services, so long as these investments promoted neighborhood revitalization, housing improvement, or economic development. The community had to explain in its application to Washington how Federal funds would further these objectives. This community development and housing plan had to identify the needs of present and expected low- and moderate-income households. All cities over 50,000 inhabitants and urbanized counties were eligible to participate in the program. Funds were distributed according to a formula that initially emphasized poverty and later (1977) gave greater weight to aged housing.

Forty billion dollars in CDBG funds flowed to over eight hundred local governments by 1988. Arlington, Massachusetts, was among the recipients. A CDBG steering committee, the town manager, and assorted official and community groups offered proposals on how to spend the town's annual million-dollar award. The Board of Selectmen approved a potpourri of requests that included repair of the Greek Orthodox Church (designated a historic landmark under Federal law), construction of a senior citizens' center and a wheelchair ramp to the public library, an alcohol education project, and red brick sidewalks for the central business district. Repairs to the homes of lower-income residents received funding, but town leaders showed greater interest in reviving the small and antiquated retail district in Arlington's center.

Officials scattered Arlington's CDBG funds over a variety of projects, many of dubious connection to the commonly understood meanings of urban policy. Other communities appeared to follow a similar pattern. A statute whose goals were written with deliberate flexibility and whose implementation was shaped by local politics virtually guaranteed that moneys would be distributed widely among many suppliants. As with previous urban programs, community development grants did not target resources on the people and the places that needed them most.[33]

Regulations of business and finance figured prominently in the expansion of civic functions in the transition and claimant eras. Two patterns concerning government oversight of business between 1946 and 1978 stand out. First, laws enacted before WWII were maintained and broadened. Most of these existing (old) regulations applied to a particular industry and dealt with the rudiments of commerce, such as pricing, business practices, and entrepreneurial competition. And second, a substantially different form of economic supervision emerged. These *new* regulations set standards of performance for all organizations, public and private, regarding social criteria that gained prominence in the 1960s and 1970s. Together the new and old regulations brought most aspects of economic life under the scrutiny of government by 1980.

The dominant features of the old regulations was sector-oriented policies whose foundations had been established decades earlier. Public utilities such as electric power and telephone service, for example, operated under the supervision of state and Federal commissions. The states had laid the basic framework of licensing professionals and the trades, the insurance industry, and liquor sales before World War II and refined these policies afterward. Energy constituted the one major addition to a federally regulated sector of the economy. In 1946 Congress created an Atomic Energy Commission, which evolved into the Nuclear Regulatory Commission (NRC) in 1974. The Federal Power Commission gained authority to set the price of natural gas at the point of production as a result of a 1954 court decision. Controls on the price of domestically drilled crude oil were imposed in the 1970s. Some observers charged that the so-called independent regulatory agencies had been captured by the industries they supervised. This perversion of the public interest, critics held, created a regulatory scheme that rewarded private enterprise at the expense of consumers. Swayed by these views, Congress assigned the administration of oil price regulation to presidentially controlled agencies.

A Department of Energy was created (1977) in part to oversee the domestic oil industry and propose remedies for the energy crisis that materialized in the mid-1970s. The Arab embargo of oil imports to the United States in 1973 had been a wakeup call for Americans, who thought of cheap gasoline as a birthright. After 1973 oil prices were set on the world market, where global demand drove up the cost of fossil fuels. In 1973 the United States imported 36 percent of its crude oil; by the 1980s the figure rose above 50 percent. Washington's reaction to the 1973 embargo included the imposition of a fifty-five-mile-per-hour speed limit on federally aided roads, a policy aimed at reducing the consumption of gasoline. But federal officials found no simple solution to the energy crisis over the next several decades, as Americans bought more cars and trucks, drove them further, and consumed more gas.

Free-market assumptions stymied most efforts to develop a national energy policy. The dairy industry, by contrast, welcomed government intervention. Beginning during the New Deal, government oversaw price-setting arrangements between dairy farmers and milk dealers. Twenty-five such marketing orders existed in 1945, covering 58 percent of the drinking milk produced. By 1973 virtually all grade-A milk brought to market arrived under one of sixty different price agreements. Price-fixing was not the only way Washington helped the income of dairymen. In 1949 Congress established their eligibility for subsidized nonrecourse loans and allowed the USDA to purchase manufactured dairy products (like cheese), which helped to prop up prices.[34] Critics charged that this two-tiered system of price support unduly pampered dairy farmers, milked the consumers' pocketbook, and saddled Uncle Sam with an unnecessary bill. In 1982 the U.S. government bought 10 percent of all milk produced at the cost of $2.28 billion and owned $3.4 billion worth of dairy products. Given this civic generosity, it is easy to understand why the dairy industry was a major contributor to congressional election campaigns.[35]

The farm program illustrated how the old regulations assisted regulated industries. Washington extended direct supports to a dozen agricultural commodities in the 1970s and indirectly subsidized others by helping foreign countries, schoolchildren, and the poor buy U.S.-grown foods. Quotas limited the imports of certain commodities (beef, for instance), which raised the income of U.S. cattle producers. The Farmers' Home Administration offered a line of ten major loan programs, and the Federal Crop Insurance Corporation protected farmers from losses caused by weather and pests. These and other USDA operations were administrated by 124,000 employees, 15,000 of whom worked in research and pest control, at a cost of $22 billion in 1983. The irony was that federally funded research and loans helped to make agriculture more productive, which in turn reduced the number of farmers, who dwindled to less than 3 percent of the workforce by 1980. The real beneficiaries of agricultural policy were a comparatively few successful farmers and many businesses that processed and sold their commodities.[36]

The broad reach of modern regulation was symbolized by President Nixon's imposition of controls on wages, salaries, and prices in 1970 and 1971. Ideologically at least, Nixon opposed price controls, but pressure from Congress and the president's fear of the political consequences of failing to restrain inflation prompted his acceptance of wage and price controls, which were soon terminated. But not regulation generally. One expert estimated that between 1965 and 1975 the regulated sectors of the economy increased from 8 to 24 percent of the GNP. Business complained about increased interference from government, but ignored the fact that the United States controlled a smaller segment of the economy than did other industrialized nations.[37]

A new regulatory impulse arose in the 1960s. The old commercial regulation had emphasized relationships between firms (i.e., competition) and their behavior as producers (e.g., pricing and wage practices). The new regulations set standards concerning the obligation of businesses and organizations toward society and toward individuals as consumers and employees. Moreover, the new controls applied to nonprofit as well as profit-making organizations and lodged additional authority in the hands of national regulators. These added powers were conveyed in scores of statutes that mandated a cleaner environment; protection of consumers' health, safety, and pocketbook; more secure working conditions for employees; and equal job opportunities for racial minorities, women, and the elderly. Table 5.2 lists leading developments on these four regulatory arenas. The table does not show analogous state laws, some of which exceeded Federal standards.

The new regulations were partially the product of a cultural fermentation that swept society during the sixties and early seventies. This period of introspection and outspoken criticisms spawned some of most significant mass-

Table 5.2. The New Federal Regulations

Presidential Administration	Environment	Consumers	Workers	Nondiscrimination
Kennedy 1961–1963	Air pollution	Drug pretesting		Equal pay for women
Johnson 1963–1968	Water pollution guidelines Auto emission standards Endangered species protected Solid waste disposal rules	Cigarette warnings Truth in package labeling and lending Auto seatbelts required Meat and poultry inspection rules	Coal mine safety	Job discrimination on basis of race and gender prohibited Job discrimination against 40–65-year-olds prohibited
Nixon 1969–1974	Environmental impact statements required Environmental Protection Agency (EPA) Clean Air Act Water and noise pollution rules	National Highway Traffic Safety Administration Consumer Product Safety Commission	Occupational Safety and Health Administration (OSHA)	Gender discrimination in education prohibited Job and access protection for the handicapped Privacy in school records
Ford 1974–1976	Hazardous waste disposal rules Safe drinking water	Toxic substance safety	Employment Retirement Income Security Act (ERISA)	
Carter 1977–1980	Superfund for waste site cleanup	Fair debt collection		Job discrimination against 65–70-year-olds prohibited

based protest movements in American history. The largest of these popular campaigns—the quest for equal rights by blacks and women, and the opposition to the Vietnam War—were instrumental in challenging social and political conventions. The roots of several movements extended back for several decades, but more recent events fueled their energy. The investigation of Richard Nixon in the Watergate scandal (1973–1974), which culminated in the president's resignation, reinforced beliefs that high officials abused their authority. Criticism of the business community fed upon a steady stream of media revelations about the misuse of the environment and deceptions of consumers. From Ralph Nader's expose (in *Unsafe at Any Speed*, 1966) of auto manufacturers' indifference to vehicle safety to the near-disastrous accident at the Three Mile Island nuclear power plant in 1979, evidence surfaced that sustained charges of corporate irresponsibility. News that the bald eagle was headed for extinction and that the local swimming hole was unsafe seemed to offer proof that leaders took a blasé attitude toward protecting their society.

Another strand of influence behind the new regulations lay in growing affluence. Americans were better off financially in the 1960s than ever before. This economic well-being seemed to change attitudes about civic priorities. Widening affluence meant that middle-class Americans were less preoccupied with keeping their job and making ends meet than prior generations had been. This "good times" economy afforded the luxury of placing greater emphasis on social goals. The growing enrollments in college, itself a by-product of the robust economy, helped to nurture elevated concerns about misdirection in social and economic policy. Changing curriculums stimulated consideration of how greater production and consumption not only grew an economy but also bred harmful social by-products, such as environmental pollution. Sensitivity to the environment peaked during Earth Day in 1970, when college students and others paused to reflect on ecological damages done to the planet. An increasingly active cadre of public-interest lobbying groups carried the message of Earth Day and related consumer concerns to Congress.[38] The upshot of these crosscurrents of thought and activity was widening agreement among citizens and legislators that government should enact policies that would made society fairer, cleaner, and safer.

The demand for a cleaner environment generated a harvest of statutes. Experts had warned about degradations to the air, water, soil, and their natural inhabitants with greater frequency in the 1950s. Except for small grants of aid to state and local governments for air pollution research and sewage treatment

facilities, Congress had given the environment scant attention during the decade. National priorities began to shift in the mid-1960s, in part following the
lead of California, which established clean air standards. In 1965 Congress declared clean water to be a national objective, authorized the Department of
Health, Education, and Welfare to set limits on the emission of automobile ex-
haust fumes, and took preliminary steps in formulating a program for the safe
handling of solid wastes.

From these modest beginnings lawmakers went on to expand Federal environmental protection policy during Nixon's first administration (1969–1972).
The National Environmental Policy Act (1969) required all public and private institutions that received Federal funds (few didn't by the 1970s) to file
environmental impact statements before beginning new construction projects. President Nixon created the Environmental Protection Agency (EPA)
in 1970 by executive order to administer the growing body of environmental
law whose oversight had been scattered among numerous agencies. The Clean
Air Act of 1970 and the Water Pollution Control Act of 1972 substantially expanded the EPA's powers and objectives. These laws boldly called for virtual
elimination of air and sewage pollution in the foreseeable future. Later statutes broadened EPA's mission to include the control of pesticides and radia-
tion, the abatement of noise pollution, the safe disposal of hazardous wastes
(such as used nuclear fuel), and the regulation of toxic substances. By 1980 the
agency's 15,000 employees had written a battery of technical standards for industry and government, assessed fines for violation of environmental laws, and
spent the largest share of the $7.6 billion that Congress appropriated for pollu-
tion control.[39]

Another area of emerging policy concerned safeguarding health and safety
of consumer products. A stimulant to this new policy direction was the U.S. surgeon general's announcement in 1964 that smoking cigarettes was unhealthy.
Washington's chief medical officer reported that years of research, focused
in particular on the connection between cigarettes and lung cancer, demonstrated that smoking harmed health. Congress reacted to this news by requiring that cigarette packages display the warning "Cigarette smoking may be
hazardous to your health." Five years later lawmakers stiffened the language
to "is dangerous" and banned cigarette advertising from radio and TV. In the
1980s the antitobacco campaign persuaded numerous local and state governments to prohibit smoking in public places, such as bars and restaurants, and
to allow private establishments to do likewise.

Unlike its stringent ban on narcotic drugs, however, Washington's approach to cigarettes was ambivalent. Faced with formidable opposition from cigarette manufacturers and from congressman who represented tobacco-producing constituencies, antismoking advocates had to settle for public disclosure rather than more sweeping restrictions.[40] Still, the modest Federal effort seemed to have some effect. The surgeon general reported in 1989 that in the twenty-five years since the first official warning about smoking the use of cigarettes had dropped from 40 to 29 percent of the adult population. Product liability suits against tobacco companies accused of misleading smokers about the hazards of cigarettes contributed to the negative publicity about the nicotine addiction. Yet the fact that cigarette smoking remained the "single most important preventable cause of death" at the end of the 1980s highlighted limitations of anti-smoking policies.[41]

As with the warnings on cigarette packages, Congress relied on public disclosure to address other consumer issues. Lawmakers required manufacturers and food processors to print germane information on the labels of product packages and told lenders to inform borrowers of the true cost of loans. Congress instructed administrators to establish standards of design or performance for certain products and to recall goods that failed these tests. Both the National Highway Traffic Safety Administration (1970), which set safety requirements for autos, and the Consumer Product Safety Commission (1972), which did the same for many smaller items, gained recall powers. Some goods were deemed hazardous and banned outright. The consumer commission, for example, forbade the sale of lead paint for use in homes, the treatment of children's sleepwear with a brand of flame retardant, and the use of urea-formaldehyde for home insulation.

The creation of OSHA, the Occupational Safety and Health Administration (1970), extended the new regulations into the workplace. This agency's mission was to ensure that employers made their place of business free from recognized hazards. Simply identifying the dangers of the workplace was a formidable task, given the many kinds of occupations and the growing number of chemical substances used in manufacturing and agriculture. Business complained about the burden of complying with OSHA's many rules. But with four million firms to inspect, OSHA's bark was worse than its bite. The average business would see an inspector "about as often as we see Halley's Comet."[42] This was not the case with the Employee Retirement Income Security Act (ERISA), the Federal law (1974) that regulated private pension plans. The statute imposed strict and explicit reporting requirements on employers and regulated numerous aspects of pension fund management. Administration was divided between the Department of Labor and the Internal Revenue Service (IRS), Washington's junkyard dog when it came to tough law enforcement. The IRS reviewed the handling of pension finances, including the premiums that employers had to deposit with the Pension Benefit Guaranty Corporation. Created to ensure pension benefits if a company folded, this government corporation paid a quarter of a billion dollars to 88,000 retired workers in 1986.[43]

Goals as ambitious as the ones articulated in the new regulations were bound to encounter practical difficulties. The tendency of Congress to enunciate general performance standards regardless of whether technical solutions were feasible created recurrent administrative dilemmas. Consider the desire to rid the environment, consumer products, and the workplace of cancer-causing agents. Everyone agreed with the objective in theory. But administrators needed to know which substances in fact were carcinogens and what level of contamination was dangerous. The scientific community had no conclusive answer to these questions. Few of the hundreds of chemicals and millions of compound substances had been comprehensively screened for carcinogenic effects. The magnitude of this problem is illustrated by the National Cancer Institute's testing procedures. Its research into a single compound customarily required six hundred animals, took two years, and cost $400,000 or more.[44] And results for animals do not necessarily hold for humans. Faced with scientific uncertainties, policy makers were forced into granting exemptions and delays in implementing health and safety standards.

The new regulations also increased paperwork for businesses and nonprofit organizations. Environmental, consumer, and work protection laws routinely required periodic submission of reports. Some, such as environmental impact statements, could run into volumes. The Commission on Federal Paperwork estimated that the cost of complying with national documentary requirements cost $100 million a year in the middle 1970s.[45] Business alone filled out ten billion sheets of paper in complying with informational rules of the fifty to a hundred Federal regulatory agencies (depending on who was counting). The paperwork burden was proof positive to some critics of the new regulation that Washington now told managers how to run their business.

State and local officials voiced similar complaints, because many of the new regulations applied to them. By one count Washington required subnational governments to observe 1,260 Federal rules. Most were attached as conditions to grants-in-aid. The broadest in coverage were the so-called crosscutting policy standards, such as the prohibition against racial and gender discrimination and environmental protection rules, which applied to every recipient of Federal money. Other rules were tied to a distinct program, such as Federal highway aid. In this latter instance, Washington threatened to reduce the grants if a state failed to enforce the speed limit. Congress used the same financial lever to force state adoption of the twenty-one-year-old legal drinking age.

Most of the new regulations imposed compliance or enforcement requirements on state and local governments. The result placed more power over policy design in Washington and vastly complicated Federal relations. OSHA illustrates a dimension of the complexity introduced by regulatory federalism. The law offered state governments the option of enforcing OSHA rules. Under these terms Washington would pay 50 percent of the costs but the state had to observe twenty administrative conditions. States could also opt to contract inspections out to private consultants, for which Washington would underwrite 90 percent of the cost. By 1980, twenty-one states chose the grant approach to OSHA implementation.[46] As national policy requirements and compliance costs for subnational governments increased, so did complaints of unreasonable Federal intrusiveness. Uncle Sam, critics sniped, was trying to play both governor and mayor in addition to chief of state.

The boundaries of the managed economy widened between 1940 and 1980 as policy makers built upon the regulatory, promotional, and stabilization functions begun in the transition and New Deal eras. To this policy base lawmakers added a permanent defense establishment, enlarged urban and suburban programs, and set new social standards for all organizations. As these commitments grew and as income assistance and public insurance programs increased, so did the size of public budgets, the level of taxation, and the economic roles assigned to fiscal policy. The publicly managed economy of the 1980s was a mammoth yet complexly intricate task that bore little resemblance to the job Grover Cleveland took on.

The quest to correct imbalances in the economy ironically created additional political problems. The numerous objectives of modern economic policy greatly complicated the task of policy implementation. The more goals that politicians put on the agenda of government, the greater the range of issues the public expected the polity to resolve. As rising productivity in the economy conditioned people to anticipate increases in their standard of living, the public also assumed rising expectations about the efficacy of public economics. A new and implied political contract had evolved during the claimant years. The terms of this revised understanding between the rulers and the ruled stated in effect that the public would bestow more power on government in exchange for effective sponsorship of the good economy. This was an instrumental standard by which political performance was judged. The republican era's apprehensions about how much power officials possessed became much less relevant in the modern era, although the old rule retained pertinence for conservatives. Now the principal criterion for judgment was how successfully lawmakers addressed economic needs. The standard for political success is always gauged within a particular political climate. In the postwar era good economic policy meant to a majority of Americans that government would insure a growing economy that maximized individual opportunity, minimized financial risk, and protected health and safety.

Yet the new ideology came with a catch. The multiplication of goals in the claimant polity hindered government's ability to fulfill many of them. The problem lay in conflicts between goals. The desire for clean air and water, for example, could slow economic growth and compromised the nation's quest for cheap energy. Guaranteeing the safety of motor vehicles limited their ability to reduce manufacturing costs. Fighting inflation through higher interest rates forced housing costs up and the number of construction jobs down. Building superhighways fostered suburban development but displaced poor people in the inner city. Washington told Americans not to smoke and simultaneously subsidized tobacco growers and cigarette manufacturers.

The proliferation of incompatible policy aims resulted from the way government had grown. New programs were added in piecemeal, ad hoc fashion, not according to a coordinated master plan or with thorough consideration of their effect on public administration. Modern economic policy was the cumulative product of many separate policy-making episodes, in which powerful special interests and their legislative allies were often the critical dynamic. The result did not add up to policy in the sense of a planned and integrated set of controls that guided the operation of the economy. Even if coordination among goals and administration had been politically feasible, officials lacked the technical capability to fine-tune the economy.[47]

Harmonizing economic objectives encountered another obstacle in the claimant polity. In theory, economic policy served everyone's well-being, and no doubt it did to some extent in practice. But the accomplishments of claimant politicians also benefited special-interest groups. Analogous to the expectations of Americans concerning system-wide goals, such as a stable and growing economy, a claimant mentality developed that expected the distribution of benefits at the micro level, that is, to individuals and groups. Modern economic policy, especially programs crafted to fit the conditions of specific sectors, was justified as beneficial for the public interest. But the greatest popularity of each particular policy decision occurred among the groups that reaped the most economic gain from it. In the claimant polity virtually every special interest demanded special treatment, and most got it.

These rewards were spread broadly among consumers and producers. Agricultural policy offers a classic illustration. The claimant polity produced numerous examples of such favoritism. In the name of national security the Pentagon signed sweetheart contracts with defense suppliers. Urban-renewal projects made profitable business for builders, bankers, and big realtors. Numerous industries have a vested interested in keeping highway funds flowing. College campuses eagerly courted Federal grant dollars to expand research activity, which enhanced the reputation of their institutions. Granting a license to operate a business (like a TV station), a profession (like a medical doctor), or a trade (like a plumber) protected the economic interest of the licensee as well as the public. Government conveys things of value in various ways. Congress counted 140 different subsidy programs in 1960 and created more later. Lawmakers especially liked the tax code and Federal grants as devices to confer benefits (see chapter 8).

Given human nature, the consequence of bestowing policy favors was fairly predictable. Because people are reluctant to give up things of value, they worked to protect their largess. Theorists of the republican polity identified this proclivity long ago. But efforts to prevent class legislation, as republicans had called special-interest actions, waned in the claimant polity. It became expected if not actually acceptable behavior to lobby actively in defense of a public benefit. Everyone did it—liberals, conservatives, independents, business, and nonprofits. This list can go on.

6

The New Income Security

"I SEE ONE-THIRD of a nation ill-housed, ill-clad, ill-nourished." That sobering observation was the keynote of Franklin Roosevelt's second inaugural address in 1937. Despite the improvement in conditions during the first four years of the New Deal, the president admitted that millions of individuals still scratched out an existence "on incomes so meager that the pall of family disaster hangs over them day by day." Most Americans in 1937 did not need a reminder that depression lingered in the land. But announcement of such widespread poverty seemed a contradiction in a country renowned for opportunity and plenty.

Difficult too for some to accept was the president's recommendation that government should "provide enough for those who have too little." Was it Washington's obligation to assist people who were in need? Who would be eligible for public benefits? How much should they receive and for how long? These questions raised some of the most intractable policy issues in modern American history. In the eyes of some if not most people in the 1930s, financial help from government subverted time-honored reliance on individual initiative, private charity, and local responsibility. And if income assistance was accepted as a legitimate exercise of national authority, the thorny problems of who deserved help and what was an adequate level of support remained. The national government had begun to consider these issues several years before Roosevelt reported on poverty. During the next sixty years the United States constructed an array of economic security programs upon this foundation. Yet the polity never achieved a philosophic consensus about income inequality or government's responsibility to ensure a decent standard of living for every individual.

Skeptics thought that Roosevelt had exaggerated the number of poor in the country. Actually the president may have erred on the conservative side. The facts of the matter were unclear because at the time government collected no comprehensive data on the subject. Knowledgeable observers thought that considerable poverty and near-poverty existed. The "old poor," as social workers termed pre-Depression poverty, referred to people who suffered financial misfortune due to family disruption, physical inabilities, ethnic prejudices, and weak spots in the economy. The so-called unemployables among this group were the elderly, the chronically ill or lame, and children of widowed or deserted mothers. Poverty was also a product of economic transitions, wherein traditional trades became outmoded or certain localities stagnated. This structural unemployment received considerable attention during the early 1960s when policy makers rediscovered low incomes and high joblessness in the Appalachian Mountains and urban ghettos. Ethnic background could cause persistent poverty too; the plight of black sharecroppers and day laborers in the South epitomized the connection between race and low income.[1]

The Great Depression added a class of "new poor" to the groups that had been habitually in need. But unlike the old poor, whom society tended to overlook or ignore, the millions of unemployed in the early 1930s were very visible. These newcomers to hard times were mainly males and family breadwinners, accustomed to regular paying jobs as industrial and service workers, professionals, and proprietors, and to the community respect that went with stable employment. The unparalleled magnitude and duration of unemployment during the Depression cast poverty into new and shocking prominence. Farmers too suffered disastrous income declines, but their plight was less visible than masses of jobless workers milling outside factory gates. Because the farm was home as well as workplace for farmers, rural poverty was less visible across America's agricultural landscape. The least fortunate country folk were forced off their land and onto the highways in search of a new start, often in another region.

Whether new or old, the poor had received little help from the national or state government before the 1930s. Social thinking common during the nation's preindustrial period held that the impoverished—adult males in particular—were victims of their own negligence and that government assistance would undermine the work ethic. The ideology of the republican polity reinforced these axioms and helped to explain the absence of measures to counter poverty and unemployment. With sporadic local exceptions prior to the 1930s, accelerated public works had not been used as a remedy for joblessness during declines in the business cycle. Help for the indigent was offered through county poorhouses and local almsgiving. In the 1910s state government began to allow (although not necessarily require) localities to institute widow's aid for the children of destitute mothers. Some states authorized similar options for old-age pensions in the next decade. But implementation of these laws was limited and the amount of this support on the eve of the Great Depression was meager.[2]

Federal assistance was similarly undeveloped, although Washington did extend support to two groups, military veterans and Indians on reservations. Prodded by the competitive bidding of political parties during the transition era, pensions for Civil War veterans evolved into a widespread program that provided stipends to a third of the elderly men in the north in 1910.[3] Congress helped veterans of later wars too, including a bonus voted for the doughboys of World War I. In 1920 national lawmakers established a retirement plan for Federal employees, financed entirely by deductions from their salary. The motivation for the program emerged as much from a desire to improve administrative efficiency (by retiring superannuated workers) as a desire to provide a comfortable retirement.[4] Notwithstanding these exceptions, Washington lagged considerably behind Europe's economic security programs and thus did not have programs in place to combat the personal hardships of the 1930s.[5]

The magnitude of impoverishment brought on by the Depression overwhelmed the resources of private charities. Local government provided much larger amounts of assistance through unprecedented relief spending, but the cities and counties were caught in their own financial bind. Their revenues fell as joblessness rose and incomes declined. Unemployed workers and destitute farmers could not pay their property taxes, from which local government derived most of its funds. City and county officials lacked independent authority to impose alternate taxes, and loans became unattainable as bankers took a dim view of extending credit to municipalities on the verge of bankruptcy or in it. Local officials needed help, so they turned to state government.

Perhaps no development gave more impetus to the drift of power to Washington than the perception that state lawmakers turned their backs on the needy during the Depression. Actually the states greatly increased spending on welfare between 1930 and 1933. By the standards of New Deal assistance, however, the amounts were minuscule. Yet the contrast between the states and Washington reaffirmed stereotypes about the conservatism of state governments, whose reputation for parsimoniousness was partially deserved. Many state officeholders shared President Hoover's disdain for the dole, as cash assistance was derisively nicknamed. Moreover, efforts to enact state relief legislation were frequently stymied by impasses between Democrats and Republicans or by disputes between localities over how to raise and allocate the funds. Only a handful of states voted any assistance for individuals before Franklin Roosevelt entered the White House. Many Americans expected no better from governments long reputed to be corrupt and inept.[6]

Such assessments oversimplified a complex political problem. State lawmakers were enmeshed in a set of restrictions inherited from the old political order. The most formidable of these constraints were embedded in state constitutions, which limited ways of raising and spending public funds. Amending these constitutions was close to impossible in some states, and everywhere the process took time. Moreover, judges sometimes interpreted these documents with strict literalness, which placed innovative statutes at risk of court rejection. Even the biennial schedule of legislative meetings, another legacy of the republican polity, hampered the ability of state governments to address problems of the Depression. Economic realities, in short, outpaced the traditional casualness of state policy making.

Yet deteriorating conditions put tremendous pressure on governors and mayors to do something. Suppressing their ideological reservations, many state and local officials called on Washington for help. The first response came in 1932 in the form of loans to the states for relief (channeled through the Reconstruction Finance Corporation), but administrative red tape prevented most of these dollars from reaching their destination during Hoover's term in office. New Dealers brushed aside these bureaucratic snags in the spring of 1933 and made much larger amounts of money available for immediate emergency relief around the nation. Federal officials then distributed these doles themselves in instances where state politicians proved unable or unwilling to do the job. Several crash Federal employment programs temporarily put millions of the jobless to work in 1933 and 1934. Relief allotments and wages on public jobs were modest and subject to meddlesome rules. Even at its peak, Federal job programs never hired more than a third of the idle workforce. Still, for the first time Washington had lent a helping hand in a significant way to individuals who were unemployed.

Franklin Roosevelt was never happy with the dole, which he saw as "a subtle destroyer of the human spirit." Nor was the president content to run up continuous budget deficits. These premises prompted him to advocate a new approach to income-assistance policy that would allow the Federal government to "quit this business of relief." The widening popularity of several income security plans that circulated in the nation in 1934–1935 and the approach of national elections in 1936 appeared connected to the timing of FDR's proposal for reform. These inducements, lingering unemployment, and the problem of pre-Depression poverty, along with pressure from the White House, moved the Congress in 1935 to pass the Social Security Act and to appropriate funds for a massive Federal employment program.

The jobs program was run by the Works Progress Administration (WPA), which Roosevelt created by executive order. Its objective was to provide temporary work for jobless individuals who were fit for work. Over its eight-year history WPA put 8.5 million individuals to work on more than a million separate projects. State and local government supervised most of the work, but Washington paid most of the bills. The many public buildings, miles of roads and sidewalks, recreational and sanitary facilities, artistic and literary creations, and other community endeavors sponsored by this intergovernmental collaboration left a tangible record of WPA's extraordinary scope and achievement. Less visible but equally influential was WPA's effect on public opinion regarding the Federal role. Critics called WPA projects boondoggles, but public employment was a godsend to millions of men and women who could not find jobs in the private sector. This appreciation of Federal assistance probably disposed many people to support permanent income-assistance policy. Public-sector employment had always been seen as a short-term measure. The long-term solution to income deficiency, New Dealers reasoned, lay in economic recovery and the Social Security Act.

The Social Security Act (1935) addressed both concerns within three different income-assistance plans. The old-age benefit program, which Americans now call Social Security, was the most innovative feature of the 1935 law. It provided financial assistance to retired workers in commerce and industry who qualified for benefits at age sixty-five by having paid a "tax" on their income for a designated period of their employment. Employers paid an "excise" of equal amount per worker. A second form of assistance aided three distinct categories of indigent (the "old poor"): the aged, the blind, and dependent children, whose eligibility for assistance depended on the demonstration of financial need. Welfare, as these programs came to be known, was administered by the states (sometimes aided by local government), which established the standards of eligibility and the level of benefits. The national government reimbursed states for a portion of these costs, contingent upon each state's compliance with certain Federal standards. Unemployment compensation, the third leg of the 1935 economic security package, taxed employers to create a fund from which to pay benefits to full-time workers who had been laid off from their jobs. Each state ran its own program under Federal guidelines.

The Social Security Act combined traditional governmental practices with policy compromises dictated by the politics of 1935. The scheme that emerged from Congress was partly national and partly local, partly financed with new special-purpose taxes and partly dependent on revenue arrangements already in place. Policy makers had envisioned some coordination between the components of the package, such as the eventual reduction of welfare pensions to the needy aged as workers qualified for retirement benefits. But no comprehensive logic bound the pieces of the security network together into a neatly integrated system. Holes in coverage existed, leaving certain classes of individuals, such as domestic and farm workers and dependent spouses (usually wives), excluded from assistance. The amount of welfare stipends varied according to the decisions of state officials and Federal aid formulas. Social Security pensions not only sought to ensure income security in old age but also to reduce unemployment by requiring mandatory retirement.[7] These inconsistencies reflect the circumstances of the Social Security Act's birth. Old and new ideas were rushed together in response to the political and economic pressures of the mid-1930s. Fundamental as it was to the formation of the welfare state, the passage of the 1935 act represents only the initial design of the program and not the finished form of U.S. income-assistance policy.

On January 30, 1940, Ida Fuller of Ludlow, Vermont, received $22.54 in the first old-age benefit check issued by the Social Security Administration. She had paid $22 in retirement taxes since 1937 during her employment as a legal secretary, and at age sixty-six she claimed her stipend. A hardy New Englander who eventually reached her one-hundredth birthday, Fuller collected $20,940 from Social Security during the thirty-four years of her retirement.

Fuller's experience highlights the ironies in America's most popular and most expensive public program. Fuller was a female recipient in a plan conceived in terms of a male-dominated workforce. Contrary to the popular perception that Social Security assistance supported family men who had worked at urban factory jobs, Fuller was an unmarried woman who had held a "pink-collar" position in a small town. She lived three times longer in retirement than the actuarial prediction of thirteen years of additional life for a white female who had reached age sixty-five. Whereas Fuller was one of a handful of elderly who received Social Security in 1940, roughly nine of every ten Americans over age sixty-five did so by the time of her death in 1975.

Social Security grew dramatically between the date of Ida Fuller's first check and 1980. In this year roughly one out of six Americans (over thirty-five million) received assistance from Social Security, compared with one in forty-three (about 3.5 million) in 1950 (see table 6.1). Social Security spending increased twenty-seven times (in per-capita constant dollars) during those three decades, accounting for 5.6 percent of the GNP in 1980, twenty times more than in 1950. In 1989 the system grew to 7.4 percent of the GNP. One-quarter of the Federal budget was devoted to funding the program's fiscal commitments when Ronald Reagan won the presidency in 1980; its share of national domestic spending (excluding defense) was substantially greater. Twenty years later 37 million people received Social Security checks (see table 11.3 in chapter 11).

The scale of this transformation exceeded the expectations of most early planners, who clearly forecast only one of the three primary factors that fueled Social Security's growth. The original policy makers realized that the number of recipients would increase annually for several decades as eligible workers reached retirement age. The retirees who joined Ida Fuller as Social Security's original beneficiaries in 1940 had been born in 1875. The largest cohort of males known to the drafters of the security plan had been born in years surrounding 1920 and would not reach benefit eligibility until the 1980s. Calculations for this actuarial peak rested on the demographic record known to planners in the early 1930s, when white males at age sixty-five lived on average into their middle seventies. By 1980, however, retiring white men had gained nearly six years of expected life, extending (actuarial) survival into their early eighties. This lengthening of life increased the number of Social Security beneficiaries, which in turn placed greater fiscal pressure on the system and increased the system's fiscal obligations.[8]

Increased longevity among women had an even greater impact on the program, because the life span of women lengthened more than men's and be-

Table 6.1. Social Security, 1950–1990

	1950	1960	1970	1980	1990
Beneficiaries (millions)					
Retired workers	1.8	8.1	13.3	19.6	24.8
All	3.5	14.8	26.2	35.6	39.8
Total expenditures (annual in billions)					
Retired worker benefits	.6	7.0	18.4	70.4	157
Medicare	—	—	7.6	35.0	107
Total OASDHI	1.0	11.2	39.0	152.1	419
Average annual benefit per retired worker (1980 dollars)	1,632	2,196	2,712	4,092	4,668
Average annual FICA tax on employees (1980 dollars)	84	213	413	637	763

Sources: Social Security Administration, *Social Security Bulletin, 1990–91: Annual Statistical Supplement, 1991* (Washington, D.C.: GPO, 1991), 108, 134; U.S. Bureau of the Census, *Statistical Abstract of the United States 1993* (Washington, D.C.: GPO, 1993), 369, and earlier years, various tables.

cause of changes in women's roles. Labor shortages during World War II and the breakdown of gender barriers in employment after the 1960s drew millions of women into the workforce. The flow of married women into the paid labor market in particular symbolized the changing mores. By 1980 the steady feminization of the labor force meant that jobs in commerce and industry by 1980 were no longer a male preserve. The transformation of employment, plus women's lengthening life spans, had a major impact on the gender composition of Social Security beneficiaries. Eventually Social Security counted more women than men among its recipients. The effect of this shift on Social Security's fiscal obligations was accentuated by the extension of benefits to spouses (1939) regardless of their work history.

Amendments to the Social Security Act constitute the third dynamic in the program's growth. Social Security has two legislative histories: first, the adoption of the initial act in 1935 and second, legislative revisions in later years. The 1935 law consumed only four pages; forty years later the Social Security law had two hundred pages. Only a few of these changes, such as assistance for workers forced into retirement by a medical condition (disability) in 1956 and health insurance for the elderly (Medicare) in 1965, were major additions. Viewed individually, most legislative changes represented minor incremental benefit increases, yet the cumulative effect of numerous add-ons compounded over the years into a wholesale expansion of the program.[9]

Revision of the 1935 act began before the first retirement check was mailed. The original law scheduled benefits to begin in 1942. Amendments enacted in 1939 advanced the starting date to 1940 and authorized payments for dependents (spouse, minor children, and widowed mother) of retired workers and for survivors of a covered worker who died. The 1939 amendments changed the name of the program from Old Age Benefit (OA) to Old Age, Survivors, and Dependent Insurance (OASI), which reflected the new categories of coverage, and severed the direct link between a worker's taxes and benefits. The addition of disability and Medicare later lengthened Social Security's acronym to OASDHI. Subsequent legislation widened coverage (by assisting dependent grandchildren and parents, for example) and lowered the age of eligibility. Retirement benefits at age sixty-two were approved for women in 1956 and for men in 1961. The 1935 act had covered only workers in commerce and industry, or about 60 percent of the labor force. The 1939 amendments began the process of folding other occupations into the system. Coverage was extended to farm workers, most state and local government employees, domestic employees, self-employed professionals, military personnel on active duty, and others. By the mid-1980s only Federal workers hired before 1983 and some state and local governmental employees remained outside the program.

Besides widening eligibility, Congress also increased Social Security benefit amounts, doing so on eight occasions between 1950 and 1972. In the latter year Congress adopted a plan that pegged benefit increases to the rise in the cost of living. (These COLAS—cost-of-living allowances—began in 1975.) Lawmakers also revised the income replacement level, which set the relationship between prior earnings and benefit amounts; these actions usually increased the value of retirement checks. The increases in benefit payments were partially financed by higher taxes on workers' incomes; Congress raised these taxes on numerous occasions in the postwar decades. The 1935 act had levied a 1 percent tax on the first $3,000 of a worker's income, which produced a maximum tax of $30 a year for an individual. By 1980 the rate had been increased to 6.13 percent, with income subjected to the tax raised to $25,900, which rendered a maximum annual tax of $1,588. Fourteen years later the maximum tax (exclusive of the levy for Medicare on high incomes) had grown to $4,635. (For more on Social Security see chapter 8.)

Under Social Security's initial design the number of beneficiaries would increase as successive cohorts of workers reached benefit age, until an equilibrium between new retirements and deaths was reached. The lengthening of life spans and the movement of women into the workforce introduced an unforeseen influence on Social Security's growth. The third growth factor— legislative modifications of the program—represent the most controllable element in the program's expansion. Why did policy makers choose to enhance the program? Part of the explanation lies in the country's robust economic growth in the three decades after World War II. This extraordinary expansion of affluence created a climate conducive to liberalizing the modest income-assistance plan contained in the 1935 act. At its inception the old-age benefit was seen as a supplementary, not the principal, source of retirement income. But Congress never firmly resolved the issue of how much of a worker's income should be replaced via Social Security.[10] This ambiguity, coupled with optimistic economic forecasts, generated drivers of program expansion. Social Security grew because a legitimate case could be made that the income of older Americans remained inadequate, and that the money to increase pensions seemed available.

Compassion and affordability appeared to have been contributing factors in Social Security's expansion, but they were not sufficient in themselves. Policy makers made a series of discrete choices concerning the composition of America's income security plan. Three considerations played critical roles in these decisions: the basic design of the program's financial mechanism, the aspirations of the system's administrators, and political dynamics in Congress.

Workers qualify for Social Security retirement benefits by earning credits, which accumulate through deductions from their wages and salaries. These payroll taxes (the FICA—Federal Insurance Contributions Act—on pay stubs) are placed in trust accounts, which can be spent only for OASDHI purposes. Congress may not tap these moneys for other programs (although the U.S. Treasury has borrowed from the trust fund), nor does Social Security have to compete with other programs for appropriations. Pension benefits are "entitlements," earned by workers paying into the system. The special-purpose FICA tax is a critical element in the program's design. Unlike the disposition of most taxes, citizens know how FICA dollars are spent—they go entirely for

Social Security functions. This link between an earmarked tax and a guaranteed stipend goes far to explain Social Security's popularity. President Roosevelt sensed the potency of this idea when he insisted that the system operate according to insurance principles, whereby payroll taxes would be dedicated exclusively to benefits.[11]

The financial windfall enjoyed by retirees during the program's formative decades also helped to build a supportive constituency behind the program. Early beneficiaries contributed less proportionately to their pensions than did later recipients. Robert Ball, a commissioner of Social Security, estimated that beneficiaries and their employers (who match their workers' contributions) had paid about 10 percent of the value of the average entitlement in 1967; twenty years later retirees recovered their own financial contributions in two and a half years.[12] This high return-to-contribution ratio resulted in part from a decision early in the program's history to pay benefits before a sizable trust fund had accumulated. Putting Social Security on a pay-as-you-go basis, wherein dollars collected from current employees were rerouted as checks to beneficiaries, proved immensely popular during Social Security's early decades when FICA taxes were minimal.

Few people paid much attention to the system's funding arrangement until the 1970s, when Social Security's bill grew more visible. In 1965 the average worker paid $113 a year in FICA taxes, while the average annual stipend was $1,008. The benefit was higher if additional dependents existed. Social Security was a bargain in its first twenty-five years, and that helped to promote a claimant outlook wherein people saw the program principally in terms of its benefits rather than its costs.

Social Security administrators repeatedly assured Congress that they could cover the costs because the program was "actuarially" sound. It was virtually impossible for most observers to verify these reassuring assessments. The program's fiscal mechanism was exceedingly complex, beyond most people's ability to verify the assumptions on which forecasts of the program's prospects rested. Social Security is a plan for the future as well as the present. Conversing knowledgeably about the relationship between current and future tax rates, projected economic growth, rates of survival, and various income replacement models requires highly specialized knowledge. Moreover, long-range demographic, social, and economic conditions can be estimated, but they cannot be gauged precisely. Despite the confidence that Social Security administrators exhibited in their projections, the system's actuarial soundness turned out to be based on government's ability to collect FICA taxes to pay for Social Security's rising costs.[13]

The complexity of the system discouraged public dialogue about its inner mechanisms and put the program's administrators, who had the most expertise about it, in an advantaged position. Publicly these executives portrayed themselves as impartial superintendents of the nation's retirement plan. In reality, Social Security administrators were committed to an ambitious agenda that began with ensuring the system's permanence. Building income security from a secured base was, as several informed observers put it, their mission. As Arthur Altmeyer, a designer of the system and one of its early commissioners, expressed the aspiration: "Social Security will always be a goal, never a finished thing." The leaders of the Social Security Administration pursued these goals patiently but persistently, settling for small gains. They understood the political utility of recommending incremental additions to the system that could be justified as minor technical adjustments. Faced with conservatives' criticism of accumulating a reserve fund, program executives dropped their advocacy of building a surplus from which to pay future scheduled benefits. Although they saw the creation of a reserve fund as the fiscally prudent course, the administrators placed greater priority on political goals, namely, winning public and congressional loyalty to the program.[14]

A key strategy for building this popularity was depicting Social Security as the antithesis of welfare, a dirty word to many in American society. The administrators likened old-age pensions to insurance whereby employees prepared for their own retirement by paying premiums that earned benefits redeemable in the future, similar to a private annuity plan. The program promoted this notion with slogans such as "you get what you pay for." The fallacious belief that Social Security held an individual's money in a personalized account probably was the dominant conception that most Americans had about the system.

Cultivating public approval of the program proved useful in deflecting challenges to the administrators' agenda. Social Security managers labeled proposals that originated from outside their network as cutbacks, a term guaranteed to send shock waves through the elderly community. The administrators pointed to their unique expertise as proof that rival plans lacked technical feasibility. They reinforced their position by loading Social Security advisory commissions with individuals who shared the bureaucrats' agenda. Program executives frequently turned to the AFL-CIO, the nation's biggest labor union, which had high interest in the system, to carry the administrators' message to Congress and the nation.

Congress played a critical role in Social Security's growth. Lawmakers altered the program in some fashion in every congressional session after 1935. The allure of building further financial security for the family, and bureaucratic assurances that additional benefits rested on a sound fiscal basis, proved compelling to politicians anxious to please their constituents and win reelection. Congress customarily deferred to the judgment of the Ways and Means Committee of the House of Representatives, which had jurisdiction over Social Security financing. A taxation rather than an appropriation committee, Ways and Means had a reputation for fiscal caution. The program administrators understood this fiscal conservatism, which they witnessed repeatedly in public and private meetings with committee members. They cultivated a special relationship with Wilbur Mills, a member of Ways and Means for thirty-four years (1942–1976) and its chair for sixteen years (1958–1974). His hard work, sharp mind, and regular contacts with the administrators earned Mills congressional recognition as the legislature's expert on Social Security. The Arkansas congressman not only understood most technical intricacies of the program but also pursued a political strategy designed to build a consensus among his colleagues on Ways and Means, so that amendments to Social Security could be presented to the full House as committee bills.[15]

Social Security proposals were considered by the full House under a closed rule that prohibited amendments by members on the floor. In effect, accommodations reached between the leaders of the Ways and Means Committee and Social Security's executives were presented to the House on a take-it-or-leave-it basis. Representatives generally took it. Senators usually seconded decisions reached in the House. Lawmakers apparently saw this legislation as a no-lose proposition, because Ways and Means bills offered expanded benefits without incurring exorbitant new costs. A key to this persuasion during the 1950s and 1960s was optimism that new benefits could be financed by reliance on a "level earnings" assumption. This projection of revenue flows into the system was a deliberately conservative estimate, because it assumed that no growth in real wages would occur. As Congress was well aware, the economy boomed in the postwar decades, filling the trust fund faster than predicted. When the system converted to a dynamic (growth-oriented) income assumption in 1972, Congress used the occasion to finance another major expansion of benefits.

As long as the system appeared fiscally sound, Congress was satisfied that higher benefits would not require substantially higher taxes. The slowdown in economic growth during the 1970s and later dispelled this fiscal illusion. Americans were surprised to learn in the mid-1970s that Social Security faced financial shortfalls. In 1977 Congress raised FICA rates in the largest peacetime tax increase in U.S. history to enhance the trust fund, yet the corrective proved only a stopgap measure. Six years later Social Security taxes were raised again. This time Congress trimmed back on benefits as well.[16] From the 1980s onward Americans learned the unpleasant truth about Social Security: older workers had not personally purchased the benefits they enjoyed. Most of the cost of their stipend was passed on to their children and grandchildren.

Popular dislike of welfare made it easier for policy makers to vote additions to Social Security. Providing public assistance for America's poor never came easy. The issue always seemed to stir up visceral emotions. Policy remedies for the problem of poverty invariably were political compromises that covered only a portion of the need that social activists said existed. Traditional thinking had seen poverty as a product of individual laziness and a defect of character, a view that remained robust in the second half of the twentieth century. Although most Americans seemed to approve of unemployment relief as a temporary expedient during the Great Depression, making public assistance available in normal times was far less popular. A commonly voiced complaint after World War II was that "welfare cheats" milked the system at the expense of hardworking taxpayers. Such critics reiterated the pre-Depression homily that the poor should work their way out of destitution. The welfare skeptics advocated good moral behavior, individual perseverance, and a healthy economy as the way to overcome poverty.[17]

The "good times economy" that spread affluence in the quarter century after World War II seemed to affirm the wisdom of this prescription. Low unemployment and rising personal income in the postwar decades bred a complacency about poverty, which experts predicted would "wither away" with the continuation of economic growth, the availability of social insurance programs like Social Security, and technical adjustments in the categorical assistance (welfare) programs. Revision of Federal welfare policy began with the 1939 amendments to the Social Security Act, which increased the national contribution to state-run Aid to Dependent Children (ADC) from one-third to one-half of the reimbursable stipend per child. In 1950 Congress changed ADC to Aid to Families with Dependent Children (AFDC) by authorizing benefits for a caretaker (mainly mothers) and offered grants to states for assistance to the permanently disabled. The Federal government also increased its rate of welfare support to individual recipients and to poorer states. A controversial action adopted in 1961 made additional Federal money available to states that provided welfare assistance to a second caretaker (usually male) if the person was unemployed. Only half of the states accepted the offer.

These incremental revisions of welfare were intended to remove inequities in the existing law and to ease the financial burden on states as much as they were to reduce poverty. Admitted pockets of dependency remained in economic backwaters of the country, such as the Appalachian Mountains and older industrial cities, but the experts explained that existing income-support programs and the dedication of social workers to the rehabilitation of the poor would correct this residual poverty.

The 1960s produced contradictory evidence. Several social scientists announced the rediscovery of poverty, less than FDR's estimate in 1937 but unacceptably widespread nonetheless. A poverty index devised in 1964 recorded nearly 40 million persons, over one-fifth of the nation, with incomes insufficient to provide a "modest" standard of living in 1959. The contention that the surging economy had passed by some groups, leaving large pockets of invisible poor, was the subject of Michael Harrington's book *The Other America* (1962), which attracted wide attention. The new focus on poverty stimulated President Kennedy shortly before his assassination to consider legislation that would address the question of income deficiency in the richest country on earth.[18]

Picking up where the slain president had left off, Lyndon Johnson announced in his State of the Union message in 1964 an "unconditional war on poverty" aimed at the "forgotten fifth" below the poverty line. Johnson's War on Poverty became part of his vision of a Great Society, which the president unveiled in May 1964. The president called on policy makers to "advance the quality of our American civilization" and provide "abundance and liberty for all." The Great Society reaped a harvest of legislation between 1964 and 1967, a period that produced the greatest burst of social reform since the New Deal. Congress adopted civil rights protections for racial minorities, women, and the elderly; substantially increased national assistance for the nation's cities and educational institutions; took significant steps toward initiating environmental and consumer protection policies; and confronted important public health issues, such as the use of tobacco and the cost of medical care for the elderly. A center-piece of this ambitious agenda was a commitment to make income adequacy a matter of national policy.

Great Society antipoverty policies emphasized rehabilitation of the poor, not large increases in cash assistance to welfare recipients. The legislative foundation of this strategy was the Economic Opportunity Act (1964), which authorized the executive branch to encourage the organization of grassroots community action boards whose function was to get the poor to find ways to help themselves. Other programs, such as Head Start (cultural enrichment for disadvantaged preschoolers) and legal services for the poor, were aimed at the same objective. A change in the Aid to Families with Dependent Children program allowed welfare parents who worked to retain a portion of their earnings without suffering a reduction in benefits. The food stamp program (1964) offered subsidies to low-income persons for food purchases. Medicaid (1965) began federal reimbursements to the states for provision of health care for the poor, and the Housing Act of 1965 inaugurated an experiment in rental supplements for needy families. Food stamps Medicaid, and rent supplements all were in-kind benefits whereby qualifying individuals received goods or services rather than cash grants. Other federally funded in-kind programs enacted during the 1960s included worker training, public health services, additional public housing, and day care. The passage of the Elementary and Secondary Education Act of 1965, a subject on the congressional agenda for decades, owed a lot to its advertisement as an antipoverty measure.[19] This law authorized Federal grants to school systems based on the number of low-income children.

The poverty watch over the next fifteen years revealed a puzzling development. On one hand, the rate of poverty dipped steadily, falling to its modern low of 11 percent in 1973. On the other hand, welfare caseloads and costs leapt higher (see table 6.2). Contrary to the predictions and hopes of policy makers, who wanted to reduce the welfare rolls and expenditures, the data trended in a different direction. Expenditures for public aid (welfare) rose from $2.5 billion in 1950 to $4.1 billion in 1960, then jumped to nearly $72 billion by 1980. In inflation-adjusted per-capita dollars, welfare costs climbed sixfold in thirty years, tripling as a percentage of the GNP. The big three welfare programs—Aid to Families with Dependent Children, food stamps, and Medicaid—accounted for two-thirds of these costs in 1980 (up to 85 percent by 1990). Nearly a tenth of the population received food stamps and Medicaid assistance in 1980. AFDC led growth rates among the older categorical aid plans contained in the 1935

Table 6.2. Welfare, 1950–1990

	1950	1960	1970	1980	1990
Expenditures (billions of $)					
AFDC	.5	1.0	4.9	12.5	21.2
Medicaid (1965–)	—	—	4.8	25.8	72.2
Food Stamps (1964–)	—	—	.5	9.1	14.2
Total Public Aid	2.5	4.1	16.5	71.8	127
Average monthly payment per recipient (1990 dollars)					
AFDC	112	127	169	150	136
Social Security: retired workers	234	332	397	529	602
Recipients (millions)					
AFDC	2.2	3.1	9.7	11.1	11.4
Families	.65	.8	2.5	3.8	4.2
Medicaid	—	—	18.3*	27.7	25.3
Food Stamps	—	—	6.4	21.1	20.1
Poverty rate					
(% U.S. population)	—	22.2	12.6	13.0	13.5

Sources: U.S. Bureau of the Census, *Statistical Abstract of the United States 1993* (Washington, D.C.: GPO, 1993 and earlier years), various tables; Social Security Administration, *Social Security Bulletin, 1990–91; Annual Statistical Supplement, 1991* (Washington, D.C.: GPO, 1991), 108.
Note: * For 1972.

Social Security Act, with a tripling of recipients during the 1960s. The extraordinary rise of these numbers fueled a welfare backlash that helped Ronald Reagan win the presidency in 1980.

The welfare explosion represents one of the most unexpected twists in history of American government. Contrary to widespread allegations, massive chiseling did not cause the swelling of the welfare rolls, although the tidal wave of new recipients overtaxed the administrative capacity of some state and local agencies. Nor did a faltering economy explain the rise in welfare costs; economic signs were generally positive until the recession of the mid-1970s. Rather, a variety of social and political factors converged during a ten-year period beginning about 1964 to put mounting pressure on public aid programs. Statutory revisions and administrative policies during the Johnson (1963–1969) and Nixon-Ford (1969–1977) presidencies contributed to this expansion, but these actions were not the sole cause of the explosion. Social and demographic developments, whose roots reached backed into the nation's socioeconomic past, played important roles.

The return of prosperity after the Depression had not eliminated poverty among groups historically prone to hard times. Race or a female-headed household substantially increased the probability of poverty. The potency of these attributes was magnified when combined, and they were accentuated further when joined with other factors, such as age and region. Some population groups, such as African American females with children but no husband, were poor virtually by definition, even in the 1960s and 1970s. Elderly black women in the South were in similar straits. Actual or near poverty existed among some traditional families too (the working poor), where the male head received very low wages. At the other end of the spectrum of affluence were households headed by middle-aged white males in metropolitan areas. Beneficiaries of the nation's postwar economic miracle, their incomes seldom fell below the poverty threshold. This was especially the case in the suburbs, where poverty among households headed by a white male was as rare as upper-class status among single-parent black females in Mississippi.[20]

Poverty became more visible after World War II, partly because it moved. The most dramatic relocation of low-income people was of southern blacks who headed for cities in the North and West between the 1940s and 1960s. This epic migration resettled one-mule sharecropper farmers from the Mississippi bottomlands and other rural areas in the South as low-skilled residents of Harlem (New York), Watts (Los Angeles), and the south side of Chicago, which became symbols of black impoverishment. Pushed out of Dixie by the mechanization of the cotton picker and lured to the cities by labor scarcity during World War II and employment opportunities later, blacks abandoned sharecropping in search of better jobs. Few went north to collect welfare checks, yet their pattern of resettlement had profound repercussions on the nation's welfare system. Black newcomers to the cities, like migrants generally, tended to be concentrated in their child-raising years. This age profile contributed to a high birthrate among urban African Americans, whose increased fertility paralleled the rest of society during the baby boom decades (1950s and 1960s). The fathers of these black children, however, faced economic obstacles in racial discrimination, low skills, and diminishing employment opportunities as manufacturing plants moved out of the central cities. The result of these socioeconomic dislocations swelled AFDC rolls with more children, especially from inner-city neighborhoods.[21]

African Americans settled into states that had not only manufacturing and service economies but also liberal welfare policies. Southern states tended to set restrictive barriers against public aid, whereas northern industrial states made welfare easier to get and paid higher benefits. Most growth in AFDC cases during the 1960s occurred in urban states, such as New York, Michigan, and California, whose affluence permitted their welfare systems to expand with the growing caseloads. Black residents in these states, moreover, displayed a new assertiveness in claiming benefits, which was a consequence of their youthful age structure, the greater political openness than in the South, and the effects of the civil rights movement of the 1960s.[22] The deadly urban riots of the sixties (e.g., Watts, 1965; Detroit, 1967) manifested an ugly side to this new aggressiveness in a racially divided society.

The welfare explosion, however, was not a story just about African Americans. Most recipients of public assistance were white. The growth of welfare was largely a social phenomenon that reflected fundamental changes in the composition of families, the role of women, and birthrates. The extraordinary upsurge of births during the baby boom (1947–1964) produced a large increase in the number of women of childbearing age by the late 1960s. This enlarged reservoir of potential mothers kept the annual number of births high even after the baby boom peaked in the late 1950s. Had nothing else changed, the number of female-headed households, the primary characteristic of welfare families, would have grown in the 1960s and 1970s.[23]

But social conditions did not stay the same. Female lifestyles changed tremendously, particularly among younger women. Many rejected traditional roles that had made husbands, children, and the home the center of their mothers' and grandmothers' world. Abetted by the erosion of barriers to female employment, divorce and separation rose markedly, and so in consequence did female-headed households. Rationales from the progressive era that had been offered in support of pensions for widowed mothers did not fit the conditions of needy families in the late twentieth century. By the 1970s, families headed by females were widespread, especially among groups in urban slums; half of all children in female-headed households in the central cities lived in poverty.[24] The changes in female attitudes, cultivated in part by women's organizations that campaigned for gender equality and by lobbies of senior citizens, combated old stigmas that had been attached to acceptance of public assistance. As the perception of welfare changed from an embarrassing handout to an entitlement, participation rates increased; individuals who were eligible to receive welfare actually signed up for benefits, especially during the 1960s. Demonstrations by welfare mothers during the decade symbolized the transformation of poor women from docile victims of circumstance to an interest group of claimant recipients.

Federal policy also helped to reshape attitudes toward poverty and welfare. Although the War on Poverty's goal of weaning the poor from the welfare rolls was a nominal failure, it did publicize the availability of public assistance. The Department of Health, Education, and Welfare pressured state governments to relax eligibility rules and to advise the needy of available benefits. The Federal courts reinforced these mandates by striking down state laws, such as long residency requirements, that impeded welfare participation. The adoption of new income-assistance programs during the Johnson years contributed to the increased awareness of government benefits. The food stamp program, for example, required states to advertise the plan as a condition of getting Federal assistance. Medicaid came with a similar publicity requirement. By the mid-1970s both Medicaid and food stamps reached twice as many recipients as were aided by AFDC, the classic welfare program. By these and other steps government played an instrumental role in transforming welfare into an economic right.

The provision of income assistance to the poor, the elderly, and the unemployed in the United States trailed the development of the welfare state in Europe by several decades. But once the Social Security Act laid the foundation of America's economic security policy, the system grew fairly rapidly. Excluding the special case of military veterans, few individuals received income support from government before New Deal; in the early 1980s nearly half of all households were recipients of some public financial assistance. Income security consumed an increased proportion of the national wealth in the latter half of the twentieth century; its cost in the late 1980s was over half a trillion dollars annually (see chapter 11 for developments since 1990). Public expenditure on social welfare functions, a comprehensive category that includes education and health and medical care as well as income security, ranged between 2 and 3 percent of the GNP before the Great Depression, compared with 18 percent in the 1980s. Washington was at the forefront of this revolution in social spending, and the elderly were its favored recipients. One-fourth of the Federal budget during the years of Reagan's presidency benefited the aged, mainly through Social Security, which accounted for nearly half of all national domestic expenditures.

Public assistance has helped millions of people weather the travails of unemployment, family disintegration, physical impairment, old age, college expenses, and housing costs. Social Security meant the difference between humiliating dependency on public charity or one's children and minimal self-sufficiency for many of the country's elderly, whose poverty rate dropped as Social Security coverage spread. Income-assistance policy offered a partial hedge against total destitution. It did not, however, assure everyone a standard of living above the official poverty line, and there was no political consensus that it should do so. A substantial portion of Social Security retirement beneficiaries, both now and in the past, lived below the poverty line. In the last year of her life (1974–1975), Ida Fuller received $1,310 from Social Security, which was hardly enough to keep body and soul together. And welfare always paid less than Social Security.

Some observers saw jobs and economic growth as the most effective weapon against poverty. Evidence in support of this proposition, they argued, appeared in the decline of the poverty rate, which began before income support spending accelerated in the late 1960s. Critics of the U.S. assistance policy have argued that welfare promoted the breakup of families, the erosion of the work ethic, and the cultivation of welfare dependency. Other commentators questioned the propriety of increasing Social Security and other non-means-tested benefits (the social insurance programs), which subsidized the middle class, and in the opinion of some, discouraged personal savings.[25]

Debate about the merits of income-assistance policy has raged since its birth in the 1930s. Yet behind the babble of these voices some economic and political contrasts in program features have persisted. Government spent three times more on insurance programs such as Social Security pensions, which do not require demonstration of financial need, than on welfare. Members of the middle class, not the poor, were the principal beneficiaries of the new income security. Social Security constituted the largest subsidy to middle-income families, who also received financial assistance from civil service and military pensions, college aid programs, unemployment compensation, and veterans' benefits. Tax deductions and Federal loan guarantees for home mortgages are other valuable subsidies to middle-class pocketbooks. Generous retirement plans existed for government and military personnel, some of whom took advantage of early retirement options to qualify in addition for Social Security from private-sector employment. Beginning in the late 1970s large companies and nonprofit institutions began to offer their employees tax-deferred retirement options, such as 401(k) plans. With so much at stake, beneficiaries of these support programs have organized interest groups to protect their public largess. The American Association of Retired Persons (AARP, founded in 1947), one of the largest such organizations, vigorously defended Social Security against benefit reductions. When cutbacks were considered as part of a package of changes to the system in 1983, the AARP's chief lobbyists announced that "we'll fight anything we don't like to the bitter end ... pull out all the stops."[26] Congress could not ignore the challenge of AARP, with its 14 million members.

Welfare, by contrast, was the unwanted stepchild of the nation's income support policy. It lacked a constituency of middle-class beneficiaries and heavyweight pressure groups working on its behalf. After World War II, it became increasingly perceived in terms of racial stereotypes. In contrast to the positive reinforcement that accompanied the expansion of Social Security benefits, lawmakers sought to reduce welfare caseloads and contain the cost of public aid. Whereas officials intimated for years that Social Security cost the government nothing, politicians saw welfare more in terms of expenses than as an opportunity to reduce poverty. Derisive reference to the welfare "mess" frequently put legislators on the defensive when they reviewed assistance for the poor. As a result, the gap between the amount of support extended to welfare families and to Social Security recipients has widened over the years. Although no one gets rich on Social Security and although the system leaves some people, particularly widowed women, vulnerable to poverty, the vast majority of elderly Americans by the 1980s received social insurance assistance. By contrast, only a third of the poor receive welfare payments.[27]

The structure of the federal system put the poor at a considerable political disadvantage in comparison to Social Security beneficiaries. The retirement system is financed and managed exclusively by the national government, has its own stream of (earmarked) revenue, and requires no demonstration of financial need to receive a benefit. Welfare eligibility and stipend amounts, by comparison, vary considerably from state to state but paid much less than Social Security everywhere. Few states adopted the Federal criterion of poverty as a standard for welfare payments. On average among the states, AFDC payments and food stamps provided a needy family with only 74 percent of the income necessary to meet the official poverty threshold in 1987; in Mississippi and Alabama the figure was 46 percent.[28] Unlike Social Security spending, which required no appropriation by the Congress, welfare had to compete with many other functions to obtain its slice of the pie. And this task often proved difficult in the tempestuous atmosphere of state politics, where financial policy making faced obstacles that did not trouble Federal lawmakers (see chapter 8). The working of American federalism, in short, assigned welfare to an uncertain and sometimes hostile policy-making environment.

Despite these disparities, Social Security and welfare have come to bear greater resemblance to each other. In several respects Social Security is another form of welfare. Most OASDHI recipients purchased only a small fraction of their total benefit. Like welfare, taxes levied on current workers fed the system's trust funds. Low-income workers received a larger payback from their FICA contributions than did higher wage earners. One-third of all OASI recipients gain entitlement to a stipend by virtue of a social relationship to a worker and not by earning eligibility through their own employment. Conversely, welfare underwent changes after World War II that removed some of its localism. In the 1960s and 1970s Washington pressed the states to modify their Victorian postures toward welfare and to establish procedures that made public aid a matter of individual entitlement. In the 1980s Congress continued to set standards concerning the provision of AFDC, Medicaid, and food stamps. The Family Support Act of 1988, for example, required the states to observe Federal rules regarding the collection of child-support payments from absent fathers and making job training available for welfare recipients. State officials contributed to this nationalization of welfare policy by pleading their own poverty to Congress, which increased the Federal contribution to welfare costs from 39 percent in 1950 to 68 percent in 1980. The poor had not gained income parity with the elderly and their dependents, but public aid and social insurance came to look more like one another before the welfare reform act of 1996 (see chapter 11). Both sets of programs allocated public funds according to politically determined rules that subsidized the income of individuals. Their differences lay more in the mind of the public than in their actual policy designs.

7

~

The New Equality

ONLY SIX HUNDRED miles lay between Clarksdale, Mississippi, and Chicago, Illinois. For the aspiring bluesman Muddy Waters and other African Americans who left the delta region for the Windy City, however, the two areas were worlds apart. Whether their destination was the upper Midwest or another location, the refugees fled the South's four curses: social segregation, the denial of political rights, poverty, and violence. These outcroppings of racial oppression had hardened into a comprehensive system of discrimination in the South during the half-century after *Plessy v. Ferguson* (1896). Racial prejudice among whites existed nationwide; in the South discrimination was legal.

Racial segregation symbolized the South's traditional legal culture. State statutes and local ordinances created a network of Jim Crow rules that kept blacks physically separated from whites. These laws applied both to privately owned establishments, such as factory washrooms and restaurants, and public facilities, such as city parks and schools. Seventeen southern states mandated that black children attend separate schools, which received a fraction of funds invested in schools reserved for whites. An analogy existed in the North, where public officials colluded with realtors and bankers in erecting racial barriers to property transactions, which put entire communities off-limits to African Americans. Even the Federal government had allowed racial discrimination, most conspicuously in the military (until 1948) and in certain programs (such as wage agreements under the New Deal).

Despite their large numbers, blacks had no hope of overturning Jim Crow at the ballot box in most southern states. Whites controlled southern political institutions, and they barred the doors to minorities. Procedural subterfuges, such as complicated poll taxes and literacy tests, coupled with white dominance of Democratic Party affairs, prevented virtually all African Americans from voting, including in primary elections, or from serving on juries in court. The Supreme Court struck down all-white party primaries in 1944 (*Smith v. Allwright*), but the decision had little actual effect because African Americans were denied the opportunity to register. No black sat in the U.S. Congress between 1900 and 1929, and none won a seat in the Deep South until the 1970s. An African American did not preside as a permanent Federal judge in the United States until 1961. Service on state high courts, even in the North, was rare.

Political power ultimately rests on economic resources, which were scarce commodities in the black community. The South was the nation's poorest section and African Americans ranked at the bottom of the region's economic ladder. Most black men and many black women toiled in the fields as day laborers or sharecroppers on cotton or tobacco farms owned by whites. A labyrinth of peonage statutes virtually bound black farmers to their landlords. Vagrancy and convict labor laws kept unskilled laborers unorganized and in some instances in virtual slavery. This was the case of many blacks assigned to work at turpentine stills isolated deep in the pine forests.[1] African American workers in the North were clustered in menial service jobs, frequently the last hired and the first fired. Surveys of unemployment always had registered much higher joblessness among blacks than whites. Economic opportunity remained elusive for African Americans, most of whom were forced into low-paying jobs by inadequate schooling, a biased legal system, and exclusion from political power. The result was widespread poverty in black communities, particularly in the South. Infant mortality rates, a useful measure of comparative well-being, consistently showed death among black babies occurred twice as frequently as among whites. In effect, racial discrimination shortened black life spans.

Infant deaths symbolize the violence that stalked life in black communities. Lynching was the most terrifying manifestation of these risks. An average of fifty African Americans a year were hung by mobs in the 1910s, mainly in the South. Race riots, which broke out regularly in northern and southern cities, claimed many lives, most black. Conflicts in Springfield, Illinois (1908), East St. Louis (1917), Chicago (1919), Tulsa (1921), and Detroit (1943) collectively tallied scores of fatalities. The law afforded African Americans little protection from these hazards. In the South they were convicted for trivial offenses or for no offense at all, which allowed them to be leased to private employers or assigned to chain gangs that worked on the roads.[2] Juries usually would not convict a white man who killed a black person. Nor did law enforcement officials intercede consistently when a black assaulted another black. Only when a black was accused of harming a white did southern courts levy penalties.[3]

The idea of equal treatment before the law was a fundamental tenet of American ideology. Enshrined in the Declaration of Independence, the principle was reiterated in the Preamble to the Constitution of the United States, which cited justice and liberty as reasons for the formation of "a more perfect Union." The Fourteenth Amendment (1868) prohibited the states from denying "to any person . . . the equal protection of the laws." The Fifteenth Amendment (1870) forbade the states from withholding the right to vote on account "of race, color, or previous condition of servitude." These principles were oratorical staples at public gatherings in subsequent decades. The Democratic Party platform of 1932, for example, promised "equal rights to all." Despite the rhetoric, a wide gap existed between the theory of equality and legal reality for African Americans and other historic minorities, such as women, Native Americans, and the aged. One hundred years after the Emancipation Proclamation (1863) the national government had no effective mechanism to challenge racial discrimination in the South or the unequal treatment of women in employment.

In light of this historical background the enactment of the Civil Rights Act of 1964 must be seen as a monumental achievement. Its significance ranks with the inauguration of Federal regulation of business in 1887 and the beginning of national income assistance policy in 1935. Along with the Voting Rights Act of 1965 and the Open Housing Act of 1968, the Civil Rights Act laid the legal basis to prosecute racial discrimination nationwide. During the 1960s and 1970s lawmakers also declared discrimination illegal on account of gender, age, and physical handicaps. These laws did not immediately end inequality in America, but they did put new statutory muscle behind old civic ideals. And they created an administrative apparatus that held out the hope of reducing blatant discrimination against the nation's historic minorities.

The 1964 Civil Rights Act declared several forms of discrimination illegal on the basis of race, color, religion, and national origin. Individuals could not be denied access to commercial establishments such as restaurants and theaters, nor could state and local governments segregate facilities according to race. The attorney general of the United States was authorized to sue local schools that continued to segregate. Federal agencies that granted financial assistance were instructed to issue rules that prohibited discriminatory practices and allowed termination of the aid if a recipient failed to comply. Title VII of the law outlawed racial, religious, and gender criteria in hiring, firing, and setting the conditions of work. The section created a five-member Equal Employment Opportunity Commission (EEOC) to hear complaints from applicants and employees, who also could sue privately. The attorney general was also permitted to file suits where "a pattern or practice" of employment discrimination was detected. Although the enforcement mechanism of the job discrimination section was relatively weak, the 1964 law and the civil rights statutes of 1965 and 1968 represented a major assertion of Federal power into matters formerly controlled at the state level or by private citizens.[4]

The Voting Rights Act authorized the appointment of Federal voter examiners who were to investigate interference with voter registration or the right to vote in any election, national or local. Examiners could draw up a fair list of qualified voters and order local officials to register them. This process was automatically triggered in designated states where less than half of the voting-age population was registered or had voted in the 1964 presidential election. Localities within these designated states were required to submit new electoral procedures to the U.S. government for approval (called "preclearance"). Literacy tests and similar devices that had blocked suffrage were restricted. Initially aimed at enfranchising southern blacks, the act was amended in 1975 to include Spanish-speaking and Native American populations. The Civil Rights Act of 1968 declared racial discrimination in the sale or rental of most housing illegal and extended civil rights protections to American Indians who lived under tribal jurisdiction.

Enactment of the 1964 Civil Rights Act raises two questions. Why did it take so long for the United States to honor its ideological commitment to equality? And what prompted Congress finally to act in 1964? Three factors go a long way in answering the first question. First obstacle to civil rights was the lingering hold of racial prejudice. As late as the 1940s public opinion polls showed that the majority of whites favored racial segregation and opposed Federal action to prevent discrimination.[5] White opposition to the prospect of black neighbors continued to be widespread throughout the country in the 1950s and 1960s. Vociferous critics of civil rights branded efforts to undo segregation a communist plot. Second, reverence for the "blessings of local government," as President James Garfield worded his praise of a decentralized federal system, still influenced people's thinking at the middle of the twentieth century. Democrats had been the leading defenders of local autonomy until the 1930s, when they swung behind national initiatives on economic issues, while Republicans increasingly embraced noncentralization as a strategy to block the growth of Federal power. Regardless of party, however, southerners were the staunchest adherents of states' rights.

The South's unique political history constituted the third obstacle to civil rights. Resentment of Republican prosecution of the Civil War and GOP control of state governments during Reconstruction drove white southerners into the Democratic camp. The region gave virtually all its electoral votes to Democratic presidential candidates between 1880 and 1944. With Dixie in his hip pocket, Grover Cleveland only needed to capture a handful of northern states to win the presidency in 1884. He took four. The loss of two of them in 1888 cost him reelection. Only New Yorker Al Smith's run for the presidency in 1928 broke the Democrats' hold on the solid South. After the Populist uprising of the 1890s, Democratic control of state offices and congressional seats was complete and durable.

The Democrats' one-party monopoly gave the South unique leverage in Congress. Lacking viable Republican challengers, individual southerners repeatedly won reelection to Congress, which built up their seniority and thus their power in the Democratic delegation. Counting the Border States (such as Kentucky and Maryland), southerners constituted between 40 and 70 percent of the party's membership in the House, depending on how Democrats fared in the North. Southerners held the speakership, the top post in the House, for forty-two of the forty-four years that the Democrats were the House majority between 1883 and 1961. Seniority put southerners in control of a disproportionate number of committee chairs, which were positions of considerable personal power. The critical positioning of southerners in Congress explains Franklin Roosevelt's timidity on civil rights during the New Deal. Needing their votes on economic legislation, the president avoided antagonizing southerners with proposals on race.

Civil rights advocates succeeded in squeezing an antilynching bill through the House in 1937, only to see southerners kill the measure in the Senate with their ultimate parliamentary weapon: the filibuster. The rules of the upper house permitted individual senators to speak for an unlimited time unless the members voted cloture to terminate debate. Between 1917 and 1974 cloture required a two-thirds (three-fifths since 1975) vote, which worked to the advantage of southern filibusters. Senators from the fifteen former slave states constituted almost one-third of the upper chamber. Between 1917 and 1963 all attempts to silence filibusterers on civil rights failed.[6]

The solidarity of southern Democrats and the lever of filibustering dimmed the prospect for a civil right law. How was this resistance overcome? Several developments, some long in the making and others more immediate, coincided to produce a historic legislative breakthrough in 1964. The key elements in this story were the activities of civil rights organizations, the impact of World War II, the migration of blacks out of the South, the commitment of liberal Democrats, and a dramatic legislative battle in the Congress.

The prologue to this struggle began in 1938, when the Supreme Court ruled that Missouri's refusal to admit a black to the state law school violated the equal protection clause of the Fourteenth Amendment. The justices did not overturn the separate-but-equal doctrine of *Plessy v. Ferguson,* but the Missouri decision did crack its foundation. Lawyers for the National Association for the Advancement of Colored People (NAACP) attacked this legal fissure. Founded in 1910, the NAACP was the oldest black civil rights group in the United States and one of the most conservative in operational style. Later groups, such as Congress of Racial Equality (1941) and the Student Nonviolent Coordinating Committee (1960), used confrontational tactics, such as marches and demonstrations, to combat racial injustice. The NAACP relied heavily on its Legal Defense Fund, which used litigation to attack discrimination.

As Roosevelt and Truman court appointees took their seats, the national judiciary became receptive to the Legal Defense Fund's challenge. The Supreme Court struck down segregation on interstate railroads (1941), on buses (1946), and in all-white primary elections (1944). In 1948 the court disallowed restrictive-covenant provisions in private contracts that prohibited the sale of homes to blacks. Two years later it prohibited a southern law school from isolating a black student from white classmates. Then the court took a giant step by repudiating the separate-but-equal doctrine in *Brown v. Board of Education* (1954). "Separate educational facilities are inherently unequal" and thus violated the equal protection standard of the Fourteenth Amendment, wrote Chief Justice Earl Warren, an Eisenhower appointee. With this crucial legal bridge crossed, state and local laws that barred blacks from various types of public facilities failed the test of constitutionality.

Legal Defense Fund strategists correctly predicted that the Federal courts would be more receptive to civil rights than would the Congress and the president. Legislators and executives had little to gain politically from taking up the cause before the 1960s, given the low interest that most whites showed in advancing black interests. But their appointment to life terms afforded Federal judges relative insulation from public opinion. This independence helps to explain why the national judiciary struck the first decisive blow at segregation. The justices' willingness to use Federal authority to do so, moreover, no doubt was influenced by the court's tendency since the late 1930s, which removed older constraints on the uses of national power. Federal disapproval of state restrictions on personal freedom can be seen as part of this new judicial course. Yet the court was limited in its ability to change policy. Judges interpret the meaning of the law, but they have a limited ability to implement these decisions.

For ten years national officials did little to transform *Brown* from legal theory into policy practice. Most public schools and commercial facilities in the South remained segregated. Blacks continued to be excluded from the electorate. Many southern whites supported a strategy of massive resistance to block desegregation. Neither the Eisenhower nor the Kennedy administration showed much willingness to buck these trends, which placed greater obligation on civil rights activists to initiate reform. A boycott of segregated buses in Montgomery, Alabama, in 1955, followed by the organization of the Southern Christian Leadership Conference (SCLC) by Martin Luther King Jr. and other civil rights leaders in 1957, indicated that African Americans would take the lead in applying new pressure to combat racism. A sit-in at the segregated lunch counter in the Greensboro Woolworth five-and-dime store by four black college freshmen from the North Carolina Agricultural and Technical College in 1960 ignited demonstrations throughout the South. The following year black and white Freedom Riders braved brutal beatings and arrests in an attempt to desegregate bus terminals in Alabama and Mississippi. The scale of racial tension and violence escalated in 1963 when the SCLC decided to target Birmingham, Alabama, which King called "the most segregated city in America." Black leaders counted on a newsworthy performance from the city's notorious hardline segregationist, Eugene "Bull" Connor, Birmingham's public safety commissioner. Bull not only lived up to his reputation but unwittingly advanced the cause of civil rights by putting King in solitary confinement and by authorizing his officers to attack demonstrators, including women and children, with high-pressure water hoses and police dogs. Millions of Americans were shocked at these scenes, which the revolution in televised news broadcasting brought into homes across the nation.[7]

John Kennedy could not ignore the brutality in Birmingham. The president announced in a televised address that the nation faced "a moral crisis" that required action by national lawmakers. Eight days later the Justice Department sent a civil rights bill to Congress. Kennedy understood the political snares that awaited the legislation. To avoid exacerbating these problems he urged black leaders to call off plans for a massive demonstration in Washington.[8] But the March on Washington brought a quarter of a million people to the capital in August 1963. With the civil rights bill pending in the House, Martin Luther King Jr. articulated the aspirations of the gathering in his "I have a dream" speech, which he delivered from the veranda of the Lincoln Memorial.

The roots of black political activism of the 1950s can be traced to the influence of World War II. During the conflict more than a million African Americans served in the armed forces, which were still racially segregated. An equivalent number of blacks found work in defense plants around the country. Yet President Roosevelt said that the purpose of the fight was "to uphold the doctrine that all men are equal in the sight of God." Black leaders noted the contradiction. At the onset of the defense buildup, civil rights leaders persuaded the president to issue an executive order that forbade companies engaged in war business from discriminating in employment. Efforts in Congress after the war to make this rule permanent wilted before filibusters. New York State, however, enacted an Anti-Discrimination Act (1945) that prohibited the use of racial criteria in employment. By 1961, twenty-one northern states had adopted similar statutes.[9]

These laws were partially the by-product of the war, which had an enormous impact on U.S. society and politics. The mobilization of defense production functioned like a giant magnet, luring thousands of blacks out of the rural South and redistributing them in cities across the country. The rapid pace of mechanization in the southern cotton fields and tobacco farms in the 1950s sustained this outmigration after the war. In 1940 three of every four African Americans resided in the South. A million and a half left Dixie in the next ten years, and a similar number followed in the 1950s, most resettling in New York, Philadelphia, Detroit, Los Angeles, and other industrial centers. Chicago's black population increased by half a million in these two decades. By 1960 nearly a quarter of Chicago's inhabitants were African Americans, most of whom were crowded into the Windy City's south side. Chicago's black ghetto was replicated throughout metropolitan America.

Despite de facto segregation and barriers to economic opportunity, African Americans experienced token gains in the North, especially in sports and entertainment. The Brooklyn Dodgers' decision to bring Jackie Robinson across the color line in major league baseball in 1947, just as television was gaining popularity, was a momentous achievement given the sport's tradition of strict segregation. Robinson's success on and off the field opened the way for a succession of other black players, such as Willie Mays, Ernie Banks, Roy Campanella, and Hank Aaron, in the 1950s and 1960s. Baseball was the national pastime, and millions of Americans young and old worshiped the game's stars. Now they saw blacks in person and on TV playing on the same field and just as well as whites. The integration of baseball may have been as influential as any development in the 1950s and early 1960s in changing northern attitudes about blacks and segregation. The popularity of black singers such as Chuck Berry, Little Richard, and Fats Domino during the early days of rock and roll (1950s) may have had a similar effect on white opinion, although their appeal was limited largely to the young at first.

Large population shifts invariably produce social and political repercussions, and this was certainly the case with the black exodus from the rural South. The relocation to the central cities of industrial states, where blacks could vote, afforded them new political leverage. Black migrants to the North tended to be young, and that stimulated feelings of greater political effectiveness and higher turnout at the polls than was true for older blacks who remained in the South.[10] By the 1950s African Americans were winning seats on city councils and in state legislatures. A "black" congressional seat was established in Chicago in 1928, in New York City in 1944, and in Detroit in 1954. Six African Americans sat in Congress in 1964. All were Democrats who represented big northern cities that had large minority populations.

African Americans had supported Republicans for generations after the Civil War, but the New Deal weaned them away from the party of Lincoln and emancipation. In addition to enrolling them in relief programs, the Roosevelt administration appointed a few blacks to positions in the executive branch and created a civil rights section of the Justice Department in 1941. Harry Truman appointed a president's committee in 1946 to recommend improvements in civil rights, and in 1948 he took the bold step of ordering desegregation of the military. Blacks responded to these gestures by remaining loyal to Democrats in the 1950s and providing crucial support for John F. Kennedy in 1960. Kennedy won razor-thin victories in several industrial states, such as Illinois, Michigan, and New Jersey, where black votes may have provided the margin of difference.[11] The movement of blacks into the Democratic camp was a symptom of the changes that had altered the party of Grover Cleveland. Nineteenth-century Democrats had championed local autonomy, resisted national encroachment on state rights, and opposed expanded uses of public power. A retreat from these positions began during the early twentieth century and gave way to support of centralized authority during the New Deal. Democratic presidents were at the nation's helm during World War II and the Korean War, both of which enhanced Federal power. Liberals and internationalists, as supporters of these policy developments were called, sided with the Democratic Party in the 1950s and 1960s.

Modern liberalism has been defined as a willingness to use government to address a range of problems confronting society. Because liberals saw state government as unable to fill this role adequately, they advocated the expansion of Federal activity. This strategy had a critical bearing on civil rights, given southern states' defense of the racial status quo. Liberal Democrats, whose constituencies were in northern industrial states and who enjoyed the backing of most labor unions, constituted the core of congressional support for civil rights legislation. The United Auto Workers (UAW), which had opened its doors to blacks in Detroit and elsewhere, and Walter Reuther, its president (1947–1970), were instrumental in linking racial justice to the Democrats' policy agenda.[12] Many northern Democrats adopted this position by 1948, when they pledged in the party platform "to eradicate all racial . . . discrimination." Alabama's and Mississippi's delegates, Birmingham's "Bull" Connor among them, responded by bolting the national Democratic convention and nominating a homegrown Dixiecrat, J. Strom Thurmond of South Carolina, for president. This widening sectional fissure within the Democratic Party and its cliffhanger victory in 1960 help to account for President Kennedy's hesitancy on civil rights—until events in Birmingham forced his hand.

The Civil Rights Act of 1964 provoked one of the epic struggles in congressional history. The bill that the Kennedy administration sent to lawmakers faced a formidable obstacle in the conservative coalition. This bloc consisted of southern Democrats, who opposed the merits of civil rights, and Republicans, who tended to resist the expansion of Federal authority in domestic affairs; they had joined in common cause on numerous issues since the late 1930s. The coalition's power in the House in 1963 pivoted around the Rules Committee, which could prevent legislation from progressing to the full membership for consideration. Howard W. Smith, an eighty-year-old Virginian who chaired the committee, denounced the civil rights bill as a "monstrous instrument of oppression."

The bill was assigned to the House's Judiciary Committee, headed by Emanuel Celler, a Brooklyn Democrat. This veteran of forty-one years in Congress became the point man for the northern Democrats, who represented the largest block of lawmakers in favor of the Kennedy legislation and who added a tough section on employment discrimination to the bill. Aiding their fight was a broadly based network of lobbyists, made up of civil rights organizations, labor unions, church groups, and liberal political organizations such as Americans for Democratic Action. Their coordinated pressure was a critical factor in the bill's passage. They assiduously courted moderate Republicans, whose support was crucial to the success of any civil rights legislation. William McCulloch, Judiciary's ranking Republican, embraced the antidiscrimination principle of the legislation and rallied enough of his colleagues behind a compromise measure to squeeze it through the Judiciary Committee. Its revisions to the bill alarmed the Kennedy administration, which feared that strengthened employment provisions would jeopardize the president's chances for reelection. These apprehensions were never put to a test. Kennedy was assassinated in November 1963, and executive leadership transferred to Johnson.

A southerner as well as a Democrat, LBJ had been cool to civil rights as a congressman, although he warmed to the idea as vice president. Above all, Johnson was an astute politician with a desire for national acceptance and a knack for persuasion, a talent he had honed during his years as the Senate's majority leader. He applied this skill to his "first priority" as president—passage of a civil rights act. Johnson urged the civil rights coalition to redouble its pressure on Republicans, whose votes were mandatory for moving the bill through the Rules Committee. After clearing this hurdle the measure endured nine days of debate in the full House. McCulloch worked the Republican side of the aisle. "The Constitution," he reminded his colleagues, "doesn't say that whites alone shall have our basic rights." When the votes were tallied, over three-quarters of the Republicans in the House joined northern Democrats in passing the legislation.[13]

This victory forced southerners to play their trump card: they would try to talk the bill to death in the Senate. They pursued this strategy for thirteen weeks in the spring of 1964. Richard Russell, dean of the Senate Dixiecrats, punctuated his dilatory monologues by equating the bill with socialism. A. Willis Robertson waved a small Confederate flag during one of his stints on the Senate floor. Silencing the filibusterers required a two-thirds vote, which meant that northern Democrats needed help from Republicans. President Johnson and Hubert Humphrey, the bill's sponsor in the Senate, focused their attention on Everett Dirksen, the leader of the Senate Republicans. Dirksen opposed the increased use of Federal power in domestic affairs but at the last minute decided to make civil rights an exception to this rule. It was, he explained, "an idea whose time had come." Political realism probably had as much to do with Dirksen's conversion as moral principle. He and other Senate Republicans were besieged with appeals from constituents to stand up to the southerners. Especially effective as lobbyists were church leaders, many of whom traveled to Washington to visit Republican senators.[14] After 524 hours of stalling, the southerners succumbed to the civil rights coalition. Twenty-seven Republicans (of the thirty-three in the Senate) and forty-four northern Democrats voted to cut off the filibuster, the first time ever on a civil rights proposal. But cloture did not end southern opposition to the bill. The southerners offered ninety-nine amendments in a futile effort to emasculate it and supplied most of the nay votes at its passage.

Johnson signed the act in a ceremony covered by live TV. Four months later he overwhelmed Barry Goldwater, one of the six Republicans who had voted against cloture, in the 1964 presidential election. Johnson's coattail effect on the congressional elections helped to add forty northerners to the Democrat's House delegation. The gain diminished southern power in Congress and facilitated the enactment of the 1965 Voting Rights Act. By launching a voter registration drive in Selma, Alabama, a bastion of segregation, Martin Luther King Jr. and the Southern Christian Leadership Conference, not the president, made the strongest case for Federal protection of suffrage rights. Sheriff Jim Clark set loose his posse, wielding clubs and cattle prods, on Selma blacks who came to register. A protest march from Selma to the state capital resulted in more assaults on demonstrators, this time by the state police. National outrage at this brutality, which resulted in several fatalities and received nationwide television coverage, spurred Johnson to propose the voting rights bill. Virginia's

Congressman Smith denounced the measure as an unconstitutional vendetta on the South, but he was unable to attract sufficient Republicans to his cause. Southerners in the Senate launched another talkathon. But with massive public opinion behind it, the civil rights coalition prevailed.

Housing discrimination was the last item on the civil rights agenda of the 1960s. Attempts to pass open-housing legislation in 1966 and 1967 fell victim to a combination of obstacles—opposition from the real estate industry, Democratic losses in the 1966 congressional elections, and riots in dozens of cities that left scores dead during the summer of 1967. Armed with the recommendations of the National Advisory Commission on Civil Disorders, whose 1968 report on the urban disturbances described widening racial division in the country, the president reiterated his advocacy of an open-housing law. Once again liberal Democrats and the civil rights coalition held the key players in line. The House Rules Committee, now under the command of Democrat William Colmer of Mississippi, came close to killing the measure. But Martin Luther King's assassination during the committee's deliberations helped to create a narrow majority behind the bill, advancing it to the full House. An antiriot amendment that levied Federal criminal penalties on convictions for civil disturbances probably influenced some moderates to vote for the measure. Timing was instrumental in the enactment of the open-housing bill, as the window of opportunity to pass legislation that prohibited discrimination against African Americans was closing rapidly. Growing hostility in the country to liberal social policies dimmed the prospect of reviving a successful civil rights coalition in the foreseeable future. In the presidential election of 1968 segregationist candidate George Wallace carried five southern states and won considerable support in the North.

Traditional social conventions and political inequities came under attack from numerous quarters during the 1960s. Most minorities mounted efforts during the decade to remove obstacles that blocked their opportunities. The African American drive for civil rights, the vanguard of this demand for reform, generated political momentum that helped women, Hispanics, Native Americans, the elderly, the handicapped, and gays with their own campaigns against discrimination. Protest against the war in Vietnam, which focused criticism on the political establishment, contributed to these advocacy movements. Although the war and other crosscurrents eventually undercut the impetus for social reform, the Congresses of the 1970s did not repeal the civil rights law written during the Great Society years.

The new equality assumed two forms. One expression was a heightened consciousness among historic minorities about their subordinate status in society. Middle-aged white males traditionally held the most social, economic, and political power in the United States. Challenges to this domination and the institutional forms that sustained it were notable features of the social turmoil of the 1960s. During the decade blacks, women, and other minorities became more insistent on receiving fair and impartial treatment from government and private institutions as a fundamental right.

In addition to the cultural dimension of the new equality, which rested on new attitudes and expanded expectations of individuals, the concept also refers to revisions in the law. Not only were outdated state statutes overturned, but also numerous new policies concerning individual opportunity, political rights, and social behavior were adopted. President Johnson's vision of the Great Society, which established "liberty for all" as a criterion for improving the "quality of our American civilization," put executive support behind nondiscrimination policy. Congress, the federal courts, and the states sustained the president with a sequence of statutes and judicial decisions aimed at achieving his objective.

Some of these actions attacked social and legal obstacles that had long frustrated women. Although women had gained the vote in 1920, few held places of power in government during the next forty years. Females endured discrimination in hiring, promotion, job classification, and compensation. Their rights in marital and social relationships regarding the control of property, physical abuse, and rape were subordinate to male authority. Lawmakers incorporated some of these double standards into public policy. During the Great Depression Federal and state policy makers forced spouses, which usually meant wives, off the public payroll in an effort to cut costs. The need for workers during World War II prompted Federal administrators to reverse course and actively recruit females into the workforce.[15] Responding to Uncle Sam's patriotic solicitations and promises of equal pay, three million women took jobs at defense plants during the war. But when employers turned them out to make way for returning GIs in 1945, Federal officials looked the other way. Congress did not forget the men, however, as the GI Bill lavished benefits on military veterans, most of whom were males.

Unwilling to resume an inferior position in the workplace after "manning" the assembly lines, active feminists pressed for a national equal pay law, similar to Massachusetts' 1945 statute. This early campaign for women's rights was stymied by the conventional image of women as mothers and homemakers that experienced a resurgence in the 1950s. In 1963, however, President Kennedy signed the Equal Pay Act, which prohibited wage discrimination by gender for equal work. Most states adopted similar laws during the next twenty years. Some statutes went beyond the Federal law and addressed the issue of comparable worth—the requirement that equal pay be given for equivalent responsibilities.

The 1964 Civil Rights Act also gave women an unexpected boost, thanks to Howard Smith, the Virginia congressman. As much a supporter of female equality as rights for blacks, Smith offered an amendment to the employment section (Title 7) of the bill that added sex to the forms of prohibited discrimination. Smith had hoped to taint the title in a way that would make it unacceptable to his colleagues. But the women on the House floor seized the moment and fought to keep gender in the employment section of the law.[16] In 1972 Title 7 protection was extended to employees in state and local government, a high percentage of whom were women. A separate measure in the same year banned sex discrimination in admission to professional schools and colleges. Later in the decade Congress forbade employers from denying health care benefits to women because of gender-related conditions, such as pregnancy. State laws that prohibited gender discrimination in employment, in the extension of loans, and in housing transactions offered another level of protection for women. Legal decisions reinforced some of these provisions. Federal courts, for example, disallowed unequal pension benefits for men and women and classified sexual harassment as a form of employment discrimination.

The court's attack on gender discrimination was part of a broader reexamination of fairness in social and criminal policy. In 1965, for example, the Supreme Court struck down a Connecticut law that prohibited the sale of contraceptives and the distribution of birth-control information to married couples. The statute was deemed to violate the right of personal privacy, which the justices held (*Griswold v. Connecticut*) was protected by the First, Fourth, Fifth, and Ninth Amendments. Their reasoning reflected an important change in the legal definition of federalism. Generations of jurists had held that the Bill of Rights in the U.S. Constitution applied only to actions of Federal officials and not to actions of the states. After 1930, however, the Supreme Court began to hold state and local governments accountable to some provisions in the first eight Amendments. The overt rationale for this "nationalization" of the Bill of Rights lay in the language of the Fourteenth Amendment, which prohibited a "state" from depriving "any person of life, liberty, or property without the due process of law." The court saw First Amendment rights, such as freedom of speech, assembly, and religion, and fair trial guarantees found in the Fourth and Fifth Amendments as fundamental components of liberty in a democracy and "incorporated" them within the Fourteenth Amendment's requirement of "due process" for every citizen. This reading of the Constitution empowered the national courts to review a large number of new state and local actions.

Conservative critics complained that the court had overreached its authority, especially regarding privacy. This criticism intensified after *Roe v. Wade* (1973), in which the justices used the right to privacy reasoning to disallow state prohibitions of abortion during the first trimester of pregnancy. The legal niceties of the case became secondary to the emotional explosiveness of the abortion issue. Many women assumed active roles in the prochoice and prolife movements. The treatment of women in institutions that had traditionally catered to males also evoked impassioned responses, as occurred at Yale when the female crew team demonstrated by standing stark naked before the director of physical education with "Title 7" painted in Yale blue on their chests.[17] The legal foundation of their protest was the congressional prohibition of sex discrimination in education (1972), which the Department of Health, Education, and Welfare ruled included college athletic facilities. Emotional controversy also followed the Equal Rights Amendment, which Congress passed and sent to the states for ratification in 1972. The measure narrowly failed to gain the necessary approval of three-fourths of the legislatures, but by the end of the 1980s nineteen states had inserted gender discrimination prohibitions into their own constitutions.[18]

The treatment of women and blacks was the primary focus of the equality movement in the 1960s and 1970s, but other groups also gained new legal protections. Congress made unreasonable job discrimination against older individuals (between forty and sixty-five) unlawful and forbade mandatory retirement based solely on age. A constitutional amendment (1971) guaranteed the right to vote to individuals over eighteen and Congress afforded students greater freedom of speech and personal control over their school records. Washington required most institutions to provide physical access for handicapped people and schools to offer special programs tailored to their needs.

Ethnic biases were removed from the nation's immigration laws in 1965. Beginning with *Reynolds v. Sims* (1964) the Federal courts attacked the apportionment of state legislative districts that deviated from the principle of "one person one vote." The court disallowed long residency as an eligibility requirement for welfare and struck down state laws that mandated prayer and Bible reading in school classrooms. Empowered by its reading of the Fourteenth Amendment, the Supreme Court forced states to adopt new standards of fairness and impartiality.

A popular misconception holds that the Civil Rights Act of 1964 "gave" African Americans their rights. According to this notion the case for civil rights was closed once the appropriate law was put on the books. Unfortunately this interpretation wilts in face of social and political reality. Civil rights acts gave nothing in any literal sense. These laws were phrased in negative terms, instructing people not to distinguish between individuals on account of "suspect" categories such as race, gender, and age in the conduct of certain affairs, and empowered officials to enforce these rules. The creation of enforcement power was necessary because voluntary compliance with the law is unreliable. If everyone voluntarily observed automobile speed limits there would be little need for traffic cops. The analogy applies to rules prohibiting discrimination.

Obtaining compliance with nondiscrimination policy posed special difficulties. The new equality rules told millions of people to alter customs and habits of a lifetime. Many Americans had grown up knowing only racial segregation. Most males were only vaguely aware of the barriers in education and employment that limited opportunities for women. Some discrimination, moreover, was not the result of deliberate acts of prejudice but was embedded in the structure of customary behavior. This structural discrimination is exemplified by "pink-collar" jobs, such as secretaries, schoolteachers, and nurses, that became dominated by women and that paid lower wages than comparable jobs held by males. Prosecution of discrimination is easiest when the motivation of the perpetrator is plain and an individual victim can document a specific act of injustice. Administrators have disagreed about how to attack the manifestations of structural discrimination, which affected large classes of people.

Effectiveness in enforcing nondiscrimination rules, as well as most other regulations, depends upon a range of factors. The language with which a policy objective was stated can affect its implementation. Goals that are stated in very general terms, defined ambiguously, or set unrealistically high can undermine a program's success. Administrators need a clear understanding of the types of action that constitute illegal discrimination. The assignment of enforcement responsibility among administrative units also affects the effectiveness of policy. So does elected leaders' commitment to a policy objective. Democrats have enforced civil rights more vigorously than have Republicans. Evidence of executive interest in a program is usually visible in the amount of funding sought to implement it. As with most aspects of modern governance, money fuels the actual application of policy. Finally, the techniques of implementation made available to administrators influence their ability to guide a program to success. Three methods were commonly used to enforce national equality law. First, administrative agencies investigated complaints filed by individuals, attempted to negotiate settlements of these disputes, and monitored compliance with nondiscrimination rules. Second, the Justice Department could sue persons and institutions on the basis of findings submitted by public agencies or on its own initiative. Finally, private citizens could sue a person or institution accused of discrimination.

The enforcement of national civil rights law was distributed among numerous Federal agencies. The Office of Civil Rights (originally in HEW) monitored progress in school desegregation, gender discrimination in educational programs, and the treatment of the handicapped. Most matters concerning employment discrimination were assigned to the Equal Employment Opportunity Commission (EEOC), created by the 1964 act, and the Office of Federal Contract Compliance Programs. HUD oversaw affairs in housing. Justice's Civil Rights Division was responsible for voting rights, litigation of matters recommended to it by other agencies, and the employment practices of state and local governments. The U.S. Civil Service Commission enforced nondiscrimination rules for Federal employees. State and local agencies enforced both national and subnational law that mandated equal treatment. As one might surmise, success in upholding civil rights standards varied by the unit in charge of overseeing them.

The Office of Civil Rights (OCR) was given the task of desegregating the South's dual school systems, symbol of the region's Jim Crow laws. OCR had two principal tools in its enforcement kit: the office could ask the Justice Department to sue negligent school districts and could threaten to withhold Federal school monies. The Civil Rights Act of 1964 instructed agencies that distributed Federal funds to write rules concerning nondiscrimination for recipients and authorized the termination of payments for noncompliance. The significance of this provision for school desegregation was immensely enhanced by the passage of the Elementary and Secondary Education Act (1965), which pumped several billion dollars a year into local schools. Proposals for Federal aid to education had languished in Congress for decades, unable to overcome the fierce loyalty to the tradition of locally controlled schools (free of the strings Federal aid was feared to bring) and opposition from churches that ran their own schools. The enlargement of the Democratic congressional delegation in 1965 and some parliamentary sleight of hand, such as calling school aid an antipoverty program, finally carried the day.[19] Now staked with considerable cash, the OCR issued firm desegregation timetables for southern school districts. The Federal courts backed up these rules by turning down southern appeals for delay. In 1969 the Supreme Court ordered every school district in Mississippi to desegregate "at once." Two years later it approved the busing of students to facilitate this goal.

Schools in the South were a relatively easy target for civil rights enforcement because state laws explicitly mandated segregation. But racially separate schools existed in the North too, the result of social as well as legal causes. The concentration of blacks in the poorer sections of inner cities and the migration of whites out of the urban cores and to suburbs produced *de facto* neighborhood segregation. Acting on the assumption that racial mixture produced desirable cultural and educational results, the OCR added these racially imbalanced school systems to its caseload and ordered their integration, even where the remedy included the busing of children. Because school districts in metropolitan areas were fragmented among numerous local governments, busing was the only immediate way of achieving racially integrated schools throughout an urban region.

The attempt to integrate schools in the North reflected a broadening of civil rights objectives that went beyond the enforcement of rules that prohibited overt and deliberate discrimination on the basis of race and color. The revised emphasis included an attack on the more entrenched inequalities in society. This philosophical shift necessitated government to initiate steps aimed at producing an equality of results. The test of discrimination no longer rested solely on documented mistreatment of particular individuals but added an evaluation of actual conditions between racial groups.[20] In this expanded definition of inequality, differences in status frequently were identified on the basis of quantitative profiles of entire population groups. This broadened attack on racial discrimination pressed up against the limits of the public willingness to support equality policy. Congress placed one obstacle in this new course in 1972 by prohibiting the use of Federal funds for forced busing (required by a desegregation plan). Two years later the Supreme Court stopped school integration from spilling over city limits; in *Milliken v. Bradley* the justices said that the suburbs of Detroit were not compelled to open up their schools to inner-city blacks and other minorities.

The quest for economic opportunity also tested society's commitment to equality policy. The Equal Employment Opportunity Commission, the body created by the 1964 act to counteract discrimination in employment, had two enforcement techniques at its disposal. First, the commission could wait for individuals to file complaints, which examiners would investigate and then attempt to resolve through negotiations. In its first seven years the EEOC received 10,000 complaints and compiled an immense backlog of cases. By 1976, 80,000 complaints a year were filed; processing time averaged two years for each case. Employers usually prevailed over employees. The EEOC lacked the power to issue cease-and-desist orders as well as the authority to sue until 1972.[21] The second enforcement technique took the burden off individual minorities and placed it on employers by requiring them to file plans that established goals and timetables for hiring and promoting blacks and women. These *affirmative-action* plans grew out of language in the 1964 Civil Rights Act. Federal agencies issued guidelines in 1968 pertaining to nondiscrimination for companies that did business with Washington. By the early 1970s agencies charged with civil rights enforcement also required large businesses, nonprofit institutions such as colleges, and all governments to write affirmative-action plans. Birmingham, Alabama, adopted an affirmative-action ordinance in 1973; in 1979 Arlington, Massachusetts, appointed an affirmative-action officer to supervise its employment plan, which projected a town workforce with 7 percent minorities and 42 percent women.

Affirmative action was controversial because it provoked confrontations between divergent outlooks and interests. Proponents argued that government was morally obligated to combat historic patterns of inequality and to break down structural barriers that blocked opportunities for blacks and women. This objective entailed putting pressure on employers to take positive steps toward eradicating discrimination. But the implementation of affirmative-action plans forced government and private organizations to rely on numerical criteria that tracked the progress of socially defined groups of people. Opponents cried foul. Such a policy, they said, contradicted the American tradition of upholding opportunity for individuals. By this reasoning, affirmative-action goals were *quotas* that unfairly rewarded minorities at the expense of non-minorities. The critics observed that the law prohibited intentional acts of discrimination against distinct individuals. To go beyond this position allowed government to engage in reverse discrimination and to ignore merit as a criterion for employment.

The Supreme Court responded to these allegations in *University of California Regents v. Bakke* (1978). Bakke was a white male who claimed that he had been denied admission to a state university medical school because its affirmative-action plan allotted a designated number of slots to minorities, some of whom possessed lower qualifications than the plaintiff. The court agreed that Bakke had been treated unjustly and ordered him admitted to the school, which was forbidden from using its two-track system of admissions, one for whites and another for minorities. But the divided court ruled that it was constitutionally permissible to take race into account regarding admission decisions. In subsequent rulings the court turned aside other challenges to affirmative action, including guidelines used by private employers and government to assist women in employment.

How effective was the government's nondiscrimination policy? Did it open up opportunities for the historic minorities and reduce inequality in America? The complexity of these issues prevents a simple answer. Appraising the success of equality policy depends in part on the definition of its goals, which is a controversial subject itself. If the objective of nondiscrimination policy was the eradication of government practices that condoned unequal treatment by private or public sources on the basis of color or sex, civil rights made considerable headway after 1964. Federal officials forced southern states to desegregate their schools and oversaw the enfranchisement of southern blacks, whose level of voter registration reached parity with whites in the 1970s. Most college-bound African Americans now go to racially integrated institutions. Government and large private institutions may not legally discriminate against blacks and women in hiring and compensation. Public and educational facilities must provide physical access and special programs for the handicapped.

Holding public office affords another measure of progress in civil rights. In the 1950s blacks held less than 1 percent of the seats in the U.S. state legislatures and women represented less than 5 percent of these bodies. Had each group claimed seats proportionate to their size in the population, they would have occupied ten times as many places. By the late 1980s blacks constituted 5 percent and women 15 percent of the membership of the state legislatures.[22] These figures do not reflect complete representational parity (and democratic theory does not insist on it), but they do denote substantial gains. Although these increases are not wholly attributable to efforts of government, Federal power was critical in enhancing the electoral influence of southern blacks. Not only did federal courts uphold administrative interventions to guarantee the right to vote, but judges expanded the meaning of disfranchisement to include the dilution of black votes through such devices as redistricting, expanding municipalities by annexation, and creating multimember districts. The Justice Department used this authority to disallow local laws that reduced the electoral effect of black votes.[23] Federal officials came close to equating electoral fairness with the ability to elect minorities in proportion to their ratio among the community's population.

Civil rights policy also can be assessed by a long-run perspective on American politics. Between 1877 and the 1950s the national government rarely interfered with state treatment of minorities. The politics of the 1960s and 1970s, however, created new attitudes about subgroups of the population and empowered Washington and most states to combat overt manifestations of discrimination against them. Nondiscrimination guidelines were attached to most Federal activities, such as issuing contracts, releasing grants-in-aid to other governments and private institutions, and hiring its staff. Private employers were instructed to hire and fire without reference to color or gender. Although these standards may appear to be simply restatements of a traditional American credo concerning individual opportunity, in fact they substantially expanded the mission of government and conveyed new power to public authorities. Because the civil rights movement resulted in numerous national guidelines that conditioned the activities of the states, nondiscrimination policy has helped to shift the balance of power in the federal system toward Washington.

Despite the new civil rights law, however, full equality remains elusive for the historic minorities. Although some African Americans have enjoyed success in highly visible pursuits, such as sports and entertainment, and although a small black middle class has emerged, the fact remains that African Americans have not been fully integrated into the mainstream of the economy. In 1990 the income of African Americans averaged 63 percent of white earnings, a ratio that had not changed materially in forty years. The average net worth of white households was ten times greater than the average among black households. Blacks remained underrepresented in the professions and in the upper ranks of corporate management. They were twice as likely to be unemployed as whites throughout the postwar era and into the twenty-first century. The concentration of African Americans in the cores of America's large cities, where substandard housing is the norm, testifies to the persistence of de facto segregation and blocked economic opportunity. Many black youngsters live in female-headed households where poverty is the rule and peddling dope a common route of upward mobility. The social pathology of impoverished urban cores and backwater rural hamlets helps to explain why homicide is the leading cause of death for young black males.[24]

Nor have women achieved parity with men. They receive lower incomes, hold proportionately fewer executive positions, and experience higher rates of poverty than do males. The gender gap in the workplace persisted through the 1980s despite state and Federal nondiscrimination guidelines. Some critics argued that this slow progress resulted from lax enforcement of the law, which they attribute in part to EEOC's limited authority. Others maintained that the agency gave priority to complaints filed by blacks, and they have faulted the Justice Department for failure to initiate suits against organizations manifesting recurrent patterns of employment discrimination. The Equal Pay Act failed to address the critical issue of structural segregation in the workplace, which channeled females into low-paying jobs. Income disparity between the sexes will persist, critics predict, until government requires employers to base compensation on comparable worth.[25] Resolving this debate remains one of the perplexing challenges on the civil rights agenda.

Ensuring equality has been one of the most controversial policy arenas in modern governance, because the issues involved confront cultural norms and social relations. Not only do these matters push emotional hot buttons, but the effort to increase social equality has expanded the power of government, an issue of growing concern to conservatives.

8

⁓

Paying for Modern Government

MODERN AMERICANS GRUMBLE when they must add a dime or more sales tax to the cost of a doughnut and a cup of coffee. The approach of April 15, when income tax reports are due, can bring on apprehensions. Life in the Cleveland era had its annoyances too, but paying taxes was not one of them for most people. The average worker paid no direct levies to the government. The explanation for this astonishing situation lies in the way government used to raise its revenue. In the late 1800s the public sector levied two principal taxes—one on property and the other on imported goods. Of the two, only the property tax was levied directly on individuals and then principally on the owners of real estate. But most Americans in 1900 did not own a home or land. Roughly two-thirds of householders in the cities, where most workers lived, were renters. And a third of all farmers were tenants working and living on land they did not own. Property taxes applied to business property too, but only a small fraction of the workforce owned commercial real estate and most who did were also homeowners. Simple arithmetic shows that only a minority of Americans paid property taxes, the largest levy in the republican era.

Custom duties on imports were the federal government's main moneymaker in the nineteenth century. Importers paid these tariffs and passed their cost on to retailers and consumers indirectly in the form of higher prices of imported goods and of articles manufactured in the United States with imported materials. Tariffs also may have boosted the price of goods produced by Americans whose industries received tariff protection. No one knows how much extra customs cost the average worker, but the burden was negligible. Washington also placed excise charges on American distilled liquor and homegrown tobacco. People who neither drank nor smoked escaped these "sin" taxes. They did, however, have to buy stamps to use the mail, although these expenses are called fees, not taxes. Homeowners might be charged for water and sewer service. Businesses and some occupations paid fees for the right to ply their trades. The average tax burden in 1900 worked out to about $900 a year per family, based on 1980 dollars. But most Americans at this time never encountered the tax collector.

A revolution in tax policy during the twentieth century transformed the public accounts of Grover Cleveland's day. Over the subsequent decades policy makers adopted new ways of raising revenue and spread taxation across the ranks of the workforce. Now most full-time workers pay not one but four direct taxes. Their cost to the average family in 1980 was $4,400, or about 23 percent of the family's income. Two misconceptions about this tax revolution exist. One popular notion holds that policy makers first adopted new programs and then sought ways to pay for them. This sequence of events has occurred, but the reverse was also true, especially after 1945. Increased flows of revenue have made it easier for lawmakers to vote new spending measures. A second misconception is that lawmakers are forever increasing taxes. This presumption assumes that politicians think and act quite differently than their constituents when it comes to taxation. American citizens have a long standing aversion to taxation, especially new ones. But so do politicians, and in the modern era they have repeatedly cut some of them. Yet the costs of government continued to rise over the decades. Given this paradox, how did policy makers pay for the claimant polity?

A cardinal tenet of classical American ideology was the personal right to own property. Taxation threatened this liberty, however, because government's authority to collect revenue harbored the power to take an individual's property. Government's capacity to operate effectively, however, hinged on its ability to raise revenue. Without this power officials could not fulfill their other responsibilities, including the protection of property. Ultimately this latter function depended on government's ability to pay police, soldiers, and judges. In other words, some revenue was necessary for the preservation of the public good, but too much was illegitimate expropriation of an individual's property. The way to strike a proper balance was to observe moderation and frugality in managing government's accounts. Taxation in excess of public necessity was "legalized larceny" to Calvin Coolidge's way of thinking, and he was reiterating an old American belief.[1] Part of the reasoning behind this low-tax mentality was the suspicion that politicians were habitually tempted to misuse public money. The numerous restrictions that have been placed in state constitutions concerning public finance flowed from this conviction.

Changes in the transition era (1880s–1920) eroded the foundation of republican-era finances. On one hand, new public tasks increased the costs of government; on the other, critics charged that industrialization had outdated the old methods of raising revenue. Most complaints centered on the property tax, whose burden, detractors said, fell principally on middle-class homeowners in the cities and landowning farmers. Corporations escaped much of their obligation largely through artful tax dodging. Many urban workers did not own real estate and thus were not liable for property taxes even though they used city services. Assessment practices, whereby property was valued for taxation, were riddled with inequities. Most assessment was done by locally elected officials, who faced community pressure to keep valuations low. Wide variations in assessments between towns resulted, causing endless difficulties for state governments in collecting their share of the property tax.

Behind these complaints lay a fundamental change in the creation of wealth. Industrialization shifted the source of income away from agriculture toward the wages and salaries of employees, the profits of business, and financial investments. This transformation, coupled with the technical problems of administering the property tax, generated campaigns in the transition era to reform taxation. One line of attack was to remove the inequalities in assessments. A second thrust sought to broaden the tax base. One way to do this was to tax corporations more. This sentiment lay behind Wisconsin's income tax law of 1911, the nation's first modern (i.e., continuous) levy on individual earnings.[2] The act exempted most farmers and made manufacturers carry the heaviest burden. Few states went as far as Wisconsin in lightening the tax burden of rural residents, but most increased levies on businesses in various ways during the Progressive Era.

Washington's finances came under attack too. Tariffs, a perennial political football, lost their ability to finance the major portion of Washington's budget, especially after the Spanish-American War (1898). Congress had enacted a modest tax on personal income in 1894, but it did not survive Supreme Court review (*Pollock v. Farmers' Loan and Trust Co.*, 1894). Lawmakers looked toward excise taxes (a sort of sales tax), principally on alcohol, to make up short-falls in revenue. But neither excises nor customs satisfied reformers' desire for a fairer apportionment of federal taxes. They recommended a graduated rate structure that taxed individuals in accordance with their ability to pay. Theodore Roosevelt endorsed this idea during his second term, arguing that it would redistribute the "burden of supporting the Government more equitably than at present." Prodded by advocates of income taxation from the South and West, Congress inched toward this objective in 1909 by approving the Sixteenth Amendment to the Constitution, which authorized Washington to levy taxes on earnings. Ratification of the amendment coincided with Woodrow Wilson's arrival in the White House in 1913. The new president saw a tax on individual income as a substitute for revenues lost from custom duties, which Wilson had promised to reduce. Congress accepted this proposal by adopting a modest tax on earnings (1913). Less than 1 percent of the workforce was obligated to pay this initial federal income tax. The law's gently progressive rate scale rose to 7 percent on incomes that today qualify a person as a multimillionaire.

The timing of constitutional authority for income taxes was propitious in view of the country's entrance into the Great War. Modern wars not only have an avaricious appetite for money, but they also undermine normal reservations about raising taxes, as defense becomes the country's dominant concern. Congress had experimented with an income tax during the Civil War, and it turned to this revenue option again in 1917, when lawmakers markedly increased income taxes. By reducing the amount of earnings exempted from taxation, the new law netted a tenfold gain in workers obligated to pay. Millionaires saw the proportion of their incomes over one million dollars subject to taxation (the marginal rate) leap to 77 percent, prompting critics to decry the levy as confiscatory. But Congress raised rates again the next year and elevated the excess profits tax on corporations that reaped windfalls from war-related business. As Congress was hammering out these provisions the states were ratifying the Prohibition Amendment, which dried up revenues from taxes on the sale of liquor.

These changes in U.S. revenue policy were an aberration caused by World War I. When hostilities ended and the doughboys returned from Europe, demands arose to restore the prewar revenue regime. The history textbooks have portrayed the 1920s as a time when the Republicans clamored to slash taxes, especially on the rich. Taxes were cut in the 1920s, but not just for the wealthy and not just by Republicans. The GOP had plenty of help from Democrats, who inserted into their 1928 national platform the old axiom that the taxing function of government "requires vigilant scrutiny . . . to prevent favoritism and oppression." The financial surpluses that piled up in the Treasury whetted appetites for tax reduction among most members of Congress, which lowered rates in stages during the decade. But the income tax was not returned to its prewar level. The highest marginal rate, for instance, dropped to 24 percent of earnings over $200,000 by 1929. War had left an indelible mark on federal accounts.

The Great Depression turned the bullishness of the 1920s into the financial crisis of the 1930s. The economic rupture cut federal receipts by half between 1929 and 1932. With personal income taxes down even more, Washington ran a deficit every year of the Depression. Wedded to traditional ideas about public finance, President Hoover responded to these unbalanced budgets (in which expenditures exceeded revenues during the fiscal year) with a recommendation to increase taxes. Congress concurred and raised rates on middle- and upper-income individuals and on corporations in 1932 in an effort to cover the budgetary shortfall. It was the most extensive revision of the income tax during the Depression, but it failed to eliminate the deficit because the shrinkage of incomes exceeded the revenue gains from the new levies. Resigned to the reality of a stalled economy, New Dealers did not push for further rate increases, with one major exception. Roosevelt's plan to "soak the rich" got enough congressional backing to boost income taxes on the wealthy and corporations briefly during the mid-thirties. The chief fiscal legacy of the New Deal, however, lay in three other areas: a new attitude toward unbalanced budgets, a funding scheme for old-age pensions under Social Security, and expansion of federal aid to state and local governments. Although not taxes in the usual sense, all three developments helped to fund the claimant polity.

The Depression struck a devastating blow to state and local governments. Although their receipts dropped less precipitously than did national revenue, state and local officials faced constraints on their fiscal options that Congress avoided. Unemployed workers and marketless farmers paid no federal income taxes, yet they still owed local and state property taxes if they owned real estate. Default on these obligations could summon the sheriff to auction off a home or farm to satisfy an unpaid bill. This possibility was the dread of property owners in the early 1930s and a dilemma for local government. The solvency of local accounts was inextricably tied to the fate of the property tax. City and county officials lacked authority to impose alternative taxes, a restriction that was a legacy of the republican era's limitation on public finance. At the state levels lawmakers had little choice other than to adopt new taxes if they wished to combat the ravages of the Depression, because unlike the U.S. Constitution their own charters prohibited unrestricted borrowing and unbalanced budgets.

While New Dealers concentrated on formulating spending and borrowing programs, state lawmakers battled over proposals for new taxes. Despite widespread calls for public "economy" during the Depression, state legislators authored a series of tax innovations unmatched in their history. The search for new revenues began in 1931, peaked in 1933, and continued throughout the decade. Beginning with Mississippi in 1932, half of the states adopted a general sales tax. A third of the states enacted income taxes, usually on both individuals and businesses. The repeal of Prohibition (1933) was a financial windfall for the states, which quickly moved either to tax liquor sales or to monopolize its retailing. Existing levies were increased, particularly the tax on gasoline sales. States hesitant to tap one or more of these big three depression taxes (on alcohol, general sales, and incomes) opted for a grab bag of minor revenue raisers. Florida followed this path, placing new charges on tangible personal property, inheritances of the wealthy, documents, stocks, utilities, and horseracing in 1931 alone. And by elevating its gasoline tax to the highest in the nation (seven cents a gallon), lawmakers in the Sunshine State passed much of its costs on to vacationing "snowbirds" from the North.[3]

The New Deal deserves credit for some of this legislation. Federal grants to state and local governments usually required a contribution from recipient authorities, especially after 1934. Aid to Dependent Children grants (later AFDC), for example, were conditional on state payment of two-thirds of the minimum stipend for each beneficiary. Loans and grants for public works projects carried contributory stipulations. New Dealers urged state officials to create public authorities as a way to fund some of these projects. Public authorities originated before the 1930s but they took on added significance in the Depression. Created to manage the construction of a particular project, these special-purpose bodies were empowered to borrow money and to collect fees or tolls to repay the debt. The device had two appeals. First, the authorization of user charges to finance a specific improvement allowed lawmakers to avoid increasing general taxes. And second, public authorities offered a legal maneuver to outflank constitutional restrictions on borrowing by state government. The creation of the Triborough Bridge Authority (1934) in New York City grew out of both considerations. By floating bonds, the Triborough Authority generated the seed money necessary to snare Federal dollars. Three years later, with the boroughs of the Bronx, Manhattan, and Queens linked by a set of bridges, motorists began handing their nickels and dimes to Triborough toll collectors.[4]

Raising money in the states to aid the jobless during the depths of the Depression proved especially difficult, as Federal officials discovered in Illinois. With its large industrial workforce in Chicago and numerous smaller cities, the Prairie State faced massive urban unemployment. Nonetheless, efforts to provide relief funds to the jobless encountered fierce partisan and regional opposition at the state capitol. A "chaotic and inefficient" revenue system inherited from the nineteenth century limited tax options in the state.[5] The state's courts reinforced these constraints on revenue policy by raising various legal objections to new tax ideas. Washington had financed most of Illinois's relief bill in 1933. Then Harry Hopkins, Roosevelt's director of the Federal Emergency Relief Administration, insisted that the Prairie state carry its share of the load. Lawmakers came up with a temporary plan that borrowed against future gasoline tax receipts. This wasn't good enough for Hopkins, who renewed his threat to cut off Federal aid unless the legislature found a more reliable source of funds. Eventually Illinois legislators settled on the sales tax, first on a temporary basis and later permanently, to fund their part of the welfare bill.[6] Proposals to tax consumer purchases provoked considerable political resistance in Illinois and elsewhere during the Depression decade. Sales taxes took a proportionately larger bite out of modest incomes than out of the incomes of the well-to-do, who devoted less of their income to necessities than did people with smaller budgets.

In view of the battles over taxation across the country, the surprise is that the states doubled their revenues during the 1930s. Florida and New York each kept pace with the national average. Illinois quadrupled its tax collections. The states, not the local or the federal governments, recorded the greatest volume of tax actions during the decade. Before the Depression the states collected a fifth of all dollars taken in by subnational government. By 1940 the states accounted for nearly one-half of all state and local subnational receipts. Together the Depression and the New Deal had stimulated a giant step toward state fiscal centralization.

Whereas the Depression loosened the foundations of the nation's traditional financial arrangement, World War II demolished it. The federal government's expenditures dramatize the magnitude of the war's fiscal impact. In its most generous year (1939) the New Deal spent $9 billion. Six years later, during the last phase of the war, Washington laid out $100 billion. Borrowing paid for half of the immediate costs of war, while the remainder was financed by the pay-as-you-go method, meaning current tax collections. Where did national officials find such huge sums? They looked at a vast untapped revenue source—individual workers, the vast majority of whom had paid no federal taxes in the Depression years. Wartime changes in the revenue laws, especially the act of 1942, put the paychecks of two-thirds of the workforce within reach of income taxation. Of the $50 billion of revenue the U.S. Treasury collected in 1945, $18 billion came from levies on the earnings of individuals. Corporations, whose income taxes were also raised, accounted for another $16 billion.

The Treasury also got its hands on this money more quickly. Before the Current Payment Tax Act of 1943, people paid their income tax in quarterly installments in the calendar year *after* receiving their earnings. The system adopted in 1943 required employers to withhold taxes from employees and forward the money promptly to the Internal Revenue Service. These piecemeal deductions from each paycheck reduced the sting of the new taxes on the average worker. Employees never saw this money, and employers handled most of the paperwork connected with it. Withholding not only accelerated tax collections, but also cut down on cheating and tax defaults. To reduce the shock on the wealthy, who still owed the tax on their 1942 earnings in 1943, Congress simply erased three-quarters of their old tax bill. Offsetting this windfall was the imposition of a 94 percent tax rate on incomes of $200,000 or more. These wartime changes catapulted the federal tax on personal income to first place among revenue raisers in the United States. Three of every four tax dollars nationwide flowed toward Washington in 1944. Pearl Harbor and Hitler's madness had produced what peacetime politics had not—a mass-based federal income tax. War had promoted Uncle Sam to the nation's chief tax collector.

Tax policy after 1945 evolved along paths blazed during the Depression and the war. Three aspects of this history stand out. First, the amount of public revenue increased substantially. Adjusted for inflation, public receipts increased over two and a half times during the Depression and war decades and nearly tripled in the next thirty years. Government collected $204 per person in 1927, $548 in 1950, and $1,540 in 1980 (see table 8.1). Second, the inversion of fiscal rankings among governments that the war had produced became permanent, as Washington continued to raise more tax dollars than the states and localities. The acceleration of state revenue collections in the 1970s and 1980s trimmed the national percentage somewhat but not enough to upset the modern pattern. City, town, and county governments never regained their former preeminence in U.S. public finance. Locally derived funds continued to support important public services such as schools and police, but these moneys shrank to one-sixth of all public sector dollars by 1980 (see table 8.1).

The third tendency in postwar finances was the growing importance of the new taxes. In 1902 the tax on property raised forty-two cents of every public dollar. Customs, postal receipts, license fees, and local utility charges brought in most remaining revenues (see "all other" in table 8.2). The adoption of new tax types after 1911 and subsequent increases in their rates dethroned the property tax from its former primacy. In 1980 property taxes had shrunk to 7 percent of all public revenue. The big four modern taxes—on personal income, corporate income, general sales, and payrolls to fund insurance trusts such as Social Security—bankrolled the claimant polity. None of the big four existed in 1902. Personal income taxes and insurance trusts alone generated half of all public dollars by 1980, and their share inched up higher during the next ten years.

These details may seem superfluous, since we must pay taxes whatever their shape or form. Yet the specifics are important, because the design of each tax type, coupled with its linkage to specific public functions, played an instrumental role in the growth of government. Money became the lifeblood of the claimant polity. Budgets controlled its heartbeat, which pumped massive revenue flows through the system, allowing it to function. As much as any other characteristic, the new fiscal system distinguishes modern governance from past political history. The revenue arrangement of the republican polity was incapable of sustaining modern government.

Popular acceptance of government's tax policy had a lot to do with the way policy makers built the new revenue regime. An important consideration in writing new laws was whether a minority or a majority of the population would bear the costs of government. Lawmakers also had to decide how shares of taxation would be distributed among the upper-, middle-, and lower-income segments of the workforce, and between employees and businesses. Some forms

Table 8.1. Revenue Amount, Governmental Source, and Federal Grants, 1902–1990

	1902	1927	1938	1950	1967	1980	1990
Total revenue per person (1958 $)	86	204	306	548	1,082	1,540	1,869
Governmental Source (percent of total)							
U.S.	38	38	41	65	64	61	56
State	9	12	26	19	18	22	25
Local	53	50	32	16	18	16	19
Federal grants							
Amount (billions)	.007	.1	.76	2.4	15.0	94.6	136.9
Percent state-local own general revenue	.8	1.6	9.5	13.5	19.8	27.1	19.0
Federal debt							
Percent total debt	36	55	66	91	74	73	79
Percent GNP	5	19	44	90	41	34	59

Sources: U.S. Bureau of the Census, *Historical Statistics on Governmental Finances and Employment* (Washington, D.C., 1985), vol. 6 of 1982 Census of Governments, tables 10–14; updated with U.S. Bureau of the Census, *Statistical Abstract of the United States: 1993* (Washington, D.C., 1993), various tables; and author calculations based on U.S. Bureau of the Census, *Historical Statistics of the United States* (Washington, D.C., 1975), series F1, F4.

Table 8.2. Revenue Types, 1902–1990 (Percent of Total Revenue)

	1902	1927	1938	1950	1967	1980	1990
Property tax	42	39	25	11	10	7	8
Sales and gross receipt taxes	3	13	20	19	14	12	11
Personal income tax	0	8	8	25	27	31	28
Business income tax	0	11	9	17	14	7	6
Insurance trusts	0	2	9	8	15	21	24
All other (including customs)	55	27	29	20	20	22	23

Sources: U.S. Bureau of the Census, *Historical Statistics on Governmental Finances and Employment* (Washington, D.C., 1985), vol. 6 of 1982 Census of Governments, table 1; updated with U.S. Bureau of the Census, *Statistical Abstract of the United States: 1992* (Washington, D.C., 1993), table 450.

of taxation raise money less painfully than others. Revenue techniques that reaped profits from a robust economy, for example, are said to be dynamic in nature. Such taxes have political advantages, compared to a levy that is unresponsive to business conditions, such as the property tax. Popular appraisal of the fairness of a tax is also an influential factor in tax politics. Federalism adds an element of complexity to these calculations, because each level of government put together a different mix of tax types (which also varies *between* states). The federal government never levied property taxes, for example, but it monopolized tariffs, whereas state governments developed various tax combinations in which sales taxes on consumer purchases became primary revenue instruments. But the best tax strategy was a revenue plan that did not appear to be a tax at all.

On this score national lawmakers had a decided advantage over state and local officials. Some of Washington's special leverage resulted from the policy responsibilities assigned to each government. An axiom of tax politics illuminates this point: the more that citizens regard a public task as worthwhile, the easier it is for politicians to raise funds to pay for it. A strong defense and Social Security both won a stamp of popular approval in the claimant era. Both activities were managed solely by federal officials, and both relied on lucrative revenue sources that only Washington possessed. National security functions were funded by the national income tax, which had especially dynamic characteristics and much higher rates than state incomes taxes. Social Security had its own special income stream. These two revenue forms increased from 8.4 percent of all public revenue in 1940 to 43 percent in 1980. In contrast to this extraordinary increase, local government administered a potpourri of programs, some of which enjoyed less widespread public support and derived most of their funding from the property tax. Local responsibilities such as schools, police, and welfare thus were heavily dependent upon an inflexible tax, which became a smaller portion of the total revenue pool over the decades. Federalism, in other words, established boundaries and channels that bore upon the evolution of spending and taxing policy in the United States. This structural effect was not neutral but advantaged policy functions controlled by the central government. The expansion of the public sector was facilitated by national policy makers marrying the most lucrative taxes to the most popular policy objectives.

Two seemingly contradictory questions are central to understanding how the claimant polity paid for the growth of government after 1945. First, why didn't Congress reduce taxes after World War II to the extent it had following the First World War? And second, how did the federal government reap its remarkable revenue gains in the postwar era despite repeated tax cuts? Answers to these questions illuminate how politics, popular perceptions, and unanticipated events shaped American tax policy.

Amid choruses of "bring the boys home" after the surrender of Japan, the Truman administration slashed the armed forces to an eighth of their wartime strength by 1947. Demobilization of the military bolstered the case for termination of wartime tax levels. Republicans led this chant, which contributed to their victories in the 1946 congressional elections. Buoyed by their enlarged power base, the GOP passed two tax-reduction bills in 1947. Truman vetoed both. And he vetoed a third in 1948, only this time a sufficient number of Democrats joined Republicans to override the president. But the man from Missouri was a pugnacious politician. He defied the predictions of the press to score an upset victory in the 1948 presidential election, then asked Congress to raise taxes. Rebuffed in 1949, Truman got his revenue bill in 1950, shortly after the outbreak of the Korean War.

Why did Truman resist demands for tax reduction? The president offered a four-point defense of his stand. Reducing revenues, he said, would jeopardize the goal of balancing the budget and would retard the reduction of the national debt, which had ballooned during the war. Both arguments drew on orthodox thinking about public finance. Picking up on a Democratic charge that the Republican tax proposals meant "relief for the greedy, not the needy," the president denounced the GOP bills as unfair. Finally, Truman argued that it was unreasonable to cut taxes in prosperous times.[7] Here, the president zeroed in on an indisputable economic fact: Americans were richer. In 1936 they averaged $518 in after-tax income. In 1947 their take-home pay was $1,178. Inflation made the gain appear larger than its real increase in terms of purchasing power, but appearances count, especially in politics. Even with higher tax rates, however, Americans had more money to spend in 1947 than before the war. Because wartime price controls had ended and citizens rushed to buy consumer goods that became available, administration economists saw taxation as a way to dampen inflation.

Truman also had an ambitious agenda, which became clearer during his second term (1949–1953). His decision to get tough with the Soviets, who were seen as ruthless communist adventurers on the world scene, required a large military capability. Gutting federal revenues could thwart a new defense buildup. Truman's Fair Deal proposed an extension of New Deal social and economic programs at home. Congress did not grant the president much on his domestic agenda, but funding for ongoing federal programs itself was expensive. Spending for veterans and agriculture at the start of Truman's second administration alone equaled the entire federal budget (in current dollars) in the most generous year of New Deal expenditures.

Truman's battle with tax cutters was a turning point in the country's fiscal history. The president told the nation that Washington's determination to contain Moscow's perceived mischief around the world was going to cost unprecedented sums for peacetime. This possibility soon became reality, although the decisive influence on tax policy making did not come from the Truman White House but from abroad. In 1950 the North Koreans invaded the southern zone of the Korean peninsula, which had been partitioned into two zones at the end of World War II. Truman responded to this aggression with U.S. military intervention under the guise of the United Nations. Federal tax collections doubled as a result of the three years of U.S. participation in the Korean War. Once again, war had propelled taxation upward.

Congress's preferred course of action, however, was to lower taxes. Seven of the eight major federal tax laws enacted between 1948 and 1976 reduced the rate of federal income taxes.[8] Yet, the flow of revenue into the Treasury increased. The largest source of its funds was the tax on individual incomes, which reaped $16 billion in 1946 and $244 billion in 1980. How could Washington simultaneously cut taxes and collect more revenue? In the first place, the reductions were more cosmetic than substantial and did not approach the magnitude of the Reagan tax cut of 1981. Members of Congress liked to brag at campaign time about trimming back on taxes but their reductions never came close to returning personal income taxes to pre–World War II levels. The rate of taxation on the lowest earnings subjected to federal taxes in the 1930s was 4 percent; in 1980 it was 14 percent. The richest Americans saw their nominal (their theoretical although not necessarily their actual) tax obligation decline after World War II but not to the levels maintained in the 1920s and 1930s. Dwight Eisenhower, Truman's Republican successor in the White House, acquiesced in this postwar tax design. His election hastened the end of the Korean War, which brought a rollback of the 1950–1952 tax hikes. But Ike went no further. Committed to a balanced budget, a strong defense, and fiscal control of price increases (inflation), Eisenhower opposed further tax reduction.[9] Although he was lambasted by liberals for resisting new spending programs, Ike was hardly a fiscal conservative in the mold of Republicans during the 1920s.

Births, affluence, inflation, and brackets. These four terms symbolize the dynamics behind the postwar fiscal magic whereby the Treasury reaped windfall benefits from demographic and economic trends. Births are the first of these expansionary factors. The baby boom was a major reason for the postwar growth of the workforce, which increased 80 percent between 1946 and 1980. More Americans at work meant more incomes subjected to federal taxation. Half of the postwar gain in individual tax returns occurred in the 1970s, a decade when baby boomers flooded the job market. Affluence compounded the effect of increased employment. Both young workers and their parents profited from the "economic miracle" of the postwar period, when average personal income doubled in real (purchasing power) terms. Government siphoned off some of this economic gain, because fatter paychecks elevated individuals into categories (brackets) with higher rates of taxation.

The federal income tax code was designed so that the rate of taxation increased in relation to larger amounts of income. The law contained sixteen such rate steps (tax brackets) in 1980. This proportionate increase in rates reflected a progressive principle of taxation whereby the rich paid a proportionately greater share of their earnings to government than did the poor. Numerous exemptions of income from taxation reduced the actual effect of these nominal rates. Yet sufficient upward ratcheting remained, even with periodic tax cuts, to capture additional tax revenues as incomes rose. The beauty of the arrangement hinged on continuing economic growth. The rise in real dollars provided Americans with more after-tax income than in former years even though government took comparatively bigger bites from their paychecks.

Inflation also pushed people into higher tax categories. Much of the jump in wages and salaries after World War II occurred in response to increases in prices, which rose three and a half times (1948–1980) and accelerated during the 1970s. But federal tax law did not distinguish between earnings that grew because of real economic growth, an individual's own achievement in the marketplace, or the inflation of prices and wages. The latter dynamic caused bracket "creep," whereby inflation thrust income earners into higher tax brackets. In effect, inflation permitted Congress to increase the average rate of taxation without actually voting for it.

Congress relinquished this silent tax by indexing income brackets to the cost of living in 1981 (effective in 1985). The Tax Simplification Act of 1986 went a step further by replacing the sixteen brackets of 1980 with three basic categories.[10] Both actions robbed national policy makers of much of their ability to capitalize on affluence and inflation. Between World War II and the Reagan administration, national officials inherited a tax machine that worked on automatic pilot. As long as the economy and the workforce grew and prices increased, the federal government cashed in on the dynamics of socioeconomic change. But when stripped of its fiscal magic by law or a sluggish economy, Congress faced unpleasant choices. It was forced to either vote higher taxes to pay for the costs of claimant era policy, cut benefits, or borrow more.

Despite its dynamic design, the federal income tax was not the fastest-growing levy in postwar America. This honor went to FICA (Federal Insurance Contribution Act), the Social Security tax. From a modest $1.2 billion in 1946, FICA contributions grew to $164 billion by 1980, an increase that elevated the Social Security tax to the second-biggest levy in the country. It was also the nation's most regressive tax. A person's Social Security tax (FICA) is calculated by taking a fixed percentage (the same rate for everybody) of the individual's earnings, up to a maximum amount. The earnings on which the rate applies is called the wage base; income above this figure incurs no additional FICA tax. Together the single rate and the cap on wages subject to the tax made FICA doubly regressive. Low-income workers paid proportionately more of their earnings to Social Security, therefore, than did workers whose income exceeded the wage base. People who live off investments pay no Social Security tax, which applies only to wages, salaries, and earnings from self-employment. It is important to remember that employers pay a Social Security tax equal to each of their worker's FICA obligation; self-employed individuals pay both parts themselves.

When Social Security collections began in 1937 the wage base was $3,000 and the tax rate on earnings was 1 percent. Both variables remained unchanged for twelve years, so that the maximum tax anyone paid through 1949 was $30 (one percent of $3,000). Such easy terms made Social Security a bargain during its formative years. The maximum tax rose to $144 a year in 1960 and to $374 in 1974, higher than before but still cheap by most standards. Then Social Security's real bill came due. The maximum obligation jumped to $1,587 by the time Ronald Reagan won the presidency. In the thirty years since 1950 the tax that the average income earner paid had increased forty-five times. During Reagan's stay in the White House (1981–1989) both the maximum and the average Social Security tax doubled. (See chapter 11 for the story since 1990.)

This rapid acceleration in FICA was the legacy of decisions made early in the life of the program. On one hand, Congress expanded benefits; on the other, it cut back on the means to pay for them. The 1935 act authorized a "tax" on workers' income that was scheduled by law to rise to 3 percent of the wage base by 1949. The law also placed a matching "excise tax" on employers, who were required to withhold the tax on workers from their wages. Amendments to the Social Security Act in 1939, however, delayed the tax increase, a step that Congress repeated on later occasions. Policy makers realized that early recipients would have paid little of their Social Security through payroll taxes. In the early days of the system its administrators presumed that Congress would draw on general revenues (in the Treasury's general fund) to finance the benefits of early recipients, who had invested a minimal amount in the system.[11] Congress reneged on the deal and repealed the authorization to tap the general revenues for the OASI program in 1950. This action left the special payroll taxes as Social Security's sole source of funding.

Because Congress delayed increases in scheduled (or recommended) payroll taxes, prohibited the use of general revenues to make up for the anticipated deficiency, and repeatedly liberalized benefits, Social Security's unfunded obligations grew with the passage of time. To meet these costs the payroll tax was revised upward fourteen times between 1950 and 1981. Yet costs continued to outstrip revenues, especially in the 1970s when wage growth slowed. Even a massive bailout action in 1977, the largest tax increase in peacetime to that date, failed to remedy the anticipated deficit. Four years later President Reagan repeated warnings about Social Security's "actuarial imbalance." In 1983 Congress increased FICA taxes again and trimmed back on benefits as well.[12]

Given Congress's usual aversion to raising taxes, what explains the repeated increases in FICA? The key to the answer lies in the program's popularity, which is largely attributable to its financing scheme. For several generations most workers did not consider their FICA payments a tax. This erroneous perception was the product of decisions made by Congress, the Supreme Court, and Social Security administrators. The original Social Security statute (1935) authorized the payment of old-age "benefits" in an early section of the law (Title 2) and levied a payroll "tax" in a separate section (Title 8). This artful legislative drafting resulted from sponsors' apprehension that an explicit link between a special benefit and an earmarked tax might fail a test of constitutionality. The Supreme Court rose to this bait and upheld old-age benefit payments in 1937 (*Helvering v. Davis*). In the split five-to-four decision, the court claimed the tax provisions of Title 8 were unrelated to the spending authorization of Title 2, which itself was a permissible use of federal power. Such a segmented reading of the act was contrary to the general understanding among policy makers in 1935.[13]

Once the constitutional hurdle regarding financing was crossed, Social Security bureaucrats moved to tie the knot between funding and benefits. Rallying supporters in and out of Congress behind a statutory revision in 1939, they succeeded in renaming the Social Security tax a "contribution" (the Federal Insurance Contribution Act).[14] The 1939 amendments relabeled the old-age benefit program an "insurance" plan and created a trust fund supplied with FICA moneys to finance it. These changes substantially altered the original understanding of how Social Security would work. On one hand, the new design delayed the increase in taxes necessary to cover actuarial estimates of anticipated benefits payable in the future. On the other hand, the fiction was introduced that individuals built up a personal annuity through premiums paid into a trust account. These revisions, along with the new terminology and deceptive publicity from the Social Security Administration, nurtured the idea that Social Security contributions were not taxes in the usual sense of the word.[15] Semantic footwork obscured the reality of Social Security financial design. Just as a rose by any other name is still a rose, so any claim government makes on the earnings of an individual is a tax, whatever it might be called. A person's willful failure to pay this "contribution" can result in loss of assets, a stiff fine, and five or more years in jail—for tax evasion.

In addition to the linguistic ruse about FICA contributions, Social Security's popularity also rested on keeping its tax rate low. But repeated increases in benefits and conversion to a pay-as-you-go arrangement (taxes on the earnings of currently employed workers funded the benefits of retirees) strapped the program's solvency. Instead of becoming a fully funded pension system, Social Security accumulated a large unfunded debt (i.e., financial reserves totaling less than promised future benefits), whose cost was mainly passed on to current workers. Revision of Social Security's original plan authorized an intergenerational transfer of costs (from retirees to people currently in the workforce) and removed a critical constraint on the program's growth. The elderly and near-retirees could press for increased benefits knowing that the costs would be minimal to them. The redesign of Social Security institutionalized inducements for expanding the program and its costs.

Federal grants-in-aid became an important method of paying for the claimant polity. From Washington's perspective, grants represented expenditures, not taxes, while state and local governments counted these dollars as revenues. In some instances federal funds substituted for revenues that subnational governments might have raised themselves. But grants also stimulated additional state taxation, because most federal aid programs require a financial contribution from the recipient government. Whatever way these accounts are reckoned, intergovernmental transfers forged new fiscal linkages across the levels of the federal system.

In 1887 Grover Cleveland signed the Agricultural Experiment Station Act (Hatch Act), which was the first permanent federal cash grant program to state governments. The law allotted $15,000 a year to each state "to conduct original researches" in agriculture, carried out by an experiment station under the supervision of the state's agricultural college. Seventeen states already operated a station, and the remainder authorized research organizations soon after the passage of the act. Grant amounts were increased in 1906 and again in 1925, when Congress authorized stations to investigate a broader range of questions, such as rural living habits and the economics of farming. Ten years later Congress enlarged the research stipend again but this time required states to match the new increment and distributed the new moneys according to a formula that favored rural states. Washington enriched the research purse several times more after World War II, expanded its use to include the construction of research facilities and the investigation of all aspects of marketing (including the education of consumers to stimulate greater consumption of agricultural products), and gave the secretary of agriculture greater discretion in distributing research funds. By 1981 Washington's support of experiment stations had climbed to $290 million a year. Even researchers in the urbanized District of Columbia got a cut of these funds.

The Hatch Act established a precedent for national policy makers, who enacted hundreds of intergovernmental subsidies as the twentieth century unfolded. Five hundred and thirty-nine grant programs were on the statute books in the year Ronald Reagan won the presidency. Once adopted, most grants underwent a process of incremental expansion analogous to the history of the experiment stations. In 1980 grant costs to Washington reached $94 billion, which equaled 27 percent of state and local governments' general revenues (funds they raised themselves; see table 8.1). Because most of this money went to state governments, federal grants figured prominently in their finances. Federal aid was equivalent to nearly half of all state taxes in 1980. At that time intergovernmental transfers constituted 13 percent of federal expenditures, but the seemingly modest size of this share is deceiving. The bulk of national outlays supported a few activities, such as defense, the post office, and Social Security pensions, which were wholly under federal control. Subtraction of these big-ticket items from the national budget left a relatively small sum. Beginning with the New Deal, Washington spent a large percentage of this residual "free cash" on grants. By applying these discretionary funds to a multigovernmental approach of policy implementation, Congress used grants as its mode of access to many new civic concerns.

The evolution of grant programs provides a historical vista on Washington's expanding domestic agenda. Agricultural research and technical education dominated early grants until 1916, when federal aid priorities shifted toward highways. The Great Depression prompted policy makers to divert federal grant moneys, which increased substantially during the New Deal, to relief and income assistance. The thirty-four programs in existence at the end of the 1930s represented a doubling during the decade. World War II temporarily suspended grant making, which resumed in 1946. In this year Congress voted funding for airport and hospital construction, school lunches, and agricultural marketing services. President Truman signed legislation for forty new programs and Eisenhower approved sixty more, including a dozen grants in 1956, which ranged from interstate highways to conservation in the Great Plains, mental health in Alaska, and vocational education for fishermen. Roads and welfare, the traditional objects of intergovernmental assistance, received two-thirds of federal aid in 1960, but the 132 programs in place by this year signify Washington's involvement in a widening array of fields. These concerns widened faster and further during the Great Society years, when grant programs doubled (from 181 to 388 between 1963 and 1968). During this period Washington earmarked funds for urban mass transit, health care for the poor, local schools, crime control, and environmental cleanup.

The grant explosion of the 1960s galvanized complaints about federal aid that had simmered for decades. State and local officials charged that grants buried their governments in paperwork and ran roughshod over local priorities. Restrictions on the use of federal aid pinched the most sensitive political nerve.[16] Most grants offered to state and local governments took the form of categorical programs, which meant that the aid could be spent only for an activity designated by statute. Funds earmarked for highways, for example, could not be diverted to schools, regardless of how local officials calculated their priorities. The lengthening menu of grant offerings, to which a mounting number of regulations and conditions were attached, introduced Byzantine complexity into intergovernmental relations. One strand of this web of provisions lay in differing financial arrangements. Some grants required state contributions, although the proportion differed from program to program, while others imposed no financial requirement. Formulas for distributing moneys to recipients differed from grant to grant, and mutated over time. Formula grant moneys went automatically to all eligible governments, while other funds were released only when federal administrators approved applications for a project. After 1964, Congress attached a growing number of cross-cutting regulations, such as nondiscrimination and environmental protection standards, to most grants. Many local officials threw up their hands in frustration at the accumulation of nationalized policy mandates and stipulations that had been grafted onto a bewildering array of narrowly designed program options.

Congress responded to some of these misgivings by consolidating selected categorical programs into five block grants between 1966 and 1974. These packages of aid ostensibly gave state and local officials greater flexibility in allocating funds within general programmatic areas, such as public health, worker training, and urban redevelopment. The Community Development Block Grant (CDBG, 1974), for example, folded ten older, urban-oriented programs, including urban renewal (1949), into a multipurpose package of options available to cities with 50,000 or more people. The Department of Housing and Urban Development released funds ($11 billion over the first three years) when communities filed applications that indicated how they intended to allocate their allotment within the guidelines of the program. By including small cities and some suburbs, community development grants more than doubled the number of places eligible for funds under urban programs.

This "explosion of the eligibles," a phenomenon observable in several block grants, reached a logical conclusion with the enactment of general revenue sharing (1972). This program distributed $83.5 billion over the next fourteen years to all fifty states and 39,000 local governments, plus Indian tribes, with few restrictions on the allocation of the funds. Revenue sharing did not, however, come without strings. In fact, the program actually extended the reach of federal policy standards to virtually every government in the country. Revenue sharing and block grants notwithstanding, Congress did not lose its taste for categorical aid programs. Lawmakers created 150 more special-purpose grants during the Nixon, Ford, and Carter administrations (1969–1981). Intergovernmental activism during the 1960s and 1970s resulted in a fourfold increase in real spending for grants and a further expansion of the national policy agenda.

Why did Congress rely so heavily on grants-in-aid? Washington had other options, in theory at least. Social Security pensions offered a model for direct national administration of a program. Prior to the judicial revolution of the late 1930s, however, the constitutionality of this approach remained uncertain. Alternatively, Congress could have forsworn entrance into some new fields and simultaneously capped the growth of federal taxation. This approach would have enhanced the ability of state and local governments to finance their own policy agendas and remained faithful to the spirit of dual federalism. Yet Congress chose a middle way, one that allowed Washington to address new civic objectives without wholly abandoning the decentralized structure of the republican polity. This solution was a practical accommodation to two contradictory influences on lawmakers. One pressure pointed toward the expansion of federal power to tackle problems that many members of Congress came to define as national in scope. The other pressure directed Congress to honor old reservations about building a national bureaucracy. Grants represented a compromise that minimized tension between new policy aspirations and the nation's political tradition.

But intergovernmental transfers did challenge the traditional federal order. Through an accumulation of grant programs, Washington's increased financial investment in them, and a proliferation of regulations affecting their use, Congress expanded the federal role. A series of incremental policy steps, not a formal rewording of the Constitution, forged this development. The Supreme Court said little about grants per se. But the jurists did interpret Washington's prerogative to promote the general welfare through appropriations broadly, which was tantamount to bestowing their blessing on grants. *Helvering v. Davis* (1937), the decision that upheld Social Security pensions, illustrates the point. Although old-age benefits were paid by Washington directly to individuals (and not to other governments), defense of this spending plan relied on classic arguments offered earlier and later on behalf of intergovernmental transfers. Justice Benjamin Cardozo's majority opinion rested on three contentions. First, industrial change made many socioeconomic ills national in character. Second, objective evidence (such as statistics) established the rationale for government to assist a worthy cause, which in this instance was the plight of older workers. And third, the states could not deal effectively with this "problem."

Cardozo took pains to argue this latter point. Some states lacked the resources necessary to fund "an adequate program of security for the aged," he observed, while others showed a reluctance to increase taxes "for fear of placing themselves in a position of economic disadvantage with neighbors or competitors." Liberals in particular argued that the states possessed neither the will nor the capacity to ameliorate the economic calamity of the 1930s or problems later in the century. Although absent from his opinion, Cardozo's rationale for federally sponsored old-age pensions applied just as logically to welfare assistance, which Congress chose to subsidize through grants to the states. Notwithstanding this inconsistency, Cardozo articulated a two-pronged justification on behalf of national involvement. On one hand, certain modern problems spilled across state jurisdictions; on the other, structural and political impediments handcuffed the ability of states to mount an effective response to them.[17]

Cardozo was right about disparities among the states. Income per person in 1929 averaged four times more in New York than in Mississippi. Between these extremes lay contrasts in wealth among the states that persisted for decades. These differences meant that poor states could tax their citizens at higher rates than rich states and still end up with less revenue. New York took in three times more taxes per person in 1929 than did Mississippi, although the latter state had the heavier tax schedule of the two. These variations in tax capacity (wealth) and effort (actual rates of taxation) bolstered the case for grants as a way to equalize financial inequalities among the states. Similar variations developed between central cities and suburbs within particular states. As middle-class whites and much of U.S. industry migrated to outlying communities, blacks and other low-income groups replaced them in the urban core. The result left the central cities with less taxable real estate than suburbs, where one found the greatest concentration of affluent homeowners. This disparity was compounded by the fragmentation of local tax jurisdictions and the reluctance of state governments, often controlled by a suburban-rural majority, to offer much help to city residents. The federal urban grants of the postwar era arose partly to compensate for the central city–suburban mismatch of finances.[18]

Contrasts in the fiscal capacities of different governments, however, do not fully account for grants. The republican polity had viewed local circumstances as local concerns, under local control. In the modern polity these inequalities increasingly were seen as national issues. What qualified a subject for federal attention? Congress made the decision, and for a variety of reasons it packaged many of its policy responses as grants. Washington's fiscal advantages over subnational governments figured prominently among these persuasions. Virtually none of the legal restrictions that bound the hands of officials at lower levels of government tied down federal lawmakers. By virtue of its extensive powers to tax and to borrow, Washington could raise funds much more easily than could lesser governments. The experience of the 1950s and 1960s proved, in fact, that Congress could both cut taxes and increase intergovernmental aid.

The financial capability of government does not, nevertheless, automatically trigger the willingness to exercise this potential. Decisions concerning how to use federal funds and whether to channel them through grants were political choices. The pattern of these decisions shows that federal policy makers increasingly chose to redress needs rather than to preserve traditional conceptions of Washington's role in domestic affairs. Members of Congress learned that distributing money added up to successful politics.[19] On the surface everyone appeared to gain. Federal lawmakers took credit for responding to problems on various fronts, achieved with minimal cost to Washington since the national share of each grant program was distributed collectively over all taxpayers. State and local officials in fact played a substantial role in requesting federal financial assistance and in formulating grant legislation.[20] Moreover, new intergovernmental ventures built collections of appreciative recipients who defended their largess, often with considerable skill and aggressiveness. These interest groups created lobbying organizations, sometimes after the adoption of their program, and used these networks to help finance the reelection of their congressional champions.[21]

Behind each grant was a worthy rationale. Proponents invariably phrased the mission of a grant in terms of addressing an issue of national public interest. One could hardly expect otherwise, given the nation's ideological tradition. The old polity had condemned policy favors as class legislation. This ideological maxim retained considerable resiliency in the twentieth century, and opponents to the first grants drew on it. Dissenters to federal grants for highways, for example, warned that aid would penalize states that had developed roads on their own and would open the door to costly pork-barrel politics. Bureaucrats in league with road contractors and other special interests, some critics predicted, would be the principal beneficiaries of highway grants.[22]

The formal structure of the U.S. government shielded lawmakers from the full impact of these charges. The political escape clause was the congressional district, which is defined geographically (by whole states for the Senate and by intrastate divisions for the House) and not in terms of particular social or economic classes. Members of Congress always had a responsibility for representing the interests of their constituents. This representational function meant that philosophic condemnation of policy favoritism applied less certainly to assistance for a jurisdictional unit than to a distinct class of persons. Grants to state and local governments, in other words, could be interpreted as an extension of lawmakers' legitimate regard for their home turf. These cooperative ventures, moreover, avoided a dramatic enlargement of federal bureaucracy because state and local officials would manage most chores connected with intergovernmental programs. By going with grants, Congress chose a policy path that presented the least political resistance.

Grants ushered in a new way of promoting policy, but it is difficult to assess their overall impact on governance. Because grants eventually penetrated most areas of domestic governance, filling out their score card comes close to grading the performance of the whole political system. Despite the complications in appraising their effects, grants appear to have contributed significantly to three major developments. They helped to increase the concentration of power in Washington, reduce citizen ability to hold officials accountable for their actions, and stimulate higher taxation.

Clearly grants were not solely responsible for the growth of the federal role, as numerous factors have increased Washington's power. Still, federal aid programs leveraged further nationalized control of governance by adding new policy objectives to the national budget. As the old saw says, "He that pays the piper calls the tune." The people who authorized spending programs, in other words, gained a considerable say in how the funds were spent. Categorical grants epitomize this maxim. Their popularity in Congress derived from their narrowness of purpose, which allowed federal lawmakers to earmark intergovernmental spending priorities. This point does not deny that interest groups, including officials from state and local governments, often sought federal aid in the first place. But the enactment of more and more grants expanded the subjects under Washington's purview. Accentuating this nationalization of policy making was Congress's penchant to use grants as levers to achieve general policy goals (such as environmental protection and nondiscrimination) unrelated to the explicit purpose of the aid program.[23]

Permitting federal administrators to withhold funds if a recipient violated the terms of a grant program conveyed new authority to national officials. The potency of this power was recognized long ago. The flap over federal aid to Illinois during the Great Depression is a case in point. Relief Administrator Harry Hopkins's threat in 1935 to withhold national funds unless Illinois spent more of its own revenues to help the unemployed provoked a local legislator to charge that his state was being reduced to "a vassal province" of Washington.[24] Despite similar outbursts over the decades, few eligible recipients refused to accept federal aid. Money talked louder than reverence for old federalism.

Federal grants also diluted the linkage between the people and their representatives. The pattern of governance under dual federalism had simplified the ability of citizens to assign credit and blame to public officials. In this older era each level of government managed a relatively distinct set of functions and raised its own revenue to pay for them. Grants brought a commingling of federal and state-local funds and multigovernmental administration of individual programs. As these authorizations increased in number, objective, and conditions, intergovernmental relations grew more complex. This development enlarged the importance of hired administrators, because only they had the time, expertise, and administrative placement to oversee the implementation of each policy specialty. This bureaucratization of intergovernmental assistance inhibited the popular control of policy. Because grant administration spanned two or three levels of government and was fragmented among hundreds of specific programs, a maze of entangled jurisdiction resulted. Who was responsible when a program failed or was abused? The federal government? The states? Some invisible administrators in Washington or in scattered local agencies? The list of potential suspects was long because so many hands now steered the ship of state. And when the craft went astray, one set of officers blamed others for its errant course, leaving the average citizen understandably befuddled. Inadvertently but conveniently for Congress and special-interest recipients, grants had created a smokescreen around the delivery of governmental services that reduced the public's ability to determine who was in charge.[25]

Grants also impacted policy making in the states. A common argument on behalf of the federal aid system was that it induced states, especially the less progressive ones, to address new civic needs and to improve their administrative capacity. Many grant-in-aid statutes required state financial contributions to the program as a condition for receiving federal subsidies. Other provisions attached to these laws required state and local governments to create special administrative bodies to allocate grant moneys and enforce regulations governing their use. Despite the stimulatory effect on state lawmaking that these provisions had, the extent to which Washington pressured the states into expanding their policy repertoire remains unclear. The states did not become docile administrative appendages of Washington but remained quasi-independent political entities with considerable policy discretion. This reality complicates the identification of state actions as ones that resulted from federal inducement and ones taken on the initiative of state lawmakers.

What is clear is that state taxes rose substantially after World War II. The greatest surge in this expansion occurred in the 1960s and early 1970s, a development whose timing overlapped with the explosion of federal aid. Between 1946 and 1980 state tax collections increased over sixfold in inflation-adjusted dollars, which was twice the rate of real growth of federal taxes (but not Social Security). States raised their new moneys mainly from levies on consumer purchases (via general sales taxes) and on personal income. Whereas only thirteen states levied both taxes in 1945, thirty-seven did so by 1980, with the greatest gain registered in the 1960s. These actions markedly altered the sources of state revenue. In 1980 sales and personal income taxes accounted for more than half of all states taxes, up from a quarter in 1946.[26]

These tax innovations elevated the states to the middle rung of the nation's fiscal ladder, which Washington came to dominate after World War II. Pressure for change in the tax order came both from above, as Washington influenced state lawmakers through grant requirements, and from below, as local communities sought to lighten their tax burden. Property taxes, the chief revenue of localities, had risen considerably after 1945, in good measure owing to the cost of schooling baby boomers. Homeowners, especially elderly residents, and local businesses demanded limitations on property tax increases. State governments responded to these requests by providing larger grants-in-aid to local governments, with the largest share targeted for schools. The enactment of new state taxes often hinged on writing guarantees into statutes that earmarked the additional revenue for local governments. Bay State voters amended Massachusetts' constitution in 1948 to dedicate motor vehicle registration fees and fuel taxes to road purposes. The state earmarked many of its tax adoptions of the 1960s and 1970s to its local aid fund. Collections from a 3 percent sales tax (enacted in 1966), a state lottery (1971), a penny increase in the gasoline tax (1971), and a hike in the sales tax to 5 percent (1975) were channeled into the fund. During these years Massachusetts also assumed local government's share of welfare and county court costs. At the same time, state revenues earmarked for local aid (or any specific function) reduced flexibility in state budgets.

Setting budgetary priorities took on greater importance as the role of the states grew during the latter half of the twentieth century. While some of this expansion is explained by pressures that came from other governments, state lawmakers were hardly puppets of local and national politicos. A general feeling emerged in the 1960s and 1970s that society faced new social and economic problems that required public solutions. This sentiment permeated state as well as national politics, encouraging candidates and officeholders to place new items on the policy-making agenda. Like their colleagues in Washington, politicians in the states came to see that their electoral fate hinged on result-oriented governance.

Nelson Rockefeller was one of the new breed of can-do state activists. A Republican who served as New York's governor for fifteen years (1959–1973), Rockefeller plunged into the agenda of the 1960s with energy and passion. His priorities read like a checklist of the concerns of the Kennedy, Johnson, and Nixon years—expansion of higher education, better hospitals and mental health facilities, parks, highways and urban transit, housing, sewer treatment plants, electrical power, and expanded welfare assistance. The construction of a massive capitol complex in Albany that would solve the space needs of state government and reverse the decay of the city's downtown typified the scale on which the governor thought. His objectives were not only ambitious but costly. On eight occasions Rockefeller asked state legislators to increase taxes. Lawmakers complied with each request, in part because Rockefeller was a master at turning the screws of political pressure.[27] Eleven different taxes were either created anew or expanded in 1968 alone. Additional money was raised by borrowing, which substantially increased the state debt.

Despite the bond issues and tax increases, some goals remained unfunded. In its search for additional revenues the Rockefeller statehouse discovered public authorities. These entities provided a technique of raising funds without appearing to increase taxes or the state's legal debt. Analogous to a business corporation, authorities were quasi-independent agencies with power to borrow money and charge fees. Purposefully insulated from the usual forms of political interference, authority finances were separate from the state budgets. In

New York State even the public authorities' account books were closed to reviews by the state auditor. The authorities' fiscal autonomy was a critical technicality, because it excused them from the requirement of New York's constitution that voters approve state borrowing proposals. Rockefeller used this
loophole to transform public authorities into financing instruments for general state purposes, such as expanding the state university, health facilities, and
highways. Construction of the new office-building complex in Albany (Empire State Plaza) used a variant of this device. Albany County borrowed funds
for the project and then leased the facility to the state in exchange for rent that
financed the loan. By 1973 such lease-purchase deals and public authority activity accounted for one-third of New York's expenditures.[28] This was back-
door financing. Expanding the mission of authorities into broader fields of endeavor provided a convenient way to circumvent traditional limits on public
finance. Rockefeller was not unique among governors in seeking routes around
these obstacles. Fiscal sleight-of-hand was a hallmark of the claimant polity,
which was constrained by deep-seated antipathies to taxation, constitutional
restrictions on budget options, and a fragmented structure of government.
Rockefeller just operated on a grander scale than the others.

Grover Cleveland was the last nineteenth-century president to serve an
entire term (1885–1889) without incurring a budget deficit in any year. Only
Calvin Coolidge matched this record among twentieth-century presidents.
After Coolidge departed the White House, federal spending exceeded revenues virtually every year, with the late 1990s (the Clinton administration) a notable exception. Yet each modern president echoed his successors in expressing
abhorrence of budget deficits, although George W. Bush represents a partial
exception to this tradition. But for most politicians, an unbalanced budget was
politically unacceptable, with a partial exception for periods of crisis.

Nineteenth-century citizens realized that unusual circumstances would
cause occasional imbalances in governmental accounts. The economic depression of the mid-1890s, for example, dragged revenues below outlays during
Cleveland's second term (1893–1897). A similar imbalance followed in the years
after the Panic of 1907. World War I, of course, occasioned extensive borrowing. Since Herbert Hoover's administration, however, emergency conditions
have become more or less permanent. The Great Depression and World War II
established precedents whereby economic downturns and foreign threats were

cited as justifications for unbalanced budgets. But during growth and peaceful times the primary reason for federal deficits was that the appetite for public goods outpaced willingness to pay for them. This gap became more severe after the mid-1960s when national lawmakers devoted increased resources to both guns (especially the Vietnam War) and butter (domestic programs). The huge tax cut of 1981 elevated budget deficits to a peacetime record during the 1980s.

Repeated unbalanced budgets caused the federal debt to grow. The accumulated national debt, which stood at 9 percent of the GDP in the last year of Cleveland's presidency, had reached 35 percent by 1980. It climbed to 54 percent at the end of Reagan's two terms (1981–1989) and continued to rise after he left office. Despite the contemporary handwringing over the size of the modern debt, however, its peak relative to the GNP occurred during World War II. After 1945 the real cost (in per-capita constant dollars) of the national debt declined until the Reagan tax cut of 1981. Additional tax cuts, overseas wars, and recession drove up the debt further during the George W. Bush and Obama administrations (2001–2013; see chapter 11).

Conservatives saw deficits as the result of excessive spending. Liberals cited the failure to raise sufficient revenues and sometimes the high cost of defense as the reason for the imbalance. But the ongoing dilemma over national accounts can also be seen as a bipartisan legacy of past tax decisions. Repeated shortfalls in the U.S. Treasury during the claimant polity resulted from both insufficient taxation and the accumulation of spending programs. On the revenue side of this equation lawmakers of various ideological stripes turned the tax code into a lever of social and economic policy, by voting exemptions that excused taxation on designated personal and business purchases. Dozens of these "tax expenditures" were granted during the lifetime of federal income taxes.[29] A classic illustration was the deduction of interest payments on home mortgages and local property taxes from an individual's taxable income. A part of the national tax code since 1913, the mortgage interest exemption was designed to help people buy a home. With the exception of having a job, no other economic goal ranked as high in America as home ownership. Governmental promotion of this objective thus rested on a worthy and popular rationale. Each tax expenditure was defended as an effort to achieve an important objective, such as encouraging business investment (and therefore, indirectly, creating jobs), saving for retirement, and local construction of schools and roads.

The extent to which each tax expenditure fulfilled its ostensible purpose is hard to determine. What is clear is that tax expenditures were subsidies to particular groups of people. Deductions for a person's expenditures on mortgage interest and property taxes, for example, benefited homeowners, not renters, and thus helped the middle class more than low-income earners. Changes in economic conditions, moreover, could alter the value of this benefit. High inflation in the 1970s and early 1980s, for instance, raised middle-income individuals into higher federal tax brackets, which made tax saving from the ownership of real estate more valuable. During periods of inflation, like the 1970s, the tax break on mortgages was skewed toward older individuals who bought their home during more stable times.

Tax expenditures were not neutral. Constituting a form of hidden spending, each special tax treatment raised other people's costs. Most individual exemptions had a limited effect on overall revenue collections. But in the aggregate they totaled a large drag on governmental receipts. They are part of the reason that U.S. federal taxes are lower than those of most other industrialized nations. Home mortgage interest and property tax deductions in 1979 alone equaled 63 percent of that year's revenue shortfall. But the claimant polity accumulated tax expenditures over time, not eliminated them. Taking back preferential treatment meant increasing someone's taxes, which Congress was loath to do. Distributing benefits, not increasing taxes, had the greatest political appeal. Tax expenditures facilitated this practice because they buried favors within the labyrinth of the Internal Revenue Code, whose technicalities obscured their existence. Their accumulation prompted Wilbur Mills, long chair of the House's Revenue Committee, to call the Internal Revenue Code a "house of horrors."[30]

Tax expenditures symbolized two proclivities of the claimant era. On one hand, policy makers used revenue mechanisms to convey special benefits. On the other hand, they obscured the true costs of these favors. Labeling money withheld from paychecks for Social Security as a contribution rather than a tax and then reserving these funds for a distinct group of recipients illustrates the tendency. The exclusion of U.S. guarantees of private loans and the finances of special-purpose organizations from the basic federal budget was another variant of deceptive fiscal practice.[31] Inserting "hold harmless" clauses into revisions of federal grant formulas so that localities would not lose prior-year funding represents a more overt way of protecting fiscal largess. For generations state and local governments have offered property tax breaks to businesses and nonprofit organizations. City subsidies for building sports stadiums, often via off-budget practices, rewarded wealthy team owners at the expense of municipal taxpayers.[32] The penchant for states to earmark particular revenue streams to particular programs and to allow public authorities to operate outside the state budgetary process constituted special encumbrances on the use of public funds. Viewed over time and across the tiers of the federal system, America's plan of public finance lacked rational coherence. Its very complexity protected special-interest favoritism.

9

The New Faces of Power

J. EDGAR HOOVER lived in the nation's capital for all his seventy-seven years. Washington, D.C., still retained a southern flavor in 1895, the year that Hoover was born. The sturdy Victorian houses that lined Seward Square, his boyhood neighborhood located a five-minute walk from the Capitol, reflected the middle-class gentility of his sector of the city. The only nonwhites encountered in the area commuted daily from the district's black ghettos to work in the homes on Seward Square. J. Edgar's roots were firmly planted in this city and in its culture, which Federal politics and administration helped to shape. Both his father and his grandfather had been employees in the print shop of the U.S. Government's Coast and Geodetic Survey. Following graduation from high school J. Edgar worked at the Library of Congress as an order clerk by day and studied law at night. He lived with his mother until her death in 1938 and supported her financially in widowhood. Here in turn-of-the-century Washington Hoover formulated a social outlook that epitomized white middle-class Protestantism. Its values were the standards that Hoover worked for decades to uphold as America's most famous law officer.[1]

World War I gave Hoover his first big break. Aided by an uncle who was a Federal judge, he landed a position in the Bureau of Investigation in the Department of Justice in 1917. Hoover was assigned to the alien enemy unit, which kept tabs on German Americans and German-speaking immigrants during the war. Two years later, during the Great Red Scare, the bureau created an antiradical division to counteract groups thought to be disloyal in the United

States. Put in charge of the operation, Hoover dove into his new responsibility with gusto. He helped to document charges of political anarchism against hundreds of individuals, some of whom were deported on the basis of dubious evidence. He personally escorted 249 aliens (noncitizen immigrants) onto the "Soviet Ark," a vessel bound for the Soviet Union. By demonstrating his effectiveness at ferreting out alleged political misfits, Hoover had set his remarkable career in motion. In 1921 he was advanced to assistant director of the Bureau of Investigation, and three years later, as the scandals about corruption in the Harding administration broke, he was appointed its director. Hoover was twenty-nine. He remained at the head of the bureau, renamed the Federal Bureau of Investigation (FBI) in 1935, until his death in 1972. He served nineteen attorney generals and eight presidents, from Calvin Coolidge to Richard Nixon.

Hoover used his long reign as the nation's chief law-enforcement officer to transform the FBI from a small, unprofessional agency into a large, rationally ordered, and nationally visible bureaucracy. He aligned his bureau squarely with traditional middle-class conservatism and publicized his battles against "un-American" forces in the land, beginning with his campaign against Reds in 1919 and ending with the bureau's attack on the Ku Klux Klan in the 1960s. In the intervening years Hoover relentlessly pursued communists and supposed communists, left-wingers, and common criminals. He instituted a national anticrime program crowned with a massive collection of individual dossiers and millions of fingerprints. By a variety of calculated steps, "Mr. FBI" built a powerful, elite police organization over which he had virtually total control for two generations. No president dared challenge his power. Hoover remained in charge of the bureau until the morning his chauffeur arrived at his home to find him dead in his pajamas.

The FBI story is a caricature of what happened to office holding in the United States. Hoover's career was incompatible with the republican polity. Its citizens had opposed personal claims to public station, and they demanded short terms and the regular rotation of elected officials. Americans were equally suspicious of bureaucrats and placemen. The sentiment could be traced to the Declaration of Independence, which attacked the King of Great Britain for creating a "multitude of new offices" and sending "swarms of officers to harass our people." Republican ideology equated the establishment of executive dynasties with a threat to liberty and as contrary to the public good. The maintenance of a virtuous civil regime required the continuous infusion of new faces into the halls of power.

The claimant polity gave the managers of government a new look but not always new faces. Actually, the same faces tended to reappear. Officeholders stayed in power longer, and there were many more of them. The trend was most visible among middle-management administrators (bureau chiefs below cabinet and vice-cabinet positions) and members of the U.S. House of Representatives. Hoover and many thousands of others made government their career. Some agencies and legislative committees became indistinguishable from the personality of their head. Hoover and the FBI became fused in this way in the public mind.

Power thus took on a new look, as individuals gained immense influence, in part maintaining themselves in office. All major political institutions—legislatures, executive branches, administrative units, the court system, and even private-interest groups—offered niches where people could build personal careers around service in the public sector. As government became more bureaucratized and as personal claims to power multiplied, the process of governance changed. The initiative for governing came less from citizens and political parties and more from people who already held the reins of power.

Legislators played a pivotal role in the growth of government. Every major addition to the civic workload required legislative approval. Why did lawmakers consent to the expansion of the public sector? The question has no clear answer, because of the nature of democracy. Legislatures brought together many different personalities, each of whom possessed an individual background and temperament and represented a distinct group of constituents. The diversity of these interests makes it hard to pinpoint the causes that induced lawmakers to support policies of growth.

Several rules of thumb about legislative politics offer clues to understanding how lawmakers went about their business. First, major proposals to increase government's role usually generated divided opinions about the best way to proceed. In the absence of consensus, compromise is generally necessary to enact innovative legislation. Most new statutes of significance bear the scars of this give-and-take process. Second, the alignment of lawmakers on various sides of a policy proposal sometimes changed when they shifted consideration from one issue to another. The reason these reorderings occur is that the content of measures helped legislators arrive at policy decision.[2] Conflict between political parties did not occur on all legislation; many issues, especially in the states, evoked bipartisan voting responses. These observations support the expectation that lawmakers' relative positioning changed as their attention moved from one area of policy to another. Third, legislators usually follow at least one of three general criteria in arriving at a policy decision: their personal preferences and ideology, advice and pressure from colleagues within the legislature and executive office, and the interests of their constituents. Decisions are easiest to reach when all three criteria point in the same direction. But when these signals clash, legislators must choose between competing references. Lawmakers tend to be cautious, and thus to favor small, incremental changes in policy as opposed to decisions that promise radical departures in governmental operations. It usually takes an inducement of major proportion to jar legislators out of their customary timidity.

Fourth, lawmakers prefer to give pleasure rather than inflict pain. The distribution of benefits is therefore more appealing than the restriction of freedom or the extraction of taxes. The rise of a claimant philosophy, which held that government should respond to needs in society, has increased the political attractiveness of providing benefits. Legislative leaders understand this fact. The formation of a victorious coalition is easiest when benefits are distributed widely among legislators or constituents. On issues that lack clear benefits or will animate cohesive party opposition, parliamentary leaders resort to procedural gimmicks such as tucking controversial measures into larger omnibus bills or drafting language that disguises a program's real nature.

Over the course of a session thousands of bills may have been introduced into a legislature, and lawmakers have cast votes on hundreds of them. Fifty separate Congresses, which were each elected for two years, but which met annually (in first and second sessions, and occasionally in special sessions), convened between 1887 and 1987. Some three thousand state legislative sessions and hundreds of thousands of meetings of city councilors, county commissioners, and other local lawmakers took place during these one hundred years. The enormous number of decisions made in these countless legislative meetings undermines the hope of locating a single key that explains lawmakers' decision making. A more sensible assumption is that various factors, which changed over time and varied between circumstances and subject matters, prompted legislators to add new tasks to the functions of government.

The representatives who wrangled over tariff legislation in 1888 were relative newcomers to Washington. Most were serving their first or second term in Congress. Only a handful had been there ten years (i.e., five terms in the House). Speaker John Carlisle, who had won the House's top post in his seventh year of service, was in his sixth term. Carlisle kept his colleagues in Washington longer than usual in 1888. Haggling over whether to bestow tariff protection to "hackled flax" and "flax not hackled" and similar questions occupied the members of the first (or long) session of the 50th Congress through early fall. The desire to resume private pursuits and to escape Washington's oppressive summer heat usually motivated lawmakers to wrap up business before July. The second (or short) session that began at the end of the year customarily adjourned after three months. At the onset of the transition era Congress was still a part-time operation that made do with a few temporary employees. Most staffers clerked for a committee or aided a senator, and many moonlighted as newspaper correspondents to supplement their skimpy congressional pay.[3]

Sam Rayburn began his legislative career during the waning years of this regime. After serving as speaker of the Texas House, Rayburn won election (1912) to Congress when he was thirty years old. He held this seat until he died forty-nine years later. Rayburn ascended the rungs of the leadership ladder in the House of Representatives during his first quarter-century of service and reached the speakership in his thirteenth term (1940). Only Republican majorities in the House in 1947–1948 and 1953–1954 kept him out of the post for the next twenty-one years. His remarkable longevity is attributable in part to political tradition in the South. Republicans were as scarce as hen's teeth there, including in his rural constituency in north Texas. This partisan legacy of the Civil War meant that Rayburn faced only token opposition, if any at all, in the general election. His only real challenges came in Democratic Party primaries, which Rayburn won with the aid of a local network of supporters. One way he cultivated these loyalties was to act like one of the ordinary folks when he returned to his district. The Texas Rayburn donned old clothes, drove a battered pickup truck, and proved that he could mow a field of alfalfa. His constituents rarely saw the Washington Rayburn, who wore tailor-made suits, rode in a chauffeured limousine, and insisted that the House conduct its proceedings with formal decorum. What they did see was a steady stream of benefits, such as a dam or a military base, for the district. These favors helped Rayburn build an electorally safe seat, which gave him the political freedom to take more liberal positions on issues facing Congress than most of his voters at home did.[4]

Rayburn departed an institution that was much different from the one he entered. By 1961 most members of the House of Representatives had chosen Congress as a career. The idyllic notion of the republican polity that civic duty was the primary basis for legislative service had lost its credence by the latter half of the twentieth century. Thomas "Tip" O'Neill followed a career pattern typical of the new generation of legislators. After graduation from Boston College during the Depression, he won election to the Massachusetts House at age twenty-four and twelve years later became its speaker. In 1952, at forty years of age, he took over the congressional seat vacated by John F. Kennedy, who had moved to the United States Senate. O'Neill turned this political windfall into a safe seat by keeping in close personal touch with his north Cambridge community, by frequent returns to his district, and by newsletters, which members of Congress could mail for free. He reminded his voters, who were largely blue-collar workers, what he had done for them lately. Headlines such as "Increases in Social Security Benefits" and "Congress Extended Personal Income Tax Cut" on his newsletters left no doubt about how he used his time in Washington. Besides supporting legislation that distributed benefits, O'Neill moved up the ranks of the Democratic Party hierarchy. After a quarter of a century in the House his colleagues elevated him to the speakership. He retired ten years later, concluding a half-century of legislative service.[5]

What encouraged O'Neill, Rayburn, and legislators with similarly lengthy careers to stay in Congress so long? And what enabled them to keep their jobs? No doubt the appeal of power itself is part of the answer. As the Federal role grew and Washington became more important, the job of managing this influence appears to have become increasingly attractive. During these decades of change the tangible rewards of a congressional career multiplied. Congressional salaries never made lawmakers rich, but the job paid more than most lines of work and more than state legislators' compensation. Between 1865 and 1907 congressional salaries held steady at $5,000 a year, then rose gradually, reaching $12,500 in 1947. Thereafter raises came more often. Rank-and-file members grossed $77,000 when O'Neill gave up the speakership (1986), which paid him over $100,000 a year. O'Neill retired on a lucrative congressional pension. Congress had created its own retirement system in 1946, which was a sure sign that many members envisioned legislative service to be long-term employment.

Pensions were only one of a host of perks and privileges that lawmakers voted themselves. They received free medical care in Washington, the use of recreational facilities and private restaurants in their office buildings, a bank with checking services for House members, unlimited phone time, the use of Park Service lodges (including one in the Virgin Islands) at discount prices, and the loan of six potted plants from the Botanic Garden in Washington. Life also became more appealing in twentieth-century Washington, which acquired upscale neighborhoods, fine restaurants, and numerous cultural amenities. Air conditioning, standard after World War II, made the district a more habitable place in the hot and humid months. Air travel, also largely a post-1945 development, allowed lawmakers to visit their constituents frequently as well as more exotic destinations on official business (junkets, in the eyes of skeptics) without adjourning Congress. By the 1970s, when Congress had already become a year-round operation, members enjoyed virtually unlimited trip privileges.

The increase of full-time staff further improved working conditions in Congress. The authorization of professional assistance for committees, which began in the 1850s, and aides for individual legislators, which began for senators in 1885 and for representatives in 1893, developed at a modest pace through the 1940s. New Deal Congresses hired 1,600 employees. Thereafter the numbers rose more swiftly, especially in the 1960s and 1970s. By 1980 the congressional payroll counted 31,000 people, most of whom worked for individual lawmakers. The average senator employed thirty-seven staffers, a quarter of whom ran offices in their home state.[6] The cost of maintaining this bureaucracy dwarfed what Congress had spent on itself in the nineteenth century. In Grover Cleveland's day legislative functions cost $6 million a year. When George H. W. Bush occupied the White House (1989–1993) the congressional establishment consumed a billion dollars a year.

In writing legislation and answering constituents' inquiries, staffers did more than make the members of Congress better legislators. They also contributed to the political security of their employers. As the twentieth century progressed an increased proportion of incumbent legislators stood for reelection, an increasing proportion of them won, and more and more did so by creating safe seats that seldom fell to challengers. The 1978 elections illustrate this story. Representatives holding 382 of the House's 435 seats sought reelection, and 358 of them (94 percent) won. The large majority of these incumbents captured 60 percent or more of the vote, which qualified their district as a safe seat. Only nineteen seats changed hands because a challenger beat an incumbent in the general election. More than twice as many new faces (forty-nine) entered Congress because incumbents had voluntarily retired.[7] In the 1980s the death of representatives opened up more seats to newcomers than did upsets at the polls.

Incumbents invested considerable time and money in maintaining these favorable odds. In the Cleveland era political parties superintended much of the campaign process. Party leaders oversaw the selection of nominees and recruited party supporters, many of whom sought patronage jobs, to campaign for the party's slate of candidates. Most voters responded to the appeal for partisan loyalty by habitually supporting the party's entire ticket. The spread of primaries as a nominating device and civil service criteria for hiring government workers weakened the hold of party leaders over elections at the very time that officeholders showed greater interest in reelection.[8] In the late twentieth century congressional incumbents tended to build their own political organizations and to raise money to finance their own campaigns. Because modern campaigns relied heavily on radio and TV spots and banks of phone operators, elections became very expensive. Fund raising became the critical element in successful electioneering. Even occupants of safe seats thought it prudent to spend liberally on their reelection campaigns.

This investment earned incumbents more years on the job, or seniority, which evolved into an important criterion for elevation to leadership posts in the House. Sam Rayburn's career benefited from this development. In the late nineteenth century, power had been centralized in the hands of a few party leaders in the House. Just a few years before Rayburn entered the institution a revolt against this system stripped Speaker Joe Cannon of key powers, such as the appointment of committee members and the heads of committees (chairs). Committee jurisdiction over legislation was formalized, and committee chairs acquired greater personal control over how their panels operated. These reforms afforded rank-and-file members greater personal influence over their careers within the institution. By the 1930s the most senior member of the majority party on each committee customarily became its chair. Rayburn was appointed to the Commerce Committee in 1913, banked years of service on it during the era of Republican majorities in the 1920s, and succeeded to the chair via seniority in 1931 when Democrats regained control of the House.

Anchored by safe seats and career longevity, the seniority system kept the same faces in power in the House for long stretches of time. Just two men, Robert Doughton of North Carolina and Wilbur Mills of Arkansas, headed the

Ways and Means Committee, Congress's key tax panel, for all but four years between the inauguration of Franklin Roosevelt (1933) and the resignation of Richard 'Nixon (1974). Because they presided over powerful fiefdoms, chairs were desirable plums. Members also sought chairs of subcommittees, which proliferated after 1946 when Congress reduced the number of basic committees. By the 1970s over half of the Democratic delegation in the House held a subcommittee chair. Seniority influenced these selections as it did the majority party's choice for speaker and majority leader. Despite their personal political abilities, Rayburn and O'Neill both served long apprenticeships as party lieutenants before their elevation to the House's top spot.

Most members of Congress had staked a personal claim to their seat in the claimant era. A similar trend emerged in many states after 1945, when their legislatures underwent considerable reform. Schedules were switched from biennial to annual sessions, professional staffs were provided, antiquated legislative procedures were reformed, and compensation markedly improved. Most states adopted pension plans for lawmakers, which is a tip-off that state legislators were staying in office longer.

The growth of government and the professionalization of legislative service were parallel developments. Did individual aspirations to stay in legislative office promote the expansion of government? The connection seems likely. It is reasonable to suppose that lawmakers became more accustomed to the uses of power the longer they remained in office. A corollary assumption suggests that legislators utilized the prerogatives of their position to keep themselves in office. Circumstantial evidence sustains this speculation. The members of Congress devoted more institutional resources, such as staff, travel, and mail privileges, to reelection efforts in the claimant era. Committee assignments were sought for the same reason. Policy making offered ways, too, of enhancing electoral prospects. Voter favor could be curried with legislation that benefited segments of the electorate. Most citizens received something of value from government in the late twentieth century. Some awards, such as jobs on military bases, defense contracts to local industries, grants to state and city governments for social services and public works, and increases in Social Security checks, were highly visible and widely distributed among legislators' districts. Other favors, such as tax expenditures and exemptions from regulations, were less visible and targeted on specific groups but no less valuable.[9]

Critics of these practices charged that representatives used the public treasury to buy their reelection. However electoral motives figured into the policy making of subsidies, legislators understood the political value of name recognition. Crusading on behalf of a policy objective, aided by the resources at the disposal of subcommittee chairmanship, could enhance this visibility. So could heading a newsworthy congressional investigation. But the route to developing a reputation as an effective lawmaker lay more in legislating new solutions to pressing problems than in prying into administrative practices.

In the republican era elected officials generally and members of Congress specially relied heavily on their political party to turn an idea into a law. Party organizations were influential because they provided the mechanism for the selection of leaders within the legislature and because voters placed a heavy emphasis on party connections in evaluating candidates who stood for election. Issues reflective of the party's ideological orientation and campaign rhetoric had the best chance of gaining partisan sponsorship. A fundamental change in partisan positioning on national issues occurred in the Wilson years (1910s) when Democrats began to abandon the philosophy of limited government. By the 1930s congressional Democrats embraced the use of Federal power in numerous policy areas. In the wake of this ideological shift during the New Deal and later, southern Democrats often deserted their northern colleagues and joined Republicans in a conservative coalition that opposed liberal proposals such as labor, civil rights, urban measures, and, after World War II, expansion of some income assistance and economic stabilization policies. Lyndon Johnson's landslide victory in 1964 seated an unusually larger number of northern Democrats in Congress, which paved the way for the enactment of Great Society legislation.[10] Partisan influence on policy waned over the next fifteen years but revived in the early 1980s when Republicans rallied behind Ronald Reagan's conservative agenda and accelerated further after 1994.

Through the 1970s, however, the influence of political parties over policy formation diminished, especially in Congress, while the role of other groups grew in significance. The organization of business and nonprofit interest groups, administrators in state and national agencies, governors, and other state-local elected officials accelerated after World War II. The trend built new conduits of influence on legislative policy making. A successful politician is one who listens to the requests placed upon the political system. The rise of the new interest groups escalated policy demands on Congress and state legislatures.

Perhaps because they are political beings who seek to please and to survive in power, legislators accommodated many of them.

Congress, not the president, was "the motive power of the government," Woodrow Wilson wrote in 1885 when he was a young political scientist.[11] The future president's observation in fact fit all governments in the republican polity, whose laws usually originated from legislative initiatives. Legislators commanded as much attention, if not prestige, in the public eye as did mayors, governors, and presidents in that earlier era, when executives customarily assumed a limited policy-making role. Sometimes they pushed for a particular policy change, as Cleveland did with tariff reform, yet they lacked the institutional resources necessary to sustain consistent leadership of the legislature. Members of the Cleveland administration did not draft legislation. Grover Cleveland did not mount a public relations campaign on behalf of an administration policy agenda, and he seldom pressured individual members of Congress to vote for any specific bill.

This passive executive style did not survive the republican era. In the twentieth century, presidents, governors, and mayors became active participants in the formation of policy. In the claimant polity the public expected modern executives to devise solutions to society's problems, push for their adoption, and oversee their implementation. Executives eagerly accepted credit when government produced positive results and were tagged with the blame for its failure. Changes in the presidency epitomize this transformation. The office has evolved from a low-keyed stewardship of a small Federal establishment into the dominant institution in the nation's civic life. In the process the president has become the personal embodiment of the government. The relative political standing of governors and mayors has also risen, although they do not rival the prestige of modern presidents.

What explains the enhanced power of executives? Why did the presidency emerge as a megaoffice in U.S. politics? The origins of the change trace back to the foundations of the republic, which made legislatures the chief instrument of governing. While republican ideology saw representative institutions as the closest embodiment of the popular will, it also warned of the dangers of governmental power. This apprehension led to a series of constitutional precautions that handicapped the ability of legislators, especially in the states, to meet the policy expectations of the twentieth century. A second significant structural feature of American legislatures was the proliferation of single-member districts. These geographically defined constituencies exhibited numerous economic, social, and political differences across the many districts that made up the state legislatures and Congress. First and foremost, these bodies were forums in which divergent constituent interests could be expressed. This is the meaning of representation in a republic—the right of the people to have some say in public discourse through the medium of their elected delegates. The bicameral division of American legislatures at both the state and national levels (and in many local settings as well) reinforced this principle by maintaining dual legislative chambers. But the cost of this excess of democracy was slower lawmaking and sometimes institutional paralysis.

These structural impediments and the inability of political parties to generate the degree of unity among their legislative members than counterparts in Europe did has encouraged American lawmakers to be especially independent-minded. This fact increased the likelihood that legislative leaders turned to bargaining, reciprocity, and compromise to build the majorities needed to enact statutes. To be successful, these tactics required that delegates place practicality over principle and assent to mutually beneficial exchanges (e.g., logrolling). Because this process was eminently political and ripe with opportunities for corruption, a meeting of the legislature signaled open hunting season for high-minded critics in the republican and transition periods. During the Progressive Era the term "state legislator" practically became synonymous with "crook" and "venal" to some cynics.[12]

A second charge, that legislators were hyperactive lawmakers, surfaced at about the same time. The critics cited a growing number of unnecessary laws, poorly drafted statutes, inept administration, and the rising cost of government. They also complained about the increase in interest groups that sought public favoritism, although this phenomenon cannot be blamed solely on legislators. Scolding lawmakers, however, is an old American pastime, virtually ingrained in the nation's style of democracy. Even sophisticated observers added their voices to the general chorus. Edward Corwin, the great scholar of the Constitution, for example, called Congress in the early 1930s "corrupt amalgamations of thievish interests . . . entirely willing to buy votes . . . with somebody else's money."[13] Harry Truman, a bona fide liberal as well as president, aired similar misgivings about his former colleagues in Congress. They habitually loaded appropriation bills with special-interest favors yet were loath to vote for taxes to pay for them. "I had to watch them all the time," he said.[14] American legislators entered the twentieth century hounded by criticism from two sides, a damned if-you-do and damned-if-you-don't situation. On one hand they were seen as exercising power too freely, while on the other hand they were portrayed as incapable of fulfilling their obligation to govern in the public interest.

After 1900 reformers repeatedly urged the expansion of executive authority as a counterweight to these charges of legislative irresponsibility. Their specific solutions envisioned giving all chief executives budget-making prerogatives and governors the right to appoint the heads of departments arranged like Washington's cabinet offices. The creation of the U.S. Bureau of the Budget in 1921 represented a step toward fulfilling this reform agenda. Originally placed in the Treasury Department, the bureau was transferred to an executive office of the president by the Reorganization Act of 1939. Its staff grew from forty-five people in 1937 to seven hundred by 1974, when the bureau was restructured into the Office of Management and Budget (OMB) as a way of enhancing the president's ability to oversee the administration.[15] The 1939 act also created a White House office that provided staff assistance for the president. By Jimmy Carter's administration (1977–1981) the presidency had assembled a bureaucracy within the White House to manage a much larger Federal bureaucracy.

The growth of civic functions created a vast new administrative role for executives at every level of government. Presidents have the additional responsibility of managing foreign relations, which became a more active and complex policy arena as the twentieth century unfolded. The Constitution makes the president both the commander-in-chief of the armed forces and the head of the diplomatic corps. Presidents exercised these two powers sparingly in the nineteenth century, when the United States remained isolated from political affairs in Europe and its national security was seldom challenged. Grover Cleveland did not flex U.S. military muscle by sending the army or navy around the globe, and he opposed colonial expansion. He blocked the annexation of the Hawaiian Islands, for example, after American planters and a supportive troop of U.S. Marines overthrew the native Queen Liluokalani in 1893. Presidents McKinley, Theodore Roosevelt, and Wilson were the first presidents to deviate substantially from the isolationist tradition. By interjecting the United States into the Cuban revolution in 1898 and the fighting in World War I (1917–1918), McKinley and Wilson set precedents for later chief executives. But the credit for inventing the modern pattern of presidential activism in foreign affairs belongs to the man who had been the assistant secretary of the navy in Wilson's administration, Franklin Roosevelt.

German expansion in central Europe and the Japanese invasion of China in the late 1930s set the stage for this new level of presidential leadership. Viewing the Nazi war machine and Japanese imperialism as threats to international order and U.S. security, FDR recommended U.S. aid for Britain, China, and their allies as defensive countermeasures. On the day World War II erupted in Europe in 1939, the president called Congress into session and urged the revision of the country's neutrality law, which prohibited the sale of weapons to nations at war. FDR got his congressional victory after placing considerable pressure on Congress; he signed the amended Neutrality Act in a ceremony recorded by newsreel cameras. Publicly labeled a security measure but in fact designed to aid Britain, the new law allowed the president to approve the sales of arms to countries at war if they paid cash and transported the goods themselves ("cash and carry"). This momentous shift in policy, whereby the president was authorized to commit U.S. resources to military conflicts, culminated in the Lend-Lease Act (March 1941). Drafted by the Roosevelt administration and urged upon a reluctant Congress, this massive program, which eventually cost $54 billion, allowed the president to give arms and supplies to any country when he considered such a transfer "in the interest of national defense." Lend-lease marks the historic pivot point in America's global quest for international stability.

Roosevelt's decisions between 1939 and 1941 inched the United States into an undeclared war with Germany, and into a confrontation with Japan during a period of official U.S. neutrality. With lend-lease cargo ships at risk from Nazi submarine attacks, the president ordered search-and-destroy missions against German submarines in the North Atlantic Ocean and stationed U.S. forces in Greenland and Iceland, which lined the marine route along which lend-lease supplies traveled to Britain. Roosevelt also escalated pressure on Japan. He ordered the Japanese government to cease its military campaign in China; terminated the sale of critical materials, including oil, to Japan; approved clandestine air operations against Japanese forces in China; and allowed U.S. military planners to coordinate strategy with the British and the Dutch in the Far East should hostilities with Japan (which got wind of the talks) erupt. Formalities aside, the United States was at war before the Japanese attacked the Pacific fleet at Pearl Harbor.[16]

The wisdom of Roosevelt's policy before Pearl Harbor has been questioned, but the impact of FDR's course of action on the expansion of presidential power is clear. Roosevelt set important precedents for later presidents in the conduct of foreign affairs. He claimed that his decisions during America's period of neutrality (1939–1941) were precautionary responses to unanticipated hostile developments. The manner in which he posed the alternatives to the public— the nation must either take positive action to preserve democracy or allow totalitarianism to spread by default—was certain to win many Americans to his way of thinking. The Supreme Court had already given the president considerable leeway to manage foreign affairs personally. The justices held in *U.S. v. Curtiss-Wright Export Corporation* (1936) that presidential authority over international relations was "plenary and exclusive." In plain language this meant that the president could do pretty much as he wished on the foreign front, at least from the standpoint of the Constitution.

Presidents after FDR freely exercised this authority. Their most conspicuous application of it has been the use of military and covert power abroad. Truman stationed U.S. forces in Europe and Asia at the onset of the Cold War and committed troops to the Korean War. Eisenhower allowed Central Intelligence Agency (CIA) complicity in the overthrow of governments in Iran and Guatemala and in sabotage against the new regime in North Vietnam. Kennedy initiated a military buildup in Vietnam, and Johnson greatly escalated this involvement while also sending marines into the Dominican Republic. Nixon widened U.S. participation in the war in Indochina and permitted the CIA to aid a coup against a Marxist regime elected in Chile. Reagan invaded the tiny Caribbean island of Grenada on the flimsiest of pretexts and secretly armed the Contras in Nicaragua. George H. W. Bush ordered the temporary occupation of Panama and the bombing of Baghdad in the Gulf War. George W. Bush (2001–2009) initiated the American invasions of Afghanistan and Iraq.

Liberals and conservatives both supported presidential internationalism in its formative decades of the Cold War. Only the president, they argued, had the capacity to cope with the dangers posed by the volatility of the modern world. FDR helped to inspire this rationale. He defended, for example, his declaration of an unlimited national emergency on May 27, 1941, when he pledged greater protection for British shipping from German marauders. Announcing the policy in a national radio address heard by millions of anxious Americans, Roosevelt implied that the Nazis were poised to hop from Iceland to Newfoundland and then dart to unknown destinations on U.S. soil, threatening the safety of people in New Orleans and Chicago as well as on the Atlantic and Pacific coasts. "It would be suicide to wait until they are in our front yard," he warned.[17] Congress apparently accepted reasoning of this sort because it granted presidents special emergency powers over national security in five hundred laws between the 1930s and the 1970s. And it allowed chief executives to transact thousands of "executive agreements" with foreign leaders, a procedure that circumvented the constitutional requirement for senatorial ratification of treaties (by a two-thirds vote).[18]

Presidents defended their activism in foreign policy as a role pressed upon them in the interest of protecting American security. Skeptics often questioned the scope of power that accompanied this claim, but the public customarily rallied behind the president. Most Americans accepted the government's position because they were loyal to their country, and besides, few citizens had the expertise to second-guess the president and his foreign policy advisers. From their perspective, presidents knew that success abroad won political points at home. Only a military stalemate such as in Korea and Vietnam caused popular support of presidential foreign policy to erode. Normally the certainty of public approval combined with congressional impotence in diplomacy, and a professional military establishment groomed for action and confident of its ability held out an immense temptation for presidents to exercise power unilaterally in foreign affairs. Nearly all of them since FDR succumbed to this seduction.

The rise of executive activism in foreign affairs contributed to the growth of presidential power generally. But the rise of presidential internationalism does not explain the expanded influence of governors and mayors, whose authority did not include national security or foreign policy. In the early twentieth century, before the United States undertook an active role in global politics, executives at every level exhibited greater leadership in policy making than had their nineteenth-century counterparts. William Howard Taft was the first president to send draft legislation to Congress. President Woodrow Wilson took an active part in statute making. Franklin Roosevelt, however, established the modern standard for executive leadership in domestic affairs. He christened this new style in his 1933 inaugural address, claiming that the people demanded "direct, vigorous action.... They have made me the present instrument of their wishes." With this announcement Roosevelt embraced a role that reformers had urged for decades: executives should serve as the chief legislator and initiate policy proposals. Some governors and mayors had already headed in this direction. By 1946 orthodox opinion had embraced the axiom that elected executives should provide a policy agenda for legislators.

Executives appealed directly to voters for support in their new role. The critical instrument in this courtship was the communications media. Presidents Taft and Wilson began the practice of inviting journalists to regular news conferences. FDR developed these meetings to a high art in the thousand press conferences he held during his presidency. He was equally skillful in using radio, newspaper's new competitor. FDR's "fireside chat" broadcasts symbolized the emergence of the president whose persona became fused interchangeably with the government.

Television added an incomparable visual dimension to the media presidency. Electronic communications allowed executives to talk in person and directly to voters on prime-time TV. Polished by his years before the camera as an actor, Ronald Reagan was the master of this theatrical aspect of politics. Because presidents made good visual copy, they received disproportionate attention on TV news programs. The nature of the communications business led broadcasters to focus on newsworthy subjects, like presidents and their wives. Jacqueline Kennedy, Lady Bird Johnson, Pat Nixon, Betty Ford, Rosalynn Carter, Nancy Reagan, Barbara Bush, Hillary Clinton, Laura Bush, and Michelle Obama were better known to the average voter (viewer) than their local legislators.[19] Policy issues and congressional negotiations lacked photogenic appeal and could not be easily explained in a couple of minutes of air coverage. In the battle between well-known faces and issues on TV, the faces won.

Aware of the power of the media to shape public opinion, executives sought to control it. FDR pressured news organizations to present his foreign policy in a favorable light. The penalty for harsh criticism of his administration could be antitrust action against movie and newsreel companies and revocation of the licenses of radio stations.[20] To see how he stood with voters, FDR commissioned public-opinion polls, a technique developed in the 1930s. Later presidents and other elected executives built on the public relations foundation that Roosevelt pioneered. Few now pass up a good photo opportunity or an occasion to air a sound bite.

Executives exploited the tremendous potential of communications technology to promote their careers as well as their programs. In the nineteenth century, presidential candidates usually did not campaign directly, relying on their parties to perform this task. The presumption existed that an individual who pursued office, at least outwardly and aggressively, had put the quest for personal glorification ahead of the public welfare. Electronic media reduced candidate dependency on political parties and party chieftains, who once had been the determining factor in the selection of nominees. In the place of these powerful operatives appeared primaries in which voters chose delegates for nominating conventions and autonomous campaign organizations that aspirants for office positions created themselves. After 1945 candidates relied heavily on radio, TV, and telephones to contact voters in primary and general elections. Dwight Eisenhower established the precedent of presidential hopefuls forming their own campaign organization.[21] In 1952, when Ike first sought the nomination, 15 percent of Republican convention delegates were selected through primaries. Three-quarters of the delegates to the convention that chose Ronald Reagan as the Republican nominee had been popularly elected.

The growth of the autonomous executive campaign had several effects on politics. First, modern elections became expensive because candidates substituted costly services, such as TV, for labor formerly donated by party workers. The larger the radius of the campaign, the higher the cost. The price tag for the 1980 presidential election, including its primaries, was $155 million; in 2012 the two major parties raised $2 billion for their candidates. Financial pressure forced candidates to become aggressive fund-raisers and to solicit well-heeled special interests for donations. Contributors gave in hopes of buying a sympathetic ear, if not more, in the new administration. Second, the electoral fate of executives and legislators became separated. Abandoning their habitual support of a particular party, voters split their tickets between Democrats and Republicans with rising frequency after World War II until the 1980s. Often one party captured the executive office and the other gained control (or split control) of the legislature. Divided partisan control of the presidency and Congress existed during two-thirds of the forty years after Eisenhower's 1952 victory. Mixed partisan control also existed in the states during the postwar era.

Executives in these years could not count on cohesive support from their party in the legislature. Those who succeeded in pushing their programs through the legislature often possessed extraordinary skills of persuasion. Lyndon Johnson and Nelson Rockefeller mastered this art. But modern executives also relied on professional assistants who were hired specifically to navigate the administration's policy agenda through the legislature. Structural changes in state government gave governors more political leverage than they had possessed formerly. They gained the right to appoint heads of administrative departments and to formulate the state's budget. Four-year gubernatorial terms and the power to veto specific appropriation items (the line-item veto) spread to most states. Governors and heads of administrative departments, not legislators, controlled the local distribution of Federal grants.[22] Like presidents, modern governors understood that the public expected them to advance a problem-solving agenda. Successful executives, whether liberal or conservative, adopted this leadership style.

J. Edgar Hoover never wielded the kind of authority that presidents possess, but in his special area of operations his power rivaled that of the chief executive. Hoover's power was an extension of the agency that he built. He assumed control of the FBI at a time when the nation sought rationally managed organizations run by professionals who displayed a selfless devotion to public service. Americans in the 1920s also were alarmed by the apparent breakdown in law and order, symbolized by Al Capone–style gangland wars and violence among liquor bootleggers. Hoover responded directly to both challenges. He turned the FBI from a small, inept bureau loaded with political hacks into what appeared to be a model of bureaucratic rationality staffed with disciplined professionals. The young director ordered the systematic collection of criminal data, established working links with state and local law-enforcement officials, and developed a disciplined esprit de corps among bureau employees. Exempt from civil service regulations, Hoover became famous for his tyrannical control of agents, who faced certain discipline, including possible dismissal, for violation of a strict dress code (hats, coats, and ties) and Victorian rules of personal conduct (e.g., no drinking).[23]

Hoover also launched a timely fight against crime. A grassroots law-and-order movement emerged at the end of the 1920s, partly in reaction to violations of Prohibition. Franklin Roosevelt's attorney general called for new crime-fighting authority for the Federal government. With the escapades of "Machine Gun" Kelly, Bonnie and Clyde, and "Ma" Barker in the headlines, Congress complied with a package of laws that set new Federal crimes (e.g., robbing banks insured by the FDIC, committing extortion over long-distance telephone lines), doubled the number of FBI agents, and allowed them to carry guns and make arrests. These steps substantially expanded the police functions of the national government. Traditionally, state and local governments administered ordinary law enforcement and punishment, including the death penalty. The Federal government did not even build a civilian prison until 1902. With the rise of the Federal establishment came an expanded national concern for internal security. Signs of this trend appear in Theodore Roosevelt's executive order that created the Bureau of Investigation in 1908. Units with similar powers followed: the White House Police Force (1922), the Border Patrol (1924) of the Immigration and Naturalization Service, the Federal Bureau of Narcotics (1930). Although most prisoners remained in state and local lockups in the twentieth century, the national government continued to construct detention facilities. The list of Federal crimes also grew; by the end of the 1980s, thirty offenses carried the death penalty. The New Deal law that made robbery of a bank covered by the FDIC a crime, for example, provided for capital punishment.

The rise of a protective shield around the president symbolizes the growth of Federal efforts to ensure personal security. Presidents of the United States had no permanent guard force in the nineteenth century. The assassination of President McKinley (1901) led to the continuous assignment of agents from the Secret Service, then primarily an anticounterfeiting unit in the Treasury Department, to presidential security. Over the years Congress placed the president's immediate family, former presidents, and presidential candidates under Secret Service protection. The assassination of John F. Kennedy (1963) stimulated another expansion of the agency, especially regarding its intelligence-gathering capability and authority to make arrests. By the late twentieth century all branches of the Federal government had their own special police forces. Even the Supreme Court Police are armed and accompany justices on their trips out of Washington. Not to be outdone, governors gained personal protection from their capitol police forces and special details of the state police.[24]

Hoover's power was partly a spinoff of this developing effort to protect the personal safety of officeholders and civilians. But even before Congress increased Hoover's crime-fighting authority the director was in hot pursuit of America's best-known crooks. His most famous catch was John Dillinger, whose daring bank robberies and escapes from justice momentarily distracted Americans from the burdens of the Great Depression. Hoover's talent lay less in nabbing top underworld figures, however, than in publicizing FBI exploits. He sought opportunities to boast about the ability of his G-men to always get their man and the effectiveness of the FBI's scientific methods of fighting crime. Hoover gave advice to authors who wrote about the agency for popular magazines and reviewed radio and movie scripts about FBI cases. He appeared on-camera for numerous promotional films about the bureau. And he shamelessly took personal credit for the successes of his agents. He rewrote the history of the John Dillinger affair, for example, robbing agent Melvin Purvis of the credit for the apprehension. By cleverly orchestrating publicity, Hoover made himself one of the most widely admired figures in the 1930s.[25]

While Hoover offered the public assurances that he was battling crime, he provided services of a different sort for his superiors. At Franklin Roosevelt's request, in 1935 the FBI began to gather information about the political views of individuals and organizations that had criticized the president. FDR said his objective was to monitor the activities of fascists and communists, but he understood the value of more ordinary political intelligence. Despite the absence of clear statutory authority, Hoover interpreted this presidential charge broadly, using it as the foundation for building an elaborate surveillance operation that included illegal wiretaps, burglaries, and infiltration techniques. Over the next thirty years FBI agents eavesdropped on innumerable prominent figures, including Prime Minister Winston Churchill, Eleanor Roosevelt (FDR's wife), former president Herbert Hoover, Martin Luther King Jr., and Robert Kennedy (Hoover's boss at the time of the snoop). The NAACP, the civil rights organization, was placed under surveillance in 1941 because Hoover considered it a threat to American values.[26]

In the name of fighting communism the director expanded his secret program of domestic surveillance into an elaborate spy operation code-named COINTEL in the 1950s. In the 1960s COINTEL targeted civil rights and antiwar groups. The agency used assorted undercover tactics, such as infiltration of organizations with the mission of provoking an incident that would publicly discredit a group. From the late 1930s through the 1960s the FBI was the chief adversary of left-wing and social reform movements in the United States. Operating in the shadows of the Capitol as well as the law, Hoover even spied on members of Congress.

Hoover got away with these excesses by putting the FBI in a position of virtual legal immunity. He achieved this feat partly by legitimate bureaucratic means, such as building an efficient agency, and partly by smoke and mirrors, as in his complicity in the making of G-men movies. He exploited fears of un-American conspiracies in the land and aggressively courted conservatives who defended Hoover's political agenda. For added security, Hoover stocked his files with possibly incriminating evidence against actual and potential critics.

He had little to fear from the top because he ingratiated himself with presidents from Roosevelt to Nixon, who found the director's ability to supply intelligence on political rivals useful. Presidents lacked either the inclination or the nerve to fire him.

J. Edgar Hoover had a counterpart in Robert Moses, who matched Hoover's knack at turning a career in civil service into a personal fiefdom. Moses was born in 1888 to upper-middle-class parents, who moved to New York City in 1897. After private school and Yale University, Moses spent two years at Oxford University in England and then completed a PhD degree in political science at Columbia University. Before graduation he signed on with the Municipal Research Bureau in New York, which was the ideal outlet for Moses's passion to advocate a merit system for administrative appointments. After a change of mayors blocked possibilities for this reform, Moses landed a position as chief of staff on the Commission to Reorganize New York State Government, created by Governor Al Smith. Young Moses's sharp intellect, boundless energy, and dedication to the principles of administrative efficiency and executive leadership appealed to Smith's reform instincts. This was the beginning of a long and fruitful relationship between the two. When Smith won a second term in 1922 he took Moses with him to Albany, where Moses became the governor's master bill drafter.

Moses applied his skill as a legal draftsman to a new passion: creating parks. In 1924 a Moses bill that established the Long Island State Park Commission sailed through the legislature and gave the governor the prerogative of picking its director. Smith of course chose Moses for the position, which automatically gave him a seat on the commission's supervisory body, the State Council of Parks. Moses quickly maneuvered himself into the chair of the parent organization. He held both posts for the next thirty-eight years. Staked with these two seemingly innocuous, nonpaying positions and a $15 million bond issue, Moses embarked on a frenetic campaign of building parks and connecting parkway roads. His first major triumph, the opening of Jones Beach in 1929, secured Moses's reputation as a selfless and far-sighted servant of the people. Although Jones Beach lay only twenty-five miles from downtown New York, inadequate roads and land-use restrictions imposed by the owners of estates on Long Island had thwarted city dwellers' access to it. The combination of bravado, legal bluff, and political power plays Moses used to smash through the obstructions of land barons became trademarks of his style of getting things done.[27]

In 1934, when New Deal money was pouring into New York, Moses was appointed park commissioner for the city. Eventually he held twelve state and city posts simultaneously. Moses drew a salary from only one of these positions, the Triborough Bridge Authority. It was not the salary but the unusual nature of this job that made it Moses's most powerful post.

The Triborough Bridge Authority was a public authority, which meant that it was a semiautonomous body (not directly supervised by the legislature or the executive branch), created to undertake a specific mission. The Triborough, like most authorities, was permitted to borrow money (initially, for the construction of bridges) and to levy fees (in this instance, tolls) to repay these loans (called bonds). Normally a project became the property of a general government when its debt was retired, at which time the authority was dissolved. The legal handcuffs that restricted the flexibility of state and local finance were a primary motive for creating these organizations. New York State's constitution limited the amount of debt that city and state governments could carry, required popular approval for large loans, and allowed only one bond referendum a year. Public authorities sidestepped these legal obstacles. They offered seemingly nonpolitical ways of overcoming the fragmentation of governmental jurisdictions (and thus tax bases) and citizen opposition to additional taxation.

Moses understood these impediments and how to use the legislature to get around them. He urged state lawmakers to create the Triborough Authority, secured its chairmanship in 1934, and opened the Triborough bridges two years later. Then Moses pulled his master stroke. In 1938 he rewrote the authority's charter to permit the refunding of its bonds. Lawmakers failed to see that the revision provided a way to perpetuate the life of the authority as well as the job of its director, whose removal Moses made contingent on paying off the authority's bonds. But Moses knew exactly what he was doing. Armed with these restrictive covenants, which legally prevented public officials from negating his financial contracts, Moses refinanced his bonds again and again.

Bankers were happy to accommodate Moses for several reasons. For one, the Triborough had a steady income. The authority's complex of bridges, which connected the Bronx and suburbs to the north with Manhattan and Queens, proved to be a gold mine. Better roads encouraged more auto traffic, which generated more toll revenue. With money to burn, Moses was willing to pay prime interest rates for his bonds. Bankers liked these terms, of course, but Moses used "sweetheart" contracts to buy good will throughout the business and labor communities. He could spend his money as he chose because the law he had written prevented auditors from prying into the authority's finances.

Triborough's tolls were mere seed money for the scale of building Moses had in mind. During the first five years of Fiorello LaGuardia's stint as New York's mayor (1934–1938) Moses spent over a billion dollars of public works and other New Deal grants. Federal funding for public housing and expressways (Urban Renewal Act, 1949; Interstate Highway Act, 1956) offered equally lucrative subsidies. Much of Moses's success as a developer lay in his ability to pool sources of private and public capital behind a single project. To pay for New York's West Side improvement project (1934–1937), which included the Henry Hudson Parkway, he parlayed funds from twenty-two different city, state, and Federal agencies.

Mastering the fragmented worlds of public and private finance enabled Moses to reshape New York City's landscape. He built express highways and parkways, gigantic bridges, numerous parks, playgrounds, and swimming pools, as well as beaches, public housing, and massive civic edifices. Lincoln Center, the United Nations building, and Shea Stadium represent some of the more visible Moses landmarks. He left his signature throughout the Empire State by constructing parks, dams, and huge power-generating facilities, and on other cities that hired him as a planning consultant. Heralded as the master builder of the mid-twentieth century, Moses influenced most public works projects in New York City and its environs between the 1930s and the mid-1960s. Their cost based on the 1993 value of a dollar approached $100 billion.

Moses did all this without ever holding elective office. But he devised a structure of authority that left him virtually unaccountable to any official, including the president of the United States. In effect, he built a personal empire that gave him immense power, which he could wield as he wished. When he could not buy compliance with sweetheart contracts he resorted to deceit, slander, and intimidation. Ruined careers littered his path to get things done his way. The Moses way alarmed some people, who claimed that the dedication of billions to highways starved public transportation of funds and choked New York with automobile traffic. The critics damned his expressway projects that displaced and abandoned poor residents while lining the pockets of slick developers.

The public rarely saw this raw use of power because Moses was a master at cultivating his own public image. He fed the press endless sanitized copy about his achievements. He wined and dined important people, who reaffirmed the

Moses image as a dedicated servant of the public. Alert to the damage that charges of personal corruption could do, Moses took little financial gain from his many projects. Yet he used the prerogatives of office to live like royalty. He maintained three fully staffed offices (with complete dining facilities) and employed several chauffeurs for his white Cadillac limousine. The master road builder never learned to drive.

Moses and Hoover defied old republican fears of personal entrenchment in office. How could appointed civil servants gain such immense power and keep it for so long? Several clues emerge from an examination of Hoover's and Moses's careers.

In the first place, Hoover and Moses were in the right place at the right time when they were young men, getting in on the ground floor in fields that were destined to expand. Hoover capitalized on a public demand to protect the nation from common criminals and political radicals. Moses arrived on the scene when automobile travel exploded. Second, each man was totally dedicated to achieve his objective. Both brought a feverish energy and passion to their job. Hoover never married; Moses never took vacations or time for hobbies. Their agencies were the center of their lives. Third, Hoover and Moses understood that knowledge can be turned into power. Each man became an expert in his field, which allowed their organizations to offer valuable services. They pointed to their specialized skills as reasons why legislators should expand the authority of their agencies. Fourth, Hoover and Moses had little regard for the strict letter of the law. To them, the ends justified the means. If an action was necessary to achieve their goal and they thought they could get away with it, they did it.

Fifth, both bureaucrats carefully nurtured their public image by manipulating the flow of information. Thus the public never saw how Moses and Hoover actually operated. Secrecy shrouded much FBI and Triborough Bridge Authority business from public scrutiny. Each director spoon-fed the news media copy about his organization. Sixth, each man ran his organization with an iron fist. Nobody worked for long for Hoover or Moses who was not 100 percent loyal. This management style clamped down on internal dissent, which freed the bureaucrats to concentrate on defending their turf from rival agencies. Administrators knew that agency status grew with increased funding, personnel, and statutory authority. Moses and Hoover continually attacked their competitors in order to monopolize control over their areas. At the same time they carefully avoided the assumption of tasks that could discredit their own reputations. Finally, Hoover and Moses courted supporters. Political power does not flow solely from the law; it also depends on personal relationships. Hoover and Moses sought out allies and won them over in part with the strength of their personalities. But they also had useful things to offer. Every president between Coolidge and Nixon turned to J. Edgar Hoover for political information. Mayors considered Moses indispensable to their administrations because he could produce tangible results fast.

Bureaucratic power did not always settle into the hands of a single agency head. Sometimes it was shared by several political figures. Such was the case of Wilbur Cohen and Social Security. Born in Milwaukee in 1913, Cohen earned a degree in economics from the University of Wisconsin in 1934 and immediately went to work for the Committee on Economic Security, which formulated the Social Security program. A year later he became an assistant on the Social Security Board (later renamed Administration), where he remained until he accepted a university professorship in 1956. Although he was off the Federal payroll, Cohen never stopped working for Social Security. Dedicated to the program's mission, he continued to be its tireless advocate. He had pushed for Federal health insurance since the early 1940s and drafted several bills to provide for it. He kept up this campaign as a private citizen and then as an assistant secretary of health, education, and welfare in the Kennedy and Johnson administrations. His persistence paid off in 1965 when Congress enacted Medicare, the health insurance program for the elderly.[28]

Nixon's election in 1968 prompted Cohen to return to academia but not to abandon Social Security. The year 1978, for example, found him in Joe Califano's office at HEW denouncing the secretary's proposals to restrain Social Security costs. Cohen used his chairmanship of SOS (Save Our Security, a lobby group) to protest cuts in benefits that the Greenspan Commission on Social Security reform recommended in 1983. Four years later, on the eve of a speech on welfare for the aged, he died.

Regardless of his employer, Wilbur Cohen remained one of the high priests of Social Security. Others in this fraternity displayed similar devotion to the program. Arthur Altmeyer, who picked Cohen as his first employee in 1935, became commissioner of Social Security and stayed with the program until 1953. Another commissioner, Robert Ball, worked his way up from field representative in the late 1930s to head of the system (1962–1973) and never lost touch with the program in retirement. He was appointed to the Greenspan commis-

sion that modified the program. The group's executive director, Robert My-
ers, began his career preparing actuarial estimates for the Committee on Economic Security and went on to serve as Social Security's chief actuary until he
resigned in 1970. That year Commissioner Ball, his deputy commissioner, and
the four assistant commissioners totaled 191 years of service in the Social Security Administration.[29]

Social Security's managers were not neutral, disinterested bureaucrats as
the classical model of administration projected. Rather, its superintendents
exhibited an ideological mission to defend and expand the system they managed.[30] The administrators stayed with this program because they believed in
it. Their resulting longevity gave them immense influence to shape its future.
Years of experience in managing an exceedingly complex program allowed
the administrators to corner the market on professional understanding about
it. The managers also adopted a patient, incremental strategy toward policy
change, an approach they believed had the greatest chance of political success.
Wilbur Cohen's quarter of a century pursuit of Federal health care illustrates
this persistence. But the managers were also willing to twist the truth. They
knew that downplaying the program's eventual costs would build public and
congressional favor. Until the 1980s, they were able to sustain this mirage.

The Social Security story tells a tale instructive about the formation of the
claimant polity. Hired bureaucrats made policy. Sometimes they were the
single most important actors that caused a program to expand. Four factors
enabled bureaucrats to behave as policy makers. First, legislators delegated
considerable authority to administrators. The complexity and volume of programs in the modern state swamped legislative ability to implement policy.
Practical necessity demanded the creation of administrative units to manage
civic functions. With administrative responsibility came bureaucratic discretion over how programs were to be run. Many statutes instructed administrators to write rules that breathed life into a program. Courts had long held that
administrative directives carried the force of law. The Administrative Procedure Act of 1946 required that Federal agencies publish proposed regulations in
the *Federal Register* for eventual compilation in the *Code of Federal Regulations*.

Second, administrators became experts in their subject areas. Sometimes,
as with Social Security, the bureaucrats were the primary source of technical
information about a program. Longevity on the job was one way of acquiring

this specialized knowledge. The twentieth-century records numerous cases at all levels of government of administrators who stayed at the helm of their organization for decades. With long tenure often came a sense of ownership of the program they tended.

Third, lax oversight of administrators afforded them additional opportunities to act as policy makers. This factor is attributable in part to modern legislative service, which held out more rewards for writing new laws than for monitoring old ones. Elected executives were drawn into a similar incentive vortex. But governors and presidents had limited ability to apply hands-on management even if they had wanted to do so. The administrative layout was too fragmented to allow easy centralized control. Some matters, like nondiscrimination policy, were enforced by many agencies, which could leave a crazy-quilt pattern of administration. Oversight of Federal recreation areas, to cite another illustration, was distributed among seven different agencies. Other policies, like welfare and highways, worked through intergovernmental grants, which split responsibility for a program among people at two or three levels of government. Elected executives usually retreated into a style of crisis management, whereby they focused attention on an administrative issue only when it became a problem before the public. In the customary course of events the agencies themselves assessed the effectiveness of their program and its implementation. Few bureaucrats criticized their own job performance.

Finally, if criticism was aired, bureaucrats called for backup. Powerful administrators made it a point to ally with private or nonprofit groups and legislators who would defend the agency from attack. This fourth factor underlying bureaucratic policy making rests on the reality that political power radiates through networks of personal relationships. Because these strategic alliances were built on mutual assistance, administrators were obligated to help their supporters. The price could be advocacy of the interest group's pet policy. Sometimes the bureaucrats solicited the interest group to lobby for a policy change. Regardless of who initiated a particular tit for tat, bureaucrats had a hand in expanding the public sector.

10

The Reagan Era and the Restrained Polity

REMINISCENT OF GROVER Cleveland nearly a century earlier, Ronald Reagan warned about the crisis of his time. Rampant inflation, unfair taxation, and chronic budget deficits, he said, were sapping the nation's spirit and stifling its economic growth. "Government is not the solution to our problem," the president stated in his inaugural address (1981); it "is the problem." Citing the "unnecessary and excessive growth of government" as the cause the country's troubles, the president proposed to "curb the size and influence of the Federal establishment." Reagan entered the White House declaring war on the modern polity.

Mimicking Cleveland's attack on the tariff and unnecessary taxation, Reagan's plan of action began with Federal finances. "The Federal budget is out of control," he said, and "we face runaway deficits." Reagan urged the reduction of taxes, spending, governmental waste, and counterproductive regulations as ways to lower the cost of government and stimulate private enterprise. Removal of impediments to entrepreneurial incentive would promote economic growth and, according to "supply-side" economic theory, generate greater public revenue even with lower taxes. "Wasteful administrative overhead" should be scaled back by shifting programs to state and local control and to private management ("privatization").[1] Reagan's vision of a scaled-down Federal establishment, a decentralized political system, and economic policy based on free-market principles would have pleased Grover Cleveland.

Reagan also blamed government for undermining the family and moral values. Welfare policy was a prime cause of this decline in his view because it encouraged teenage pregnancy, single-parent families, and drug abuse. Instead of alleviating dependency, welfare had created "a permanent culture of poverty." The president claimed that liberal social policies, such as abortion on demand, toleration of pornography, limits on school prayer, and gun control, also weakened traditional values and community stability. Rekindling sound moral values required that the Federal government stop interfering with local schools, favoring minorities through affirmative action, and coddling criminals at the expense of victims. Rejecting the direction of public policy since the 1960s, Reagan vowed to "take the government off the backs of the great people of this country."[2]

Reagan's attack on big government resurrected old themes in American history. Suspicion of governmental power and the intentions of officeholders had infused early American ideology, and these sentiments had resurfaced on numerous occasions over subsequent generations. A new wave of political mistrust appeared in the mid-1970s, setting the stage for Reagan's 1980 election victory over President Jimmy Carter. Complaints about government were especially pronounced in California, where Reagan had served as governor (1967–1974). In 1978 California voters approved Proposition 13, a tax-limitation initiative, by a two-to-one margin. Howard Jarvis, a retired businessman, spearheaded the drive for this constitutional amendment, which limited increases in the assessed value of homes and capped property taxes. The following year California voters approved a cap on state and local government spending by a three-to-one ratio. Voters in Massachusetts joined the tax revolt in 1980 by accepting Proposition 2½. This initiative law (a statute put on the books by a popular referendum) limited property taxes to 2.5 percent of full cash value of real estate and capped property tax increases to 2.5 percent a year unless voters in a locality passed an exemption (override). Like many Bay State communities, Arlington went for Carter over Reagan in 1980 yet opted for Prop 2½. "People want restraints on government," an *Arlington Advocate* editorial claimed; Prop 2½ signaled that "the era of the free lunch is over."[3]

The tax revolt spread across the country in 1978–1981. Two-fifths of the states imposed limitations on local property taxes, and a slightly lesser number adopted limitations on state taxes or expenditures.[4] These actions coincided with rising complaints that government operations were saturated with waste and that taxes were too high and inequitable. Many citizens believed that a bloated, inefficient Federal bureaucracy was the main cause of chronic national deficits.[5] Doubting that Congress would act to curb the mounting debt, a grassroots campaign mounted a drive in 1975 to persuade the states to call for a constitutional convention for the purpose of adopting a balanced budget amendment. By 1979 twenty-eight of the necessary thirty-four state legislatures had approved the petition, prompting worried opponents to warn that a constitutional convention could turn into "a rogue elephant" and seriously erode basic American liberties.[6] Political discontent became so widespread in 1979 that Jimmy Carter called a domestic summit at Camp David, Maryland, to assess the malaise that gripped the country. The president concluded that a "crisis of confidence" in government prevailed across the country. Policy makers' inability to cope with the nation's "paralysis and stagnation and drift," the president reported, posed "a fundamental threat to American democracy."

What caused the tax revolt? Why had the public soured on government? If history is a guide, tax protests are a staple of American politics. They had occurred regularly since the origins of the republic, usually in conjunction with economic stress, such as depressions or unusual spikes in prices. The economic downturns of the 1840s, 1870s, 1890s, 1930s, and late 1940s all coincided with movements for fiscal retrenchment.[7] The malady of the 1970s was "stagflation," a term that described a combination of sluggish economic growth and high inflation. Between 1973 and 1978 average family income failed to increase, which set off alarm bells in a nation accustomed to rising affluence. Due largely to a sharp recession in the middle years of the decade, the wage sag of the seventies also reflected profound changes in the world economy, in which U.S. manufacturing predominance had eroded. This reversal of fortune continued in the 1980s and later, as Americans faced new competitive pressures from around the globe. Stagnant wages were troublesome themselves, but inflation also soared in the later 1970s, forcing the cost of living to race upward. *Time* magazine diagrammed the impact on the family budget, pointing out that between 1967 and 1979 the price of a loaf of bread had doubled, a woman's two-piece wool suit had tripled, and a Hershey chocolate bar had quadrupled.[8] The cost of homes went through the roof. Mortgage rates in 1978 were twice as high as they had been a generation earlier. Three years later they soared to unheard-of heights of 16 and 17 percent. These numbers added up to tough times for the millions of baby boomers who flooded the job and housing markets in the 1970s but whose incomes did not keep pace with the rise in prices. The baby bust of the same years, when birth rates plummeted, caused school enrollments to shrink, which left many classrooms empty and school hoards with a surplus of teachers. Parents in many communities were confronted with the perplexing choice of closing the neighborhood schools or facing higher education costs.

People were mad as hell, in Howard Jarvis's words, about policy makers' inability to rectify the country's maladies. Reminiscent of the cynicism toward legislators generations earlier, criticism of government grew during the 1970s. Now the cynicism was fanned by a series of disconcerting events that challenged public confidence in the capacity of officials to make government work. The war in Vietnam dragged on in the early 1970s, until U.S. troops left in 1973, leaving South Vietnam to fall to the North Vietnamese communists. Nineteen seventy-three was also the year that the Supreme Court's *Roe v. Wade* decision legalized abortions and instantly created a "right to-life" lobby that sought to overturn the law. To conservatives the abortion ruling symbolized a series of liberal social experiments, such as calls for gun control and tolerance of marijuana, that undermined traditional values. Arab nations' embargoed oil sales to the U.S. in 1973 produced long lines at gas pumps, higher energy prices, and a prolonged bear market for stock values. In 1974 the Watergate scandal preoccupied the nation and discredited President Nixon, whose part in a cover-up of a burglary of Democratic election campaign headquarters in Washington was revealed in congressional hearings carried live on national television. The fall of some of Washington's mightiest political figures packed as much drama as a daytime soap opera. Nixon resigned rather than face impeachment.

Nineteen seventy-five brought revelations that the nation's top security agencies, the FBI and the CIA, had been spying on Americans, including members of Congress. In the same year officials in New York announced that the city was on the verge of defaulting payment on its outstanding loans. Critics saw the Big Apple's fiscal woes as the result of overspending, overregulation, and caving in to selfish municipal labor unions, all of which drove business from the city. Late in the decade the government's inability to free the Americans taken hostage in Iran, the nuclear accident at the Three Mile Island power plant in Pennsylvania, and the U.S. boycott of the summer Olympics in Moscow after Soviet troops occupied Afghanistan raised questions about the ability of the Carter administration to cope with contemporary problems.

Whatever the causes of the new cynicism, policy makers sensed the public dissatisfaction in the late 1970s. Congress and the executive branch shied away from creating new programs and trimmed back on the goals of some existing ones. Encouraged by the Carter administration, which sought to stem stagflation, legislators voted to deregulate trucking, railroads, airlines, domestic oil production, telecommunications, and banking, removing many restrictions on competition in these industries.[9] Lawmakers delayed the timetables for achieving clean water and air, increased emergency exemptions to the regulation of insecticides, backed off forcing Detroit to install air bags in new cars, and limited the authority of the Occupational Safety and Health Administration to order new regulations. Congress slowed the growth of Federal spending, reduced grants to state and local governments, and ended the state portion of general revenue sharing. Responding to charges that it had buried Americans in red tape, Congress directed officials to reduce needless paperwork. Even before Reagan brought his antigovernment crusade to Washington, Carter and Congress had slowed the growth of the Federal government.

Riding the wave of political cynicism into the White House, Reagan proceeded to attack the size of government. First on his hit list was the Federal budget. Appealing to his own party and southern Democrats, the president corralled enough congressional votes to enact the Economic Recovery Tax Cut Act of 1981, which reduced the rate of personal income taxes by 25 percent and provided additional tax breaks for businesses. Congress tacked on an indexing provision that ended "bracket creep," by which inflation had pushed incomes into higher categories of taxation. The Tax Reform Act of 1986 went beyond these changes by collapsing the numerous tax rate brackets into three categories, capping the maximum rate at 31 percent and exempting six million low-income individuals from Federal taxes.

The second prong of Reagan's budgetary attack in 1981, the Omnibus Budget Reconciliation Act, sliced 5 percent out of contemplated expenditures. Most cuts fell on need-based programs such as food stamps, housing assistance, Medicaid, and public-sector jobs; urban programs (especially mass transit and community development); and aid to local schools. The act eliminated numerous Federal grant programs and folded others into generalized block grants. Reagan argued that the "jungle of grants-in-aid" distorted the functions of government and undermined the accountability of public officials.[10] He proposed to return certain programs such as AFDC to the exclusive care of the states in exchange for a Federal takeover of Medicaid (the need-based medical assistance program), an idea that Congress killed. Yet intergovernmental aid remained vulnerable to the budget ax. Between 1978 and 1988 Federal aid to local government fell by one-half and to state government by one-quarter.

The downsizers also targeted regulations that impinged on private enterprise. Many were removed during Reagan's first year, resulting in a condensation of the *Federal Register* by a third. Staff reductions occurred in the Federal Trade Commission, the Food and Drug Administration, the Antitrust Division of the Justice Department, and other regulatory bodies. Reaganites were especially hostile to the regulations that established environmental, health and safety, and nondiscrimination policies. Administration officials stressed private economic development and industry self-regulation over stringent public surveillance. The Reagan White House opposed vigorous enforcement of nondiscrimination policy. It called affirmative-action guidelines unfair quotas, avoided legal actions against apparent patterns of discrimination in the workplace and housing, and opposed busing to promote the racial integration of schools.[11] The idea that government should promote "comparable worth" for female compensation in relation to wages paid to males found no reception in the Oval Office.

Reagan's attack on "excessive" government zeroed in on means-tested programs. Eligibility requirements for Medicaid, AFDC, disability, and unemployment compensation were tightened. The Family Support Act of 1988 mandated that welfare recipients sign up for job training or work as a condition of financial assistance and pressured states to expedite the collection of child-support payments from negligent fathers. Federal grants for urban programs were cut by 50 percent, housing subsidies fell by 75 percent, and the Federal contribution to public school budgets declined from 10 to 6 percent.[12]

Even Social Security did not escape readjustment. Reagan announced in 1981 that an "actuarial imbalance" threatened the "fiscal integrity" of Social Security. The system faced "bankruptcy" unless revenues were accelerated and benefit payments were slowed. The political sensitivity of tampering with this sacred cow persuaded the president to create a bipartisan commission to manage the problem. After two years of wrangling, the Greenspan Commission members negotiated a compromise solution behind closed doors. The 1983 amendments to Social Security raised the age of eligibility for full retirement benefits in stages from the prevailing sixty-five years to age sixty-seven by the year 2027, revised downward the cost-of-living adjustment, and subjected one-half of the benefit for upper-income recipients to Federal taxes. Even the president, future members of Congress, and new Federal employees were forced to join the system. Although hardly earthshaking, these changes constituted the most substantial cutbacks in the life of the program.

The downsizers brought exuberance and zeal to Washington during the 1980s, but did they reduce the size of the Federal establishment? And did the antigovernment fever result in contraction of the public sector generally? Answering these questions is as perplexing as identifying the causes of the expansion of the public sector prior to 1980. By its nature political power is a slippery entity that defies straightforward accounting. We must rely, therefore, on surrogate indicators that approximate the exercise of authority. Examination of three aspects of governing—policy-making actions, public costs, and administrative capacity—suggests directions in governance during the Reagan era.

In keeping with Reagan's own priorities, the analysis can begin with the cost of government. Contrary to a general belief, expenditures did not decrease during Reagan's presidency. In fact, total government spending increased 11 percent between 1980 and 1988 (in per-capita constant dollars). Both Washington and state-local governments registered greater outlays, with the largest increase recorded at the subnational level. Some Federal programs laid out substantially more money: real expenditures per person for Social Security and other insurance programs rose 21 percent, defense went up 42 percent, and payments for interest jumped a whopping 86 percent during the Reagan years. Federal spending for grants-in-aid and veterans' benefits, on the other hand, declined, while the national contribution to welfare held constant. Yet real welfare outlays in 1988 were more than twice the amount spent in 1970. Although Federal officials shifted national dollars toward defense, Social Security, and interest payments during the Reagan years, these big-ticket items consumed a smaller share of the national budget in 1988 than in 1970. Still, Reagan budgeters could boast that they slowed the rate of growth in Federal outlays in the 1980s.[13]

Policy makers also maintained government's customary programmatic objectives. None of the eight major Federal functions nor any of their component subfunctions was discontinued (see table 3). Nor did the states jettison their basic tasks, which encompassed a smorgasbord of activities that ranged from education and the protection of life and property to the promotion of business and the maintenance of parks and wild lands. Viewed from a historical perspective, the most conspicuous feature about public policy in the 1980s was its continuity with past civic activity. Much like the 1920s and the 1950s, government neither added new functions nor shed its old ones during the decade. Instead, the polity downshifted to a slower pace; small, incremental adjustments to existing law became the norm.

Termination of some specific programs did occur. Moreover, Washington dragged its feet in enforcing nondiscrimination, environmental protection, worker safety, and banking standards. But balanced against these administrative slowdowns was increased attention applied to other goals. This tradeoff affects the net accounting of public power. Besides devoting greater resources to the military and high-tech weaponry like Star Wars, which cost $27 billion between 1983 and 1991, Reagan and the Congress expanded the Federal role in fighting street crime. This effort included greater use of Federal courts to try criminal cases, more pretrial detentions, and mandatory minimum jail sentences. In a war on drugs, national officials increased the size of the Border Patrol, authorized more wiretaps, appointed more prosecutors, filled the courts with drug cases, and squeezed more inmates into crowded Federal prisons. The FBI initiated a program of undercover sting operations that netted dozens of allegedly crooked state and local politicians. In California Federal agents posed as businessmen and bribed stare legislators to pass a law favorable to the phony enterprise. The FBI's Operation Lost Trust scored indictments against fourteen South Carolina state legislators.[14] Critics questioned whether this extraordinary use of police power was compatible with constitutional democracy.

The Executive Office of the President itself engaged in novel uses of administrative authority. President Reagan allowed the Office of Management and Budget to expand its review of new regulations that Federal agencies proposed. Contrary to general administrative practice, however, the OMB did not open its decision-making process to the public. The Iran-Contra affair represented another unusual exercise of presidential power: with the apparent knowledge of the president and in conflict with national law, White House officials secretly sold military weapons in the Middle East and used the profits to buy arms for antigovernment guerrillas in Nicaragua (Reagan called them Freedom Fighters). The Irangate scandal was stopped just short of directly implicating the president himself in illegal gunrunning, contempt of Congress, and paying ransom to terrorists.

Administrative capacity, the third criterion by which to assess government's scope and scale, underwent no radical housecleaning. Most agencies survived the decade, and public employment in fact grew at each level of government. Although some regulatory bodies experienced staff reductions, others grew. Even before the savings and loan banking debacle broke into the news at the end of the 1980s, for example, the FDIC had tripled its staff. Although generalization about administrative procedures must be speculative, public agencies appear to have shed little of their bureaucratic red tape. By 1991 the *Federal Register* had regained the pages shed during Reagan's presidency.

Relations between levels of governments show the survival of bureaucratic complexity. President Reagan called the patchwork of grant-in-aid programs a confused mess and urged decongestion of the federal system. He ordered Federal agencies to be more respectful of state prerogatives and persuaded Congress to eliminate some grant programs. But entanglements across the layers of the federal system did not unravel. The number of grant-in-aid programs rebounded to 492 by 1988 (up to 557 by 1991), and most regulations concerning their use remained. One set of rules made the release of Federal money contingent on local compliance with national policy standards. This tactic had been used for years in connection with highway funds, as in the instance of the Interstate Highway Act (1956), which authorized the withholding of payments if a state failed to enforce limits on truck weights. Congress added further stipulations to highway grants in the 1960s and 1970s, pressuring states to regulate roadside billboards (1965), set up highway safety programs (1966), and require motorists to wear seatbelts (1976). During the Reagan years the states were told to raise their legal drinking age to twenty-one years (1984) and enact strict license tests for truck and bus drivers (1986). Most states quickly complied.[15]

Besides continuing to hold state governments accountable to many national standards, Congress increasingly *preempted* state policy-making authority. Preemption occurred when national lawmakers forbade state officials to act in a particular policy area or to exceed a national policy standard. The 1970 amendments to the Cigarette Labeling and Advertising Act (1965), for example, prohibited all state and local health regulations of cigarette advertising. As a result, only Washington could specify the content of warnings that appeared on cigarette packages. Fearful of harsher treatment from state and local officials, tobacco companies had pushed for this muzzle. Mushrooming in the 1970s, Federal preemptions kept coming in the 1980s; Reagan signed seventy-six acts that contained preemption provisions. For example, the Cable Telecommunications Act of 1984, which partially deregulated the industry, prevented state and local governments from controlling certain aspects of the cable TV business, even though they licensed these enterprises to operate in their communities. Other preemptions prevented states from enacting standards, such as environmental protection provisions, that surpassed Federal requirements. The Justice Department continued to use the preclearance section of the Voting Rights Act in the 1980s to disallow local ordinances that potentially diluted the effect of minority votes. However phrased, preemptions furthered the centralization of authority in Washington and increased intergovernmental complexity.[16]

The spread of information data banks about individuals constituted an ominous sign of expanding government control. Over the course of the twentieth century and especially since the 1930s, Washington had increased its capacity to keep tabs on Americans, creating what might be called a surveillance state. Law after law allowed Federal agencies to create files about private citizens. The FBI, the Internal Revenue Service, the armed services, and the Social Security Administration stored several trillion records about individuals. The expanding use of Social Security numbers symbolizes the tendency. Originally intended to verify worker eligibility for retirement benefits, Social Security numbers spread to other uses, such as federal income taxes, state automobile drivers' licenses, and private health care plans and university IDs. The Internal Revenue Service's requirement in the 1980s that parents obtain Social Security numbers for their infant children demonstrated that Washington had taken major steps toward maintaining a national system of personal enumeration. The advent of high-speed data-processing technology allowed Federal agencies to link records and integrate them with other data, such as driver's licenses and criminal records maintained by the states. These developments, coupled with continuing advances in computer capability, steadily enlarged government's ability to track the activities of its citizens.[17]

Government did not contract during the 1980s. If anything its power held constant and perhaps even expanded slightly. Why did the antigovernment crusade fail to downsize the public sector? Ronald Reagan had an answer to this question. He pointed at the Washington "colony," which he claimed had a vested interest in supporting the status quo. Joining together members of Congress, lobbyists, and journalists, each an influential group in its own right, the colony gained additional clout by its defense of special-interest programs.

These Washington insiders were a durable lot, as the predictable reelection of congressional incumbents showed. "There is less turnover in the House," the president quipped at his retirement, "than in the Supreme Soviet [in Russia]." For emphasis, Reagan singled out the Democrats and a Congress "that is out of control" for America's fiscal excesses.[18]

The president's rap on the special interests echoed a refrain heard in the 1880s. While Ronald Reagan may have sounded at times like Grover Cleveland, he was not a slash-and-burn radical. Reagan and Cleveland lived in very different eras in regard to ideas about government. Cleveland had been born at the end of Andrew Jackson's presidency, when a widely accepted axiom depicted officeholders as prone to act in their self-interest to the detriment of the general good. This conviction had animated the republican polity's insistence on limitations on political power. Reagan gave lip service to this old saw, but his effort to downsize government was limited. His agenda was selective, focused on lowering taxes, reducing welfare rolls, and eliminating particular value-oriented social policies.

When it served their purposes, Reaganites were willing to use and even expand public power. Two top administration priorities were strengthening the military establishment and broadening the campaign against narcotic drugs. The legacy of the Reagan years was record budget deficits and a mounting national debt. The administration pushed harder for reducing taxes than it did for trimming expenditures or eliminating major programs. Such a strategy followed the course of least political resistance. Tax reduction is always popular. The reduction of benefits and an increase in taxes is always painful. National officials wanted the best of both political worlds. Thus they decreased Washington's revenue flow, borrowed money to continue benefits at a constant level, and passed on unfunded mandates to the states. Interest to service the debt equaled 3 percent of the GNP in 1988, more than twice its burden in 1970.

People like paying lower taxes, which made the revenue side of Reaganomics appealing. Between 1978 and 1982, when mistrust in government peaked, many voters saw tax reduction as a way to eliminate waste in government and to streamline inefficient bureaucracies. By the mid-1980s, however, the national mood had begun to shift. Opinion polls showed a decline in voter hostility to big government and increased support for spending on environmental protection, jobs creation, universal health care, schools and day care, and the maintenance of drug rehabilitation facilities. Even during the height of the tax revolt, surveys revealed that the public preferred the continuation of services over the reduction of taxes when given a choice between these options.[19]

Reagan had opened his presidency with the claim that "we are in the worst economic mess since the Great Depression." His remedy to rekindle business activity was a package of tax, spending, and regulatory cuts.[20] Economic recovery from the 1980–81 recession, however, limped ahead slowly. The growth of the GDP lagged behind the rate of prior decades; only upper-income groups reaped substantial gains during the 1980s. The average family saw no improvement in its purchasing power; lower-income groups lost considerable ground.[21] The average hourly wage for manufacturing jobs, an area of employment that had catapulted millions of blue-collar workers into the middle class during the postwar decades, fell during the 1980s. The signs were not encouraging for stalwarts of the middle class, such as college-educated males between the ages of forty-five and fifty-four. Their median income peaked in 1973 and then declined, including a 17 percent drop between 1986 and 1992, years that encompassed a recession (1990–1991).[22] Policies of the 1980s may have aggravated American economic anxieties as much as relieved them. The total tax burden on the middle class grew during the 1980s, because the combined result of increases in Social Security, state and local levies, plus the failure to index exemptions from Federal income taxes, exceeded the amount of the Reagan tax cuts. The tax reduction laws of 1981 and 1986 turned out to be windfalls for the wealthy, not the middle or working classes.[23]

Reagan's defense buildup helped to lure the Soviet Union into an arms race that hastened its bankruptcy, allowing George H. W. Bush to boast in 1992 that "by the grace of God, America won the Cold War." But the downside to the new peace was the elimination of high-paying civilian jobs in defense industries; procurement for military goods peaked in 1985, and employment in military-related jobs shrank perceptibly after 1989. The combined impact of the skewed benefits of Reagan fiscal policy and the widespread economic insecurity sapped considerable pep from the antigovernment populism that had peaked between 1978 and 1982.

Behind the crosscurrents of perceptions of government in the 1980s unfolded some larger political rhythms. First, public opinion polls suggest that voters approved of the broad, general goals that government had acquired during the twentieth century. Although they rejected big government in the abstract and thought that the public sector was laden with fat and the private sector was overregulated, Americans were unwilling to disengage government from seeking remedies to specific problems in society or to give up their individual benefits.[24] This instrumental view of power, in which government is allowed to adopt risk-reduction policies, is the essence of claimant politics. Second, confidence in the public sector's ability to deal effectively with contemporary issues has waxed and waned over the decades. In some periods, such as the 1910s, 1930s, and 1960s, considerable public support materialized for the adoption of new civic functions. At other times, such as the 1870s, 1920s, 1950s, and 1980s, the tempo of new policy formation had slowed and cautious incrementalism prevailed. The dynamics that underlay these political shifts are imperfectly understood. Nonetheless, it is apparent that American history has experienced contrasting cycles of governmental activism and restraint. The Reagan era embodied limited success in downsizing the civic sector.

The fragmentation of power in the United States goes far to account for why Reagan did not reduce government further. The heart of claimant politics is acquiescence in government's risk-reduction strategies. Few people willingly consent to the reduction of their own benefits in the name of political reform. The fragmented structure of the American polity offered numerous tactical platforms from which to combat cutbacks and preserve programs. Four of the most important reservoirs of this power were interest groups, the Congress, the courts, and the states. These conglomerations of influence could marshal sufficient strength to divert or defeat attacks on individual programs.

Interest groups possessed special potency. They had a greater motivation to work to preserve a policy from which they received direct benefit than the general public or officeholders had in focusing the necessary energy to cut or terminate it. If the number of political action committees (PACs) was any indication, the volume of interest-group activity mounted during the 1980s. Formed to dispense money to candidates running for election, PACs increased by 63 percent during the decade.[25] Most voters could name only a few of the thousands of specialized interest groups active in the 1980s. Some of these heavy hitters—farmers, defense contractors, public employee unions, the National Rifle Association, the Real Estate Association, bankers, the tobacco and cable TV industries, the American Association of Retired Persons, medical doctors, and hospitals—had enough political muscle to dilute if not deflect attempts to harm their programs. Historically weaker groups, such as the poor, minorities, the young, and urban dwellers, were the biggest policy losers during the decade.

Congress still had plenty of kick left in the 1980s to thwart much of the president's agenda. Focused in good part on staying in office, distributing benefits to constituents, and defending pet programs, members of Congress tended to tread old paths. Reelection rates to the House, for example, remained extremely high. In 1988, for example, 408 of 431 representatives chose to run (95 percent of incumbents) and 402 of them won (98.5 percent), most by margins that classified their seats as safe. Only one incumbent was defeated in a primary.[26] Awash in donations, incumbents outspent challengers by wide margins. PAC contributions to House incumbents in 1987–1988 were eight times greater than the amount given to challengers and usually were allocated among friends of the PAC's special policy interest.[27] Critics sniped that Americans got the best Congress money could buy.

The continuation of Federal budget deficits in the 1980s and 1990s underscored Congress's reluctance to change course radically after Reagan came to power. Lawmakers voted no major new spending initiatives, but they also level-funded most big-ticket items, such as Social Security, Medicare, and other middle-class income-assistance programs. Legislators continued to tuck greater parts of the Federal budget into the "relatively uncontrollable" category, which made it more difficult to decrease total expenditures, and they left tax expenditures—Congress's back-door spending technique—largely untouched. Party opposition to a Republican president explained some of the resistance to downsizing the Federal establishment. Democrats held a majority of seats in the lower House during all of Reagan's eight years and through the Bush presidency, while Republicans maintained a slender advantage in the Senate between 1981 and 1986. Republican–southern Democratic coalitions helped the administration in Reagan's first year, but the alliance splintered afterward. But congressional Republicans too lacked the enthusiasm to tackle spending sacred cows, to the consternation of David Stockman. As Reagan's budget director, Stockman had helped to engineer the 1981 tax cut that he later said "shattered the nation's fiscal stability." In his view Republicans were as much to blame for perpetuating the politics of distribution as were Democrats. Instead of moderating its overzealousness in reducing revenues, Stockman complained, the GOP continued to poison "the political debate with a mindless stream of anti-tax venom."[28]

Congress resisted the attack on the public sector on other fronts as well. Lawmakers showed slight interest in implementing suggestions of the Grace Commission to streamline Federal operations. President Reagan had appointed this panel to investigate the national government's management of administration, with an eye to improving its efficiency. Grace Commissioners reported that the system lacked "control or rational management" and offered 2,478 cost-cutting ideas, including recommendations for privatization of many government activities.[29] Because most of the proposals threatened somebody's vested interest, few won congressional approval. Senators and representatives welcomed the flow of defense dollars into their districts when the military budget rose during Reagan's first term. The end of the Cold War, on the other hand, sent members scrambling, Republicans and Democrats alike, to claim a portion of the dwindling procurement budget for their constituencies. The savings and loan scandal in the late 1980s evidenced the resurgence of classic risk-reduction policy making when major economic interests were at stake. Deregulation of banking in the early 1980s lured many savings and loan institutions into making risky investments in commercial real estate ventures and so-called junk bonds. The financial collapse of hundreds of these banks imposed a huge debt on the Federal Deposit Insurance Corporation and sister insurance agencies that compensated depositors for their losses. Congress came to the rescue of the agencies and ultimately the bankers with a multibillion-dollar bailout package, whose cost was charged to taxpayers.

The courts were a third mechanism that preserved features of claimant politics. Following the constitutional revolution of the 1930s the national courts approved most public intervention into economic and social affairs over the next several generations. This judicial permissiveness continued in the 1970s and 1980s, and opened up new avenues to secure rights and benefits. Plaintiffs turned to the courts with great frequency in the later twentieth century, sometimes with class-action suits that encompassed numerous individuals, to challenge administrative restrictions on their benefits or the failure of executives to protect constitutional rights. A case in point occurred in the early 1980s over the termination of Social Security disability. The Reagan administration had implemented congressional authority to apply more stringent eligibility standards, an action that removed nearly half a million people from the disability rolls. Two hundred thousand individuals—many through class action suits—challenged the termination procedures in Federal court, which restored coverage in more than half the cases.[30]

In addition to upholding affirmative action and overturning arbitrary administrative procedures, courts also issued remedial decrees that ordered agencies to perform certain tasks. Federal courts took this path concerning prisoners' rights. State and local jails traditionally had operated independently of national interference. But in 1969 a Federal district court declared the Arkansas prison system unconstitutional because it violated the Eighth Amendment's guarantee against cruel and unusual punishment. Similar suits followed in the 1970s, resulting in district court orders that mandated remedial actions to reform penal practices and to alleviate prison overcrowding. In 1989 jails in forty-one states operated under judicial caps on the size of their inmate populations or were ordered to improve conditions. State and local governments were faced with the unhappy choice of spending scarce dollars to build more prisons or permitting the early release of convicts.[31]

Federal courts also ordered compliance with environmental rules, including the cleanup of Boston Harbor. The Water Pollution Control Act (1972) had mandated the elimination of untreated sewer discharges and had instructed the states to oversee its implementation. But Massachusetts dallied in updating its antiquated sewer system, which periodically dumped raw wastewater into Boston Harbor. Officials in the harbor city of Quincy sued, an action that prodded state legislators to establish the Massachusetts Water Resource Authority (MWRA). The authority's slow progress in cleaning up the harbor prompted further legal action, this time in Federal district court, which held Massachusetts in violation of national water pollution standards. The judge in the case set a timetable for implementation of the MWRA's antipollution plan. When the authority fell behind schedule in 1991 the judge banned further hookups of new commercial buildings to the metropolitan sewer system until progress was demonstrated. The order effectively put business construction on hold in the region.[32] Plaintiffs used the Federal courts, in other words, to apply pressure on state government to comply with national environmental standards. In exchange for the promise of cleaner water, Boston-area residents received much higher water and sewer charges.

The water pollution and prison cases illustrate the expansion of judicial federalism, in which national judges set policy guidelines for officials at lower levels. In Massachusetts, for instance, Federal justices issued orders that affected the operation of Boston's schools, local jails in a majority of the state's counties, mental health facilities, and two water control agencies.[33] The state's own courts also set policy guidelines, such as the specification of minimum welfare benefit levels and maximum numbers of public parking spaces in certain cities. They enjoined the state from terminating assistance to disabled people without an impartial medical review. The courts didn't always side with plaintiffs, but they offered a recourse for citizens to challenge decisions made by legislatures and administrators.

Despite Federal mandates and preemptions, the states retained considerable policy autonomy in the Reagan era. They used this maneuverability to initiate their own policy innovations, to replace much of the revenue lost in Federal grants, and to find legal protection for individuals' rights in their own constitutions. These state actions constitute the fourth restraint on reducing the size of government. The groundwork for these developments had been laid by steady improvement in policy-making capabilities of state governments, including the adoption of new revenue mechanisms. By the end of the 1980s the states collected more taxes than local government, reversing the historic fiscal relationship between the two levels.[34] These innovations raised the capacity of the states as the service workhorses of the Federal system. Besides directly administering or overseeing the local implementation of human resource, social service, and regulatory programs, the states ran most programs undertaken collaboratively with Washington, such as Medicaid and environmental protection programs. Once the weakest link in the federal system, state governments had evolved into the linchpins of America's multitiered structure of public services and regulations.

Federal judges offered reinforcement for the resurgence of the states. "The essence of our federal system," Justice Blackmun wrote in *Garcia v. San Antonio Metropolitan Transit Authority* (1985), is that "the states must be . . . free to engage in any activity that their citizens choose." At issue in *Garcia* was whether the Federal government could subject a local public agency to the wage and hours regulations of the Fair Labor Standards Act. The court said yes, although it held that Congress, not the Supreme Court, should be the final arbiter of what the limits of national power were. In the same breath, Blackmun reminded lawmakers that the states "unquestionably do 'retain a significant measure of sovereign authority.'" The Supreme Court reiterated this position more emphatically in *New York v. United States* (1992). Explaining the court's rejection of a Federal law that compelled the states to provide sites for radioactive wastes, Justice Sandra Day O'Connor held that "States are not mere political subdivisions of the United States." The Constitution, she observed in language penned by James Madison, "leaves to the several States a residuary and inviolable sovereignty."

While the justices renewed the continuing debate over the division of power in the Federal system, state policy makers had been busy in the 1980s working on many issues, such as education, worker training, economic development, health care, human services, transportation, crime, and the environment. The states picked up some of the slack in environmental protection enforcement left loose by the Reagan administration. They developed wild areas programs, conducted research on acid rain, and required the recycling of cans and bottles.[35] A few states, most notably California, established environmental standards that surpassed Federal requirements.[36] Some states sponsored incubator programs to promote new businesses and experimented with day care centers. Voters in both Massachusetts and California authorized their governments to increase taxes on tobacco products and to spend the proceeds on antismoking campaigns. Despite media attention on Washington in the war on drugs, state and local law-enforcement officials patrolled the front lines against street crime, prosecuted most lawbreakers, and had custody of the largest number of prison inmates.

The states also picked up the slack in the fiscal system, which was buffeted by fiscal crosswinds after 1977. At the local level the tax revolt slowed revenue collection, while efforts in Washington to reduce the budget deficit stripped funds from Federal grants. The states made up much of this shortfall and dramatically increased financial aid to their local partners. California more than doubled its fiscal assistance to local government in the ten years after Proposition 13. Massachusetts followed a similar financial path in the aftermath of Proposition 2½. Middle-class residents gained from these shifts, because caps on property taxes represented benefits for homeowners, who were concentrated in the suburbs. The reduction in Federal aid, on the other hand, drained dollars from welfare and the inner cities. State-run lotteries and revenues from legalized gambling, schemes that swept the country in the 1980s, contained similar consequences. Lotteries were a form of regressive taxation that benefited affluent communities more than low-income neighborhoods.[37]

But there was a limit to how far the states could carry these new fiscal burdens. One perennial problem was the sensitivity of state revenues to recession. The economic slump of 1990–1991 cut into state tax collections and presented state policy makers with deficits in budgets they were legally required to balance.[38] Fiscal woes became particularly acute in Massachusetts, where first Democratic governor Michael Dukakis and then Republican governor William Weld slashed local aid in the face of dwindling tax receipts. The option for many communities in the Bay State was either to lay off teachers, police, and firefighters and close libraries and senior-citizen centers or approve overrides of property tax caps in referenda questions. The 1980s were not, however, conducive to popular approval of higher taxes; most override proposals failed, including referenda questions on three separate occasions in Arlington, Massachusetts. But persistence can pay off. Arlington's voters turned out in record numbers for a special election in 1991 and narrowly approved a $2.5 million increase in property taxes, earmarked mainly for education. But it took a spirited campaign in which school kids played an active role to convince townsfolk that the addition to their tax bill was a good investment.[39]

The structure of federalism permitted such local expressions of democratic policy making. Policy referenda offered voters a convenient way of venting their frustration with civic affairs. Even if state and local governments were not the chief cause of ineffective governance, they were convenient targets for criticism. In the traditional polity each level of government had functioned as semi-independent entities in which the demands on them were modest and their costs were low. In the claimant polity public functions multiplied and civic expenditures rose manifold. A labyrinth of intergovernmental programs confused the locus of administrative accountability. Because these developments blurred the policy distinctiveness between jurisdictions, the states often became the scapegoats for complaints about the way the system worked.

The states faced increased fiscal pressure in this new civic arrangement. They came to shoulder the lion's share of civic services but were handicapped in their ability to pay for them. The historic evolution of governance under federalism, in other words, left functions such as schools, much of health care, support for poor children, and police protection dependent on income sources whose stability was closely tied to the uncertainties of the business cycle and to the political fallout from recurrent tax revolts. Washington, by contrast, had captured the polity's most lucrative tax resources, half of which it allocated to defense and Social Security. National outlays for these two functions in the Reagan years equaled all state and local tax collections, on which scores of programs were dependent. And this was not the only financial inequity between the two governments. Washington could (and did) borrow at will, whereas forty-nine states were prevented by their constitutions, statutes, or both from budgeting deficits.[40] And to add insult to injury, citizens had no direct say in how Congress and the president distributed public money, but they could (and did) vote down state and local tax increases and bond propositions in many localities.

These imbalances between the national and subnational levels of government were the structural legacy of a political philosophy formed in the eighteenth century and refined in the 1800s. The rules of this older regime had been forged out of the conviction that government was a danger to liberty. Americans had attempted to outlaw the abuse of power with legal restrictions, but over the generations they also sought solutions to a myriad of concerns that emerged from social and economic changes. In response lawmakers approved the first modern expansion of civic functions between the Civil War and Grover Cleveland's first administration. They continued this pattern of programmatic response over the next hundred years. Despite the accumulation of an enormous new policy load, however, the old structural political framework remained largely intact. The irony of the Reagan-era reforms was the downloading of many modern policy objectives to the states, whose capacity to manage public affairs continued to be handicapped by republican-era restraints.

Few Americans appeared to be troubled by this contradiction between policy goals and governing capability. They grumbled about the travails of big government and its costs, but they did not demand comprehensive reform of administrative and financial structures. Nor did they want government to abandon risk-reduction programs. The dynamics of the restrained polity thus resembled the crosscurrents of sentiment that had bedeviled politicians since Grover Cleveland's day. Americans have always been of two minds about their government. One voice insisted that individualism should be allowed to flourish, free from nettlesome public interference. The other replied that government should create a secure environment and a stable society. The history of the growth of government in America documents the repetition of this conversation time and again.

11

The Debate over "Big" Government

"READ MY LIPS: no new taxes." Taking a cue from a Clint Eastwood movie, George Herbert Walker Bush pledged to hold the line on taxes in his presidential nomination acceptance speech at the Republican National Convention in 1988. Bush's promise is among the most memorable political remarks uttered in recent decades. His antitax stand echoed the advice of his predecessor Ronald Reagan and probably helped him beat Michael Dukakis, the Democratic presidential candidate, in 1988. But his "Read my lips" remark came back to haunt the president, who angered supporters by agreeing to tax increases in 1990. Although the president proposed to lower the budget deficit by both a reduction in spending and an increase in revenue, conservatives saw Bush's budget maneuvering as a betrayal of his antitax pledge. Here was evidence for the Right that the president was not a real conservative. This resentment cost George H. W. Bush votes in 1992, when he lost his reelection bid to Bill Clinton and to Ross Perot, the billionaire independent candidate who focused on the deficit issue.

President Bush's budget concession hurt his standing among Republicans, yet ironically it reinforced his party's commitment to fiscal prudence. During the next two decades Republicans intensified their opposition to tax increases, making it the core of their policy agenda. Coupled with the advocacy of reductions in public spending, the elimination of budget deficits, and a decrease in the national debt, Republicans hoped to scale back "big" government. They believed that the key to this dismantling process was to deny Washington more money. To a remarkable extent they achieved their objective over the next quarter-century. They kept taxes low, but did not shrink government.

The battle over the budget in 1990 symbolizes the great debate over government in the late twentieth and early twenty-first centuries. Financial issues were not the only issue in this dispute. Nor did every legislative measure pit a united Republican party against Democrats. Yet the Republican demand to tax and spend less generated cohesive partisan conflict in Congress more regularly than other issues and more in the 1990s and 2000s than in prior sessions. Inadvertently, George H. W. Bush had stiffened the backbone of the GOP, especially its conservative (Right) wing, helping to position the party for future election campaigns and encouraging an increasingly impassioned attack on American government.

Debate about the role and size of government has raged on and off since the formation of the American republic. How much power should be allotted to government, especially the national government, and how that power should be used, provoked repeated disagreement in the first decades of American history. Conservative Republicans of the late twentieth century were echoing Thomas Jefferson, who repeatedly warned against the power of the national government. The expansion of the public sector after the Civil War intensified this dialogue. Edward Bellamy's and William Graham Sumner's divergent positions on the subject at the end of the nineteenth century (see chapter 3) foreshadowed debates to come in the twentieth century, when the public sector underwent bursts of expansion in the Progressive, the New Deal, and the Great Society eras. World War II and the Cold War produced additional growth, especially in military power and Social Security. In each of these episodes government had assumed new functions, increased its costs, expanded its administrative capacity, and assumed a greater presence in society. By the 1970s government had grown immensely, measured by financial cost and programmatic objectives, in comparison with earlier generations.

Generally speaking, most citizens acquiesced in this enlarged public mission, in large part because they wanted government to reduce risks and increase security in their lives. Governmental intervention at times of crises, such as economic depressions, foreign threats, and natural disasters, seemed logical in the face of common dangers. The robust economy of the three decades after World War II, which raised family incomes, increased financial equality, and reduced poverty, made the financial costs of the new statecraft easier to bear. Still, there was little unanimity over the emergence of "big" government. Citizens welcomed aid and assistance but complained about bureaucracy and red tape.

Conservative complaints have emphasized these negative aspects of state expansion. Their criticism drew on an old American apprehension that public officials would misuse their power and spent money inappropriately. Since the nation's Revolution commentators have viewed their rulers as potentially tyrannical, susceptible to acting capriciously, and thus compromising individual liberty. Thomas Jefferson frequently emphasized this theme, encapsulated in the Declaration of Independence, which he charged that the king of England had conspired to "enslave" Americans. After 1776 Jefferson wrote elegantly about the imperative to limit the powers of the national government. His contemporary John Adams agreed, warning that the human "love of domination, selfishness, and depravity" threatened the preservation of individual rights. As a safeguard against "tyrannical laws" Adams's solution was a balanced republican government whose principles rested on "laws not men." Delegates at the Constitutional Convention in 1787 agreed that stronger national powers were necessary, but they differed over how much authority to lodge in the new government. Their compromise produced a federal arrangement of divided authority, a decision that became a bedrock principle of American statecraft. But the debate over how much power to allot between the center and periphery was not fully resolved in 1787 or later.

America's frontier experience, where pioneers lived by their wits taming the wilderness and creating new governments, reinforced the commitments to the early axioms of governance—noncentralization, limits on terms of service, bills of rights, careful watch over public treasuries, and very low taxes. Yet over the course of the nineteenth century civic power grew, most dramatically by the Federal government's defeat of the southern Confederacy and the first the regulations of modern business during the Gilded Age. The scope of public aid and restrictions expanded during the Progressive Era, when partisan positions on statecraft took a major turn. During the presidential campaign of 1912 incumbent president William Howard Taft denied the Republican presidential nomination to Theodore Roosevelt, a step that purged many progressives from the GOP and enabled Woodrow Wilson to win the presidency, from which he articulated an enhanced vision of the Federal role. Henceforth Republicans customarily opposed Federal expansion, while Democrats became the primary partisan sponsor of the social service–administrative–military state.

This partisan divide was clear during the New Deal, when the national government combated the Great Depression and provided income assistance to the unemployed, elderly, and needy. Conservative victories in the elections of 1938 and America's entrance into World War II suspended the New Deal reform impulse. Yet the war was instrumental in the redesign of federal taxation and in demonstrating the efficacy of Keynesian-styled fiscal policy, whereby deficit spending helped pay for war and restore the nation to economic health. Military Keynesianism (as national defense expenditures were sometimes called) continued during the Cold War, muting Republican criticism of Democrats during the postwar struggle with communist powers (1946–1973). Republicans stood shoulder to shoulder with Democrats on the containment of global communism and took the lead in the hunt for subversives at home. On occasion Republicans joined Democrats on some domestic initiatives, such as civil rights and environmental protections in the 1960s and 1970s.

Republicans were the minority party at the national level for most years between 1932 and 1972. During the postwar period liberal Republicans, especially from the Northeast, supported some Democratic domestic goals. But this Republican "me-tooism" (such as supporting larger Social Security benefits) alienated dedicated members of the Right.[1] Conservative objection to the creation of the social service–regulatory state had been muted but not silenced since 1933. Writing in 1934, former president Hoover rejected the contention that the Depression could be cured by legislation. He saw worrisome signs of centralization, bureaucratic regimentation, welfare dependence, and diminished opportunities lurking in New Deal legislation. The Liberty League, a group of industrialists and others opposed to the New Deal, provided a short-lived organization that supported Hoover's complaint.

Friedrich A. Hayek, an Austrian-born economist on the faculty of the University of Chicago, was instrumental in creating a philosophic touchstone for conservatives. His book *The Road Serfdom* (1944), a surprise bestseller, warned of a drift toward absolutist government that would stifle individual freedom. Influenced by the political trajectory of Russia, Germany, and Italy, which had adopted authoritarian regimes between 1917 and the 1930s, Hayek viewed small steps taken in the name of providing stability and security as precursors to totalitarianism. He argued that state control of the economy (so-called planning in Western democratic countries) reduced the freedom of choice for individuals. The liberty of individuals, he believed, was critical to the survival of capitalism. Even democratic social welfare regimes, such as arose in the United States, planted seeds that could sprout into autocracy. Hayek's warning about an inadvertent descent into socialism influenced the way many conservatives characterized liberal Democrats. Ronald Reagan's "A Time for Choosing" speech in 1964 on behalf of Barry Goldwater, the Republican presidential nominee, alluded to the dangers of following this slippery slope. Conservatives did not universally accept everything in Hayek's book, but his celebration of individual "freedom of choice" resonated widely with people with antistatist attitudes.

Hayek's phrasing caught the eye of Milton Friedman, whose book *Free to Choose* (1979) build on Hayek's warnings about the dangers of bureaucratic creep toward socialism. A central figure among the "free market" economists, Friedman venerated an economy that minimized economic controls, which he contended stifled enterprise and initiative. Friedman's book, written in conjunction with a public television series about the growth of government, capped an illustrious career as an economist at the University of Chicago, a bastion of conservative thinkers. Much of Friedman's economic analysis had a political connection. He argued that federal bureaucrats, who sought power and job security, and special interest lobbyists, whose objective was to secure sinecures, drove governmental expansion. They were instrumental, Friedman argued, in moving government the toward "the collectivist side."[2] Friedman's advocacy of a capitalist regime with minimal regulation and no policy favors for special interests won over many economists by the 1980s.

Nonacademic writers also kept conservative aspirations alive. One of the most successful was novelist Ayn Rand, who wrote *The Fountainhead* in 1943. Celebrating the freedom of individual action, the book became a favorite among dedicated antistatists. Other conservative authors of the 1940s and 1950s, most notably Albert Jay Nock and Russell Kirk, joined the conversation among a small band of dedicated conservatives. The key figure in popularizing conservative principles in the postwar era was William Buckley, who established the *National Review* in 1955. The magazine became a principal outlet for conservative commentary on public affairs for the next several generations. An engaging personality, Buckley became something of media cult figure, hosting a television talk show where he jousted with liberals for many years. The *National Review* and other periodicals provided outlets for the "neoconservatives," such as Irving Kristol and Daniel Bell, most of whom were disillusioned liberals.

The academics and the authors usually stood apart from the politicians. Barry Goldwater was an exception. A senator from Arizona, Goldwater published *The Conscience of a Conservative* (1960), a small book that made a big splash. Ghostwritten by William Buckley's brother-in-law, the book provided a pithy synopsis of postwar conservatism. The book is still in print, which testifies to its literary vitality. Goldwater added little new to the conservative credo, but he tailored its axioms to the politics of the 1950s in a way people could understand. Like Hayek, he saw "welfarism" as a backdoor road to "socialism." The "stifling omnipresence of government" was causing "our vanishing freedoms" he wrote. Because "the people's welfare depends on self-reliance," Goldwater rejected the proposition that his legislative role was to pass new laws: "my aim is . . . to repeal them."[3] Many of Ronald Reagan's sound bites echoed lines in *Conscience of a Conservative*.

In various forums and formats between the New Deal and 1992, authors, academics, and politicians had discussed the principles of conservatism. These writings and speeches built a reservoir of ideas on which modern conservatives drew. A summary of these premises helps to characterize the ideological impetus behind the increased visibility of conservatism after 1992. First, however, one must realize that there is no *single* philosophy of conservatism. Rather than a rigid set piece, conservatism contains varied perspectives, whose emphases have changed over time. Any brief summary necessarily homogenizes these variations. Second, one must be mindful that conservatism as a philosophic outlook is not necessary synonymous with the actions that politicians took. Politics remains the art of the possible; it demands that groups unify around a single candidate, such as a nominee for president, and that candidates recognize who their supporters are. When issues reach the voting stage in a legislature the choice for lawmakers is restricted to voting yes or no (or abstaining) on the motion before them. Ideologies take on varied hues and colorations; politics forces decisions on particular matters at specific moments.

The root idea of modern conservatism begins with liberty. As with the American revolutionaries, liberty meant the preservation of freedoms for individuals. The term includes the legal protections conveyed in the concept of "rights," but its scope is broader. Fundamental to liberty was citizens' right to elect political representatives. This prerogative and the ability of individuals to find their own way in an economy based on the ownership of private property constituted core principles of a republican polity. In short, a good society rests on individual self-reliance. Beyond an individual's personal choices, the family, the local community, and the church, following Judeo-Christian morality, offer the primary precepts to guide behavior. Self-reliance and equality of opportunity give a capitalist economy its distinctive advantages. Markets should function with minimal regulation and little or no governmental planning. The phrase "free markets" encapsulates the rudiments of this system, in which individual initiative and competition generates economic growth and renders benefits for society.

Conservatives express a deep pride in their nation and its heritage. They see America as exceptional, with a distinctive core of values, and are not embarrassed to boast that the United States stands as a beacon of hope and fairness in a troubled world. They believe their country's principles must be defended at home and abroad. This worldview put American conservatives in the forefront of opposition to communism after World War II. Right-wing conservatives are skeptical that government can do much good beyond providing order at home and security from foreign threats. The best government is one closest to home; the "central" government is the most likely to curtail liberty. Barry Goldwater called the states "the cornerstone of the Republic, our chief bulwark against the encroachment of individual freedom by Big Government."[4] Thomas Jefferson would have seconded the sentiment.

Practical politics requires a transition from ideology to policy positions. Generally speaking, the Republican Party has served as the conduit for conservative ideas since 1912. The party's overriding goal has been the reduction in the scope of governmental action. "This government is too big," George H. W. Bush intoned at his 1992 inauguration.[5] Other Republicans over the next two decades echoed this conclusion, concurring that the Federal government was unrestrained and "ever-expanding." These charges have animated Republican proposals to slash expenditures, taxes, and the federal bureaucracy. John R. Kasich, chair of the House Budget Committee, defended large proposed budget cuts in 1998 with the argument that the Federal government "is without question the most bloated, inefficient, duplicative red-tape organization on the face of the earth."[6]

Republicans claimed that big government threatened individual freedom, impeded business, and fueled an inefficient bureaucracy. This condition had become institutionalized over the years because Democrats had accommodated pet interest groups that extracted "handouts" in exchange for votes.[7] Republicans singled out labor unions, which were a major component of the Democratic voter coalition from the 1930s through the 1960s. Cutting off the flow of funds to privileged special interests would disrupt this corrupting process, a strategy that Representative Kasich and House Speaker Newt Gingrich pursued in the late 1990s. In 1992 George H. W. Bush promised "to set the economy free" by reducing "high taxes, high regulation, red tape, and yes, wasteful governmental spending."[8] After 2000 Republicans increasingly justified budget cutting as a stimulus measure for the economy. In 2011 House Budget chair Representative Paul Ryan of Wisconsin supported massive budget reductions with the prediction that more federal spending meant more borrowing, which would require higher taxes and thus stifle job creation.

Conservatives zeroed in on Federal taxes because they provided the funds that supported profligate spending. Tax reduction not only would force government to contract its activities but also was good in principle because taxes were an "attack on property rights," as Barry Goldwater put it. He called the graduated income tax a "confiscatory" one that punished success. Some libertarians saw income taxes as "plunder" and likened the IRS to the Mafia.[9] Most Republicans adopted less extreme positions, but they did unite behind President George W. Bush's tax reduction bills in 2001 and 2003. The younger Bush redeemed the legacy of his father.

After taxes and the federal bureaucracy, welfare was high on Republicans' list of programs in need of reform, if not elimination. Public assistance to the poor and unemployed had never been popular in America, even in the depths of the Great Depression. Barry Goldwater saw welfare as "the elimination of any feeling of responsibility" for a person's own welfare. It transformed "the individual from a dignified, industrious, self-reliant, spiritual being into a dependent animal creature."[10] Charles Murray, a social observer, argued that welfare undermined the work ethic and should be scrapped. Economist Milton Friedman thought a negative income tax (a kind of reverse tax) was a better way than welfare checks to address income deficiencies; he predicted that his plan would also eliminate welfare fraud.

Social Security, the giant among the "entitlement" programs that distribute benefits to individuals, was a target for GOP reformers. Republicans recognized the popularity of the program, which offered modest yet rising stipends to millions of retirees, their spouses, and disabled persons, and thus were cautious about it. Yet Republicans criticized U.S. Treasury borrowing from the Social Security Trust Fund to cover the deficit. They questioned the prospect that Congress would repay the loan, thus leaving the program strapped for funds in the future. The Republican solution for what they saw as a "crisis" in Social Security was privatization, whereby individuals would contribute FICA taxes to personal accounts that would be invested in private financial markets. President George W. Bush floated the idea in his second term, but he dropped the plan when it failed to generate sufficient support. Thereafter the GOP pushed to reduce benefits.

Republicans have stood for a traditional view of social morality. They opposed abortion, legal recognition of gay marriage, the decriminalization of narcotic drugs, and easy access to pornography. Schools should allow prayer and the teaching of "intelligent design" but prohibit sex education—and there should be no Federal taxation of private religious schools that violated national nondiscrimination policy. The evolution of a "rights" society in which nondiscrimination standards were enacted to protect the rights of racial minorities, women, and gays draw lukewarm support from Republicans. They criticized "liberal judicial activism" that undermined "family values" and was soft on criminals. Conservatives tended to support aggressive surveillance techniques (like wiretapping and phone monitoring) that were advertised as antiterrorist measures; the 9/11 attacks and Boston Marathon bombing (2013) intensified this sentiment. Most Republicans supported the National Rifle Association's opposition to gun restrictions.

The modern liberal perspective, which emerged during the New Deal and expanded during the Great Society years, contends that government plays a beneficial role in society. Drawing on the commonwealth conception of community in early American history, liberals contend that government has an obligation to promote social wellbeing and help individuals who fall on hard times. They question the wisdom of a society that place exclusive reliance on the individual, for whom private and personal concerns dominate, or on an unregulated market place, where profit motives rule. Such an unregulated society will undermine the community's interest. Responsible governance requires an open and transparent democracy, where voters have an effective voice in public affairs. Because massive amounts of money entered politics since 1992, liberals support restrictions on campaign contributions, including donations to political action committees (PACs).[11]

Liberals agree that government should help individuals who fall on hard times, whether due to economic recession or to personal misfortune. They pushed the adoption of Medicare and Medicaid in the 1960s and generally favor universal health coverage, with many advocating a single payer system (i.e., government, like western European nations). Liberals argue that investment in public goods, such as infrastructure (roads, bridges, airports, dams, schools, health facilities) and basic research (biomedical, technology, energy) reaps social and economic returns for society. They also expect government to keep the environment clean and safe, and to maintain public spaces, such as playgrounds and national parks. Liberals increasingly embrace the conviction that government should guarantee the equal protection of law for racial minorities, women, the elderly, the disabled, and gays.[12]

The liberal outlook accepts private enterprise as the foundation of the economy. They join conservatives in the belief that individual achievement deserves reward and that private property should be protected, but they also insist that government should keep the economic playing field open to all and fully competitive. Acceptance of the "free market" should not mean a license to manipulate the system for individual or corporate gain. A fair economy requires regulations that seek to promote competition (and thus a counter to monopoly) and punishments for violations of law concerning business and banks. Liberals express reservations about privatization, where public functions are contracted to the private enterprise, and are skeptical of claims that private firms are more efficient than government. Since the 1930s liberals have viewed labor unions as a legitimate counterweight to corporate power, and accept the economic and moral basis for minimum-wage laws and unemployment compensation. From a larger philosophic perspective, liberals give greater emphasis to economic justice than do conservatives, who place a higher value on economic efficiency. They also see the Federal government as more likely to support liberal objectives than will state governments.

Finally, liberals take a pragmatic position on how and when to tax. Most liberals support a "progressive" schedule for the income tax code, whereby the rich pay a higher proportion of their earnings to government than do lower and middle income groups. In keeping with Keynesian economics (see chapters 4 and 5), liberal economists believe that government can rekindle economic recovery during recessions by (temporary) deficit spending. Conservative Republicans criticized the George W. Bush administration for authorizing a financial bailout for large financial institutions (TARP 2008) and the Obama administration for sponsoring the Stimulus Act (2009) to combat the Great Recession. Historically, liberals have not agreed about the details of these and other policy developments. Nonetheless, in general they have supported the idea that government has a responsibility to promote economic growth and to moderate extreme income inequality.

This sketch of conservatives and liberals has remained relatively constant since the 1970s. Opinion polls on ideological self-identification record that moderates (middle-of-the-roaders) were the largest group, encompassing roughly 38 percent of respondents, while about 35 percent of interviews called themselves conservative, compared to 27 percent who identified as liberal. More individuals identified with Democrats than with Republicans in the post–World War II era, although the gap between the parties has narrowed since the 1980s. From the fifties to the early 2000s the proportion of independents has doubled. In other words, neither the liberals/Democrats nor the conservatives/Republicans have a political headlock on political sentiments of Americans.[13]

Yet this story has several additional dimensions. For one, conservatism has gained a firm foothold among many opinion leaders, including the media, members of Congress, and perhaps a majority of economists since the 1970s. Spokespersons affiliated with these groups are influential in persuading the public that government intervention carries negative effects. And second, conservatism has achieved considerable electoral success since 1992, primarily through the Republican Party. But how? What explains the Republican revival?

Four factors can tell much of this story. The economy is the place to start because it is the most important domestic influence on politics. Because four-fifths of Americans work at a wage or salaried job, the condition of the economy has a critical bearing on employment and thus on individual well-being. For most Americans the loss of their job can produce a financial catastrophe. Public opinion polls show that voters have regarded the economy as the most important domestic issue facing the nation over the past quarter of a century. These concerns spike higher when the economy lapses into a recession.

The historical record demonstrates that major economic downturns have triggered changes in American politics. The depressions of the late 1830s–early 1840s, the 1870s, 1890s, the panic of 1907 (which includes a pair of recessions between 1910 and 1915), and the Great Depression of the 1930s all produced partisan or policy changes, and often both.[14] The recessions of 1974–1975 and 1980 helped to swing voters against the incumbent party. The downturns of 1991–1992, 2000–2003, and 2008–2010 influenced the elections that put Bill

Clinton, George W. Bush, and Barack Obama into the White House.[15] Polls documented that effects of the 1991–1992 recession helped Republicans gain their stunning victory in the 1994 congressional elections.[16] Unemployment reached 10 percent in the Great Recession; perhaps as large a proportion of the workforce consisted of discouraged workers (dropouts from the workforce) and part-time workers (many of whom wanted full-time jobs). The slow recovery from the Great Recession and resentment of Federal antirecession spending helped Republicans regain the majority in the U.S. House in 2010.

Recessions can be considered short-run events, with a declining and a recovery phase during each business cycle. These ups and downs, however, play out within the rhythms of longer trends. Since the 1970s the long-run economic story has brought numerous disappointments. Whereas the incomes of most Americans rose steadily between 1948 and 1973 (the "good times" postwar economy), the decades since the oil embargo of 1973 have seen slower gains for most Americans. Median household income was lower in 2011 than in 1989 (adjusted for inflation) according to the Census Bureau. It was only 5 percent higher than in 1973, largely on the strength of women, and especially mothers with young children, going to work.[17] The "feminization" of the workforce lowers overall wages, because women make less than men (even when they work at the same positions). The earnings of male workers who lack education beyond high school has declined over the past three decades. Many good-paying jobs of the postwar economy (1948–1973) have vanished during the slower-growth years (1973–), in part due to the contraction of manufacturing in the United States. Manufacturing employed more than a quarter of the labor force in late 1940s; in 2009 the proportion had dropped to 8 percent. Service jobs, which pay less, have expanded substantially.

New corporate strategies have contributed to this new economic uncertainty. Businesses have moved many manufacturing and service operations abroad, and have taken a more aggressive policy toward labor. Labor union membership, which had fought for wage increases and formed a backbone of the Democratic coalition during the good-times economy, has shrunk from over a third of the private sector's workforce (1950s) to less than 10 percent. Corporations have also reduced private safety nets, replacing company pensions with 401k plans that require employee contributions, and made employees pay a larger share of health-care coverage. Many businesses have followed Walmart's practice of hiring part-time workers at low wages without benefits and aggressively warning away labor unions. Most economic gains of the last three decades have flowed to the Fortunate Fifth of the workforce, and especially to the top 5 and 1 percent of income earners. Some observers speak of an emerging caste system in the United States where two Americas exist: those who have been able to remain in the middle class and those who see their economic status slipping or at risk.

The good-times economy (1948–1973) featured rising incomes, a major expansion of the middle class and homeownership, and corporate policy that accommodated labor. This was the period when the claimant polity reached its apex. Since then the United States has experienced slow economic growth, income stagnation, growing financial inequality, corporate strategies focused primarily on short-term profitability, and repeated recessions. This recent period has overlapped the restrained polity, which took shape in the 1980s. Arguably, an age of economic uncertainty has fueled attacks on traditional liberalism.

Political changes do not necessarily flow directly or automatically from economic circumstances. Voters must see viable alternatives to the people and policies in place. Conservatives have worked diligently to provide these options, a development that constitutes a *second factor* behind the conservative revival. Much of the groundwork for nurturing an antistatist perspective was laid in the 1970s by research institutes, businesses, and religiously based organizations. These groups became institutionalized in the following decades, evolving into a network of well-funded entities that disseminated conservative ideas. The American Enterprise Institute and the Heritage Foundation (1973–) were important conservative think tanks, rivaling to the liberal-leaning Brookings Institution. The Cato Institute (begun 1974–1976 as the Charles Koch Foundation) sponsored publications with a libertarian bent. All three of these conservative groups were headquartered in Washington, D.C., as were many of the groups created during later years. Also located in the capital city was Grover Norquist's Americans for Tax Reform (1985–), a group that got most Republican members of Congress to sign an antitax pledge. Norquist promised to support primary opposition to Republicans who backslide from their antitax commitment. The *Wall Street Journal,* the nation's most influential business newspaper, functioned as a conduit for conservative ideas through its editorial page.

The 1970s was a transitional decade for business, which mounted a more organized approach to government and politics. In 1970 most of the nation's 500 largest corporations did not have a public affairs office; in 1980 four-fifths did.[18] In 1972 CEOs from a number of large firms formed the Business Round-table, which became a powerful lobbying group. A much older organization, the Chamber of Commerce, underwent a transformation from a low-profile federation into a zealous advocate of private enterprise. Aiding this energized political campaign was the loosening of restrictions on political contributions, whereby corporations were allowed to solicit their employees for donations and to fund political action committees (PACs). With more money and better coordination, business became a formidable adversary for regulators and liberal candidates for office.

The Christian Right formed an instrumental organizational lever for the conservative resurgence. Evangelical Protestants (sometimes called "born-again" or fundamentalist Christians) constituted over 20 percent of the electorate. A number of evangelically oriented religious groups, such as the Christian Coalition and the Moral Majority, became active in politics in the last quarter of the twentieth century. Evangelical ministries used radio and television to broadcast religious services that pitched support for traditional "family" values. The tax code allowed many religious organizations to qualify as non-profit entities (tax-free status) that could use a portion of their donations for political advocacy. The evangelical political movement helped to wean working-class voters away from the Democrats, especially in the South. In the 2004 presidential election 78 percent of "born-again and evangelical Christians" voted for President Bush.

Money has long been a part of elections and lobbying in American politics. But the amount of political funds has grown enormously, and the rules governing their use have changed since the 1970s. Congress, the states, federal courts, and the Federal Election Commission (created 1971) have combined to create a byzantine complex of rules concerning campaign finance. The result has significantly diluted the effect of restrictions on campaign donations. Money from business, wealthy donors, and labor unions poured into the election campaigns in the 2000s. The two parties raised over $2 billion in 2012 for their presidential candidates. Republicans have been the chief beneficiary of corporate donations. In the 2010 elections, when Republicans regained the majority in the U.S. House of Representatives, business groups outspent labor unions $1.3 billion to $79 million. Businesses and the finance industry have pumped billions into lobbying Congress. In *Citizens United v. Federal Election Commission* (2010) the Supreme Court struck down spending limitations on

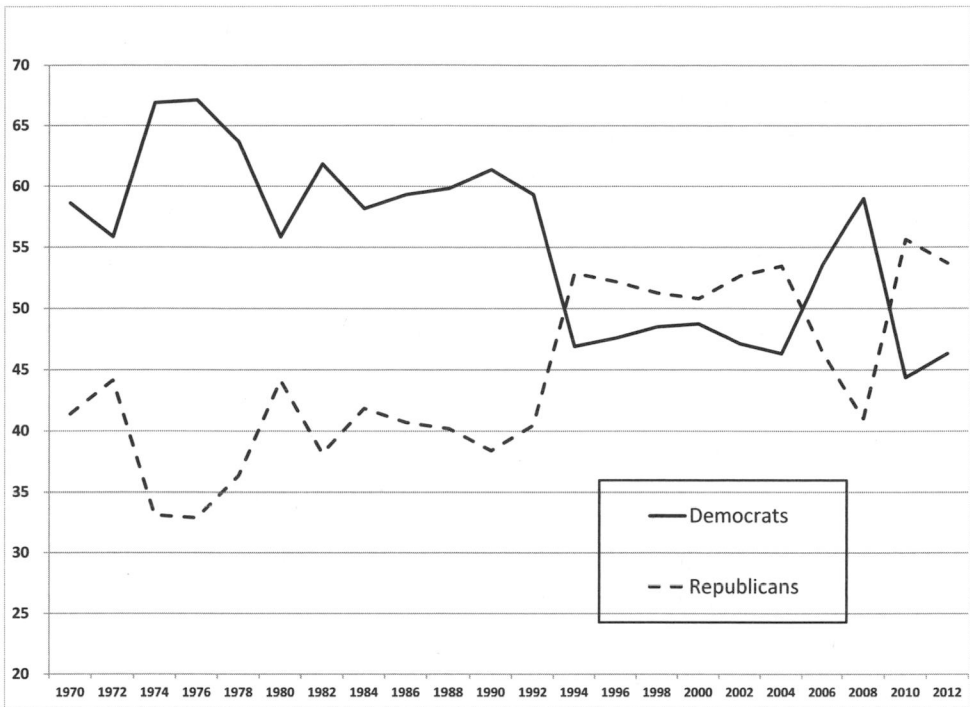

FIGURE 11.1. Party Balance in the U.S. House, 1970–2013: % of Seats Held

corporations, private associations, and labor unions for political advertising during election campaigns.

Winning elections requires organization and a strategy. Republicans have honed their skill in these arts since the 1980s, a development that constitutes the *third factor* behind the conservative revival. This story can begin with Congress. Democrats controlled the House of Representatives from the election of 1954 through the election of 1992, the year when Bill Clinton won the presidency (see figure 11.1). The congressional election of 1994 broke the Democratic hold on the House, with Republicans taking fifty-four seats from Democrats to claim the majority. The largest partisan turnover in the House since 1938, this reversal of fortune is remarkable in light of the high rate of incumbent reelection and few remaining competitive seats (districts in which each party had a reasonable chance of winning). How had it happened?

Newt Gingrich was key to this electoral earthquake. A former college professor, Gingrich won a seat in the House in Georgia on his third try in 1978.

Once in Washington, Gingrich set his sights on upending the liberal regime in the House. Gaining the chair of GOPAC, an organization devoted to advancing Republican political fortunes, Gingrich recruited candidates for the 1994 election, schooled them in tactics, and helped solicit financing for their campaigns. To punctuate the conservative orientation of the Republican attack on liberalism, the Gingrich group offered a campaign platform called the "Contract with America." The document pledged to cut spending and taxes, insert a balanced budget requirement in the Constitution, get tough with criminals, revamp welfare (with their "Personal Responsibility Act"), and set term limits for national legislators. Rush Limbaugh, with his 20 million listeners, and other conservative talk-show radio hosts, acted as cheerleaders for the Gingrich group, which struck pay dirt. Republicans garnered 52 percent of the popular vote in 1994 compared with 44 percent in 1990 (the previous "off-year" congressional election). Republicans gained a whopping nine million additional votes over 1990. His extraordinary electoral achievement earned Gingrich election as Speaker of the House. A year later *Time* magazine selected him as "Man of Year."

Gingrich's strategy was a key, but not the only factor behind the 1994 surprise. Post-vote polls showed a customary portrait in which Republicans outdrew Democrats among whites, men, Protestants (evangelicals especially), independents, and more affluent voters. But the surveys also showed that voters whose saw their financial situation as "worse" voted Republican by nearly a two-to-one margin; voters who saw their financial situation as "better" went Democratic. Moreover, Republicans improved their standing among low-income voters, which encroached on a traditionally Democratic constituency.[19] What the Gingrich campaign was able to do is convert voter frustration with the economy and social trends into a reproach of liberalism, and attract a substantial number of white male workers. Republicans drew on these sentiments in varying degrees over the next several decades.[20]

Many of the party-defector voters in the Gingrich "Revolution" were southerners. Whites in the south tended to be conservative, especially on civil rights and social issues (like abortion, crime, and welfare). Until the early 1980s, however, they had remained Democrats in voting for Congress and state offices. In 1976 Republicans took only 27 of 108 U.S. House seats in the eleven former states of the Confederacy. In 1994 the GOP won 64 House seats in the region versus 61 for Democrats, gaining an additional 16 seats in the 1994 election alone. Republicans also registered major gains for southern state legislatures, traditionally Democratic institutions. The Gingrich Revolution was instrumental in accelerating the historic transformation of the south from a Democratic to a Republican region.

The GOP hold on the south grew stronger over the next two decades. In 2003, the third year of the George W. Bush presidency, when Republicans controlled both congressional chambers, the House Speaker and majority whip were southerners, as were the majority leader and whip in the Senate. The election of 2010 put 94 southern Republicans in the House, compared with 37 Democrats. In Texas, where Republicans gerrymandered congressional district lines to their advantage, the GOP Republicans held a 23 to 9 advantage; in Florida Republicans held 19 of the state's 25 House seats. The south's partisan transition to Republicanism benefited from the regional redistribution of Americans. Between the end of World War II and 2000 the population of the South and the West grew faster than that of the East and Midwest.[21] Republicans gained in popularity in the two regions of the nation that had expanded the most.

The Gingrich Revolution also reshaped the organization of the House, and in the process, changed some public policy. Bypassing senior Republicans for some committee assignments, Gingrich imposed more centralized control over his legislative party. Tight Republican organization facilitated House passage of most of the Contract with America, including a balanced-budget amendment to the Constitution, but it and most other Contract bills died in the Senate. Gingrich rallied congressional Republicans to reject President Clinton's budget. When Clinton continued to resist Republican fiscal demands late in 1995, the GOP forced two shutdowns of the Federal government in weeks around the Christmas holidays. In addition, the Gingrich movement persuaded President Clinton that the time was right to "end welfare as we know it." The reform substituted federally guaranteed welfare reimbursements to states under AFDC for a plan that gave more discretion to the states and mandated that aid beneficiaries accept a work requirement.

Although the public blamed Republicans for forcing the shutdowns of the national government, Gingrich was successful in pushing the president to the right politically. Sensing voter frustrations with traditional liberalism, Clinton pronounced in this 1996 State of the Union message that "The era of big government is over . . . we need a smaller, less bureaucratic government . . . one that lives within its means." He spent much of his presidency on the defensive, deflecting Republican attacks on the liberal policy establishment. The level of party disagreement in Congress reached one of the highest levels in the twentieth century. But Gingrich overreached, alienating moderate Republicans with his ideological attacks on liberalism. The Speaker also stumbled in his condemnation of Clinton's sexual encounter with a White House intern, a tactic that Gingrich thought would win votes for his party. But his assumption proved faulty, as Republicans lost seats in the 1998 midterm election. The House Ethics Committee fined the Speaker $300,000 for misusing campaign donations in his political activities leading up to the 1994 election. Facing diminished confidence among Republicans, Gingrich resigned from Congress.

Although his own congressional career ended with startling swiftness, Gingrich played a pivotal part in the resurgence of the Right in America. His ideological condemnation of the social service–managerial state set the tone among Republicans for the next generation. Gingrich's demand for tighter central control in Congress produced increased party cohesiveness and consistent opposition to Democratic measures. Partisan voting disagreement in the national legislature reached levels not seen since early in the twentieth century.[22] The Gingrich Revolution broadened the establishment of Republicanism in the South. This transformation played a major role in forging ideological consistency in the GOP, whereby districts that voted for a Republican presidential candidate also elected Republicans to Congress. President George W. Bush and Karl Rove, his key political adviser, pursued a strategy that nurtured the party's conservative base rather that develop wider political appeal that would attract independents. In the process moderate Republicans, many from the Northeast, were weeded from the party. Democrats, too, trended toward greater liberal homogeneity in districts they won. These trends contributed to a "sorting out" of party and ideology within the United States, whereby constituencies tended to elect both congressional and presidential candidates of the same party. Split ticket voting declined. Districts thus became more distinctly conservative or liberal, leaving fewer party moderates or toss-up congressional districts, and thereby abetting ideological conflict between the two parties. The result was "hyperpartisanship" in Congress from the mid-1990s though the Obama presidency (2009–2017).[23] When partisan control of Congress and the presidency was split, policy gridlock occurred frequently, as witnessed during President Obama's administration.

Hyperpartisanship also divided the Supreme Court of the United States, notably when William Rehnquist served as chief justice (1986–2004) and since John Roberts was appointed as chief justice (2005–). On various subjects but particularly cultural issues, a liberal bloc of four justices faced four conservatives. Anthony Kennedy, a Reagan appointee, emerged as the most frequent "swing" justice, whose vote determined the outcome of many close cases. The Supreme Court upheld the Obama health-care law, ruled the 1996 Defense of Marriage Act unconstitutional (regarding gay couples), nullified a key provision of the 1965 Voting Rights Act, and allowed corporations to contribute unlimited sums to non-candidate PACs by 5–4 decisions.[24]

Economic conditions and social trends, interest organizations, and partisan strategy account for much of the dynamic behind the revival of Republican electoral success. In general, these were long-term factors that evolved over the years. Unexpected events, on the other hand, occurred with episodic randomness and provided a single, one-time shock to the body politic. These "random intrusions" (see chapter 2) had immediate, and usually shorter-run, impacts on governance, in part because their effect disrupted the status quo. Because politics tends to settle into a balance of power, changes at the margins of this equation can have magnified effects. The implosion of the Soviet Union (1988), which ended the Cold War, removed an issue that had unified Republicans. The Clinton sex scandal (1998), which galvanized Republicans in a cohesive attempt to impeach the president, posed a mini-crisis for a Democratic administration. Politically salient events—the *fourth factor* in the conservative revival—arguably worked in favor of Republicans, especially in the twenty-first century.

George W. Bush's election (or "selection" as some critics saw it in light of the Supreme Court's 2000 decision) was a curious end to the twentieth century. A ruling by the Florida Supreme Court on disputed votes in certain precincts of the state was overturned on a 5–4 vote by the U.S. Supreme Court, thereby blocking a recount (which might have produced a Gore victory) and confirming Bush's victory. The new president began his term under a cloud of doubt about his political legitimacy. But within months the 9/11 attack transformed his presidency. Beginning with Bush's dramatic defiance of terrorism from the rubble of downtown Manhattan, 9/11 converted his administration into a wartime presidency and reversed his sagging public approval rating. The U.S. invasions of Afghanistan and Iraq followed, aiding Bush's reelection in 2004. Then he hit unexpected snags, including scandals involving Republican members of Congress and his administration's clumsy response to Hurricane Katrina (2005). Rising skepticism over the war in Iraq helped Democrats regain the majority in the House of Representatives in 2006. The Great Recession, which began in 2008, was a key factor in Barack Obama's presidential victory over Republican John McCain.

Barack Obama's appeal for a less partisan politics resonated among many voters, but it did nothing to restore bipartisan harmony in Washington. Congressional Republicans stood virtually shoulder to shoulder opposing administration proposals, such as the Stimulus Act to boost economic recovery (2009), a health reform law ("Obamacare," 2010), and the Wall Street Reform Act (2010). Conservative anger at Federal intervention into the economy and the new spending coalesced into the Tea Party movement that helped Republicans gain 63 seats in the House of Representatives in 2010. Committed conservative ideologues, the Tea Party identifiers sparked unified Republican opposition to the Obama administration.

Still, random events could disadvantage either party. The Deep Horizon (BP) oil spill off the Louisiana coast (2010) temporarily quieted Republican demands for accelerated drilling in the Gulf of Mexico. Congressional refusal to enact tougher regulations of firearms following the shooting massacres at Aurora, Colorado, and Newtown, Connecticut, in 2012 confirmed for liberals the influence of the National Rifle Association among Republicans. On the other hand, TV viewers saw a Republican governor (Chris Christie) and a Democratic president (Obama) chatting amicably on their inspection tour of the north Jersey shore that Superstorm Sandy had devastated. Many Republicans crowed "I told you so" when the launch of Obamacare in 2013 became ensnarled in computer problems.

Many conservatives alleged that the Federal government spent lavishly, killed jobs with taxes, racked up an unsustainable debt, and was simply "out of control." They contended that liberal bias led to overregulation of business and stifled incentive to work among millions who received checks from Washington. These charges invite examination and amplification. The first step is to summarize the key developments in governance since 1992. This reconnaissance will help answer the question: did government grow in the past two decades?

The place to begin the review is with public finances, for money is the lifeblood of modern government. Budgeting has triggered intense partisan conflicts since President Bush's concession on taxes in 1990. Figure 11.2 shows the

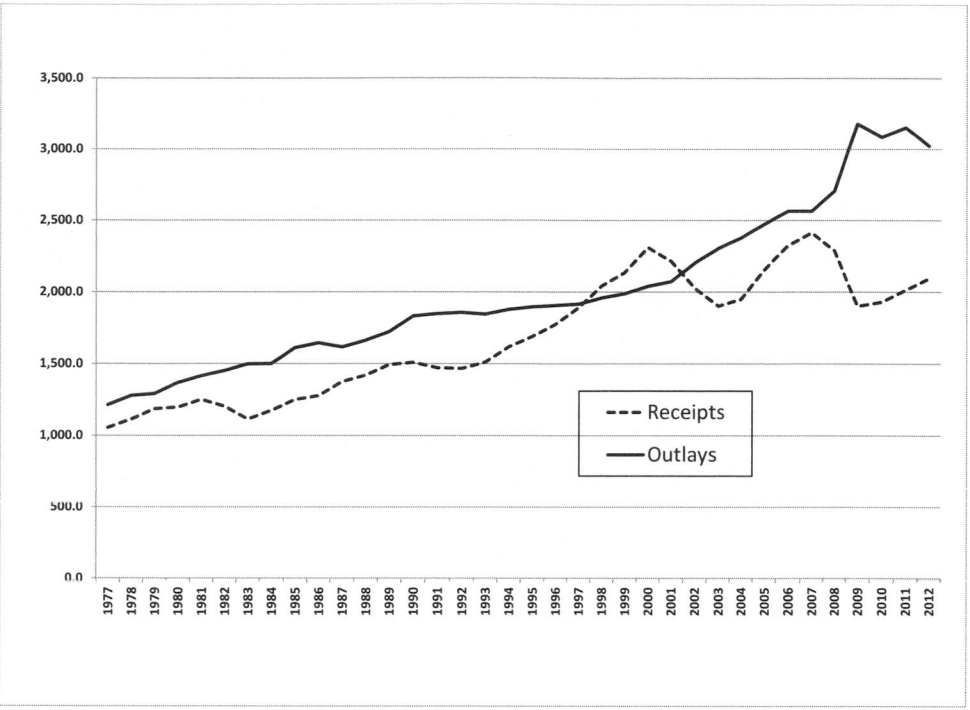

FIGURE 11.2. Federal Government Receipts and Outlays, 1977–2012 (billions of 2005 dollars). Office of Management and Budget, the President's Budget for FY 2014: Historical Tables (www.whitehouse.gov/omb/budget), tab. 1.3.

trend in Federal finances from the late 1970s to 2012, expressed in inflation-controlled dollars.[25] In the three decades from 1977 to 2007 Federal outlays increased at 3.6% a year on average, and then spiked upward during years of the Great Recession. National receipts (all sources of governmental revenue) rose more or less in tandem with expenditures through twin peaks in early twenty-first century, but ended the decade with a lower intake than in the late 1990s. National accounts look less expansive when expressed as a percentage of the gross domestic product (see figure 11.3). By this standard Federal expenditures declined from the earlier Reagan administration through the last year of the George W. Bush administration (2008), when the Great Recession began. Revenues essentially flatlined until 2001, when the combination of Bush tax cuts (2001, 2003) and the Great Recession took a huge bite out of Federal receipts relative to the GDP. At the state levels tax revenues equaled between 5.1

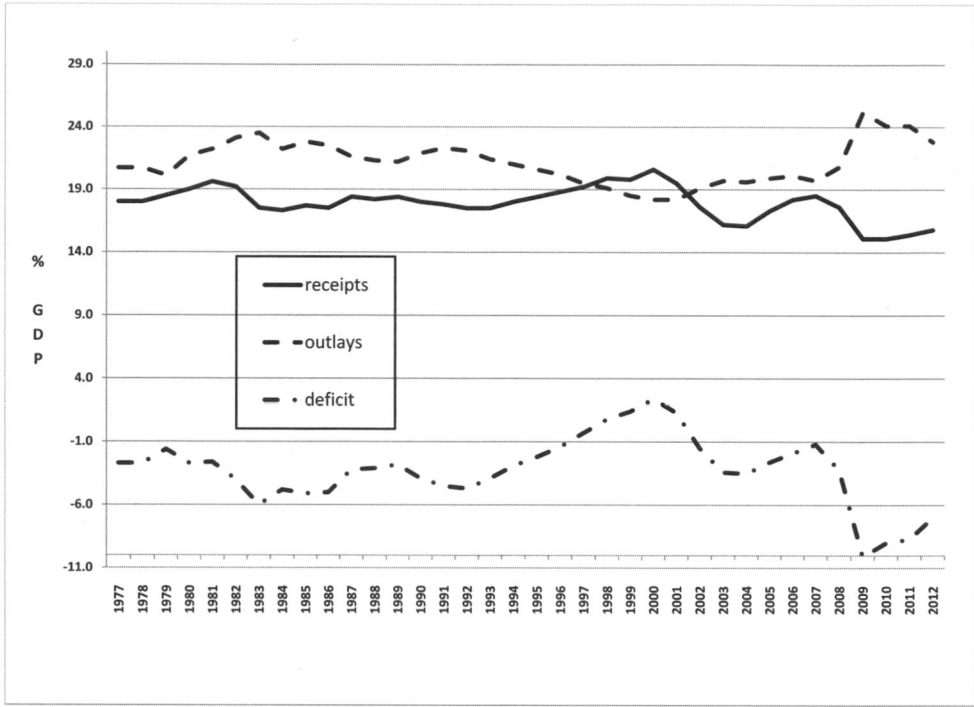

FIGURE 11.3. Federal Budget, 1977–2012 as a Percent of GDP. Office of Management and Budget, the President's Budget for FY 2014: Historical Tables (www.whitehouse .gov/omb/budget), tab. 1.3.

and 5.5 percent of the GDP through 2008, and then dipped to 4.8 in 2010, a recession year.[26]

Assessing trends in the national budget in terms of averages per person (per capita) in constant dollars controls for both inflation and population growth (see table 11.1). By this measure expenditures ("Outlays") increased modestly between 1980 and 2000, and then jumped noticeably in the early twenty-first century. Revenues ("Receipts"), grew substantially during the two decades after 1980, and then fell markedly, reflecting the Bush tax cuts and the Great Recession effects. Individual income taxes represented 8 to 10 percent of the GDP from the late 1970s through 2001, after which they declined noticeably, bottoming out at 6.3 percent in 2010. Corporate income taxes remained a negligible part of the economy (around 1 to 3 percent of the GDP) throughout the period. Taxes for social insurance (primarily Social Security and Medicare) ranged between 6.5 and 6.9 percent of the GDP in the 1990s and 2008, until the

Table 11.1. Federal Outlays and Receipts: Per Capita, Constant (2005) Dollars 1970–2010

Year	1970	1980	1990	2000	2010
Outlays	4,834	6,041	7,365	7,251	9,933
Receipts	4,763	5,286	6,066	8,208	6,215

Source: U.S. Bureau of the Census, Statistical Abstract of the United States, 2012 (Washington, D.C.), tables 1, 2, 469; author per capita calculations.

Table 11.2. Federal Outlays as Percent of GDP, 1990–2010

	1990	2000	2010
Total	21.9	18.2	23.8
Defense	5.2	3.0	4.8
Payments to individuals	10.2	12.0	15.8
Grants	1.9	2.2	2.7

Source: U.S. Bureau of the Census, Statistical Abstract of the United States, 2012 (Washington, D.C.: GPO, 2012), table 471.

recession and the Obama administration's reduction of the FICA tax (2010 and 2011) cut this stream of revenue.

Critics questioned the wisdom of the Obama administration's FICA tax suspension in light of the rising costs of Social Security, Medicare, and Medicaid. These programs represented the largest outlay in the federal budget, and were projected to be a greater financial burden over the next decades.[27] Less was spent on national defense and the military, which consumed 17 percent of the Federal outlays in 1992 but rose to 19 percent in 2012 (see table 11.2). The American wars in Afghanistan and Iraq cost $1.4 billion in direct appropriations and another billion in related costs (2001–2012), including assistance to the governmental regimes the U.S. supported.[28] At home, Federal expenditures for the "administration of justice," which includes correctional facilities, increased tenfold, 1980–2010, reflecting a quadrupling of prisoners in federal custody, many for drug-related offenses.[29] Washington also spend $136 billion on disaster relief between 2011 and early 2013; crop insurance related to droughts and violent storms like Katrina were part of the reason for these emergency outlays.

Aside from "entitlement" assistance paid to individuals through Social Security and the like, much of government's spending supports public employees and officials. Surprisingly in light of claims to the contrary, the Federal civilian workforce has not grown over the four decades since 1970 (see figure 11.4). By contrast, state workers increased at a gradual pace during this period. The largest gain in public employees occurred at the local level, where its workforce grew noticeably until the Great Recession forced a wave of pink slips. Overall on a per capita basis, however, public employment generally demonstrated no significant change, averaging 7.3 public sector workers per 100 persons.[30] The vast majority of public employees work in education, health-care, and criminal justice jobs (such as teachers, hospital administrators and nurses, and police). In this respect recent decades differ little from the historical pattern.

Balanced budgets have been a hot-button topic for conservatives, especially during the Clinton and Obama administrations. Annual deficits, the customary budgetary pattern after World War II, increased in size between 1981 and the early 1990s, when they equaled 4.3 percent of the GDP. Thus it was a pleasant surprise that the Treasury ran budget surpluses in the late 1990s. Tax increases in 1993, Clinton's fiscal chastening after the Gingrich Revolution, and a robust economy accounted for this good news. But the extra money did not last long. The combination of Bush tax cuts, American military actions in Afghanistan and Iraq, the Great Recession (2008–2009 and its slow recovery), and the Obama administration Stimulus Act of 2009 cut the revenue flow below outlays.[31] The large deficits during the first Obama administration added considerably to the national debt, which grew to 103 percent of the nation's GDP in 2012.

The budget was the most partisan topic in Washington since 1992. Since Ronald Reagan launched his attack on big government and the Bush revenue concession in 1990, Republican lawmakers have demonstrated intensified commitment to the reduction of taxes, spending, deficits, and the debt. When the opportunity arose, they turned ideology into practice with unified voting against fiscal compromises with Democrats. On the other side of the aisle, most Democrats have opposed deep tax cuts and budget slashing, labeling them bad economic policy, harmful to the poor and elderly, and unneeded windfalls for the wealthy. If voters thought they had heard this story over and over again they were right. Details changed from time to time but the basic partisan plot remained fixed.

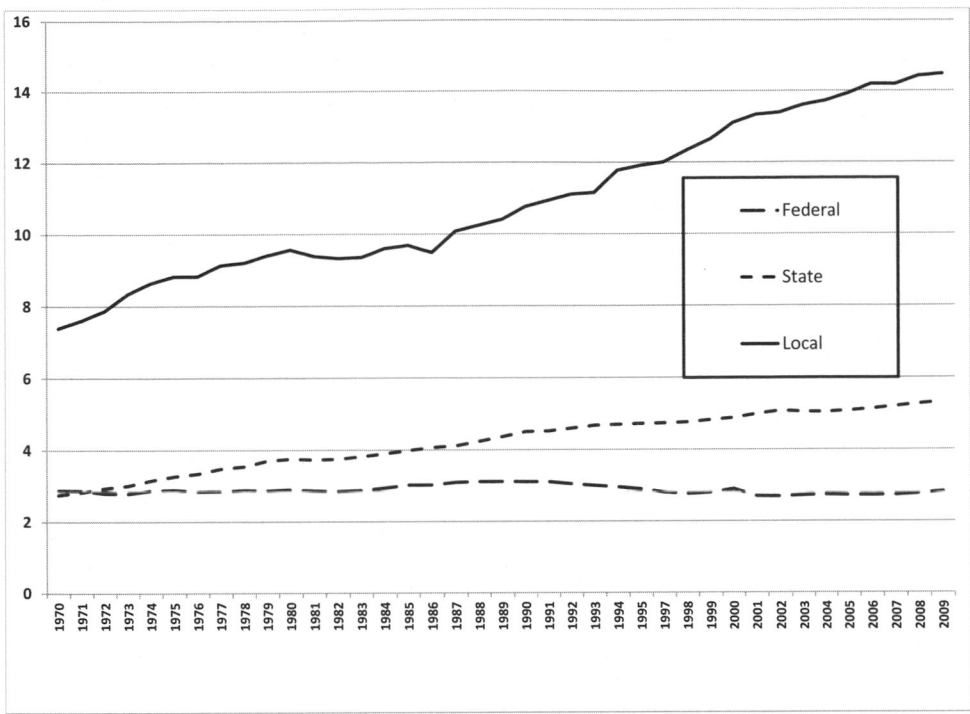

FIGURE 11.4. Federal, State, and Local Governmental Employees, 1970–2009 (millions). *Vital Statistics on American Politics 2011–2012,* edited by Harold W. Stanley, and Richard G. Niemi, CQ Press, 2011. Tab. 8–7

The 1994 Republican election victory and the subsequent government shutdown had pushed President Clinton toward a more conservative financial position. Clinton had announced in his 1996 State of the Union address that "the era of big government is over," but Republicans sought much deeper retrenchment, not a maintenance of the status quo. Robert Dole, Clinton's opponent in the 1996 presidential race, lambasted the Washington establishment as "our runaway Government" and called for larger tax cuts, including a 50 percent reduction on capital gains (stock market earnings). The surplus budgetary windfall that materialized by 1998 did not deter the GOP budget hawks, who continued to push for tax cuts. Rejecting Clinton's plan to devote the extra funds to shoring up the future obligations of Social Security and Medicare, House Republicans urged the return of the "extra" revenue to voters, because it was "the people's" money.

The election of George W. Bush fulfilled Republican hopes for major tax cuts, but not budget deficits. The president pushed through massive tax reduction packages in 2001 and 2003, claiming that lower taxes stimulated the economy and created jobs. Critics replied that the tax changes would produce deficits and cause a wholesale transfer of wealth to richest Americans.[32] From a political perspective, liberals saw revenue reduction as a tactic to "starve the beast" whereby tax cuts would enlarge deficits unless countered by reductions in spending. Bush, however, waved aside worries about aligning spending and revenues. The wars in Afghanistan and Iraq, new antiterrorism initiatives, and then the Great Recession brought back deficits. When congressional Republicans questioned the president on this financial laxity, he answered, "We're at war."[33]

Barack Obama inherited the Bush era deficits when he entered the White House, and drove them higher with the Stimulus Act of 2009, which only three Republicans (all senators) supported. The Tea Party congressional victory in 2010 further sharpened partisan rancor over fiscal issues, including veiled threats to shut down the Federal government rather than to raise the U.S. debt limit (a statutory threshold set by Congress). Partisan tensions over the budgetary matters continued for the next two years through New Year's Day 2013, the date when the Bush tax cuts expired. At the eleventh hour Democrats and Republicans struck a bargain that extended the Bush cuts except for the wealthiest taxpayers. Partisan gridlock had produced repeated stalemates, a partial federal government shutdown in 2013, and eleventh-hour, crisis-born compromises.

The battle over the budget prompts several observations about financial politics in contemporary America. First, the United States is not a high-tax nation in terms of an international comparison. The U.S. tax burden on families is lower than in other industrial countries, including those of the European Union.[34] This ranking is consistent with the American antitax tradition. But one should also recognize that the code tax, which was amended 4,680 times between 2001 and 2012 and is 74,000 pages long, hides innumerable "loopholes." Some of these provisions allow corporations and the very wealthy to hide their assets in offshore accounts, beyond reach of tax collectors.

Second, some economists contend that the composition of the Federal budget presents a misleading picture. The U.S. budget counts spending on capital goods (such as buildings and highways) as part of the operating costs, not as investments. Businesses and homeowners, by comparison, consider only the interest on loans and a portion of the principal, not the whole amount borrowed (like a mortgage for a home), as a current expenditure. Grants to state and local government are also entered as consumption in the U.S. budget, but state and local revenues are not taken into account. Recessions reduce tax collections and trigger automatic spending, such as unemployment benefits, but reduce revenues. These rules of national financial accounting increase the prospects of annual deficits.[35]

Third, the argument that lower taxes, balanced budgets, and less debt will promote economic growth is a hypothesis, not a fact. Considerable historical and cross-national evidence does not sustain the contention that particular tax rates and the size of a national debt determine the fate of an economy.[36] Most economic historians hold that numerous factors shape how an economy performs. No infallible model of economic growth exists that arranges the critical factors in a foolproof causal scenario. A reasonable conclusion to draw from these observations is that the claim of an invariant connection between the combination of lower taxes and a smaller debt and a more affluent economy is part of an ideological dispute, in which different assumptions drive policy positions.

Agreement does exist that social welfare programs have grown in size and cost during the last quarter century. The largest share of federal spending goes for entitlements, which are income assistance programs for individuals, such as Social Security, Medicare, and grants to state and local governments for Medicaid and income assistance to low-income families. Roughly 37.5 million Americans, 11 percent of the U.S. population, received Social Security in 2010, at a cost of $471 billion, in current dollar values (see table 11.3). The program had 28 million recipients in 1990, with an outlay of $172 billion. However, the proportion of Americans sixty-five years or older remained unchanged at 12.5 percent during this period, but is projected to increase to 20 percent in 2030 when most baby boomers have retired. By then the ratio of recipients to workers, whose taxes fund current Social Security outlays (on the "pay as you go" principle, discussed in chapter 6) will be about two to one, considerably lower than before 1990. This outlook and the fact that the U.S. government borrows from the federal Social Security Trust fund has alarmed budget hawks. President George W. Bush, among others, said Social Security was in "crisis." His solution was to "privatize" the program, whereby workers' FICA contributions

Table 11.3. Social Security, Medicare, and Disability (OASDHI), 1990–2010

	1990	2000	2010
Beneficiaries (millions)			
Retired workers and dependents	28.37	31.76	37.49
Medicare	34.3	39.7	47.5
Total expenditures (annual in billion $)			
Retired workers and dependents	172	274	471
Medicare	107	219	521
Average annual benefit per retired worker	7,236	10,140	14,114
Average annual OASD tax on employees	1,035	1,524	1,978

Source: U.S. Bureau of the Census, *Statistical Abstract of the United States*, 2012 (Washington, D.C.: GPO, 2012), tables 544, 546.

would be invested in the private equity market. The plan culminated years of debate over the long-term financial viability of retirement income for seniors. Liberals refuted the charges that Social Security was going broke and that the program contributed to the national debt, and fought attempts to scale back benefits. Opposition from liberals and moderates, plus the public's uneasiness with privatization, scotched his proposal. Nonetheless, the financial sustainability of Social Security remained contentious.[37]

Medicare, the second of the two big income assistance programs for seniors, grew faster in its number of recipients and costs than Social Security (see table 11.3). Whereas Social Security expenditures were predicted to top out at 6 percent of the GDP around 2030, Medicare was projected to cost 8 percent by 2040. Accelerating Medicare (and Medicaid) expenditures were driven in part by greater demand from affluent Americans for medical services and the rising prices of treatments. The cost of specific health-care procedures in the United States was considerably more expensive than elsewhere in the world. Despite America's outsized health-care costs, however, the United States ranked near the bottom of developed countries on measures of healthiness. Another factor that pushed health-care costs up was congressional failure to impose limits on federal reimbursement rates for Medicare services; critics claimed that lawmakers bowed to lobbying by the health-care industry.[38]

President Obama cited the escalating price of health care and the one-seventh of the population who lacked health-care insurance (such as part-time workers) as major reasons for his health reform, enacted in 2010. The Patient Protection and Affordable Health Care Act, a long and complex statute, provides health coverage for the uninsured, mechanisms to drive down health-care costs, and new revenues for the program. The measures passed on a strict party vote. Republicans opposed the law's requirement that all individuals obtain health coverage, calling the mandate unconstitutional, an intrusion on individual freedom, and a job-killer for small business.

Congress's failure to address the health consequences of cigarette smoking spurred the states to take action. The attorney generals of forty-six states sued the tobacco industry for Medicaid costs incurred for tobacco-related health problems, and won a $206 billion judgment in 1998. The settlement included an agreement that tobacco companies restrict advertising and merchandizing, steps aimed at preventing young people from getting hooked on nicotine. The deal proved timely in light of the Supreme Court 5–4 ruling in 2001 that the FDA, which had held that nicotine was an addictive drug, lacked regulatory authority over tobacco products.

"Obamacare," as the health-care reform act was nicknamed, was one of two major changes in income assistance policy since 1992. The other was welfare reform, enacted during the Clinton administration in 1996. The law abolished AFDC, the program that obligated Washington to reimburse states for welfare recipients that they deemed eligible and at benefits levels they set. The new policy provided national eligibility standards, which included work requirements for recipients. Faced with pressure from the Gingrich Revolution and eyeing his reelection bid, Clinton consented to the change, which was designed to reduce welfare costs. Senator Daniel Moynihan (Democrat, New York), called the new welfare law a "repeal," not a "reform" of assistance for the poor. But the Federal government still maintained numerous programs that assisted low-income individuals. Researchers writing in *National Review Online* in 2012 counted eighty means-tested programs that served about 100 million Americans at an average cost of $9,000 per person. All such programs should have a work requirement, they contended, to end "the self-defeating cycle of dependency."[39]

The policy trend concerning business since 1992 was deregulation, which continued the pattern begun in the late 1970s. The Federal government did not consistently investigate potential antitrust violations or closely monitor the evolving trading practices of the financial industry. In 1999 Congress repealed the separation of commercial banks from investment units that had been law since the New Deal. Federal approval of a trade pact with Mexico and Canada (North American Free Trade Agreement, 1994) and normalization of trade relations with China (2000) opened up new opportunities for American corporations; critics charged that these deals exported jobs abroad. Neither Democratic nor Republican administrations took aggressive steps to slow the offshoring of American jobs to low-wage countries, such as China, India, and Bangladesh. Nor did national lawmakers adopt new environmental rules; no substantive action was taken in response to alarms about the effects of global warming, which the Bush administration claimed was based on uncertain science. Some states were more active in creating stronger environmental regulations.

Two dramatic setbacks for business and finance occasioned exceptions to this lax oversight. The spectacular collapse of Enron, a huge energy-trading corporation, and conviction of its top executives for illegal accounting, prompted Congress to enact the Corporate Fraud Act (2002). The law imposed stiffer penalties for corporate executives who "cooked" their books to hide questionable practices. The involvement of banks and brokerages in the meltdown of the housing market and collapse of stocks that triggered the Great Recession formed the backdrop for the Wall Street Reform and Consumer Protection Act of 2010. The 848-page statute, which regulated numerous areas of financial activity and created the Consumer Financial Protection Bureau, faced unified opposition from Republicans and most large banks and brokerages. This coalition continued its resistance to the imposition of stiff restrictions during the rule-making phase of the new law.

"There is a religious war going on in our country for the soul of America. It is a cultural war," stated Patrick Buchanan, a journalist and presidential contender, at the Republican National Convention in 1992. Republicans and their allies in the evangelical community urged governments to legislate against the erosion of moral standards that they believed were weakening families and communities. Religious conservatives opposed abortion, legalized marriages for gays, sex education in the schools, and access to illegal drugs, including medical uses of marijuana. They favored bans on pornography, tough sentences for convicted criminals, capital punishment, and prayer and the teaching of "intelligent design" (a derivation of biblical versions of creation) in the schools.

The Right opposed aggressive enforcement of nondiscrimination policy for minorities and opposed leniency toward illegal immigrants, who were viewed as a drain on public welfare. Liberals and Democrats usually either flatly rejected these views or were willing to compromise. With the exception of enforcing civil rights laws already on the books, the conservative cultural agenda frequently called for a positive exercise of governmental power that codified its version of morality.

Tallying the score on the cultural wars defies neat summary, for two reasons. First, the states possess predominant authority over social policy, based on their constitutional authority to guard the health and morals of their residents. Faced with varied state actions in these subjects, conservatives at times have pocketed their defense of local prerogatives by supporting mandates that imposed national uniformity on cultural issues. And second, the federal structure brings both the national and state courts into the debate over cultural policies. As the United States Supreme Court has taken a more conservative turn under the aegis of appointments from three Republican presidents (Reagan and the two Bushes), liberals have turned to state courts to oppose the conservative social agenda. In combination these two features of the political process have produced a varied set of cultural rules. However, a regional patterning of policies is discernible. Conservative positions tend to prevail in the South, the midsection of the country and mountain region. The Pacific Coast and the Northeast lean toward the liberal side of the cultural debate. Hawaii and Massachusetts, for example, took the lead on legalizing same sex marriage.[40] New England, the Pacific Coast, Illinois, and Minnesota provided public funding for abortions, while the remainder of America did not. Southern states lead the nation is the exercise of capital punishment. The South and mountain region fiercely opposed strict regulation of guns. The conservative emphasis on stiff sentencing and aggressive enforcement of narcotics laws goes a long way to explain why the United States has an incarceration rate more than four times higher the countries in the European Union. The high cost of housing the two million–plus inmates in U.S. prisons has persuaded some conservatives to find cheaper solutions to the criminal justice process.[41]

The end of the Cold War did not lead to a ratcheting down of military intervention or defense spending. With varying support from liberals, conservatives supported a robust and sometimes proactive use of American military force, for which they have made an exception to their demands for smaller budgets. Since the Persian Gulf War (1991) American armed forces participated in engagements in Somalia, Yugoslavia, Afghanistan, Iraq, and the drug wars in Colombia. The military and CIA have eliminated known and suspected terrorists by clandestine raids (navy special forces killed Osama bin Laden, the Al Qaeda leader, in Pakistan) and unmanned aircraft ("drones"). The Pentagon reported that the nation supported 611 overseas bases, not counting those in Iraq and Afghanistan, and 580,000 uniformed and defense contractors in fifty-seven countries. The 2011 defense bill was just under $1 trillion.[42]

The 9/11 attacks on the United States provided the immediate justification for the invasion and occupations of Afghanistan and Iraq. But each intervention underwent "mission creep," whereby democratic state building replaced the original public justifications for the actions. The notion that the United States served as the "global policeman" in the post–Cold War decades became accepted dogma to Republicans and many Democrats. The American response to the Al Qaeda 2001 attacks enhanced a presidency that already possessed wide discretion to act in the world arena. Following the 9/11 attacks Congress quickly approved military action against Al Qaeda in Afghanistan. President George W. Bush contended that he did not need congressional approval to invade Iraq, although he thought it political prudent to gain it; lawmakers passed Bush's war "resolution" (2002), with numerous Democrats voting no.[43] President Obama withdrew the remaining "combat" troops from Iraq, but increased the American forces in Afghanistan during his first term. Because they have the option of using the defense apparatus with minimal political restrictions, in some instances in secret, and because of wide public acceptance of the idea that America is the world's primary peace-keeper, presidents face a nearly irresistible temptation to wield military power.

Antiterrorism legislation, particularly the USA Patriot Act (2001), has added to executive powers. A broad and complex law, the 2001 statute gave federal officials wide authority to gather information from wiretapping, phone monitoring, and financial records such as credit cards, in the name of forestalling terrorist attacks. The unauthorized disclosure in 2013 of National Security Agency data on electronic eavesdropping provided a glimpse at the scope of these intelligence operations. The NSA revelations worried both libertarians and many liberals. The former group saw the Federal government moving closer to creating a national ID system, which they dreaded; the latter group favored stricter controls on government snooping in order to safeguard individual privacy.[44]

This survey of governance only skims the surface of a complex historical record. While brief, the outline highlights developments that bear on the debate over "big" government. We should recognize that complaints about the growth of the Federal government have been around for a long time. Some conservatives argue that unwarranted expansion began with the adoption of the Federal income tax and the Federal Reserve System in 1913. Nonetheless, the years since 1992 have brought an intensification of antistatist complaints. This heightened ideological animus against big government puts the 1990s and 2000s into sharp contrast with the politics of the 1950s and 1960s.

Given this elevation of political conflict, who won the debate over big government? Were there *any* winners? The answer to the first question is that the debate ended in a tie. This conclusion is partially an educated guess, because there is no simple or foolproof method of adding up all the pluses and minuses in the exercise of public authority. Governance embraces the adoption of new laws and administrative actions, judicial rulings, and a complex system of public finance involving three tiers of government and independent authorities. The political landscape in which this process unfolded changed periodically, especially when elections brought turnovers of party majorities.

Nonetheless, the last quarter of a century shows that conservatives have been successful in popularizing a new paradigm about the role of government. The debate about governance has elevated certain assumptions, such as the utility of market-based economics, the drag that deficits and debt put on it, and the imperative of relaxing federal mandates, to a regular place at the bargaining table. On the policy front, Republicans have blocked most efforts to add new civic functions to the Federal agenda and have slowed enforcement of certain policies, as in the case of civil rights, environmental protection, and business. The GOP denied President Obama and Democrats a second economic stimulus package that was designed as a further boost to economic recovery. The Reagan and George W. Bush administrations reduced federal taxation, leaving the wealthy much better off as a result.[45]

On the other side of the ledger, liberals and some moderates have successfully defended virtually all major functions of government adopted since 1887 (see table 2.1). None of the major tasks that Congress assigned to the national government since the Cleveland era have been terminated, although a few, such as business regulations and enforcement of civil rights law, have been modified. Traditional Federal welfare policy underwent a major revision. None the less, conservatives continue to fault the *existing* policy regime, pointing to excesses such as the level of entitlement spending, the intrusiveness of Federal mandates on lower governments and business, and rulings that offend evangelical Christian morality.[46]

Viewed from a different angle, one finds victors in the sweepstakes for governmental favors. Business has shaken off much of the burden of regulation, especially in banking and investment firms, and for multinational corporations, which contract for manufacturing and services in other countries. Conservatives have said little about giants such as Google and Apple sheltering billions of profit from taxation in offshore accounts.[47] Defense industries have received generous financial support, a portion of which was paid to private contractors who operated in hot spots like Iraq and charged exorbitant fees. Providing flexibility to the states has allowed localities to shape their own social programs. Retirees still get their monthly checks, which have increased in dollar amounts and have pushed the poverty rate down for individuals over sixty-five. Liberal-leaning states have adopted protections for gays, women, children, and low-income individuals. Some states—California, Massachusetts, and Maine, for example—have taken innovative steps toward protecting their environments.

The winners in the struggles over public policy include many groups backed by powerful, well-funded lobbies. Too often, some say, the public interest is only the sum of victories won by special interests. The intense partisan gridlock in Washington and in some states facilitates special-interest government. Organized interests have the resources to mobilize voters and fund political campaigns, thus earning the gratitude of officeholders and political hopefuls. This moneyed investment in politics helps to perpetuate divided partisan control, which in turn facilitates legislative deadlock, policy stalemates, and eleventh-hour crisis solutions. Democracy has suffered from these political logjams, creating doubt about the capacity of public officials to govern effectively. This is not the first time in American history that a crisis of confidence in government has gripped the country. Periodically reforms have addressed these past challenges to the political system. One wonders when the next round of correctives will come and what they will look like.

NOTES

INTRODUCTION

1. Richard L. McCormick, "The Party Period and Public Policy: An Exploratory Hypothesis," *Journal of American History* 66 (1979): 279–98; Harry N. Scheiber, "Federalism and the American Economic Order, 1789–1910," *Law and Society Review* 10 (1975): 58–118, and "Government and the Economy: Studies of the 'Commonwealth' Policy in Nineteenth-Century America," *Journal of Interdisciplinary History* 3 (1972): 135–51; Joel A. Tarr, "The Evolution of the Urban Infrastructure in the Nineteenth and Twentieth Centuries," in *Perspectives in Urban Infrastructure,* ed. Royce Hanson (Washington, D.C.: National Academy Press, 1984); Richard F. Bensel, *Yankee Leviathan: The Origins of Central State Authority in America, 1859–1877* (New York: Cambridge University Press, 1990).

2. Robert A. Dahl, *Modern Political Analysis* (Englewood Cliffs, N.J.: Prentice-Hall, 1970), 25.

3. On the enumeration of civic functions, see Robert M. MacIver, *The Web of Government* (New York: Macmillan, 1949); William H. Riker, *Federalism: Origin, Operation, Significance* (Boston: Little, Brown, 1964), ch. 3; Theodore Lowi, "American Business, Public Policy, Case-Studies, and Political Theory," *World Politics* 16 (1964): 677–715; Gabriel A. Almond and G. Bingham Powell Jr., *Comparative Politics: A Developmental Approach* (Boston: Little, Brown, 1966), ch. 8; Carl V. Harris, *Political Power in Birmingham, 1871–1921* (Knoxville: University of Tennessee Press, 1977), 6–11; Bensel, *Yankee Leviathan,* 111–14.

4. Deborah A. Stone, *Policy Paradox and Political Reason* (New York: HarperCollins, 1988).

5. Samuel P. Huntington and Jorge I. Dominguez, "Political Development," in *Handbook of Political Science,* ed. F. Greenstein and N. Polsby (Reading, Mass.: Addison-Wesley, 1975), 3:15–16.

1. GOVERNING THE CLEVELAND ERA

1. James D. Richardson, comp., *Messages and Papers of the Presidents* (Washington, D.C.: Bureau of National Literature and Art, 1910), 7:5165–76, quoted at 5166 and 5169.

2. Davis R. Dewey, *National Problems, 1885–1897* (New York: Harper and Brothers, 1907), 57–75; H. Wayne Morgan, *From Hayes to McKinley: Party Politics, 1877–1896* (Syracuse, N.Y.: Syracuse University Press, 1969), 277–291; Sidney Ratner, *The Tariff in American History* (New York: D. Van Nostrand, 1972).

3. Ballard C. Campbell, "Did Democracy Work? Prohibition in Late Nineteenth-Century Iowa: A Test Case," *Journal of Interdisciplinary History* 8 (1977): 87–116; Richard J. Jensen, *The Winning of the Midwest: Social and Political Conflict, 1888–1896* (Chicago: University of Chicago Press, 1971), ch. 4; Paul Kleppner, *The Third Electoral System, 1853–1892: Parties, Voters, and Political Culture* (Chapel Hill: University of North Carolina Press, 1979), chs. 6–8; Norman H. Clark, *Deliver Us from Evil: An Interpretation of American Prohibition* (New York: W. W. Norton, 1976).

4. Ballard C. Campbell, "The Good Roads Movement in Wisconsin, 1890–1911," *Wisconsin Magazine of History* 49 (1966): 273–93.

5. Clay McShane, *Down the Asphalt Path: The Automobile and the American City* (New York: Columbia University Press, 1994).

6. Carl V. Harris, *Political Power in Birmingham, 1871–1921* (Knoxville: University of Tennessee Press, 1977), ch. 9.

7. I have used the convention of capitalizing the word *Federal* to refer to the national government in order not to confuse it with *federalism*, which is a shorthand expression for the federal system of government.

8. Gordon A. Wood, *The Creation of the American Republic, 1776–1787* (New York: W. W. Norton, 1972), 529, from the debates in the Constitutional Convention, 1787. Madison expressed the same idea in the 39th and 51st Federalist papers, contained in *The Federalist*, ed. Jacob E. Cooke (Cleveland: World, 1961).

9. Madison in the 51st Federalist paper, contained in Cooke, *The Federalist*, 351.

10. Richard F. Bensel, *Sectionalism and American Political Development, 1880–1980* (Madison: University of Wisconsin Press, 1984), ch. 3; David W. Brady, *Critical Elections and Congressional Policymaking* (Stanford, Calif.: Stanford University Press, 1988), ch. 3; Carl V. Harris, "Right Fork or Left Fork: The Section-Party Alignment of Southern Democrats in Congress, 1873–1897," *Journal of Southern History* 42 (1976): 471–506; Theda Skocpol, *Protecting Soldiers and Mothers: The Political Origins of Social Policy in the United States* (Cambridge, Mass.: Harvard University Press, 1992), ch. 2.

11. John Adams, "Thoughts on Government" (1776), in Michael Kammen, *Deputyes and Libertyes: The Origins of Representative Government in Colonial America* (New York: Knopf, 1969), 199–203; James Madison, debate in the Constitutional Convention, 1787, in *The Federal Convention and the Formation of the Union of America States,* ed. Winton U. Solberg (Indianapolis: Bobbs-Merrill, 1958), 236, and 10th Federalist paper (1787), in Cooke, *The Federalist;* and generally, Wood, *The Creation of the American Republic.*

12. Chs. 3 and 9 examine opinion about legislators in the transition era and provide citations on the topic.

13. Roscoe L. Ashley, *The American Federal State* (New York: Macmillan, 1902), 584–85. See the bibliography for references to writing about the state legislatures and state constitutions.

14. Ballard C. Campbell, *Representative Democracy: Public Policy and Midwestern Legislatures in the Late Nineteenth Century* (Cambridge, Mass.: Harvard University Press, 1980); Philip R. VanderMeer, *The Hoosier Politician: Officeholding and Political Culture in Indiana, 1896–1920* (Urbana: University of Illinois Press, 1984); Jon C. Teaford, *The Unheralded Triumph: City Government in America, 1870–1900* (Baltimore: Johns Hopkins University Press, 1984), 39–41; Morris P. Fiorina, David W. Rhode, and Peter Wissel, "Historic Change in House Turnover," in *Congress in Change: Evolution and Reform,* ed. Norman J. Ornstein (New York: Praeger, 1975), 24–57.

15. Teaford, *Unheralded Triumph,* ch. 6; Leonard D. White, *The Republican Era, 1869–1901: A Study in Administrative History* (New York: Macmillan, 1958), 244, 246. Assessments of administrative capacity at the national level appear in White, *Republican Era,* esp. chs. 17 and 18; Stephen Skowronek, *Building a New American State: The Expansion of National Administra-*

tive Capacities, 1877–1920 (New York: Cambridge University Press, 1982); Wallace D. Farnham, "'The Weakened Spring of Government': A Study in 19th-Century American History," *American Historical Review* 68 (1963): 62–80.

16. Terrence J. McDonald, *The Parameters of Urban Fiscal Policy: Socioeconomic Change and Political Culture in San Francisco, 1860–1906* (Berkeley: University of California Press, 1986).

17. Alfred H. Kelly, W. Haribson, and H. Belz, *The American Constitution: Its Origin and Development* (New York: W. W. Norton, 1983), chs. 19, 20; William R. Brock, *Investigation and Responsibility: Public Responsibility in the United States, 1865–1900* (New York: Cambridge University Press, 1984), ch. 3; W. Brooke Graves, *American State Government* (Boston: D. C. Heath, 1946), 647.

18. Morton Keller, *Affairs of State: Public Life in Late Nineteenth Century America* (Cambridge, Mass.: Harvard University Press, 1977), 407; Brock, *Investigation,* ch. 3; Melvin I. Urofsky, "State Courts and Protective Legislation during the Progressive Era: A Reevaluation," *Journal of American History* 72 (1985): 63–91.

19. The court decisions discussed in the next several paragraphs, unless otherwise noted, are excerpted in Stanley I. Kutler, ed., *The Supreme Court and the Constitution: Readings in American Constitutional History,* 2nd ed. (New York: W. W. Norton, 1977). For comments on the context of the decisions see the bibliography under Constitutional and Legal.

20. http://supreme.justia.com/cases/federal/us/92/542/case.html. Also see Hans L. Trefousse, *Reconstruction: America's First Effort at Racial Democracy* (New York: Van Nostrand Reinhold, 1971), 189–194.

2. THE COURSE AND CAUSES OF GROWTH

1. Charles A. Beard, *American Government and Politics* (New York: Macmillan, 1928; originally published 1910), 3–4, 6; Walter E Dodd, *State Government* (New York: Century, 1923), 5–8; Robert Luce, *Legislative Assemblies* (Boston: Houghton Mifflin, 1924), 132, 147; Leonard D. White, *Introduction to the Study of Public Administration* (New York: Macmillan, 1926), 79, 466.

2. *President's Private Sector Survey on Cost Control. A Report to the President* (Washington, D.C.: GPO, Jan. 15, 1984), vol. 1, nicknamed the Grace Commission report (a short synopsis was prepared by Thomas O. Donlan, "Amazing Grace: Baring Washington's Monumental Waste," *Barron's,* Nov. 28, 1983); Murray L. Weidenbaum, *Business, Government, and the Public* (Englewood Cliffs, N.J.: Prentice-Hall, 1981), 198–200.

3. The rise in national expenditures and its relation to spending on social security is succinctly reviewed by Rudolph G. Penner, "Federal Government Growth: Leviathan or Protector of the Elderly?" *National Tax Journal,* 14 (1991): 437–50.

4. C. E. Black, *The Dynamics of Modernization: A Study in Comparative History* (New York: Harper and Row, 1967), (esp. ch. 3); G. Ross Stevens, "State Centralization and the Erosion of the Local Autonomy," *Journal of Politics,* 36 (1974), 44–76; David R. Cameron, "The Expansion of the Public Economy: A Comparative Analysis," *American Political Science Review,* 72 (1978): 1253.

5. Advisory Commission on Intergovernmental Relations, *A Crisis of Confidence and Competence* (Washington, D.C., 1980), 115, and *Regulatory Federalism: Policy, Process, Impact and Reform* (Washington, D.C., 1984), 63; Congressional Quarterly, *Congress and the Nation* (Washington, D.C.: Congressional Quarterly, 1981), vol. 5, 862.

6. Advisory Commission, *Regulatory Federalism,* 64.

7. Federal grants are discussed in ch. 8.

8. For reviews of the literature on explanations of the growth of government, see Patrick D. Larkey, Chandler Stolp, and Mark Winer, "Theorizing about the Growth of Government: A Re-

search Assessment," *Journal of Public Policy*, 1 (1981): 157–220; Advisory Commission on Intergovernmental Relations, *The Condition of Contemporary Federalism* (Washington, D.C., 1981), ch. 5; David B. Robertson, "The Return to History and the New Institutionalism in American Political Science," *Social Science History*, 17 (1993): 1–36.

9. Black, *Dynamics of Modernization*; Richard F. Bensel, *Yankee Leviathan: The Origins of Central State Authority in America, 1859–1877* (New York: Cambridge University Press, 1990), 4–10; Melvin L. Adelman, "Modernization Theory and Its Critics," in Mary K. Cayton et al., eds., *Encyclopedia of American Social History* (New York: Scribner, 1993).

10. Louis Galambos, "Technology, Political Economy, and Professionalization: Central Themes of the Organizational Synthesis," *Business History Review*, 57 (1983), 471–93. Earlier exponents of this outlook were Samuel P. Hays, *The Response to Industrialism, 1885–1914* (Chicago: University of Chicago Press, 1957), and Robert H. Wiebe, *The Search for Order, 1877–1920* (New York: Hill and Wang, 1967). Paul Starr, *The Social Transformation of American Medicine* (New York: Basic Books, 1982), is an excellent case study.

11. For an international perspective, see Phillips Cutright, "Political Structure, Economic Development, and National Security Programs," *American Journal of Sociology*, 70 (1965), 537–50; Harold L. Wilensky, *The Welfare State and Equality* (Berkeley: University of California Press, 1975); and Cameron, "The Expansion of the Public Economy." For a cross-sectional view of the American states and cities, see Thomas R. Dye, *Politics, Economics, and the Public: Policy Outcomes in the American States* (Chicago: Rand McNally, 1966); Richard I. Hofferbert, *The Study of Public Policy* (Indianapolis: Bobbs-Merrill, 1974); and J. Rodgers Hollingsworth and Ellen Jane Hollingsworth, *Dimensions of Urban History* (Madison: University of Wisconsin Press, 1979). For a cross-sectional view of the states at past periods, see Richard E. Dawson, "Social Development, Party Competition, and Policy," in William N. Chambers and Walter D. Burnham, eds., *The American Party Systems* (New York: Oxford University Press, 1967); Jack L. Walker, "The Diffusion of Innovations among the American States," *American Political Science Review*, 63 (1969): 880–99; and Virginia Gray, "Models of Comparative State Politics: A Comparison of Cross-Sectional and Time Series Analyses," *American Journal of Political Science*, 20 (1976): 235–56. Time series of national expenditures are examined in Michael S. Lewis-Beck and Tom W. Rice, "Government Growth in the United States," *Journal of Politics*, 47 (1985): 2–30, and William D. Berry and David Lowery, *Understanding U.S. Government Growth: An Empirical Analysis of the Postwar Era* (New York: Praeger, 1987).

12. Richard Rose, "How Exceptional Is the American Political Economy?" *Political Science Quarterly*, 194 (1989), 91–115; Andrew Abbott and Stanley DeViney, "The Welfare State as Transnational Event: Evidence from Sequences of Policy Adoption," *Social Science History*, 16 (1992): 245–74.

13. John W. Kingdon, *Agendas, Alternatives, and Public Policies* (New York: HarperCollins, 1984), 99–105. Business cycles occur periodically; what is not predictable is their timing and severity. On long-term cycles, see Brian J. L. Berry, *Long-Wave Rhythms in Economic Development and Political Behavior* (Baltimore: Johns Hopkins University Press, 1990).

14. Robert Higgs, *Crisis and Leviathan: Critical Episodes in the Growth of American Government* (New York: Oxford University Press, 1987).

15. James L. Sundquist, *Dynamics of the Party System: Alignments and Realignments of Political Parties in the United States* (Washington, D.C.: Brookings Institution, 1973); Everett Carll Ladd, Jr., *The Transformations of the American Party System* (New York: W. W. Norton, 1978); Richard Jensen, "The Last Party System: Decay of Consensus, 1932–1980," in Paul Kleppner, ed., *The Evolution of American Electoral Systems* (Westport, Conn.: Greenwood Press, 1981). Also see Richard Oestreicher, "Urban Working-Class Political Behavior and Theories of American Elections, 1870–1940," *Journal of American History*, 74 (1988): 1257–86.

16. Allan H. Meltzer and Scott F Richards, "Why Government Grows (and Grows) in a Democracy," *Public Interest*, 52 (1978): 111–18.

17. Beard, *American Government and Politics*, 5; Leonard D. White, *Introduction to the Study of Public Administration* (New York: Macmillan, 1954; first published in 1926), 3; Ladd, *The Transformations of the American Party System*, 211.

18. Lloyd A. Free and Hadley Cantril, *The Political Beliefs of Americans: A Study of Public Opinion* (New York: Simon and Schuster, 1968); Linda L. M. Bennett and Stephen E. Bennett, *Living with Leviathan: Americans Coming to Terms with Big Government* (Lawrence: University of Kansas Press, 1990).

19. E. E. Schattschneider, *The Semi-Sovereign People* (Hinsdale, Ill.: Dryden Press, 1960); John C. Wahlke, "Policy Demands and System Support: The Role of Represented," in Heinz Eulau and Wahlke, eds., *The Politics of Representation* (Beverly Hills, Calif.: Sage Publications, 1978); Benjamin. Ginsberg, *The Captive Public: How Mass Opinion Promotes State Power* (New York: Basic Books, 1986); Thomas R. Dye, *Understanding Public Policy* (Englewood Cliffs, N.J.: Prentice-Hall, 1984), 320.

20. Richard L. McCormick, "The Party Period and Public Policy: An Exploratory Hypothesis," *Journal of American History*: 66 (1979), 279–98; Theda Skocpol, *Protecting Soldiers and Mothers: The Political Origins of Social Policy in the United States* (Cambridge, Mass.: Harvard University Press, 1992), 82–83; Mark L. Kornbluh, *From Participation to Administration: A Social and Political History of the Emergence of Modern American Politics, 1880–1918* (Baltimore: Johns Hopkins University Press, 2000), ch. 3. The concept of distributional policy originated in Theodore Lowi's policy schema in "American Business, Public Policy, Case-Studies, and Political Theory," *World Politics*, 16 (1964): 677–715.

21. Walter Dean Burnham, *Critical Elections and the Mainsprings of American Politics* (New York: W. W. Norton, 1970); William N. Chambers and Walter D. Burnham, *The American Party Systems: Stages of Political Development* (New York: Oxford University Press, 1972, 2d ed.); Jerome Clubb, William H. Flanigan, and Nancy Zingale, *Partisan Realignment: Voters, Parties and Government in American History* (Beverly Hills, Calif.: Sage Publications, 1980); Richard L. McCormick, "The Realignment Synthesis in American History," *Journal of Interdisciplinary History*, 13 (1982): 85–105; David W. Brady, *Critical Elections and Congressional Policymaking* (Stanford, Calif.: Stanford University Press, 1988).

22. Berry, *Long-Wave Rhythms*, ch. 8; Samuel P. Huntington, "Paradigms of American Politics: Beyond the One, the Two, and the Many," *Political Science Quarterly*, 89 (1974): 22–25. To the list of cycles one might add sunspots.

23. See the citations to voting studies in the essays by Brady, Collie, and Thompson in Gerhard Loewenberg and others, eds., *Handbook of Legislative Research* (Cambridge, Mass.: Harvard University Press, 1985), and in the essays by Shade, Alexander, Mayhew, and Cox in Joel H. Silbey, ed., *Encyclopedia of the American Legislative System* (New York: Scribner, 1994), 3 vols. Ballard C. Campbell, "Party, Policy, and Political Leadership in Congress during the Nineteenth Century," *Legislative Studies Quarterly*, 6 (1981): 622.

24. Richard L. McCormick, *From Realignment to Reform: Political Change in New York State* (Ithaca, N.Y.: Cornell University Press, 1981); Martin Shefter, "Party, Bureaucracy, and Political Change," in Louis Maisel and Joseph Cooper, eds., *Political Parties: Development and Decay* (Beverly Hills, Calif.: Sage Publications, 1978); Kornbluh, *From Participation to Administration*, chs. 4–6. On the decline of partisanship and turnout, see Walter D. Burnham, "The System of 1896: An Analysis," in Kleppner, *American Electoral Systems*; Paul Kleppner, *Who Voted? The Dynamics of Electoral Turnout, 1870–1980* (New York: Praeger, 1982); John F. Reynolds, *Testing Democracy: Electoral Behavior and Progressive Reform in New Jersey* (Chapel Hill: University of North Carolina Press, 1988).

25. David R. Mayhew, *Divided We Govern: Party Control, Lawmaking, and Investigations, 1946–1990* (New Haven, Conn.: Yale University Press, 1991), esp. 124, 126.

26. Jerome M. Clubb and Santa A. Traugott, "Partisan Cleavage and Cohesion in the House of Representatives, 1861–1974," *Journal of Interdisciplinary History*, 7 (1977): 375–401.

27. Assessments of policy consequences of party realignment face two unresolved but formidable empirical challenges. First, vast segments of policy-making history in America, especially in the states and cities, remain unexplored or under-researched. My position regarding the state legislatures on this issue remains as valid today as it was when I wrote "The State Legislature in American History: A Review Essay," *Historical Methods*, 9 (1976), 185–94. Even less systematic research on historical aspects of policy making in cities exists; Teaford in Silbey, *American Legislative Systems*, reviews the literature. And second, neither roll-call votes nor expenditure data offer sufficient information for analyzing the contours of policy development. Also see Allan J. Lichtman, "The End of Realignment Theory? Toward a New Research Program for American Political History," *Historical Methods*, 15 (1982): 170–88; and Mayhew, *Divided We Govern*, esp. ch. 6.

28. See, e.g. Theodore J. Lowi, "Party, Policy, and Constitution in America," in Chambers and Burnham, *American Party Systems*.

29. Leonard D. White, *Trends in Public Administration* (New York: McGraw-Hill, 1933), ch. 20; Thomas J. Anton, "Intergovernmental Change in the United States: An Assessment of the Literature," in Trudi Miller, ed., *Public Sector Performance* (Baltimore: Johns Hopkins University Press, 1984), 28.

30. Jack L. Walker, "Origin and Maintenance of Interest Groups in America," *American Political Science Review*, 77 (1983): 390–406. The pluralist perspective on U.S. politics sees interest groups as a driving dynamic of policy making; Huntington, "Paradigms of American Politics," examines this interpretation in relation to the consensus and the progressive (class-conflict) theses. David Nachmias and David H. Rosebloom, *Bureaucratic Government USA* (New York: St. Martin's Press, 1980), ch. 8, succinctly reviews the literature on interest groups.

31. On Congress, see Margaret Susan Thompson, *The "Spider Web": Congress and Lobbying in the Age of Grant* (Ithaca, N.Y.: Cornell University Press, 1985). On the states, see Robert Harrison, "The Hornets' Nest at Harrisburg: A Study of the Pennsylvania Legislature in the Late 1870s," *Pennsylvania Magazine of History and Biography, 103* (1979): 334–55; Ballard C. Campbell, *Representative Democracy: Public Policy and Midwestern Legislatures in the Late Nineteenth Century* (Cambridge, Mass.: Harvard University Press, 1980). On cities, see Jon C. Teaford, *The Unheralded Triumph: City Government in America, 1870–1900* (Baltimore: Johns Hopkins University Press, 1984), ch. 6.

32. The literature on the capture thesis is summarized in Thomas K. McCraw, "Regulation in America: A Review Article," *Business History Review*, 49 (1975): 159–83. The classic statement of the theory from an economist's perspective is George J. Stigler, "The Theory of Economic Regulation," *Bell Journal of Economics and Management Science*, 2 (1971): 3–21. A penultimate complaint that American government has been given over to private interests is Theodore J. Lowi, *The End of Liberalism: The Second Republic of the United States* (New York: W. W. Norton, 1969, 1979); for an updated reiteration of this point, see David Cay Johnston, *Free Lunch* (New York: Portfolio, 2007).

33. For example, see David R. Mayhew, *Congress: The Electoral Connection* (New Haven, Conn.: Yale University Press, 1974); Richard Gid Powers, *Secrecy and Power: The Life of J. Edgar Hoover* (New York: Free Press, 1987). Also see the citations in ch. 9.

34. James M. Buchanan, "Easy Budgets and Tight Money," in James M. Buchanan and Robert D. Tollison, *Theory of Public Choice: Political Applications of Economics* (Ann Arbor: Uni-

versity of Michigan Press, 1972). A more elaborate version of his argument appears in Buchanan and Richard E. Wagner, *Democracy in Deficit: The Political Legacy of Lord Keynes* (New York: Academic Press, 1976). Public-choice and other economic perspectives on the growth of government are surveyed in Carolyn Weaver, *The Crisis in Social Security: Economics and Political Origins* (Durham, N.C.: Duke University Press, 1982), ch. 1.

35. Leonard D. White, a political scientist at the University of Chicago between 1920 and 1956, was a pioneer in the movement to expand formal (university-based, professional) training for public servants; see the four editions (1926–1955) of his *Introduction to the Study of Public Administration* (New York: Macmillan). See also Ballard C. Campbell, "Leonard D. White," *American National Biography* (New York: Oxford University Press, 1999).

36. Stephen Skowronek, *Building a New American State: The Expansion of National Administrative Capacities, 1877–1920* (New York: Cambridge University Press, 1982). Bensel, *Yankee Leviathan*, and Skocpol, *Protecting Soldiers and Mothers*, also emphasize the view that considerable initiative for policy innovation came from within government. For a recent review of this perspective among social scientists, see Robertson, "The Return to History and the New Institutionalism."

37. Gordon Tullock, *The Politics of Bureaucracy* (Washington, D.C.: Public Affairs Press, 1965); William A. Niskanen, *Bureaucracy and Representative Government* (Chicago: Aldine-Atherton, 1971). For a review and critique of the public-choice theory of budget maximizers, see Gary J. Miller and Terry M. Moe, "Bureaucrats, Legislators, and the Size of Government," *American Political Science Review*, 77 (1983): 297–322.

38. Huntington, "Paradigms of American Politics." Instructive on this issue is Margo Anderson, "The Language of Class in Twentieth-Century America," *Social Science History*, 12 (1988), 349–76.

39. Richard E. Dawson and Kenneth. Prewitt, *Political Socialization* (Boston: Little, Brown, 1969); David Easton, *A Systems Analysis of Political Life* (Wiley, 1965).

40. Schattschneider, *Semi-Sovereign People*, 37.

41. Thomas R. Dye, *Understanding Public Policy*, 7th ed. (Englewood Cliffs, N.J.: Prentice-Hall, 1992), ch. 2, summarizes incrementalism and other paradigms of politics.

42. Schattschneider, *Semi-Sovereign People*, 128.

43. Martha Derthick, *Policymaking for Social Security* (Washington, D.C.: Brookings Institution, 1979), 377. The incremental expansion of policy can be consider in regard to the law of compound growth, which states that increases at a constant rate eventually double the size of an entity, then double it again in a shorter period; see Henry Tenue, *Growth* (Newbury Park, Calif.: Sage Publications, 1988), 74. The expansion of public expenditures provides some confirmation of the principle. Christopher Howard, "The Hidden Side of the American Welfare State," *Political Science Quarterly*, 108 (1993): 403–36, argues that both incrementalism and structure account for the growth of tax expenditures.

3. THE TRANSITION ERA

1. Edward Bellamy, *Looking Backward, 2000–1887* (New York: Random House, 1951; originally copyrighted 1887), 36, 70, 76–77. The quotations in the next three paragraphs come from Bellamy's book.

2. Ibid., 39–41, 45, 52, 225.

3. William Graham Sumner, "The Absurd Effort to Make the World Over," originally published in *Forum* (1894) and reprinted in *War and Other Essays*, ed. Albert G. Keller (New Haven, Conn.: Yale University Press, 1911), 106; W. G. Sumner, *What Social Classes Owe to Each Other* (Caldwell, Idaho: Caxton, 1961; originally published 1883), 88, 95, 104; W. G. Sumner, "Reply to

a Socialist" (1904), in *American Issues: The Social Record*, 4th ed., ed. Merle Curti et al. (Philadelphia: Lippincott, 1971), 2:309.

4. Governor's message of 1900, in *Messages from the Governors*, ed. Charles Z. Lincoln (Albany: New York State, 1909), 10:80–101; James D. Richardson, comp., *Messages and Papers of the Presidents* (Washington, D.C.: Bureau of National Literature and Art, 1910), 7353–7355, quoted at 7364.

5. Richardson, *Messages*, 7355; Clifford L. Staten, "Theodore Roosevelt: Dual and Cooperative Federalism," *Presidential Studies Quarterly* 23 (1993): 129–43.

6. Winston Churchill, *Mr. Crewe's Career* (New York: Macmillan, 1908),180.

7. Clifton K. Yearley, *The Money Machines* (Albany: State University of New York Press, 1970), ch. 10. Generally, see David Mark Chalmers, *The Muckrake Years* (New York: D. Van Nostrand, 1974); Ray Stannard Baker, *American Chronicle: The Autobiography* of Ray Stannard Baker (New York: Scribner, 1945).

8. Paul Kleppner, *Who Voted? The Dynamics of Electoral Turnout, 1870–1980* (New York: Praeger, 1982), ch. 4; Peter H. Argersinger, "'A Place on the Ballot': Fusion Politics and Antifusion Laws," *American Historical Review* 85 (1980): 287–306; John F. Reynolds and Richard L. McCormick, "Outlawing 'Treachery': Split Tickets and Ballot Laws in New York and New Jersey, 1880–1910," *Journal of American History* 72 (1986): 835–58.

9. Leonard D. White, *Trends in Public Administration* (New York: McGraw-Hill, 1933), ch. 20; William R. Brock, *Investigation and Responsibility* (Cambridge: Cambridge University Press, 1984).

10. Martin J. Schiesl, *The Politics of Efficiency: Municipal Administration and Reform in America, 1800–1920* (Berkeley: University of California Press, 1977); Jane S. Dahlberg, *The New York Bureau of Municipal Research* (New York: New York University Press, 1966); Peri E. Arnold, "Executive Reorganization and the Origins of the Managerial Presidency," *Polity* 8 (1981): 586–99.

11. Paul Kleppner, *The Third Electoral System, 1853–1892* (Chapel Hill: University of North Carolina Press, 1979), and *Continuity and Change in Electoral Politics, 1893–1928* (New York: Greenwood Press, 1987); Lewis L. Gould, *Reform and Regulation: American Politics from Roosevelt to Wilson* (New York: Knopf, 1986).

12. Wilson's messages to Congress are contained in Richardson, *Messages and Papers of the Presidents*; quoted in *Inaugural Addresses of the Presidents of the United States* (Washington, D.C.: United States Government Printing Office, 1961), 201. Also see excerpts from Wilson, *The State* (1889) in *The Transformation of American Society, 1870–1890*, ed. John A. Garraty (New York: Harper and Row, 1968), and Woodrow Wilson, *Constitutional Government in the United States* (New York: Columbia University Press, 1908), 173–97.

13. Woodrow Wilson, "The Study of Administration," *Political Science Quarterly* (1887).

14. Ch. 8 traces changes in tax policy.

15. J. Rogers Hollingsworth and Ellen Jane Hollingsworth, *Dimensions in Urban History: Historical and Social Science Perspectives on Middle-Sized Cities* (Madison: University of Wisconsin Press, 1979); Thomas R. Dye, *Politics, Economics, and the Public: Policy Outcomes in the American States* (Chicago: Rand McNally, 1966); Norman Walzer and Glenn W. Fisher, *Cities, Suburbs, and Property Taxes* (Cambridge, Mass.: Oelgeschlager, Gunn, and Ham, 1981).

16. White, *Public Administration*, chs. 14, 15; Dahlberg, *New York Bureau of Municipal Research*; W. Brooke Graves, *American State Government* (Boston: D. C. Heath, 1946), 584–90.

17. *Arlington Town Report for 1927*, Arlington, Mass., 1928.

18. Arlington Cooperative Bank, "Helping Arlington Home Owners for 50 Years" (1939), reprinted in the *Arlington Advocate Centennial Edition*, September 28, 1972, 17.

19. Lawrence M. Friedman, *A History of American Law* (New York: Simon and Schuster, 1974), 397. Ballard C. Campbell, "Public Policy and State Government," in *The Gilded Age: Essays on the Origins of Modern America*, rev. ed., ed. Charles W. Calhoun (Lanham, Md.: Rowman and Littlefield, 2006).

20. Herbert Hovenkamp, *Enterprise and American Law, 1836–1937* (Cambridge, Mass.: Harvard University Press, 1991), chs. 12, 13; Thomas K. McCraw, *Prophets of Regulation* (Cambridge, Mass.: Harvard University Press, 1984), ch. 1; George H. Miller, *Railroads and the Granger Laws* (Madison: University of Wisconsin Press, 1971); and Albro Martin, "The Troubled Subject of Railroad Regulation in the Gilded Age—A Reappraisal," *Journal of American History* 61 (1974): 339–71.

21. W. Brooke Graves, "Professional and Occupational Restrictions," *Temple Law Quarterly* 13 (1939): 334–63; Paul Starr, *The Social Transformation of American Medicine* (New York: Basic Books, 1982), chs. 3–6.

22. White, *Public Administration*, ch. 6; John W. Meyer, David Tyack, and others, "Public Education as Nation-Building in America: Enrollments and Bureaucratization in the American States, 1870–1930," *American Journal of Sociology* 85 (1979): 591–613.

23. Ballard C. Campbell, "The Good Roads Movement in Wisconsin, 1890–1911," *Wisconsin Magazine of History* 49 (1966): 273–93.

24. John C. Burnham, "The Gasoline Tax and the Automobile Revolution," *Mississippi Valley Historical Review* (now *Journal of American History*) 68 (1961): 435–59; Bruce E. Seeley, *Building the American Highway System: Engineers as Policy Makers* (Philadelphia: Temple University Press, 1987).

25. W. Brooke Graves, *Uniform State Action: A Possible Substitute for Centralization* (Chapel Hill: University of North Carolina Press, 1934). Elihu Root made the comment about "regrettable" centralization (1907), printed in W. Brooke Graves, *American Intergovernmental Relations* (New York: Scribner, 1964), 799.

26. Ari and Olive Hoogenboom, *A History of the ICC* (New York: W. W. Norton, 1976); Carroll H. Wooddy, *The Growth of the Federal Government, 1915–1932* (New York: McGraw-Hill, 1934), 254–55.

27. Martin Sklar, *The Corporate Reconstruction of American Capitalism, 1890–1916: The Market, the Law, and Politics* (New York: Cambridge University Press, 1988); Richard Hofstadter, "What Happened to the Anti-Trust Movement," in *The Paranoid Style in American Politics and Other Essays* (New York: Vintage Books, 1964).

28. John M. Gaus and Leon O. Wolcott, *Public Administration and the United States Department of Agriculture* (Chicago: Public Administration Service, 1940); Wooddy, *Growth of the Federal Government*, esp. ch. 12; Charles E. Rosenberg, "Science, Technology, and Economic Growth: The Case of the Agricultural Experiment Station Scientist, 1875–1914," *Agricultural History* 45 (1971): 1–20; Grant McConnell, *The Decline of Agrarian Democracy* (New York: Athenaeum, 1969).

29. Seeley, *Building the American Highway System*.

30. William Preston Jr., *Aliens and Dissenters: Federal Suppression of Radicals, 1903–1933* (Cambridge, Mass.: Harvard University Press, 1963); Paul L. Murphy, *World War I and the Origin of Civil Liberties in the United States* (New York: W. W. Norton, 1979).

31. Wooddy, *Growth of the Federal Government*, ch. 4 and 37, 392.

4. THE GREAT DEPRESSION AND ECONOMIC POLICY

1. Studs Terkel, *Hard Times: An Oral History of the Great Depression* (New York: Washington Square Press, 1970), presented a prize-winning collection of personal stories, quoted 50.

2. Albert U. Romasco, *The Poverty of Abundance: Hoover, the Nation, the Depression* (New York: Oxford University Press, 1965), ch. 8; John Braeman, *The New Deal: The State and Local Levels* (Columbus: Ohio State University Press, 1975), vol. 2; "State Aid for Unemployment Relief," *State Government* (August 1932) 8.

3. Florence Peterson, "Unemployment Relief—Local and State," in John R. Commons et al., *History of Labor in the United States* (New York: Macmillan, 1935), vol. 3; Paul Studenski and Herman Krooss, *Financial History of the United States* (New York: McGraw-Hill, 1963), 432–33; David J. Mauer, "Unemployment in Illinois during the Great Depression," in *Essays in Illinois History*, ed. Donald J. Mauer (Carbondale: Southern Illinois University Press, 1968), 120–32.

4. James T. Patterson, *The New Deal and the States: Federalism in Transition* (Princeton, N.J.: Princeton University Press, 1969), chs. 1 and 2; Arthur E. Buck, *Modernizing Our State Legislatures* (Philadelphia: American Academy of Political and Social Science, 1936); Robert B. McKay, *Reapportionment: The Law and Politics of Equal Representation* (New York: Twentieth Century Fund, 1965).

5. B. U. Ratchford, "Constitutional Provisions Governing State Borrowing," *American Political Science Review* 32 (1938): 694–717; Byron R. Abernethy, *Constitutional Limitations on the Legislature* (Lawrence: Governmental Research Center, University of Kansas, 1959). Two instructive illustrations of the fiscal problems of the early 1930s in the states are Richard T. Ortquist, "Tax Crisis and Politics in Early Depression Michigan," *Michigan History* 59 (1975): 91–119, and Harold Gorvine, "The New Deal in Massachusetts," in Braeman, *New Deal,* vol. 2.

6. Herbert Stein, *The Fiscal Revolution in America* (Chicago: University of Chicago Press, 1969), ch. 4; Albert U. Romasco, *The Politics of Recovery: Roosevelt's New Deal* (New York: Oxford University Press, 1983), ch. 11; William D. Leuchtenburg, *Franklin D. Roosevelt and the New Deal* (New York: Harper and Row, 1963), 37.

7. Stein, *Fiscal Revolution,* 50.

8. Kenneth S. Davis, "The Birth of Social Security," *American Heritage* 30 (1979): 38–51; Alan Brinkley, *Voices of Protest: Huey Long, Father Coughlin, and the Great Depression* (New York: Knopf, 1982); Romasco, *Recovery,* 126–28.

9. Samuel Rosenman, ed., *The Public Papers . . . of Franklin D. Roosevelt: 1937* (New York: Russell and Russell, 1941), 45–46, 37.

10. Arthur M. Schlesinger Jr., *The Age of Roosevelt: The Coming of the New Deal* (Boston: Houghton Mifflin, 1959), 102.

11. Arthur M. Schlesinger Jr., *The Age of Roosevelt: The Politics of Upheaval* (Boston: Houghton Mifflin, 1960), 280.

12. Christopher L. Tomlins, *The State and the Unions: Labor Relations, Law, and the Organized Labor Movement in America, 1880–1960* (New York: Cambridge University Press, 1985), 136–37.

13. Howard W. Odum, *Southern Regions of the United States* (Chapel Hill: University of North Carolina Press, 1936), a classic study of comparative regional characteristics, offers a rich description of race and poverty in the South. Robert A. Margo, "The Competitive Dynamics of Racial Exclusion: Employment Segregation in the South, 1900–1950," National Bureau of Economic Research Working Paper No. 14 (August 1990), presents an econometric analysis.

14. Romasco, *Recovery,* 161–79; Theodore Saloutos, *The American Farmer and the New Deal* (Ames: Iowa State University Press, 1982), 34–45; Pete Daniel, *Breaking the Land: The Transformation of Cotton, Tobacco, and Rice Cultures since 1880* (Urbana: University of Illinois Press, 1985), 94–104.

15. Paul Abrahams, "Agricultural Adjustment during the New Deal Period: The New York Milk Industry, a Case Study," *Agricultural History* 39 (1965): 92–101; Murray R. Benedict and Oscar C. Stine, *The Agricultural Commodity Programs: Two Decades of Experience* (New York:

Twentieth Century Fund, 1956), 444–52, 468; Brigitte Young, "The Dairy Industry," in *Governance of the American Economy*, ed. John L. Campbell and others (New York: Cambridge University Press, 1991), 236–58.

16. Benedict and Stine, *Agricultural Commodities*, 468; Richard A. Ippolito and Robert T. Masson, "The Social Cost of Government Regulation of Milk," *Journal of Law and Economics* 21 (1978): 33–65; Harmon Zeigler, *The Florida Milk Commission Changes Minimum Prices* (Tuscaloosa: University of Alabama Press, 1963). Marketing orders provided that dealers agreed to pay dairy farmers a specified minimum price for each unit of milk delivered. Since these agreements hinged on price arrangements negotiated between cooperatives and dealers, dairy regulation in effect ratified the pooling price scheme that existed in the industry. Dairy cooperatives were granted authority to act as a kind of labor union for farmers, much like the NLRB legitimized the bargaining units of industrial workers. The intent of this policy was, as the Florida law (1933) stated, to guarantee a "reasonable return" to milk farmers.

17. William R. Childs, *Trucking and the Public Interest: The Emergence of Federal Regulation, 1914–1940* (Knoxville: University of Tennessee Press, 1985), 129–38.

18. Childs, *Trucking*, 158–59; John W. Snow, "The Problem of Motor Carrier Regulation and the Ford Administration's Proposal for Reform," in *Regulation of Entry and Pricing in Truck Transportation*, ed. Paul MacAvoy and John Snow (Washington, D.C.: American Enterprise Institute, 1977), 7.

19. Thomas K. McCraw, *Prophets of Regulation* (Cambridge, Mass.: Harvard University Press, 1984), 259–65.

20. Katie Louchheim, *The Making of the New Deal: The Insiders Speak* (Cambridge, Mass.: Harvard University Press, 1983), 315–50; McCraw, *Prophets of Regulation*, 59, 171.

21. Thomas McCraw, "With the Consent of the Governed: SEC's Formative Years," *Journal of Policy Analysis and Management* 1 (1982): 355–56.

22. See ch. 9 for references to literature concerning changes in the presidency and Congress.

23. Patterson, *New Deal and the States*, 94–101; Advisory Commission on Intergovernmental Relations, *Significant Features of Fiscal Federalism, 1976–1977*, vol. 2: *Revenue and Debt* (Washington, D.C., 1977), 99–103. Also see James A. Maxwell, *Financing State and Local Governments* (Washington, D.C.: Brookings Institution, 1965).

24. Patterson, *New Deal and the States*; Braeman, *The New Deal: The State and Local Levels.*

25. Patterson, *New Deal and the States*, ch. 6; John M. Allswang, *The New Deal and American Politics* (New York: Wiley, 1978). For three illustrations, see Robert E. Burton, "The New Deal in Oregon," in Braeman, *The New Deal*; John Miller, *Governor Philip LaFollette and the Wisconsin Progressives* (Columbia: University of Missouri Press, 1982); David R. Colburn and Richard Scher, *Florida's Gubernatorial Politics in the 20th Century* (Tallahassee: University Presses of Florida, 1980), esp. chs. 5–9.

26. Patterson, *New Deal and the States*, 104, 112–13, 121–23; W. Brooke Graves, "Federal Leadership in State Legislation," *Temple Law Review* 10 (1936): 385–405.

5. THE MANAGED ECONOMY SINCE THE NEW DEAL

1. Robert Palmer, *Deep Blues* (New York: Penguin Books, 1982), 135–36.

2. Harold G. Vatter, *The U.S. Economy in World War II* (New York: Columbia University Press, 1985), presents the conventional view; Robert Higgs, "Wartime Prosperity? A Reassessment of the U.S. Economy in the 1940s," *Journal of Economic History* 52 (1992): 41–60, argues that conditions weren't as rosy as commonly believed.

3. John F Witte, *The Politics and Development of the Federal Income Tax* (Madison: University of Wisconsin Press, 1985), ch. 6. See ch. 8 for additional references concerning taxation and budgeting.

4. Vatter, *Economy in World War II*, ch. 1; Witte, *Federal Income* Tax, 131.

5. John Morton Blum, *"V" Was for Victory* (New York: Harcourt, Brace, Jovanovich, 1976), reviews the presidency and society during the war.

6. Thomas G. Patterson, *On Every Front: The Making of the Cold War* (New York: W. W. Norton, 1979), ch. 1, vividly describes this devastation.

7. Stephen K. Bailey, *Congress Makes a Law* (New York: Columbia University Press, 1950), 43; Herbert Stein, *The Fiscal Revolution in America* (Chicago: University of Chicago Press, 1969), 172–75.

8. Stein, *Fiscal Revolution*, 173 (Dewey quoted), 174.

9. Joseph Duncan and William Shelton, *Revolution in U.S. Government Statistics, 1926–1976* (Washington, D.C.: U.S. Department of Commerce, Office of Federal Statistical Policy and Standards, 1978). Also see William Abraham, *National Income and Economic Accounting* (Englewood Cliffs, N.J.: Prentice-Hall, 1969), 3–4.

10. For example, see Stein, *Fiscal Revolution*; George P. Schultz and Kenneth W. Dam, *Economic Policy: Beyond the Headlines* (New York: W. W. Norton, 1977)

11. Schultz and Dam, *Economic Policy*, 202. Also see Stein, *Fiscal Revolution*, chs. 15, 16.

12. James L. Sundquist, *Politics and Policy: The Eisenhower, Kennedy, and Johnson Years* (Washington, D.C.: Brookings Institution, 1968), 38–54; Stein, *Fiscal Revolution*, 449–50.

13. Johnson's remarks are printed in *Economic Report of the President . . . 1964* (Washington, D.C.: U.S. Government Printing Office, 1964), 3–18.

14. Congressional Quarterly, *Budgeting for America: The Politics and Process of Federal Spending* (Washington, D.C., 1982), 48–49. On the process of Federal fiscal expansion generally, see Advisory Commission on Intergovernmental Relations, *A Crisis of Confidence and Competence* (Washington, D.C.: 1980), and John W. Ellwood, *Reductions in U.S. Domestic Spending* (New Brunswick, N.J.: Transaction Books, 1982), 7–31.

15. Herman B. Leonard and Elisabeth H. Rhyne, "Federal Credit and the 'Shadow Budget,'" *Public Interest* 65 (1981): 40–58.

16. Larry Berman, *The Office of Management and Budget and the Presidency, 1921–1979* (Princeton, N.J.: Princeton University Press, 1979).

17. Carl M. Brauer, "Kennedy, Johnson, and the War on Poverty," *Journal of American History* 69 (1982): 98–119.

18. Advisory Commission on Intergovernmental Relations, *Reducing Unemployment: Intergovernmental Dimensions of a National Problem* (Washington, D.C.: Advisory Commission on Intergovernmental Relations, 1982), 85, 97.

19. Jacques S. Gansler, *The Defense Industry* (Cambridge, Mass.: MIT Press, 1980), 4, 300n44, and ch. 4 generally. Also see James Fallows, *National Defense* (New York: Vintage Books, 1981), 62–69 and ch. 5; John H. Mollenkopf, *The Contested City* (Princeton, N.J.: Princeton University Press, 1983), 217, 239. Almost 60 percent of the 435 congressional districts contained or were adjacent to the 3,868 military bases in the United States in 1981, according to Cait Murphy, "Unfinished Business: Who Is Holding Up Grace Commission Reform?" *Policy Review*, Fall 1986, 60–65.

20. Eisenhower's "Farewell Address," January 17, 1961, quoted in this and two paragraphs below, is printed in Henry Steele Commager, ed., *Documents of American History* (Englewood Cliffs, N.J.: Prentice-Hall, 1973), 2:653–654.

21. Gansler, *Defense Industry*, 15 and ch. 4; Nancy J. Bearg and Edwin A. Deagle Jr., "Congress and the Defense Budget," in *American Defense Policy*, ed. John E. Endicott and Roy W. Stafford Jr. (Baltimore: Johns Hopkins University Press, 1977), 335–54; Common Cause, *Defense Dollars and Sense* (Washington, D.C.: Markrovner, 1983), 46–47.

22. On the culture of military procurement and its linkage to costs, see Gansler, *Defense Industry*, esp. chs. 3, 6; Fallows, *National Defense*; and Bearg and Deagle, "The Defense Budget."

23. Mollenkopf, *Contested City*, chs. 1, 6.

24. James Gilbert, *Another Chance: Postwar America, 1945–1968* (New York: Knopf, 1981), 23; Kenneth A. Jackson, *Crabgrass Frontier: The Suburbanization of the United States* (New York: Oxford University Press, 1985), 215.

25. Jackson, *Crabgrass Frontier*, ch. 11, esp. 204–205.

26. Mollenkopf, *Contested City*, 115–21; Alan. Lupo and others, *Rites of Way: The Politics of Transportation in Boston and the U.S. City* (Boston: Little, Brown, 1971), 191, 200; Alan Altshuler, "Changing Patterns of Policy: The Decision Making Environment of Urban Transportation," *Public Policy* 25 (1977): 171–203.

27. K. H. Schaeffer and Eliot Sclar, *Access for All: Transportation and Urban Growth* (New York: Columbia University Press, 1980), ch. 6; James F. Fish et al., *An Analysis of Arlington, Massachusetts* (1978), 45; Michael P. Conzen and George K. Lewis, *Boston: A Geographical Portrait* (Cambridge, Mass.: Ballinger, 1976), 54.

28. Ronald C. Kahn, "Political Change in America: Highway Politics and Reactive Policymaking," in *Public Values and Private Power in American Politics*, ed. J. David Greenstone (Chicago: University of Chicago Press, 1982), 139–72; Robert A. Caro, *The Power Broker: Robert Moses and the Fall of New York* (New York: Vintage Books, 1974), esp. chs. 37–39. Generally, see Mollenkopf, *Contested City*, and Lupo, *Rites of Way*.

29. Norman Walzer and Glenn W. Fisher, *Cities, Suburbs, and Property Taxes* (Cambridge, Mass.: Oelgeschlager, Gunn and Hain, 1981); Matthew Edel, Elliott D. Sclar, and Daniel Luria, *Shaky Palaces: Homeownership and Social Mobility in Boston's Suburbanization* (New York: Columbia University Press, 1984), 251. U.S. Bureau of the Census, *County and City Data Book 1983* (Washington, D.C.: 1983) documents the contemporary differences in wealth between places within metropolitan areas.

30. Marian Lief Palley and Howard A. Palley, *Urban America and Public Policies* (Lexington, Mass.: D. C. Heath, 1981), surveys the political consequences of local governmental fragmentation.

31. Marc A. Weiss, "The Origins and Legacy of Urban Renewal," in Pierre Clavel and others, *Urban and Regional Planning in an Age of Austerity* (New York: Pergamon Press, 1980), 55–72; Herbert J. Gans, "The Failure of Urban Renewal," in *Urban Renewal*, ed. Jewel Bellush and Murray Hausknecht (Garden City, N.Y.: Anchor Books, 1967), 465–84; Mollenkopf, *Contested City*, chs. 5 and 6.

32. Mollenkopf, *Contested City*, 179 and ch. 4; Weiss, "Urban Renewal"; Caro, *Power Broker*, chs. 41, 43.

33. My reflections on community development block grants in Arlington are based on reports in the *Arlington Advocate*, town reports, and personal observation. See Donald F. Kettl, *Managing Community Development in the New Federalism* (New York: Praeger, 1980); Paul R. Dommel and Michael J. Rich, "The Rich Get Richer: The Attenuation of Targeting Effects of the Community Development Block Grant Program," *Urban Affairs Quarterly* 22 (1987): 552–79.

34. Willard W. Cochrane and Mary E. Ryan, *American Farm Policy, 1948–1973* (Minneapolis: University of Minnesota Press, 1976), 234–40; Richard A. Ippolito and Robert T. Masson, "The Social Cost of Government Regulation of Milk," *Journal of Law and Economics* 21 (1978): 33–65.

35. W. P. Welch, "Campaign Contributions and Legislative Voting: Milk Money and Dairy Price Supports," *Western Political Quarterly* 35 (1982): 478–95. Welch found little overt connection between policy making and financial contributions.

36. Cochran and Ryan, *American Farm Policy*, 359–81. Charles Schultze indicated that 7 percent of American farmers received an estimated 40 percent of all agricultural benefits in 1969, with government providing about 43 percent of their net income. On the other hand, the least successful half of farm operators received only 9 percent of Federal farm subsidies; see "U.S. Farm Policy: Who Gets the Benefits," in *The Political Economy of Federal Policy*, ed. Robert H. Haveman and Robert D. Hamrin (New York: Harper and Row, 1973), 189–90.

37. Paul W. MacAvoy, *The Regulated Industries and the Economy* (New York: W. W. Norton, 1979), 25; Louis Galambos and Joseph Pratt, *The Rise of the Corporate Commonwealth* (New York: Basic Books, 1987), 46.

38. David Vogel, "The 'New' Social Regulation in Historical and Comparative Perspective," in *Regulation in Perspective: Historical Essays,* ed. Thomas K. McCraw (Cambridge, Mass.: Harvard University Press, 1981), 155–85; Jack L. Walker, "The Origins and Maintenance of Interest Groups in America," *American Political Science Review* 77 (1983): 390–406; Samuel H. Beer, "In Search of a New Public Philosophy," in *The New American Political System,* ed. Anthony King (Washington, D.C.: American Enterprise Institute, 1978), 5–44; *Boston Globe,* "Earth Day Special," April 22, 1970.

39. Advisory Commission on Intergovernmental Relations, *Protecting the Environment: Politics, Pollution, and Federal Policy* (Washington, D.C.: ACIR, 1981).

40. A. Lee Fritschler, *Smoking and Politics: Policy Making and the Federal Bureaucracy* (Englewood Cliffs, N.J.: Prentice-Hall, 1983).

41. *New York Times,* Jan. 11, 1989; James T. Patterson, *The Dread Disease: Cancer and Modern American Culture* (Cambridge, Mass.: Harvard University Press, 1987), ch. 8.

42. Steven Kelman, "Occupational Safety and Health Administration," in *The Politics of Regulation,* ed. James Q. Wilson (New York: Basic Books, 1980), 247; Jerome J. Hanus, "Authority Costs in Intergovernmental Relations," in *The Nationalization of State Government,* ed. Jerome J. Hanus (Lexington, Mass.: Lexington Books, 1981), 24–28.

43. Congressional Quarterly, *Social Security and Retirement* (Washington, D.C.: CQ, 1983), 117–27.

44. *New York Times,* Nov. 2, 1983, A26.

45. *New York Times,* Oct. 5, 1977. Also see *President's Private Sector Survey on Cost Control* (Jan. 15, 1984), 3:108ff.; Murray L. Weidenbaum, *Business, Government, and the Public* (Englewood Cliffs, N.J.: Prentice-Hall, 1981), ch. 11.

46. Jerome J. Hanus and Gary C. Marfin, "State Dependency and Cooperative Federalism," *State Government* 53 (1980): 174–75.

47. Herbert Stein, *Presidential Economics: The Making of Economic Policy from Roosevelt to Reagan and Beyond* (New York: Simon and Schuster, 1984), 22.

6. THE NEW INCOME SECURITY

1. James T. Patterson, *America's Struggle against Poverty, 1900–1986* (Cambridge, Mass.: Harvard University Press, 1986), chs. 1, 3; Anthony J. Badger, *The New Deal: The Depression Years, 1933–1940* (New York: Noonday Press, 1989), 23–29.

2. Theda Skocpol, *Protecting Soldiers and Mothers: The Political Origins of Social Policy in the United States* (Cambridge, Mass.: Harvard University Press, 1992), esp. 424–64, 472; Advisory Commission on Intergovernmental Relations, *Public Assistance: The Growth of a Federal Function* (Washington, D.C.: ACIR, 1980), 10–17.

3. Skocpol, *Protecting Soldiers and Mothers,* 132,135.

4. William Graebner, *A History of Retirement: The Meaning and Function of an American Institution, 1885–1978* (New Haven, Conn.: Yale University Press, 1980), ch. 3.

5. Skocpol, *Protecting Soldiers and Mothers,* 9; Carolyn Weaver, *The Crisis in Social Security: Economic and Political Origins* (Durham, N.C.: Duke University Press, 1982), 34–35; Paul Starr, *The Social Transformation of American Medicine* (New York: Basic Books, 1982), 237.

6. See notes 2–5, ch. 4.

7. Graebner, *Retirement,* 184–90; Weaver, *Crisis in Social Security,* chs. 4, 5.

8. On assumptions underlying Social Security old-age pensions, see Weaver, *Crisis in Social Security,* chs. 4–6; J. Douglas Brown, *An American Philosophy of Social Security: Evolution and Issues* (Princeton, N.J.: Princeton University Press, 1972); Arthur J. Altmeyer, *The Formative Years of Social Security* (Madison: University of Wisconsin Press, 1966).

9. Martha Derthick, *Policy Making for Social Security* (Washington, D.C.: Brookings Institution, 1979); Carolyn L. Weaver, "The Social Security Bureaucracy in Triumph and Crisis," in *The New American State: Bureaucracies and Policies since World War II,* ed. Louis Galambos (Baltimore: Johns Hopkins University Press, 1987), 54–84. A comprehensive listing of statutory changes to Federal income assistance programs appears in Social Security Administration, *Social Security Bulletin: Annual Statistical Supplement, 1991* (Washington, D.C.: GPO, 1991).

10. Derthick, *Policy Making for Social Security,* chs. 10–13.

11. Mark H. Leff, "Taxing the 'Forgotten Man': The Politics of Social Security Finance in the New Deal," *Journal of American History* 70 (1983): 359–81, esp. 366, 372.

12. Derthick, *Social Security,* 6; *New York Times,* Nov. 24, 1987.

13. Derthick, *Social Security,* esp. chs. 1, 2, 11, and 19.

14. I have closely followed Derthick, *Social Security,* regarding the behavior of the program's administrators. Also see Weaver, "Social Security Bureaucracy" and *Crisis in Social Security;* Katie Louchheim, *The Making of the New Deal: The Insiders Speak* (Cambridge, Mass.: Harvard University Press, 1983), 151–59.

15. Derthick, *Social Security,* chs. 2, 16.

16. Ch. 8 discusses social security taxes; ch. 10 reviews the benefit reductions in the 1983 act.

17. Patterson, *Struggle against Poverty,* ch. 2; Michael B. Katz, *In the Shadow of the Poorhouse: A Social History of Welfare in America* (New York: Basic Books, 1986).

18. Carl M. Brauer, "Kennedy, Johnson, and the War on Poverty," *Journal of American History* 69 (1982): 98–119.

19. James L. Sundquist, *Politics and Policy: The Eisenhower, Kennedy, and Johnson Years* (Washington, D.C.: Brookings Institution, 1968), ch. 5.

20. U.S. Bureau of the Census, "Characteristics of the Population below the Poverty Level: 1974," *Current Population Reports,* P-60, no. 102 (Washington, D.C.: GPO, January 1976), esp. tables 8, 23.

21. Patterson, *Struggle against Poverty,* chs. 10, 11; Frances F. Piven and Richard A. Cloward, *Regulating the Poor: The Functions of Public Welfare* (New York: Vintage Books, 1971), chs. 8, 9.

22. Dwaine Marvick, "The Political Socialization of the American Negro," *Annals of the American Academy of Political and Social Science* 361 (1965): 112–27.

23. Leon D. Platky, "The Effect of Recent Demographic Trends on the AFDC Program," Population Reference Bureau, *Intercom* 6 (November 1978): 7–9.

24. Bureau of the Census, "Characteristics of the Population below the Poverty Level: 1974," 43.

25. Charles Murray, *Losing Ground: American Social Policy* (New York: Basic Books, 1984); Michael Harrington, *The New American Poverty* (New York: Holt, Rinehart and Winston, 1984); Peter G. Peterson, "No More Free Lunch for the Middle Class," *New York Times Magazine,* Jan. 17, 1982, 40–41, 56–63.

26. *Newsweek,* Jan. 24, 1983, 23. Also see Paul Light, *Artful Work: The Politics of Social Security Reform* (New York: Random House, 1985), esp. 75–77.

27. William P. O'Hare, "Poverty in America: Trends and New Patterns," *Population Bulletin* 40 (1985): 1–44; David B. Robertson and Dennis R. Judd, *The Development of American Public Policy: The Structure of Policy Restraint* (Glenview, Ill.: Scott, Foresman, 1989), 226; *Boston Globe*, Sept. 22, 1992.

28. William P. O'Hare, "America's Welfare Population: Who Gets What?" in Population Reference Bureau, *Population Trends and Public Policy* 13 (1987), 10; Advisory Commission on Intergovernmental Relations, *Public Assistance*, 112–13.

7. THE NEW EQUALITY

1. Pete Daniel, *The Shadow of Slavery: Peonage in the South, 1901–1969* (New York: Oxford University Press, 1973); William Cohen, "Negro Involuntary Servitude in the South, 1865–1940: A Preliminary Analysis," *Journal of Southern History* 42 (1976): 31–60.

2. Alex Lichtenstein, "Good Roads and Chain Gangs in the Progressive South: 'The Negro Convict Is a Slave,'" *Journal of Southern History* 59 (1993): 85–110.

3. Albert B. Hart, *The Southern South* (New York: D. Appleton, 1912), 182–83.

4. In *Heart of Atlanta Motel v. United States* (1964) the Supreme Court held the 1964 Civil Rights Act constitutional based on the congressional power to regulate interstate commerce.

5. Thomas R. Dye, *Understanding Public Policy*, 2nd ed. (Englewood Cliffs, N.J.: Prentice-Hall, 1975), 42–43; Robert S. Erikson and Norman R. Luttbeg, *American Public Opinion: Its Origins, Content, and Impact* (New York: Wiley, 1973), 46–49; George H. Gallup, *The Gallup Poll: Public Opinion, 1935–1971* (New York: Random House, 1972), 748, 810, 1333, 1723, 1827; Jacob K. Javits, *Discrimination U.S.A.* (New York: Washington Square Press, 1962), esp. ch. 8.

6. Charles and Barbara Whalen, *The Longest Debate: A Legislative History of the Civil Rights Act* (New York: New American Library, 1985), 127; Richard F. Bensel, *Sectionalism and American Political Development, 1880–1980* (Madison: University of Wisconsin Press, 1984), table 5.9.

7. David J. Garrow, *Bearing the Cross: Martin Luther King, Jr., and the Southern Christian Leadership Conference* (New York: William Morrow, 1986), chs. 4, 5; William A. Nunnelley, *Bull Connor* (Tuscaloosa: University of Alabama Press, 1991); Richard Polenberg, *One Nation Divisible* (New York: Penguin Books, 1980), 184.

8. Whalen, *Longest Debate*, 21 and chs. 1, 2.

9. Javits, *Discrimination*, ch. 5.

10. Dwaine Marvick, "The Political Socialization of the American Negro," *Annals of the American Academy of Political and Social Science* 361 (1965): 112–27.

11. Theodore H. White, *The Making of the President, 1960* (New York: New American Library, 1961), 397.

12. Whalen, *Longest Debate*, 107; John Barnard, *Walter Reuther and the Rise of the Auto Workers* (Boston: Little, Brown, 1983), 173, 185, 206.

13. Whalen, *Longest Debate*, ch. 2.

14. Ibid., chs. 5–7, esp. 167, 186.

15. Susan M. Hartmann, *The Home Front and Beyond* (Boston: Twayne, 1982).

16. Whalen, *Longest Debate*, 177–219.

17. *New York Times*, Mar. 4, 1976.

18. Advisory Commission on Intergovernmental Relations, *State Constitutions in the Federal System* (Washington, D.C.: Advisory Commission on Intergovernmental Relations, 1989), 63. On state statutes concerning gender equality, see John Galvin and Ethel Mendelson, "The Legal Status of Women," in Council on State Governments, *The Book of the States, 1980–1981* (Lexington, Ky.: Council on State Governments, 1980), 36–46.

19. James L. Sundquist, *Politics and Policy: The Eisenhower, Kennedy, and Johnson Years* (Washington, D.C.: Brookings Institution, 1968), ch. 5.

20. Diane Ravitch, *The Troubled Crusade: American Education, 1945–1980* (New York: Basic Books, 1983), ch. 5; Jeremy Rabkin, "Office for Civil Rights," in *The Politics of Regulation*, ed. James Q. Wilson (New York: Basic Books, 1980), ch. 9.

21. Charles S. Bullock III and Charles M. Lamb, *Implementation of Civil Rights Policy* (Monterey, Calif.: Brooks/Cole, 1984), 96–98. Regarding the constraints on equal employment policy generally, see Gary Bryner, "Congress, Courts, and Agencies: Equal Employment and the Limits of Policy Implementation," *Political Science Quarterly* 96 (1981): 411–30.

22. Harold W. Stanley and Richard G. Niemi, *Vital Statistics on American Politics* (Washington, D.C.: CQ Press, 1990), 368. The 1992 elections raised the female proportion to almost one-fifth; see Michael X. Delli Carpini and Ester R. Fuchs, "The Year of the Woman: Candidates, Voters, and the 1992 Elections," *Political Science Quarterly* 108 (1993): 35.

23. Abigail M. Thernstrom, *Whose Votes Count? Affirmative Action and Minority Voting Rights* (Cambridge, Mass.: Harvard University Press, 1987), esp. ch. 8.

24. *New York Times*, Dec. 12, 1990. U.S. Bureau of the Census, "Money, Income, and Poverty Status in the United States, 1987," in *Current Population Reports*, P-60, no. 161 (Washington, D.C.: GPO, 1988).

25. Elaine Johansen, *Comparable Worth: The Myth and the Movement* (Boulder, Colo.: Westview Press, 1984); Sara M. Evans and Barbara N. Nelson, *Wage Justice: Comparable Worth and the Paradox of Technocratic Reform* (Chicago: University of Chicago Press, 1989).

8. PAYING FOR MODERN GOVERNMENT

1. The quotation is from Coolidge's inaugural address, Mar. 4, 1925.

2. W. Elliot Brownlee, "Income Taxation and the Political Economy of Wisconsin, 1890–1930," *Wisconsin Magazine of History* 59 (1976): 299–324.

3. Advisory Commission on Intergovernmental Relations, *Significant Features of Fiscal Federalism, 1976–1977* (Washington, D.C., 1977), 2:99–103; James T. Patterson, *The New Deal and the States: Federalism in Transition* (Princeton, N.J.: Princeton University Press, 1969), 94–101; *State Government* 5 (September 1932): 8. W. Brooke Graves, *American State Government*, 3rd ed. (Boston: D. C. Heath, 1946), ch. 13, describes the state tax system shortly after the conclusion of the 1930s; the second edition of his text was published in 1941.

4. Robert A. Caro, *The Power Broker: Robert Moses and the Fall of New York* (New York: Vintage Books, 1974), ch. 28.

5. I. M. Labovitz, "The Illinois Revenue System, 1818–1936," in *Special Report* 4 (Springfield, Ill.: Illinois Tax Commission, 1936); the quotation is from "Report of Retrenchment Commission," *Journal of the House of Representatives, Fifty-ninth Illinois General Assembly* (Springfield, Ill.: 1935), 1790. On restrictions that handcuffed Chicago finances, see Marjorie Murphy, "Taxation and Social Conflict: Teacher Unionism and Public School Finance in Chicago, 1898–1934," *Journal of the Illinois State Historical Society* 74 (1981): 242–60; and William R. Biles, *Mayor Edward J. Kelley of Chicago: Big City Boss in Depression and War* (De Kalb: Northern Illinois University Press, 1984).

6. Philip G. Bean, "Illinois Politics during the New Deal," PhD dissertation, University of Illinois, Urbana, 1976; *Journal of the House of Representatives, 57th, 58th, and 59th Illinois General Assemblies* (Springfield, Ill.: 1931–1935).

7. Harry S. Truman, *Years of Trial and Hope*, vol. 2 of *Memoirs* (New York: New American Library, 1956), 54–55.

8. John F. Witte, *The Politics and Development of the Federal Income Tax* (Madison: University of Wisconsin Press, 1985), esp. 164.

9. Ibid., ch. 7; James L. Sundquist, *Politics and Policy: The Eisenhower, Kennedy, and Johnson Years* (Washington, D.C.: Brookings Institution, 1968), chs. 2, 3.

10. The Omnibus Budget Act of 1993 added two more tax brackets, which increased the total to five.

11. Martha Derthick, *Policymaking for Social Security* (Washington, D.C.: Brookings Institution, 1979), ch. 11; Carolyn Weaver, *The Crisis in Social Security: Economic and Political Origins* (Durham, N.C.: Duke University Press, 1982), chs. 4–6. Also see Mark H. Leff, "Taxing the 'Forgotten Man': The Politics of Social Security Finance in the New Deal," *Journal of American History* 70 (1983): 359–81.

12. Paul Light, *Artful Work: The Politics of Social Security Reform* (New York: Random House, 1983).

13. Weaver, *Crisis in Social Security*, 94, 109–10, 219, 225.

14. Ibid., 111–15; Derthick, *Social Security*, 199.

15. *Congressional Record*, April 14, 1969, 7.

16. Advisory Commission on Intergovernmental Relations, *Categorical Grants: Their Role and Design* (Washington, D.C., 1978), ch. 8; Deil S. Wright, *Understanding Intergovernmental Relations* (North Scituate, Mass.: Duxbury Press, 1978), chs. 8, 9.

17. Michael D. Reagan and John O. Sanzone, in *The New Federalism* (New York: Oxford University Press, 1981), cite the weakness of state fiscal capacity and ability as a justification for federal grants; their argument reiterates claims about the superior fiscal position of the national government put forth throughout the twentieth century: e.g., Charles Beard, *American Government and Politics* (New York: Macmillan, 1928), 449–50; "The Commission on Organization of the Executive Branch" and "Federal-State Relations," in *The People, Politics, and the Politician*, ed. A. N. Christensen and Evron M. Kirkpatrick (New York: Holt, 1950), 147–52.

18. John H. Mollenkopf, *The Contested City* (Princeton, N.J.: Princeton University Press, 1983), ch. 3; Kenneth Fox, *Metropolitan America: Urban Life and Urban Policy in the United States, 1940–1980* (Jackson: University Press of Mississippi, 1986).

19. See ch. 9 for citations to the literature about Congress.

20. The subnational requests for Federal aid became significant in the 1930s: Mark I. Gelfand, *A Nation of Cities: The Federal Government and Urban America, 1933–1965* (New York: Oxford University Press, 1975), 37–39, 65; Patterson, *The New Deal and the States*, 31. For similar supplications after World War II, see Daniel J. Elazar, *American Federalism: A View from the States* (New York: Harper and Row, 1972), esp. 212, and Thomas J. Anton, "Intergovernmental Change in the U.S.: An Assessment of the Literature," in *Public Sector Performance: A Conceptual Turning Point*, ed. Trudi Miller (Baltimore: Johns Hopkins University Press, 1984), 15–64.

21. The activities and influence of policy communities in the claimant era is well documented. For example, see Willard W. Cochrane and Mary E. Ryan, *American Farm Policy, 1948–1973* (Minneapolis: University of Minnesota Press, 1976), esp. 118; Joseph A. Califano Jr., *Governing America: An Insider's Report from the White House and the Cabinet* (New York: Simon and Schuster, 1981), esp. 23, 141–42, 183–84, 331; Thomas J. Anton, *American Federalism and Public Policy: How the System Works* (New York: Random House, 1989), chs. 4, 5; Theodore J. Lowi, *The End of Liberalism: The Second Republic of the United States* (New York: W. W. Norton, 1979); James T. Bennett and Thomas J. Dilorenzo, "The Role of Tax-Funded Politics," in *Prospects for Privatization*, ed. Steven H. Hanke (New York: Academy of Political Science, 1987), 14–23. Also see the citations in ch. 9.

22. Ballard C. Campbell Jr., "The Good Roads Movement and the Passage of the Federal Aid Road Act of 1916," master's thesis, Northeastern University, 1964, ch. 4. Michael Les Benedict, "Laissez and Liberty: A Re-evaluation of the Meaning and the Origins of Laissez-Faire Constitutionalism," *Law and History Review* 3 (1985): 293–331, brilliantly explained the legal-intellectual context of these charges. See too Carroll H. Wooddy, *The Growth of the Federal Gov-*

ernment, 1915–1932 (New York: McGraw-Hill, 1934), 447, 527; Leonard D. White, *Trends in Public Administration* (New York: McGraw-Hill, 1933), chs. 3, 4.

23. Advisory Commission on Intergovernmental Relations, *Categorical Grants*, esp. chs. 2, 3, 7, and *Regulatory Federalism* (Washington, D.C., 1984); David B. Walker, *Toward a Functioning Federalism* (Cambridge, Mass.: Winthrop, 1981), esp. chs. 4, 7, 8; Donald F Kettle, *The Regulation of American Federalism* (Baltimore: Johns Hopkins University Press, 1988). Leonard D. White detected these themes years ago in his brilliant lectures *The States and the Nation* (Baton Rouge: Louisiana State University Press, 1953).

24. House Resolution no. 56, *Journal of the House of Representatives of the 59th Illinois General Assembly* (Springfield, Ill., 1935), 840.

25. A good sampling of criticism along these lines appears in Advisory Commission on Intergovernmental Relations, *A Crisis of Confidence and Competence* (Washington, D.C., 1980) and *Summary and Concluding Observations* (Washington, D.C., 1978), which was a volume in the commission's study *The Intergovernmental Grant System: An Assessment and Proposed Policies* (14 vols., 1976–1978); Edward Kock, "The Mandate Millstone," *Public Interest* 61 (1980): 42–57.

26. Clara Penniman, "The Politics of Taxation," in *Politics in the American States: A Comparative Analysis*, ed. Herbert Jacob and Kenneth N. Vines (Boston: Little, Brown, 1976), 428–64; Walker, *Federalism*, ch. 6; ACIR, *Fiscal Federalism, 1976–1977*, 2:105.

27. Robert H. Connery and Gerald Benjamin, *Rockefeller of New York: Executive Power in the Statehouse* (Ithaca, N.Y.: Cornell University Press, 1979), esp. ch. 3; Peter D. McClelland and Alan L. Magdovitz, *Crisis in the Making: The Political Economy of New York State since 1945* (New York: Cambridge University Press, 1981), chs. 5–7.

28. Connery and Benjamin, *Rockefeller*, ch. 6; McClelland and Magdovitz, *Crisis*, chs. 6, 7.

29. Witte, *Income Tax*, ch. 13; Christopher Howard, "The Hidden Side of the American Welfare State," *Political Science Quarterly* 108 (1993): 403–36.

30. Witte, *Income Tax*, 369. Jimmy Carter called the Federal income tax "a disgrace to the human race" in his 1976 presidential campaign.

31. Herman B. Leonard and Elisabeth H. Rhyne, "Federal Credit and the 'Shadow Budget,'" *Public Interest* 65 (1981): 40–58.

32. David Cay Johnston, *Free Lunch* (New York: Portfolio, 2007), chs. 6–9.

9. THE NEW FACES OF POWER

1. Richard G. Powers, *The Secrecy and Power: The Life of J. Edgar Hoover* (New York: Free Press, 1987).

2. Aage R. Clausen, *How Congressmen Decide: A Policy Focus* (New York: St. Martin's Press, 1973); Ballard C. Campbell, *Representative Democracy* (Cambridge, Mass.: Harvard University Press, 1980), and "Federalism, State Action, and 'Critical Episodes' in the Growth of American Government," *Social Science History* 16 (1992): 565–66.

3. H. Douglas Price, "The Congressional Career Then and Now," in *Congressional Behavior*, ed. Nelson W. Polsby (New York: Random House, 1971); Nelson W. Polsby, "The Institutionalization of the House of Representatives," *American Political Science Review* 62 (1968): 144–68; Donald A. Ritchie, *Press Gallery: Congress and the Washington Correspondents* (Cambridge, Mass.: Harvard University Press, 1991).

4. Anthony Champagne, *Congressman Sam Rayburn* (New Brunswick, N.J.: Rutgers University Press, 1984); D. B. Hardmeman and Donald C. Bacon, *Rayburn: A Biography* (Austin: Texas Monthly Press, 1987).

5. Greg O'Brien, "Timely Rider," *Boston Magazine*, March 1983, 94, 122–33, and Robert L. Turner, "Eighth Notes," *Boston Globe Magazine*, May 26, 1985, trace O'Neill's career, as does

O'Neill's autobiography, *Man of the House: The Life and Political Memoirs of Speaker Tip O'Neill* (New York: Random House, 1987).

6. Congressional Quarterly, *Guide to the Congress of the United States* (Washington, D.C.: Congressional Quarterly, 1982), 477–80, 580; Norman J. Ornstein and others, *Vital Statistics on Congress, 1982* (Washington, D. C.: Congressional Quarterly, 1982), 105–18.

7. John F. Bibby and others, *Vital Statistics on Congress, 1980* (Washington, D.C.: American Enterprise Institute, 1980), 14, 16; Bureau of the Census, *Statistical Abstract of the United States, 1980* (Washington, D.C.: GPO, 1980), 508, 511. An important work that examines the decline of competitive House seats over time is David W. Brady, *Critical Elections and Congressional Policy Making* (Stanford, Calif.: Stanford University Press, 1988), chs. 7, 8.

8. Walter D. Burnham, "The System of 1896: An Analysis," in *The Evolution of American Electoral Systems,* ed. Paul Kleppner (Westport, Conn.: Greenwood Press, 1981); Samuel T. McSeveney, *The Politics of Depression: Political Behavior in the Northeast, 1893–1896* (New York: Oxford University Press, 1972); Mark L. Kornbluh, *From Participation to Administration: A Social and Political History of the Emergence of Modern American Politics, 1880–1918* (Baltimore: Johns Hopkins University Press, 2000).

9. Three of the best works that emphasize these themes are David R. Mayhew, *Congress: The Electoral Connection* (New Haven, Conn.: Yale University Press, 1974); Morris P. Fiorina, *Congress: Keystone of the Washington Establishment* (New Haven, Conn.: Yale University Press, 1977); D. Douglas Arnold, *The Logic of Congressional Action* (New Haven, Conn.: Yale University Press, 1990), esp. ch. 5.

10. Barbara Sinclair Deckard, "Political Upheaval and Congressional Voting: The Effects of the 1960s on Voting Patterns in the House of Representatives," *Journal of Politics* 38 (1976): 326–45; Aage R. Clausen and Carl E. Van Horn, "The Congressional Response to a Decade of Change: 1963–1972," *Journal of Politics* 39 (1977): 624–66. The bibliography cites voting studies that cover various eras.

11. Woodrow Wilson, *Congressional Government: A Study in American Politics* (Cleveland: Meridian Books, 1956, originally published 1885), 44

12. E. L. Godkin, "The Decline of the Legislature," *Atlantic Magazine* 80 (1897): 35–53; Paul S. Reinsch, *American Legislatures and Legislative Methods* (New York: Century, 1907), ch. 7; Arthur N. Holcombe, *State Government in the United States* (New York: Macmillan, 1926), ch. 9.

13. Edward S. Corwin, *The Twilight of the Supreme Court* (New Haven, Conn.: Yale University Press, 1934), 178.

14. Harry S. Truman, *Memoirs* (New York: Signet, 1956), 2:52.

15. Larry Berman, *The Office of Management and Budget and the Presidency, 1921–1979* (Princeton, N.J.: Princeton University Press, 1979).

16. Robert Dallek, *Franklin D. Roosevelt and American Foreign Policy* (New York: Oxford University Press, 1979); Robert A. Divine, *The Reluctant Belligerent: American Entry into World War II* (New York: Wiley, 1979).

17. The May 27, 1941, proclamation is printed in Henry Steele Commager, ed., *Documents of American History* (New York: Appleton, Century, Crofts, 1949), 631–33.

18. Arthur M. Schlesinger Jr., *The Imperial Presidency* (Boston: Houghton Mifflin, 1973); Louis Fisher, *The Constitution between Friends: Congress, the President, and the Law* (New York: St. Martin's Press, 1978), chs. 8, 9; James M. Burns and others, *Government by the People* (Englewood Cliffs, N.J.: Prentice-Hall, 1978), 309.

19. Eleanor Roosevelt, the wife of Franklin Roosevelt, began the trend of politically active and visible first ladies. In 1993 the U.S. Court of Appeals for the District of Columbia ruled that Hillary Clinton, wife of the president and head of the administration's Task Force on National Health Care Reform, was a de facto Federal official; *New York Times,* June 23, 1993.

20. Richard W. Steele, "The Great Debate: Roosevelt, the Media, and the Coming of the War, 1940–1941," *Journal of American History* 71 (1984): 69–92.

21. Theodore J. Lowi, *The Personal President: Power Invested, Promise Unfulfilled* (Ithaca, N.Y.: Cornell University Press, 1985), ch. 4.

22. Alan Rosenthal, *Legislative Life: People, Process, and Performance in the States* (New York: Harper and Row, 1981), 306–309; George D. Brown, "Federal Funds and National Supremacy: The Role of State Legislatures in Federal Grant Programs," *American University Law Review* 28 (1979), 279–313.

23. Powers, *Hoover,* esp. chs. 5, 6.

24. Congressional Quarterly, *Guide to the Presidency* (Washington, D.C., 1989), 905–909; *Report of the Warren Commission on the Assassination of President Kennedy* (New York: Bantam, 1964), 45–46, 433–46; Congressional Quarterly, *Congress and the Nation* (Washington, D.C., 1969), 2:649–50; *Boston Globe,* Dec. 21, 1991.

25. Powers, *Hoover,* esp. ch. 7; Kenneth O'Reilly, "A New Deal for the FBI: The Roosevelt Administration, Crime Control, and National Security," *Journal of American History* 69 (1982): 638–58.

26. O'Reilly, "A New Deal for the FBI"; Athan Theoharis, "FBI Wiretapping: A Case Study of Bureaucratic Autonomy," *Political Science Quarterly* 107 (1992): 101–22.

27. Robert Caro, *The Power Broker: Robert Moses and the Fall of New York* (New York: Knopf, 1974), esp. chs. 9–17. My treatment of Moses's career is based principally on Caro's biography.

28. Katie Louchheim, *The Making of the New Deal: The Insiders Speak* (Cambridge, Mass.: Harvard University Press, 1983), 151–59; Martha Derthick, *Policymaking for Social Security* (Washington, D.C.: Brookings Institution, 1969), 52–55, 320–23, and passim; *New York Times,* May 5, 1987 (obituary).

29. Joseph A. Califano Jr., *Governing America: An Insider's Report from the White House and the Cabinet* (New York: Simon and Schuster, 1981), 389; Derthick, *Social Security.*

30. Derthick, *Social Security,* 19, 22. Carolyn L. Weaver, "The Social Security Bureaucracy in Triumph and in Crisis," in *The New American State: Bureaucracies and Politics since World War II,* ed. Louis Galambos (Baltimore: Johns Hopkins University Press, 1987), 78, agrees with Derthick. Cohen was quite up front about the mission; see Louchheim, *New Deal,* 154. Also see Califano, *Governing America,* esp. 389–92.

10. THE REAGAN ERA AND THE RESTRAINED POLITY

1. My synopsis of Reagan's political economy is drawn principally from his first inaugural address (Jan. 20, 1981), his address to the nation on the economy (Feb. 5, 1981), his budget message of Feb. 18, 1981, and his first State of the Union message (Jan. 26, 1982).

2. My representation of Reagan's position on social issues is drawn from his speech to the National Association of Evangelicals (March 6, 1984), his weekly radio address as paraphrased in the *Boston Globe* (Feb. 16, 1986), his speech from the White House on drug abuse (Sept. 14, 1986), and his 1988 State of the Union address.

3. David O. Sears and Jack Citrin, *Tax Revolt: Something for Nothing in California* (Cambridge, Mass.: Harvard University Press, 1982); "Sound and Fury over Taxes," *Time,* June 19, 1978; and Lawrence Susskind and Cynthia Horan, "Proposition 2½: The Response to Tax Restriction in Massachusetts," *Proceedings of the Academy of Political Science* 35 (1983): 158–71.

4. Advisory Commission on Intergovernmental Relations, *Significant Features of Fiscal Federalism,* 1982–1983 ed. (Washington, D.C.: ACIR, 1984), tables 65 and 66.

5. Sears and Citrin, *Tax Revolt,* 40–45; Linda L. M. Bennett and Stephen E. Bennett, *Living with Leviathan: Americans Coming to Terms with Big Government* (Lawrence: University Press of Kansas, 1990), 81–87.

6. *Boston Globe,* Feb. 13, 1979; *Washington Post,* Feb. 25, 1979; *New York Times,* Mar. 19, 1985.

7. On the nineteenth century, see Michael F. Holt, *The Political Crisis of the 1850s* (New York: Wiley, 1978), 107–108; Jon C. Teaford, *The Unheralded Triumph* (Baltimore: Johns Hopkins University Press, 1984), 287–91; and David P. Thelen, *The New Citizenship: The Origins of Progressivism in Wisconsin* (Columbia: University of Missouri Press, 1972), 138, 203–10. Terrence J. McDonald, *The Parameters of Urban Fiscal Policy* (Berkeley: University of California Press, 1986), argued persuasively for the influence of ideology and party on municipal taxes in the late nineteenth century. On the twentieth century, see David T. Beito, *Taxpayers in Revolt: Tax Resistance during the Great Depression* (Chapel Hill: University of North Carolina Press, 1989); Harold Gorvine, "The New Deal in Massachusetts," in John Braeman and others, *The New Deal* (Columbus: Ohio State University Press, 1975), 2:14; Paul Studenski and Herman E. Krooss, *Financial History of the United States* (New York: McGraw-Hill, 1963), ch. 31. Some historians contend that the writing of the U.S. Constitution (1787) was a form of tax revolt insofar as advocates of a stronger national government sought to limit the economic authority of state governments; see Gordon S. Wood, *The Creation of the American Republic, 1776–1787* (New York: W. W. Norton, 1969), chs. 10, 11; Cathy D. Matson and Peter S. Onuf, *A Union of Interests* (Lawrence: University Press of Kansas, 1990), esp. 71–72.

8. *Time,* Jan. 15, 1979, 58–59.

9. Martha Derthick and Paul J. Quirk, *The Politics of Deregulation* (Washington, D.C.: Brookings Institution, 1985).

10. Reagan's first State of the Union message, Jan. 26, 1982.

11. Norman C. Amaker, *Civil Rights and the Reagan Administration* (Washington, D.C.: Urban Institute Press, 1988).

12. Thomas R. Swartz and John E. Peck, *The Changing Face of Fiscal Federalism* (Armonk, N.Y.: M. E. Sharpe, 1990), esp. chs. by R. C. Hill, S. D. Gold, and H. F. Ladd.

13. Unless otherwise indicated, my descriptive reports of Reagan administration fiscal policy are based on data in the U.S. Bureau of the Census, *Statistical Abstract of the United States,* various issues; Advisory Commission on Intergovernment Finance, *Significant Features of Fiscal Federalism,* various issues; and the *New York Times* and *Wall Street Journal.*

14. On FBI sting operations and other investigations of state and local officials in the 1980s and early 1990s, see *Boston Globe,* Mar. 25, 1991, and Apr. 24, 1992; *New York Times,* Aug. 20, 1981, Dec. 27, 1988, and May 31, 1991.

15. John Kincaid, "From Cooperation to Coercion in American Federalism: Housing, Fragmentation and Preemption, 1780–1992," *Journal of Law and Politics* 9 (1993): 419–22, 428; Donald F Kettl, *The Regulation of American Federalism* (Baltimore: Johns Hopkins University Press, 1988).

16. Advisory Commission on Intergovernmental Relations, *Federal Statutory Preemption of State and Local Authority* (Washington, D.C., 1992); David B. Walker, "American Federalism from Johnson to Bush," *Publius* 21 (1991): 105–19.

17. *U.S. News and World Report,* July 12, 1982, 34–37; David Burnham, *Rise of the Computer State* (New York: Random House, 1983); Gary T. Marx, "We're All under Surveillance," *Los Angeles Times,* Dec. 1, 1985; "What Price Privacy?" *Consumer Reports,* May 1991, 356, 360. See chapter 11 for developments after the Patriot Act 2001.

18. *New York Times,* Dec. 14, 1988, on the Washington colony; *New York Times,* Oct. 8, 1985; State of the Union message, Jan. 25, 1988.

19. Bennett and Bennett, *Living with Leviathan,* ch. 2, 94–97; *New York Times,* Dec. 1, 1987 (Times/CBS News poll); *New York Times,* Nov. 9, 1989 (Harris poll); Sears and Citrin, *Tax Revolt,* 62–63, 67, 70.

20. Reagan's report to the nation on the economy, broadcast Feb. 5, 1981.

21. Kevin Phillips, *Boiling Point: Democrats, Republicans and the Decline of Middle-Class Prosperity* (New York: Random House, 1993), esp. 49; Michael Bernstein and David Adler, eds., *Understanding American Economic Decline* (New York: Cambridge University Press, 1994).

22. Louis Uchitelle, "Male, Educated and in a Pay Bind," *New York Times,* Feb. 11, 1994. On similar themes and accompanying anxiety, see Louis Uchitelle, "Stagnant Pay: A Delayed Impact," *New York Times,* June 18, 1991; Leonard Silk, "Why Fiscal Policy Has to Have a Soul," *New York Times,* Dec. 6, 1991.

23. Phillips, *Boiling Point,* ch. 5 and appendix B; *New York Times,* Oct. 1, 1992.

24. This ambivalence toward big government in the abstract and specific governmental policies runs throughout the opinion and voter literature. See Bennett and Bennett, *Living with Leviathan,* chs. 3, 4, esp. 107–108; Robert Shapiro and John M. Gilroy, "The Polls: Regulation," *Public Opinion Quarterly* 48 (1984): 531–42; Paul Kleppner, *Who Voted? The Dynamics of Electoral Turnout, 1870–1980* (New York: Praeger, 1982), 160; Lloyd A. Free and Hadley Cantril, *The Political Beliefs of Americans: A Study of Public Opinion* (New York: Simon and Schuster, 1968), 5, 178–79; Advisory Commission on Intergovernmental Relations, *The Condition of Contemporary Federalism: Conflicting Theories and Collapsing Constraints* (Washington, D.C., 1981), 172–87. An important statement about the utility of polls for policy makers is Benjamin Ginsberg, *The Captive Public: How Mass Opinion Promotes State Power* (New York: Basic Books, 1986).

25. U.S. Bureau of the Census, *Statistical Abstract of the United States: 1992* (Washington, D.C.: GPO, 1992), 274.

26. *New York Times,* Nov. 10, 1988; Norman J. Ornstein and others, *Vital Statistics on Congress, 1991–92* (Washington, D.C.: Congressional Quarterly, 1992), 19–20, 61, 240–41.

27. U.S. Bureau of the Census, *Statistical Abstract of the United States, 1991* (Washington, D.C.: GPO, 1991), 275; *Wall Street Journal,* Mar. 22, 1988; Robert Spitzer, "Gun Control: Constitutional Mandate or Myth?" in *Social Regulatory Policy: Moral Controversies in American Politics,* ed. Raymond Tatalovich and Byran Daynes (Boulder, Colo.: Westview Press, 1988), 115.

28. David Stockman, "The Myth of Federal 'Overspending,'" *Los Angeles Times,* Mar. 8, 1993.

29. *President's Private Sector Survey on Cost Control: A Report to the President* (Washington, D.C.: GPO, Jan. 15, 1984), vol. 1.

30. Martha Derthick, *Agency under Stress: The Social Security Administration in American Government* (Washington, D.C.: Brookings Institution, 1990), 5, 33–45, 145–47. In 1984 Congress adopted a compromise measure, the Social Security Disability Benefits Reform Act, which reduced the flood of complaints to the courts; Derthick, *Agency,* 159–60.

31. Phillip J. Cooper, *Hard Judicial Choices: Federal District Court Judges and State and Local Officials* (New York: Oxford University Press, 1988), 4–21 and ch. 8; Malcolm M. Feeley and Edward L. Rubin, "Federal-State Relations and Prison Administration," in *Power Divided: Essays on the Theory and Practice of Federalism,* ed. Harry Scheiber and Malcolm M. Feeley (Berkeley: University of California Press, 1988), 62–73; Kincaid, "From Cooperation to Coercion in American Federalism," 423–24.

32. *Boston Globe,* Feb. 27, Apr. 2 (the broader ban), 1991. I followed the Boston Harbor clean water episode in the 1980s in the *Globe* and news releases distributed by the MWRA.

33. *Boston Globe,* May 19, 1993; Massachusetts Taxpayers Foundation, *State Budget Trends, 1990* (Boston: MTF, April 1990), 38–39, 50–51; *Boston Globe,* June 9, 1991.

34. Advisory Commission on Intergovernmental Relations, *The Question of State Government Capability* (Washington, D.C.: ACIR, 1985), reviews the modernization of state government and the secondary literature about these trends.

35. Deborah A. Gona, "State of the States, 1988–1989," *Book of the States, 1990–1991* (Lexington, Ky.: Council of State Governments, 1990), 1–17.

36. Samuel P. Hays, *Beauty, Health, and Permanence: Environmental Politics in the United States, 1955–1985* (New York: Cambridge University Press, 1987), 453–56.

37. *Boston Globe*, Sept. 27, 1993; U.S. Bureau of the Census, *Statistical Abstract of the United States*, 1991, 294.

38. Steven D. Gold, "State Finances in the New Era of Fiscal Federalism," in Swartz and Peck, *Fiscal Federalism*, 105, 1 19; *Book of the States, 1990–1991*, 285. On the fiscal impact of the 1981–1982 recession, for example, see "The States' Red-Ink Blues," *Newsweek*, Feb. 28, 1983, 19–20, 23.

39. On state budget woes in the recession of 1990–1991, see *New York Times*, May 31, Oct. 30, 1991; *Boston Globe*, June 7, July 18, 1991; *Arlington Advocate*, June 14, 1990, and earlier issues.

40. The budget requirements are listed in Advisory Commission on Intergovernmental Relations, *Significant Features of Fiscal Federalism, 1984* (Washington, D.C.: ACIR, 1985), table 89.

11. THE DEBATE OVER "BIG" GOVERNMENT

1. I use the terms "conservatives" and "the Right" interchangeably, recognizing that "the Right" is often seen as extreme conservatism. On the other side of the political spectrum I use the terms "liberals" and "the Left" interchangeably, recognizing that "the Left" is a term frequently meant to identify an extremely liberal position. I follow the conventional perception that most conservatives are Republicans and most liberals are Democrats, with the reminder that each party historically has contained an array of ideological positions among its members.

2. Milton and Rose Friedman, *Free to Choose: A Personal Statement* (New York: Avon, 1980), 56.

3. Barry Goldwater, *The Conscience of a Conservative* (Shepherdsville, Ky.: Victor Publishing, 1960), 22–23.

4. Ibid., 24–25.

5. President George H. W. Bush State of the Union address, January 1992, www.gpoaccess .gov/pubpapers/ghwbush.html.

6. *New York Times*, May 21, 1998.

7. Friedman, *Free to Choose*, 279–86; Price Fishback, "Seeking Security in the Postwar Era," in *Government and the American Economy: A New History*, ed. Price Fishback and others (Chicago: University of Chicago Press, 2007), 509–18.

8. David R. Henderson, "The Case for Small Government," *Fortune*, June 26, 1995, 39–40, argues that deregulation will spur economic growth.

9. Charlotte A. Twight, *Dependent on D.C.: The Rise of Federal Control over the Lives of Ordinary Americans* (New York: Palgrave, 2002), ch. 4.

10. Goldwater, *Conscience of a Conservative*, 73.

11. Hedrick Smith, *Who Stole the American Dream?* (New York: Random House, 2012), chs. 9 and 10; David Cay Johnston, *Free Lunch: How the Wealthiest Americans Enrich Themselves at Government Expense* (New York: Portfolio, 2007).

12. Paul Krugman, "Two Cheers for the Welfare State," *Fortune*, May 1, 1995, 41–42, and *The Accidental Theorist* (New York: Norton, 1998); Steven Conn, ed., *To Promote the General Welfare: The Case for Big Government* (New York: Oxford University Press, 2012).

13. Harold W. Stanley and Richard G. Niemi, eds., *Vital Statistics on American Politics, 2011–2012*, ch. 3, especially figures 3.1–3.3 (Washington, D.C.: CQ Press, 2011), http://library.cqpress .com/vasp.

14. On the connection between economic depressions and political change historically, see Ballard C. Campbell, "Tax Revolts and Political Change," *Journal of Policy History* 10 (1998): 153–78; "Economic Causes of Progressivism," *Journal of the Gilded Age and Progressive Era* 4, no. 1 (January 2005): 7–22.

15. See *New York Times*, "Portrait of the Electorate" [1976–1992], Nov. 5, 1992. In the 2008 presidential election Obama received 71 percent of the vote among voters who indicated that their financial situation as "worse today," while McCain got 60 percent of the vote among the electorate who indicated that their financial situation was "better today." *New York Times*, Nov. 9, 2008. Also see *New York Times*, Jan. 20, 1997.

16. David M. Gordon, *Fat and Mean: The Corporate Squeeze of Working Americans and the Myth of Managerial "Downsizing"* (New York: Free Press, 1996), 22; Ruy A. Teixeira and Joel Rodgers, "Who Deserted the Democrats in 1994?," *American Prospect*, Fall 1995, 73–76; *New York Times*, Nov 7, 1996.

17. William A. Galston, "Behind the Middle-Class Funk," *Wall Street Journal*, August 7, 2013, reports a greater forty-year gain in median household income when 1970 is the baseline, but agrees that the middle-class has contracted over the period and has not fully recovered from the Great Recession. Floyd Norris, "U.S. Companies Thrive as Workers Fall Behind," www .newyorktimes.com, 8/9/2012.

18. Kim Phillips-Fein, *Invisible Hands: The Businessmen's Crusade against the New Deal* (New York: Norton, 2009), 188 and ch. 9. Also see David Vogel, *Fluctuating Fortunes: The Political Power of Business in America* (New York: Basic Books, 1990), esp. chs. 6 and 7.

19. *New York Times*, exit polls, Nov. 11 and 13, 1994.

20. Republicans served as governor in the majority of the states in eight of ten biennial elections cycles, 1994–2012.

21. In 1949 the South and West held 31 and 13 percent of the nation's population; in 2010 their proportions were 37 and 23 percent. As regional populations shifted, so did the apportionment of seats in the House of Representatives.

22. Steven Rattner, "America in 2012 as Told in Charts," *New York Times*, Dec. 31, 2012, presents the partisan voting conflict index developed by Keith Poole for the years 1879–2009.

23. I am summarizing Ronald Brownstein, *The Second Civil War* (New York: Penguin Press, 2007), ch. 6, "The Great Sorting Out."

24. *New York Times*, September 5, 2005, A19 [retrospective on the Rehnquist court]; Adam Liptak, "Roberts Pulls Supreme Court to the Right Step by Step," www.newyorktimes.com, June 27, 2013.

25. Several controls are important in assessing public finance over time. First, financial series should be compared against standardized references that remove distortions. Three such standards are used here. "Constant dollars" removes the effects of inflation and deflation on nominal dollar values. "Per person" ("per capita") calculations present finances in relation to the number of people in society. Expressing fiscal trends as a "percentage of the gross domestic product (GDP)" relates spending and taxing to the size of the total economy, and facilitates comparisons with other nations. Second, time series of financial information must embrace a sufficient time period to minimize skewing by unusual events, such as recessions, war, and other unusual costs (e.g., natural disasters). Third, revenue, expenditure, and debt should be broken down by state and local and the federal government, as their taxing and budget policies differ.

26. *Book of the States 2011* (Lexington, Ky.: Council of State Governments, 2011), 275.

27. A debate exists about whether Social Security is a part of the federal budget, as the program has its own revenue stream that is dedicated to specific individual benefits.

28. White, *American Dream*, 357–58, 510–11, based on several reports, including the Congressional Research Service, March 29, 2011, and the Watson Institute for International Studies [Brown and Boston Universities], June 2011.

29. *Statistical Abstract of the United States for 2012* (Washington, D.C.: U.S. Government Printing Office, 2012), table 348, and earlier years.

30. *New York Times*, October 22, 2012, editorial page.

31. Office of Management and Budget, *President's Budget for FY 2014* (Washington, D.C.: U.S. Government Printing Office, 2013), Historical Tables, table 1.3; Iwan Morgan, *The Age of Deficits: Presidents and Unbalanced Budgets from Jimmy Carter to George W. Bush* (Lawrence: University Press of Kansas, 2009)), table 1 and appendix. The annual deficit reached 10 percent of the GDP in 2009, a recession year.

32. For example, the comments of Paul Krugman, economist and columnist for the *New York Times*, April 4, 2001, May 7, 2003; on the Republican antitax program during the Obama administration, see January 3, 2013.

33. *Boston Globe*, Feb. 2, 2004.

34. Stanley L. Engerman and Robert E. Gallman, *The Cambridge Economic History of the United States* (Cambridge: Cambridge University Press, 2000), 3:1051–52; Douglas J. Besharov and Douglas M. Call, "The Global Budget Race," *Wilson Quarterly* 34 (Autumn 2010): 38–50; White, *American Dream*, 347; *Statistical Abstract of the United States for 2012*, table 1362, based on OECD data.

35. Robert Eisener, *The Misunderstood Economy: What Counts and How to Count It* (Cambridge, Mass.: Harvard Business School Press, 1994), chs. 4, 5; Bruce Bartlett, "Mismeasurement of Federal Spending, Investment, and Saving," www.newyorktimes.com, Feb. 26, 2013; Martin Feldstein and Kathleen Feldstein, "Need to Slow Spending Growth," *Boston Globe*, April 30, 1996.

36. Bruce Bartlett, "Tax Increases and Bull Markets," www.newyorktimes.com, Jan. 8, 2013; Peter Passell, "Do Tax Cuts Raise Revenue?" *New York Times*, Nov. 16, 1995; White, *American Dream*, 41–42, 137. Arpit Gupta, "Tax Rates and Economic Growth," *National Review*, October 15, 2012, 45–47, summarizes the conservative argument. Krugman, *Accidental Theorist*, 39–61, rebuts "supply-side" economics.

37. On the debate over Social Security, see Marcia Clemmitt, "The National Debt: Are Higher Taxes Needed to Reduce the Debt?" *CQ Researcher* 21, no. 1 (March 18, 2011), http://0-library.cqpress.com; Linda A. Jacobsen et al., "America's Aging Population," *Population Bulletin* 66, no. 1 (2011); Paul Krugman, "America's Senior Moment," *New York Review of Books*, March 10, 2005, 6–11; Jeff Jacoby, "The Social Security Scam," *Boston Globe*, December 20, 1994; *USA Today*, Nov. 28, 2012.

38. "Longer, Not Healthier, Lives," *Wall Street Journal*, July 11, 2013; *Economist*, Feb. 20, 2010, 69. Morgan, *Age of Deficits*, 258.

39. *New York Times*, Aug. 2, 1996; Robert Rector and Rachel Sheffield, "Welfare Is at an All-Time High," *nationalreview.com*, Oct. 22, 2012.

40. E.g. The *Goodridge* decision (2003) in Massachusetts was the first time that the highest court in a state had ruled that gay couples had the right to marry.

41. "As Prisons Squeeze Budgets, GOP Rethinks Crime Focus," *Wall Street Journal*, June 21, 2013; www.newyorktimes.com, March 24, 2013.

42. White, *American Dream*, 357–8, 386, 371.

43. Ballard C. Campbell, *American Wars* (New York: Facts on File, 2012), ch. 12.

44. Twight, *Dependent on D.C.*, ch. 7 on government data gathering and privacy.

45. Bruce Bartlett reviewed the Federal Reserve *Report on Wealth, Spending, and the Economy, 2013*, in "Among the Wealthiest 1 Percent," www.newyorktimes.com, March 12, 2013.

The Federal Reserve report is part of a large literature that documents widening income inequality in the United States.

46. When U.S. Health and Human Services refused to grant a waiver to Massachusetts under the 1996 Welfare Reform Act, Republican Governor William Weld shot back: "We know our own needs a lot better than a Washington bureaucrat who thinks that Martha's Vineyard is in the middle of California wine country." *Boston Globe,* Aug. 13, 1995.

47. The method of taxing the foreign profits of American multinational corporations, and proposed elimination of corporate income taxes altogether, is under debate. *Week,* Dec. 21, 2012, and June 7, 2013.

BIBLIOGRAPHY

(Note: A bibliographic supplement follows this bibliography.)
The bibliography contains works selected with two purposes in mind. First, many of the titles listed here shaped my understanding of the growth of American government. Thus the bibliography supplements the sources that are cited in the notes to each chapter. And second, I have selected items that will aid further exploration of particular aspects of the growth of government. Titles that span several political eras or a variety of policy functions are listed under General Works. The remainder of the selections are organized by the chapters of the book to which they pertain and the Supplement to the Revised Edition.

General Works

Economic and Financial

Textbooks on economic history also review historical dimensions of economy policy (once referred to as political economy). Good surveys include Lance E. Davis, *American Economic Growth: An Economist's History of the United States* (New York: Harper and Row, 1972); Ross M. Robertson and Gary Walton, *History of the American Economy* (New York: Harcourt, Brace, Jovanovich, 1979); Harold U. Faulkner, *American Economic History,* 8th ed. (New York: Harper and Brothers, 1960); and W. Elliot Brownlee, *Dynamics of Ascent: A History of the American Economy* (New York: Knopf, 1974). Economic textbooks discuss political economy in the contemporary era. For example, see Bradley R. Schiller, *The Economy Today,* 5th ed. (New York: McGraw-Hill, 1991); and Ralph Byrns and Gerald Stone, *Economics,* 4th ed. (Glenview, Ill.: Scott, Foresman, 1989). Valuable reviews of past political economy are Claudia Goldin, *Understanding the Gender Gap: An Economic History of American Women* (New York: Oxford University Press, 1990); Emmette S. Redford, *American Government and the Economy* (New York: Macmillan, 1965); Paul Studenski and Herman E. Krooss, *Financial History of the United States,* 2nd ed. (New York: McGraw-Hill, 1963); Jonathan R. T. Hughes, *The Governmental Habit: Economic Controls from Colonial Times to the Present* (New York: Basic Books, 1977); Thomas K. McCraw, *Prophets of Regulation* (Cambridge, Mass.: Harvard University Press, 1984); and McCraw, ed., *Regulation in Perspective: Historical Essays* (Boston: Harvard University Press, 1981). Joel A. Tarr, "The Evolution of Urban Infrastructure in the Nineteenth and Twentieth Centuries," in *Perspectives on Urban Infrastructure,* ed. Royce

Hansen (Washington, D.C.: National Academy Press, 1984) is a valuable overview of local public works.

Many generalizations in this book rest on quantitative indicators, especially time series of economic, social, political, and fiscal activities. The most useful sources of statistical data on public finance were publications of the U.S. Bureau of the Census (Washington, D.C.: U.S. Governmental Printing Office): Susan B. Carter et al., eds., *Historical Statistics of the United States: Earliest Times to the Present* (New York: Cambridge University Press, 2006); *Statistical Abstract of the United States* (annual); and *Historical Statistics on Governmental Finances and Employment,* which appears as a *Topical Study of the 1982 Census of Governments* (1985, and at earlier five-year intervals). The Advisory Commission on Intergovernmental Relations published useful compilations of fiscal data in its annual editions of *Significant Features of Fiscal Federalism* (Washington, D.C.). Ballard C. Campbell, "Federalism, State Action, and 'Critical Episodes' in the Growth of American Government," *Social Science History* 16 (1992): 561–77, cites sources of fiscal data for the late nineteenth century, when no national clearinghouse for compiling public finance existed. *The Book of the States* (Lexington, Ky.: Council of State Governments, biennial since 1935) and legislative manuals and bluebooks published by individual states filled in gaps in fiscal data and contained storehouses of political information.

Constitutional and Legal

Alfred Kelly, Winfred Harbison, and Herman Belz, *The American Constitution: Its Origins and Development* (New York: W. W. Norton, 1983, 1991), a text in constitutional history, also surveys a good deal of the national government's policy history and contains an extensive bibliography on numerous dimensions of governmental history. Melvin I. Urofsky and Paul Finkelman, *A March of Liberty: A Constitutional History of the United States* (New York: Knopf, 2011); Morton J. Horwitz, *The Transformation of American Law, 1870–1960: The Crisis of Legal Orthodoxy* (New York: Oxford University Press, 1992); and Joan Hoff, *Law, Gender, and Injustice: A Legal History of United States Women* (New York: New York University Press, 1991), are valuable surveys. Although dated, Benjamin F. Wright, *The Growth of American Constitutional Law* (New York: Holt, 1942) retains considerable utility, especially concerning federalism. I used Stanley Kutler, ed., *The Supreme Court and the Constitution: Readings in American Constitutional History* (New York: W. W. Norton, 1984) for the language of many court decisions. A second convenient source for leading cases and other political texts is Henry Steele Commager, ed., *Documents of American History,* 9th ed. (Englewood Cliffs, N.J.: Prentice-Hall, 1973).

State constitutions are fundamental to understanding political structure in American governmental history. No comprehensive history of these charters exists, but useful sources are Kermit L. Hall, "The Irony of the Federal Constitution's Genius: State Constitutional Development," in *The Constitution and American Political Development: An Institutional Perspective,* ed. Peter F. Nardulli (Urbana: University of Illinois Press, 1992); Morton Keller, "The Politics of State Constitutional Revision, 1820–1930," in *The Constitutional Convention as an Amending Device,* ed. Kermit Hall, H. Hyman, and L. Sigal (Washington, D.C.: American Historical Association, 1981); James Q. Dealey, *Growth of American State Constitutions* (Boston: Ginn, 1915); Byron R. Abernethy, *Constitutional Limitations on the Legislature* (Lawrence: Government Research Center, University of Kansas, 1959); Albert L. Sturm, *Thirty Years of State Constitution Making, 1938–1968* (New York: National Municipal League, 1970). Nineteenth-century state constitution are compiled in Francis N. Thorpe, ed., *The Federal and State Constitutions,* 7 vols. (Washington, D.C.: U.S. Government Printing Office, 1909).

Federalism

The history of the American polity inherently involves the federal system. W. Brooke Graves's *American Intergovernmental Relations: Their Origins, Historical Development, and Current Status* (New York: Scribner, 1964) is the most authoritative survey of the subject, but it is now dated. Other standards include William H. Riker, *Federalism: Origin, Operation, Significance* (Boston: Little, Brown, 1964); Morton M. Grodzins, *The American System: A New View of Government in the United States* (Chicago: Rand McNally, 1966); Daniel J. Elazar, *American Federalism: A View from the States* (New York: Crowell, 1972). Leonard D. White, *The States and the Nation* (Baton Rouge: Louisiana State University Press, 1953) remains a classic despite its vintage. Harry N. Scheiber has authored many important articles on the history of federalism, including "Federalism and the American Economic Order, 1789–1910," *Law and Society Review* 10 (1975): 58–118; "American Federalism and the Diffusion of Power: Historical and Contemporary Perspectives," *University of Toledo Law Review* 9 (1978): 619–80; and "Federalism and Legal Process: Historical and Contemporary Analysis of the American System," *Law and Society Review* 14 (1980): 663–722. Stimulating ideas about the historical transformation of federalism are contained in Samuel Beer, "The Modernization and American Federalism," *Publius* 3 (1973): 49–75, and John Kincaid, "From Cooperation to Coercion in American Federalism: Housing, Fragmentation and Preemption, 1780–1992," *Journal of Law and Politics* 9 (1993): 333–433. Also see Dell S. Wright, "A Century of the Intergovernmental Administrative State," in *A Centennial History of the American Administrative State*, ed. Ralph C. Chandler (New York: Free Press, 1987). Ballard C. Campbell, "Federalism and American Legislatures," in *Encyclopedia of the American Legislative System*, ed. Joel Silbey (New York: Scribner, 1994), lists additional titles on the evolution of federalism. Because the texture of federalism is woven from the governing experiences of the national, state, and local governments, most of the studies cited in the remainder of this bibliography characterize aspects of the system's configuration.

Parties, Elections, and Political History

Because no political history of the United States examines governance at all levels of government, one must turn to surrogates, such as the economic and constitutional histories previously cited. Two other scholarly traditions, the historical investigation of political parties and elections (primarily undertaken by historians and political scientists interested in patterns of voter behavior) and general surveys of American government (customarily written by political scientists who concentrate on the present), also illuminate aspects of governmental history. Important works on parties and elections are V. O. Key, *American State Politics: An Introduction* (New York: Knopf, 1956); Walter Dean Burnham, *Critical Elections and the Mainsprings of American Politics* (New York: W. W. Norton, 1970); Everett Carll Ladd Jr., *American Political Parties: Social Change and Political Response* (New York: W. W. Norton, 1970); James L. Sundquist, *Dynamics of the Party System: Alignment and Realignment of Political Parties in the U.S.* (Washington, D.C.: Brookings Institution, 1973); William N. Chambers and W. D. Burnham, eds., *The American Party Systems: Stages of Political Development*, 2nd ed. (New York: Oxford University Press, 1975); Jerome Clubb, William H. Flanigan, and Nancy Zingale, *Partisan Realignment: Voters, Parties, and Government in American History* (Beverly Hills, Calif.: Sage Publications, 1980); Paul Kleppner, ed., *The Evolution of American Electoral Systems* (Westport, Conn.: Greenwood Press, 1981); and Paul Kleppner, *Who Voted? The Dynamics of Electoral Turnout, 1879–1980* (New York: Praeger, 1982). Dewey W. Grantham, *The Democratic South* (New York: W. W. Norton, 1963) surveys the chief regional idiosyncrasy in American politics.

Historically useful explorations of American government include V. O. Key, *Politics, Parties, and Pressure Groups*, 5th ed. (New York: Crowell, 1964); Theodore J. Lowi, *The End of Liberalism: The Second Republic of the United States* (New York: W. W. Norton, 1979); and David B. Robertson and Dennis R. Judd, *Development of American Public Policy: The Structure of Policy Restraint* (Glenview, Ill.: Scott, Foresman/Little Brown, 1989); because the authors of this last work discuss the connection between structure and policy, their book also deserves to be listed in the section on federalism. Introductions to public policy, such as Thomas R. Dye, *Understanding Public Policy*, 6th ed. (Englewood Cliffs, N.J.: Prentice-Hall, 1987), review dimensions of governance in the post–World War II era. Thanks to the descriptive (or historical-institutional) orientation in political science before 1945, older textbooks on American government contain invaluable information about past policy and political practices. Three classics in this tradition are Charles A. Beard, *American Government and Politics*, 5th ed. (New York: Macmillan, 1928; originally published 1910); W. Brooke Graves, *American State Government*, 3rd ed. (Boston: D. C. Heath, 1946; originally published 1936); and Frederick A. Ogg and P. Orman Ray, *Introduction to American Government*, 10th ed. (New York: Appleton-CenturyCrofts, 1951; originally published 1922). These four political scientists, as well as their colleagues V. O. Key and Leonard D. White, cited above, integrated historical perspectives into their writing.

Documents

I drew frequently on the words of the presidents, governors, and other officials. The messages of presidents from George Washington through Calvin Coolidge are contained in James D. Richardson, compiler, *Messages and Papers of the Presidents* (Washington, D.C.: Bureau of National Literature and Art, 1910, and several later editions). The public materials of subsequent presidents were published by the U.S. Government Printing Office as *Public Papers of the Presidents of the United States* (Washington, D.C., various years), with the exception of FDR, whose papers were compiled by Samuel Rosenman, ed., *The Public Papers ... of Franklin D. Roosevelt*, 13 vols. (New York: Russell and Russell, 1938–1950). There is no central collection of the papers of the governors, which are found in more diverse publications, if compiled and printed at all. Kirk H. Porter and Donald B. Johnson, compilers, *National Party Platforms, 1840–1956* (Urbana: University of Illinois Press, 1956) supplied national platforms; state bluebooks and legislative manuals contained statements by political parties at the state level. Summaries of national statutes, congressional proceedings, and information about the presidency, including selected speeches, are published by the Congressional Quarterly Service, *Congress and the Nation, 1945–1964* (Washington, D.C.: Congressional Quarterly, 1965), and subsequent volumes for later administrations. On occasion I also used Congressional Quarterly's more detailed *Almanac* (annual since 1945). For U.S. statutes prior to 1945 I turned first to Commager, *Documents of American History*, then to specialized collections, such as Wayne D. Rasmussen, ed., *Agriculture in the United States: A Documentary History*, 4 vols. (New York: Random House, 1975) and, if necessary, consulted U.S. Congress, *U.S. Statutes at Large*. Individual states prepared their own compilation of acts (session laws) and codes (integrated compilation of session laws). My view of politics since 1960 has been informed by newspapers and magazines, particularly the *New York Times,* the *Boston Globe,* and the national news magazines. It is only fair to acknowledge that the electronic media, such as radio, television, and the Internet, have shaped my perception of contemporary governance, but I know of no convenient way of citing these reports.

For Arlington, Massachusetts, I relied principally on the *Arlington Advocate,* the hometown weekly newspaper; the annual *Town Report,* a rich source that includes tax and fiscal information; Arlington Bicentennial Book Committee, eds., *Arlington Celebrates: The Growing Years,*

1875–1975 (Arlington, Mass.: Arlington Heritage Trust, 1977); and three volumes published by the Arlington Historical Commission: *Mill Brook Valley: A Historical and Architectural Survey* (Arlington, Mass., 1976); *Northwest Arlington, Massachusetts: An Architectural and Historical Study* (Arlington, Mass., 1980); and *Ice, Crops, and Commuters: South and East Arlington's Historical and Architectural Heritage* (Arlington, Mass., 1981). The Local History Room of Arlington Public Library contains additional items that I found useful. To place the town in its appropriate contexts I turned to numerous works about the economic development, suburbanization, and political history of Massachusetts, many of which are cited in chapter 5.

1. Governing the Cleveland Era

The republican tradition in America and its influence on the structure of government bears fundamentally on governance in the nineteenth century. A classic work on this subject is Gordon Wood, *The Creation of the American Republic, 1776–1787* (New York: W. W. Norton, 1972). The bibliography in Alfred Kelly, *The American Constitution*, references titles on republican outcroppings in the politics of the revolutionary era and later. Manifestations of republicanism in the structure of state government are analyzed in Willi Adams, *The First American Constitutions: Republican Ideology and the Making of the State Constitutions in the Revolutionary Era* (Williamsburg, Va.: Institute of Early American History and Culture, 1980). Changes in state constitutions, especially the limitations imposed on state legislatures and public finance, can be traced in Hall, "State Constitutional Revision," Dealey, *State Constitutions*, and Abernethy, "Constitutional Limitations," listed previously, and Illinois Legislative Reference Bureau, "State and Local Finance," *Constitutional Convention Bulletins* (Springfield, 1920, bulletin no. 4), 207–336; and Jon C. Teaford, *The Unheralded Triumph: City Government in America, 1879–1900* (Baltimore: Johns Hopkins University Press, 1984). Insightful analyses of the law, republicanism, and business in the late nineteenth century are Michael Les Benedict, "Laissez-Faire and Liberty: A Re-evaluation of the Meaning and Origins of Laissez-Faire Constitutionalism," *Law and History Review* 3 (1985): 293–331; Herbert Hovenkamp, *Enterprise and American Law, 1836–1937* (Cambridge, Mass.: Harvard University Press, 1991); Charles W. McCurdy, "Justice Field and the Jurisprudence of Government-Business Relations: Some Parameters of Laissez-Faire Constitutionalism, 1863–1897," *Journal of American History* 61 (1975): 970–1005; and "The Knight Sugar Decision of 1895 and the Modernization of American Corporation Law, 1869–1903," *Business History Review* 53 (1979): 304–42.

Richard W. Welch Jr., *The Presidencies of Grover Cleveland* (Lawrence: University Press of Kansas, 1988), and Godffrey Blodgett, "The Emergence of Grover Cleveland: A Fresh Appraisal," *New York History* 73 (1992): 132–68, provide good introductions to Grover Cleveland and his presidential administrations. Allan Nevins, *Grover Cleveland: A Study in Courage* (New York: Dodd, Mead, 1932) is the classic longer biography of the man. Introductions to politics in the late nineteenth century are John A. Garraty, *The New American Commonwealth, 1877–1890* (New York: Harper and Row, 1968); Robert Marcus, *Grand Old Party: Political Structure in the Gilded Age, 1880–1896* (New York: Oxford University Press, 1971); Robert Kelley, *The Cultural Pattern in American Politics: The First Century* (New York: Knopf, 1979); and Joel Silbey, *American Political Nation, 1838–1893* (Stanford, Calif.: Stanford University Press, 1991). Readers seeking a greater emphasis on policy developments can consult Lawrence M. Friedman, *A History of American Law* (New York: Simon and Schuster, 1973), which concentrates on the years before 1900; Morton Keller, *Affairs of State: Public Life in Late Nineteenth Century America* (Cambridge, Mass.: Harvard University Press, 1977), which provides a richly textured overview of policy at both the national and state levels; Richard McCormick, *The Party Period and Public Policy: American Politics from the Age of Jackson to the Progressive Era* (New

York: Oxford University Press, 1986), a collection of suggestive essays; Sidney Fine, *Laissez Faire and the General Welfare State* (Ann Arbor: University of Michigan Press, 1956), a classic and still useful despite its age; and Leonard D. White, *The Republican Era, 1869–1901: A Study in Administrative History* (New York: Macmillan, 1958), which pioneered its field. Two valuable works on state-level policy and administration are William R. Brock, *Investigation and Responsibility: Public Responsibility in the United States, 1865–1900* (New York: Cambridge University Press, 1984), and Clifton K. Yearley, *The Money Machines: The Breakdown and Reform of Governmental and Party Finance in the North, 1860–1920* (Albany: State University of New York Press, 1970). James Bryce, *The American Commonwealth* (New York: Macmillan, 1890), is a classic with continuing utility once one understands the author's biases.

On Congress in the last half of the nineteenth century one can begin with Allan G. Bogue, *The Congressman's Civil War* (New York: Cambridge University Press, 1989), and H. Douglas Price, "The Congressional Career: Then and Now," in *Congressional Behavior,* ed. Nelson W. Polsby (New York: Random House, 1971). Excellent specialized studies are David W. Brady, *Critical Elections and Congressional Policymaking* (Stanford, Calif.: Stanford University Press, 1988); and Margaret Susan Thompson, *The "Spider Web": Congress and Lobbying in the Age of Grant* (Ithaca, N.Y.: Cornell University Press, 1985). David J. Rothman, *Politics and Power: The U.S. Senate, 1869–1901* (Cambridge, Mass.: Harvard University Press, 1966), is useful but should be supplemented by the voting analysis in William G. Shade and others, "Partisanship in the United States Senate: 1869–1901," *Journal of Interdisciplinary History* 4 (1973): 185–205. The state legislatures have not received the scholarly treatment that their importance in American governance warrants. The reader can begin with William G. Shade, "State Legislatures in the Nineteenth Century," in Joel H. Silbey, ed., *Encyclopedia of the American Legislative System* (New York: Scribner, 1994). Two detailed studies of the late-nineteenth-century lawmakers are Philip R. VanderMeer, *The Hoosier Politician: Officeholding and Political Culture in Indiana, 1896–1920* (Urbana: University of Illinois Press, 1984), and Ballard C. Campbell, *Representative Democracy: Public Policy and Midwestern Legislatures in the Late Nineteenth Century* (Cambridge, Mass.: Harvard University Press, 1980).

Case studies of politics in individual states and cities are essential to drawing a comprehensive profile of governance in the Cleveland era. Important titles include Dwight B. Billings Jr., *Planters and the Making of a "New South": Class, Politics, and Development in North Carolina, 1865–1900* (Chapel Hill: University of North Carolina Press, 1979); J. Morgan Kousser, *The Shaping of Southern Politics: Suffrage Restriction and the Establishment of the One Party South, 1880–1910* (New Haven, Conn.: Yale University Press, 1974); Stanley B. Parsons, *The Populist Context: Rural Versus Urban Power on a Great Plains Frontier* (Westport, Conn.: Greenwood Press, 1973); and James Wright, *The Progressive Yankees: Republican Reformers in New Hampshire, 1906–1916* (Hanover, N.H.: University Press of New England, 1987), which has a splendid chapter on governance in the late 1800s. On local governance, see Paula Baker, *Moral Frameworks of Public Life: Gender, Politics, and the State in Rural New York, 1870–1930* (New York: Oxford University Press, 1991); Carl V. Harris, *Political Power in Birmingham, 1871–1921* (Knoxville: University of Tennessee Press, 1977); Terrence J. McDonald, *The Parameters of Urban Fiscal Policy: Socioeconomic Change and Political Culture in San Francisco, 1860–1906* (Berkeley: University of California Press, 1986); and Jon C. Teaford, *The Unheralded Triumph: City Government in America, 1870–1900* (Baltimore: Johns Hopkins University Press, 1984).

2. The Course and Causes of Growth

Useful guides to the literature on the growth of government are Patrick D. Larkey, Chandler Stolp, and Mark Winer, "Theorizing about the Growth of Government: A Research Assessment," *Journal of Public Policy* 1 (1981): 157–220. A shorter version of their review appears in Trudi C. Miller, ed., *Public Sector Performance: A Conceptual Turning Point* (Baltimore: Johns Hopkins University Press, 1984). Also, Advisory Commission on Intergovernmental Relations, *The Condition of Contemporary Federalism: Conflicting Theories and Collapsing Constraints* (Washington, D.C.: ACIR, 1981); Robertson and Judd (1989), cited above, ch. 3; Theda Skocpol, *Protecting Soldiers and Mothers: The Political Origins of Social Policy in the United States* (Cambridge, Mass.: Harvard University Press, 1992), ch. 1; David R. Cameron, "The Expansion of the Public Economy: A Comparative Analysis," *American Political Science Review* 72 (1978): 1243–61; and Richard Rose, "How Exceptional Is the American Political Economy?" *Political Science Quarterly* 104 (1989): 91–115.

General treatments of public-sector expansion include Solomon Farbricant, *The Trend of Government Activity in the United States since 1900* (New York: National Bureau of Economic Research, 1952); Terry Anderson and Peter J. Hill, *The Birth of a Transfer Society* (Stanford, Calif.: Hoover Press, 1980); Charles L. Taylor, ed., *Why Governments Grow: Measuring Public Sector Size* (Beverly Hills, Calif.: Sage Publications, 1983); and Robertson and Judd (1989), cited previously. Robert Higgs, *Crisis and Leviathan: Critical Episodes in the Growth of American Government* (New York: Oxford University Press, 1987), used a shock-dislocation hypothesis to trace the expansion of the Federal government in the twentieth century. Yair Aharoni, *The No-Risk Society* (Chatham, N.J.: Chatham House, 1981), is a perceptive statement about the character of claimant-era policy.

A pioneering comparative analysis of modernization and political development is C. E. Black, *The Dynamics of Modernization: A Study in Comparative History* (New York: Harper and Row, 1966). Richard J. Jensen, *Illinois: A History* (New York: W. W. Norton, 1978), applies modernization theory to the history of a single American state. On economic development and its correlates, see Nathan Rosenberg and L. E. Birdzell Jr., *How the West Grew Rich: The Economic Transformation of the Industrial World* (New York: Basic Books, 1986); Karl Polanyi, *The Great Transformation* (Boston: Beacon Press, 1957); W. W. Roslow, *Politics and the Stages of Growth* (New York: Cambridge University Press, 1971); Louis Galambos, "Technology, Political Economy, and Professionalization: Central Themes of the Organizational Synthesis," *Business History Review* 57 (1983): 471–93; and Walter Nugent, *Structures of American Social History* (Bloomington: Indiana University Press, 1981), which places demographic patterns within a socioeconomic framework. As one might imagine, economic determinants of policy development have been studied from numerous angles; for example, see Harold L. Wilensky, *The Welfare State and Equality: Structural and Ideological Roots of Public Expenditures* (Berkeley: University of California Press, 1975); Thomas R. Dye, *Politics, Economics, and the Public: Policy Outcomes in the American States* (Chicago: Rand McNally, 1966), whose research design generated a subcommunity of research based on aggregate analysis of state-level indicators; and William D. Berry and David Lowery, *Understanding U.S. Government Growth: An Empirical Analysis of the Postwar Era* (New York: Praeger, 1987), who analyzed time series. A comparative study emphasizing cultural determinants of fiscal policy is Carolyn Webber and Aaron Wildavsky, *A History of Taxation and Expenditure in the Western World* (New York: Touchstone Books, 1986).

Studies of voters, political parties, and elections that encompass several periods are cited under political history in the general section of the bibliography. The early twentieth century was a transition era in electoral politics; see Allan J. Lichtman, *Prejudice and the Old Politics: The Presidential Election of 1928* (Chapel Hill: University of North Carolina Press, 1979); Paul Kleppner, *Continuity and Change in American Electoral Politics, 1893–1928* (Westport, Conn.: Greenwood Press, 1987); John F. Reynolds, *Testing Democracy: Electoral Behavior and Progressive Reform in New Jersey* (Chapel Hill: University of North Carolina Press, 1988); and

Mark L. Kornbluh, *From Participation to Administration: A Social and Political History of the Emergence of Modern American Politics, 1880–1918* (Baltimore: Johns Hopkins University Press, 2000). Time series analysis has been used to test partisan influence on fiscal activity: Paul Burstein, "Party Balance, Replacement of Legislators, and Federal Government Expenditures, 1941–1976," *Western Political Quarterly* 32 (1979): 203–98; Robert X. Browning, "Presidents, Congress and Policy Outcomes: U.S. Social Welfare Expenditures, 1949–1977," *American Journal of Political Science* 29 (1985): 97–216. Also see Benjamin Ginsberg, "Elections and Public Policy," *American Political Science Review* 70 (1976): 41–49.

Linda L. M. Bennett and Stephen E. Bennett, *Living with Leviathan: Americans Coming to Terms with Big Government* (Lawrence: University Press of Kansas, 1990), reviewed the literature and data concerning popular attitudes regarding the growth of government. On the life cycle of reform eras, see John J. Broesamle, *Reform and Reaction in 20th Century American Politics* (Westport, Conn.: Greenwood Press, 1990). Benjamin Ginsberg, *The Captive Public: How Mass Opinion Promotes State Power* (New York: Basic Books, 1986), argued that public officials used opinion polls to leverage their own policy objectives. In a kindred vein, James A. Morone, *The Democratic Wish: Popular Participation and the Limits of American Government* (New York: Basic Books, 1990), examined historical episodes to illustrate the contention that democratic control of policy is a mirage. Gary J. Miller and Terry M. Moe surveyed much of the literature on bureaucratic influences on growth in "Bureaucrats, Legislators, and the Size of Government," *American Political Science Review* 77 (1983): 297–332. Two opinions about the power of interest groups, the first by a conservative, the second from a radical perspective, are Milton and Rose Friedman, *Free to Choose: A Personal Statement* (New York: Avon, 1979), and G. William Domhoff, *The Powers That Be: Processes of Ruling Class Domination in America* (New York: Vintage Books, 1978).

Because the examination of governmental change entails the study of policy making and general politics, it is appropriate to call attention to important titles on these issues: R. M. MacIver, *The Web of Government* (New York: Macmillan, 1947), especially chs. 9 and 10 on changes in governmental functions; E. E. Schattschneider, *The Semi-Sovereign People* (Hinsdale, Ill.: Dryden Press, 1960), a kind of pluralist vision of American politics that contains some interesting historical observations; David Easton, *A Systems Analysis of Political Life* (New York: Wiley, 1975), whose conceptualization of political activity influenced my composition of the figure in ch. 2; and Murray Edelman, *Politics as Symbolic Action* (Chicago: Markham, 1971). John W. Kingdon, *Agendas, Alternatives, and Public Policies* (New York: HarperCollins, 1984), and Deborah A. Stone, *Policy Paradox and Political Reason* (New York: HarperCollins, 1988), present sensible and readable discussions of how the policy process seems to work.

3. The Transition Era

Because the transitional polity began in the Cleveland era, many references cited for chapter 1 are pertinent for this chapter. Two important interpretations of social and political change in the transition era are Samuel Hays, *The Response to Industrialism, 1885–1914* (Chicago: University of Chicago Press, 1957), and Robert H. Wiebe, *The Search for Order, 1877–1920* (New York: Hill and Wang, 1967). Arthur L. Link and Richard L. McCormick, *Progressivism* (Arlington Heights, Ill.: Harland, Davidson, 1983), succinctly survey early-twentieth-century politics. Alan Dawley, *Struggles for Justice: Social Responsibility and the Liberal State* (Cambridge, Mass.: Harvard University Press, 1991), provides a more critical perspective on the era. Arguments in the great debate over the role of government are examined in Robert M. McCloskey, *American Conservatism in the Age of Enterprise* (Cambridge, Mass.: Harvard University Press, 1951); Richard Hofstadter, *Social Darwinism in American Thought* (Boston: Beacon Press, 1955); Sidney Fine, *Laissez Faire and the General-Welfare State;* and James Gilbert, *Designing the Industrial State: The Intellectual Pursuit of Collectivism in America, 1880–1940* (Chicago: Quadrangle Books, 1972). Ray Ginger, ed., *American Social Thought* (New York: Hill and Wang, 1961), and H. Landon Warner, ed., *Reforming American Life in the Progressive Era* (New York: Pitman, 1971), contain selections written by leading participants in the debate over the functions of government.

The civic technocrats and their contributions to public administration are discussed in Martin J. Schiesl, *The Politics of Efficiency: Municipal Administration and Reform in America, 1800–1920* (Berkeley: University of California Press, 1977); Jane S. Dahlberg, *The New York Bureau of Municipal Research: Pioneer in Government Administration* (New York: New York University Press, 1966); Michael H. Frisch, "Urban Theorists, Urban Reform, and American Political Culture in the Progressive Era," *Political Science Quarterly* 97 (1982): 295–315; Arthur E. Buck, *The Reorganization of State Governments in the United States* (New York: Columbia University Press, 1938); Thomas Schick, *The New York State Constitutional Convention of 1915 and the Modern State Governor* (New York: National Municipal League, 1978); W. Brooke Graves, *Uniform State Action: A Possible Substitute for Centralization* (Chapel Hill: University of North Carolina Press, 1934); and William Graebner, "Federalism in the Progressive Era: A Structural Interpretation of Reform," *Journal of American History* 64 (1977): 331–57. Leonard D. White, *Trends in Public Administration* (New York: McGraw-Hill, 1933), is useful in tracing administration developments between the 1890s and 1930. Carroll H. Wooddy, *The Growth of the Federal Government, 1915–1932* (New York: McGraw-Hill, 1934) is a gold mine of information on both administrative activities and policy. Stephen Skowronek, *Building a New American State: The Expansion of National Administrative Capacities, 1877–1920* (New York: Cambridge University Press, 1982), argues that the construction of a coherent administrative foundation was a prerequisite for the rise of modern governance.

Governance at the subnational level is fundamental to understanding the expansion of the public sector in the transition era. Evidence on this point appears in Ballard C. Campbell, "Federalism, State Action, and 'Critical Episodes' in the Growth of American Government," previously cited. Writing about state and city governance has tended to take the form of case studies on particular places or policy topics. I cite only a few of the many useful titles: John D. Buenker, *Urban Liberalism and Progressive Reform* (New York: W. W. Norton, 1973); Don S. Kirschner, *City and Country: Rural Responses to Urbanization in the 1920s* (Westport, Conn.: Greenwood Press, 1970); William A. Link, *The Paradox of Southern Progressivism, 1880–1930* (Chapel Hill: University of North Carolina Press, 1992); Richard L. McCormick, *From Realignment to Reform: Political Change in New York State, 1893–1910* (Ithaca, N.Y.: Cornell University Press, 1981); Gerald D. Nash, *State Government and Economic Development: A History of Administrative Policies in California, 1894–1933* (Berkeley: University of California Press, 1964); Thomas R. Pegram, *Partisans and Progressives: Private Interests and Public Policy in Illinois* (Urbana: University of Illinois Press, 1992); Sheldon Hackney, *Populism to Progressivism in Alabama* (Princeton, N.J.: Princeton University Press, 1969); and David P. Thelen, *The New Citizenship: Origins of Progressivism in Wisconsin, 1885–1900* (Columbia: University of Missouri Press, 1972). Important urban studies include Alan D. Anderson, *The Origin and Resolution of an Urban Crisis: Baltimore, 1890–1930* (Baltimore: Johns Hopkins University Press, 1977); David C. Hammack, *Power and Society: Greater New York at the Turn of the Century* (New York: Russell Sage, 1981); Harold L. Platt, *City Building in the New South: The Growth of Public Services in Houston, Texas, 1830–1915* (Philadelphia: Temple University Press, 1983); and Stanley K. Schultz, *Constructing Urban Culture: American Cities and City Planning,*

1800–1920 (Philadelphia: Temple University Press, 1989), which contains superb chapters on the legal basis of the state-urban relationship and city powers.

Comparative cross-sectional analyses of state and urban policy actions provide useful points of reference for assessing case studies. Among the most useful studies for historical purposes are Jack L. Walker, "The Diffusion of Innovations among the American States," *American Political Science Review* 63 (1969): 880–99; Robert L. Savage, "Patterns of Multilinear Evolution in the American States," *Publius* 3 (1973): 75–108; and J. Rodgers Hollingsworth and Ellen Jane Hollingsworth, *Dimensions in Urban History: Historical and Social Science Perspectives on Middle-Size American Cities* (Madison: University of Wisconsin Press, 1979). Virginia Gray, "Models of Comparative State Politics: A Comparison of Cross-sectional and Time Series Analysis," *American Political Science Review* 20 (1976): 235–56, supplies an important caveat to the spatial studies of policy diffusion.

Detailed studies of economic policy are Morton Keller, *Regulating a New Economy: Public Policy and Economic Change in America, 1900–1933* (Cambridge, Mass.: Harvard University Press, 1900); Robert E. Cushman, *The Independent Regulatory Commissions* (New York: Oxford University Press, 1941); Robert Wiebe, *Businessmen and Reform: A Study of the Progressive Movement* (Cambridge, Mass.: Harvard University Press, 1962); Martin Sklar, *The Corporate Reconstruction of American Capitalism, 1890–1916: The Market, the Law, and Politics* (New York: Cambridge University Press, 1988); John R. Commons et al., *History of Labor in the United States,* vol. 3 (New York: Macmillan, 1935). Old but still useful are Harold U. Faulkner, *The Decline of Laissez Faire, 1897–1917* (New York: Rinehart, 1951), and John M. Gaus and Leon O. Wolcott, *Public Administration and the United States Department of Agriculture* (Chicago: Public Administrative Service, 1940). On road policy, see Hal S. Barron, "And the Crooked Shall Be Made Straight: Public Road Administration and the Decline of Localism in the Rural North, 1870–1930," *Journal of Social History* 26 (1992): 81–103; Ballard Campbell, "The Good Roads Movement in Wisconsin, 1890–1911," *Wisconsin Magazine of History* 49 (1966): 273–93; Howard L. Preston, *Dirt Roads to Dixie: Accessibility and Modernization in the South, 1885–1935* (Knoxville: University of Tennessee Press, 1991) and Bruce E. Seeley, *Building the American Highway System: Engineers as Policy Makers* (Philadelphia: Temple University Press, 1987).

Among the many excellent studies of social policy are Barbara G. Rosenkrantz, *Public Health and the State: Changing Views in Massachusetts, 1842–1936* (Cambridge, Mass.: Harvard University Press, 1972); David B. Tyack, *The One Best System: A History of American Urban Education* (Cambridge, Mass.: Harvard University Press, 1974); David Tyack, Thomas James, and Aaron Benavot, *Law and the Shaping of Public Education, 1785–1954* (Madison: University of Wisconsin Press, 1987); Theda Skocpol, *Protecting Soldiers and Mothers: The Political Origins of Social Policy in the United States* (Cambridge, Mass.: Harvard University Press, 1992); Eileen McDonagh, "The Welfare Rights State and the Civil Rights State: Policy Paradox and State Building in the Progressive Era," *Studies in American Political Development* 7 (1993), 225–275; Jack S. Blocker Jr., *Retreat from Reform: The Prohibition Movement in the United States, 1890–1913* (Westport, Conn.: Greenwood Press, 1976); Norman H. Clark, *Deliver Us from Evil: An Interpretation of American Prohibition* (New York: W. W. Norton, 1976); James C. Mohr, *Abortion in America: The Origins and Evolution of National Policy, 1800–1900* (New York: Oxford University Press, 1978); and Marion T. Bennett, *American Immigration Policies* (Washington, D.C.: Public Affairs Press, 1963). On civil liberties, see William Preston Jr., *Aliens and Dissenters: Federal Suppression of Radicals, 1903–1933* (Cambridge, Mass.: Harvard University Press, 1966), and Eldridge F. Dowell, *A History of Criminal Syndicalism Legislation in the United States* (Baltimore: Johns Hopkins University Press, 1939).

4. The Great Depression and Economic Policy

Three fine overviews of the New Deal are Anthony J. Badger, *The New Deal: The Depression Years, 1933–1940* (New York: Noonday Press, 1989); William E. Leuchtenberg, *Franklin D. Roosevelt and the New Deal, 1932–1940* (New York: Harper and Row, 1963); and Harvard Sitkoff, ed., *Fifty Years Later: The New Deal Evaluated* (New York: Knopf, 1985). Two books by Albert U. Romasco, *The Poverty of Abundance: Hoover, the Nation, the Depression* (New York: Oxford University Press, 1965) and *The Politics of Recovery: Roosevelt's New Deal* (New York: Oxford University Press, 1983), reconstruct policy responses to the Depression. Richard J. Jensen, "The Causes and Cures of Unemployment in the Great Depression," *Journal of Interdisciplinary History* 19 (1989): 553–583, analyzed joblessness in the 1930s and its relationship to relief and recovery policies. David Burner, *The Politics of Provincialism: The Democratic Party in Transition, 1918–1932* (New York: W. W. Norton, 1967); John M. Allswang, *The New Deal and American Politics: A Study in Political Change* (New York: Wiley, 1978); Alan Brinkley, *Voices of Protest: Huey Long, Father Coughlin, and the Great Depression* (New York: Knopf, 1982); and James Patterson, "A Conservative Coalition Forms in Congress, 1933–1939," *Journal of American History* 52 (1966): 757–72, review currents in election and administration politics during the decade.

Ellis W. Hawley, *The New Deal and the Problem of Monopoly: A Study in Economic Ambivalence* (Princeton, N.J.: Princeton University Press, 1966), is an indispensable guide to New Deal political economy. Also valuable are Thomas K. McCraw, *Prophets of Regulation* (Cambridge, Mass.: Harvard University Press, 1984), especially the chapters on James Landis and Alfred Kahn; and Herbert Stein, *The Fiscal Revolution in America* (Chicago: University of Chicago Press, 1969). Christopher L. Tomlins, *The State and the Unions: Labor Relations, Law, and the Organized Labor Movement in America, 1880–1960* (New York: Cambridge University Press, 1985) looks at labor in the 1930s and in the broader context of the twentieth century. Michael A. Bernstein, *The Great Depression: Delayed Recovery and Economic Change in America, 1929–1939* (New York: Cambridge University Press, 1987) examines long-term trends in various sectors of the economy and their relationship to recovery efforts.

Good introductions to the farm problem and agricultural policy are Theodore Saloutos, *The American Farmer and the New Deal* (Ames: Iowa State University Press, 1982); Grant McConnell, *The Decline of Agrarian Democracy* (New York: Atheneum, 1969); and Willard W. Cochrane and Mary E. Ryan, *American Farm Policy, 1948–1973* (Minneapolis: University of Minnesota Press, 1976). The evolution of milk controls can be followed in Jewel Bellush, "Milk Price Control: History of its Adoption, 1933," *New York History* 43 (1962): 79–104, and Geoffrey S. Shepard and Gene A. Futrell, *Marketing Farm Products* (Ames: Iowa State University Press, 1959), ch. 24. The national regulation of trucking is traced nicely in William R. Childs, *Trucking and the Public Interest: The Emergence of Federal Regulation, 1914–1940* (Knoxville: University of Tennessee Press, 1985), which one can supplement with Dudley F. Pegrum, *Transportation: Economics and Public Policy* (Homewood, Ill: Richard D. Irwin, 1968); Donald V. Harper, *Economic Regulation of the Motor Trucking Industry by the States* (Urbana: University of Illinois Press, 1959); and Thomas Gale Moore, "Beneficiaries of Trucking Regulation," *Journal of Law and Economics* 21 (1978): 327–43. Michael E. Parrish, *Securities Regulation and the New Deal* (New Haven, Conn.: Yale University Press, 1970), and American Public Works Association, *History of Public Works in the United States, 1776–1976* (Chicago: APWA, 1976), discuss important areas of policy making.

The place to begin investigation of the states during the Great Depression is James T. Patterson, *The New Deal and the States: Federalism in Transition* (Princeton, N.J.: Princeton University Press, 1969), and John Braeman and others, eds., *The New Deal: The State and Local Levels* (Columbus: Ohio State University Press, 1975). Many case studies of politics and policy making in individual states during the 1930s have appeared since Patterson's pioneering work, but they lack synthesis in a single study. My examination of subnational policy during the decade concentrated on four states: Florida, Illinois, Oregon, and New York. A published book-length account of policy making during the 1930s exists for only one of the four: Robert P. Ingalls, *Herbert H. Lehman and New York's Little New Deal* (New York: New York University Press, 1975), an excellent work. Dissertations by James W. Dunn on Florida (Florida State University, 1971), Philip G. Bean on Illinois (University of Illinois, 1976), and Judith Stein on New York Republicans (Yale University, 1968), and the chapter on Oregon by Robert E. Burton in Braeman, *The New Deal,* were principal secondary sources for these states, in which I also did archival research. The bibliographies in Badger, *New Deal,* and Allswang, *The New Deal and American Politics,* list many of the published studies for states. Recommended titles on urban localities include Jo Ann Argersinger, *Toward a New Deal in Baltimore* (Chapel Hill: University of North Carolina Press, 1988); Roger Biles, *Mayor Edward J. Kelly of Chicago: Big City Boss in Depression and War* (De Kalb: Northern Illinois University Press, 1984); Raymond L. Koch, "Politics and Relief in Minneapolis during the 1930s," *Minnesota History* 41 (1968): 153–70; and Charles H. Trout, *Boston, the Great Depression, and the New Deal* (New York: Oxford University Press, 1977).

James Patterson blazed the trail in the study of federalism during the 1930s, but a comprehensive synthesis is needed. Useful works on the topic are V. O. Key Jr., *The Administration of Federal Grants to States* (Chicago: Social Science Research Council, 1937); Leonard D. White, *The States and the Nation* (Baton Rouge: Louisiana State University Press, 1953), a brilliant essay; and the works of W. Brooke Graves cited above. A valuable compilation of information about state finances appears in the New York State Constitutional Convention Committee, *Problems Relating to Taxation and Finance* (Albany: New York State, 1938); and B. U. Ratchford, *American State Debts* (Durham, N.C.: Duke University Press, 1941).

5. The Managed Economy since the New Deal

Many of the items concerning political economy, public finance, and federalism listed among the general works in the bibliography are pertinent for this chapter. On the United States during World War II, see James M. Burns, *Roosevelt: The Soldier of Freedom* (San Diego: Harcourt Brace Jovanovich, 1970), and Harold G. Vatter, *The U.S. Economy in World War II* (New York: Columbia University Press, 1985). The political economy of defense policy is ably analyzed in Jacques S. Gansler, *The Defense Industry* (Cambridge, Mass.: MIT Press, 1980); James Fallows, *National Defense* (New York: Vintage Books, 1981); Sidney Lens, *The Military-Industrial Complex* (Philadelphia: United Church Press, 1970); and Walter A. McDougall, *The Heavens and the Earth: A Political History of the Space Age* (New York: Basic Books, 1985). Roger W. Lotchin, *Fortress California, 1910–1961: From Warfare to Welfare* (New York: Oxford University Press, 1992) is a fine historical study.

James L. Sundquist, *Politics and Policy: The Eisenhower, Kennedy, and Johnson Years* (Washington, D.C.: Brookings Institution, 1968), contains a good review of the tax cut of 1964 and related economic policy. Useful too is Herbert Stein, *The Fiscal Revolution in America* (Chicago: University of Chicago Press, 1969); George P. Shultz and Kenneth W. Dam, *Economic Policy: Beyond the Headlines* (New York: W. W. Norton, 1977); and the Advisory Commission on Intergovernmental Relations, *Reducing Unemployment: Intergovernmental Dimensions of a National Problem* (Washington, D.C.: ACIR, 1982). Guides to political economy after the war include John L. Campbell, J. Rodgers Hollingsworth, and Leon N. Lindberg, eds., *Governance of the American Economy* (New York: Cambridge University Press, 1991); Louis Galambos and Joseph Pratt, *The Rise of the Corporate Commonwealth: U.S. Business and Public Policy in the Twentieth Century* (New York: Basic Books, 1987); and Willard W. Cochrane and Mary E. Ryan, *American Farm Policy, 1948–1973* (Minneapolis: University of Minnesota Press, 1976). Theodore S. Lowi, *The End of Liberalism: The Second Republic of the United States* (New York: W. W. Norton, 1979) is a very influential critique of the modern political economy.

Until the "new" regulations of the 1960s and 1970s are synthesized in a general history, readers must turn to overviews and specialized studies. See James Q. Wilson, ed., *The Politics of Regulation* (New York: Basic Books, 1980); Paul W. MacAvoy, *The Regulated Industries and the Economy* (New York: W. W. Norton, 1979); and Lawrence P. Feldman, *Consumer Protection* (St. Paul: West Publishers, 1976). Murray L. Weidenbaum, *Business, Government, and the Public* (Englewood Cliffs, N.J.: Prentice-Hall, 1981), tracked the impact of the new regulations on private enterprise. Samuel P. Hays, *Beauty, Health, and Permanence: Environmental Politics in the United States, 1955–1985* (New York: Cambridge University Press, 1987), is a history of contemporary ideology as well as a masterful essay on the environment. A more chronological approach to Federal environmental politics is Advisory Commission on Intergovernmental Relations, *Protecting the Environment: Politics, Pollution, and Federal Policy* (Washington, D.C.: ACIR, 1981). On tobacco, see Kenneth M. Friedman, *Public Policy and the Smoking-Health Controversy: A Comparative Study* (Lexington, Mass.: Lexington Books, 1975).

Kenneth A. Jackson, *Crabgrass Frontier: The Suburbanization of the United States* (New York: Oxford University Press, 1985), is a wonderful study and comes about as close to an overview of the political economy of housing, transportation, and space in the postwar era as any existing book. Landon Y. Jones, *Great Expectations: America and the Baby Boom Generation* (New York: Ballantine Books, 1980), is a delightful portrayal of an immensely significant factor in post–World War II America. The evolution of urban policy is reviewed by John H. Mollenkopf, *The Contested City* (Princeton, N.J.: Princeton University Press, 1983); Mark I. Gelfand, *A Nation of Cities: The Federal Government and Urban America, 1933–1965* (New York: Oxford University Press, 1975); and Jon C. Teaford, *City and Suburb: The Political Fragmentation of Metropolitan America, 1850–1970* (Baltimore: Johns Hopkins University Press, 1979). Norman Walzer and Glenn W. Fisher, *Cities, Suburbs, and Property Taxes* (Cambridge, Mass.: Oelgeschlager, Gunn, and Hain, 1981) examines the imbalances in subnational finances; Peter D. McClelland and Alan L. Magdovitz, *Crisis in the Making: The Political Economy of New York State Since 1945* (New York: Cambridge University Press, 1981) is a rich case study of the political economy in the Empire State.

On housing and urban renewal policy, readers can consult Gwendolyn Wright, *Building the Dream: A Social History of Housing in America* (New York: Pantheon Books, 1981); Michael E. Stone, "Housing and the American Economy: A Marxist Analysis," in *Urban and Regional Planning in an Age of Austerity,* ed. Pierre Clavel (New York: Pergamon Press, 1980); Jewel Bellush and Murray Hausknecht, eds., *Urban Renewal: People, Politics, and Planning* (Garden City, N.Y.: Anchor Books, 1967); Donald F. Kettl, *Managing Community Development in the New Federalism* (New York: Praeger, 1980); and Kenneth Fox, *Metropolitan America: Urban Life and Urban Policy in the United States, 1940–1980* (New Brunswick, N.J.: Rutgers University Press, 1986).

My synopsis of the linkage of automobile transportation, highways, housing, and suburban development in the Boston area drew on several excellent studies, including Sam Bass Warner, *The Way We Really Live: Social Change in Metropolitan Boston since 1920* (Boston: Boston Public Library, 1977); K. H. Schaeffer and Eliot Sclar, *Access for All: Transportation and Urban Growth* (New York: Columbia University Press, 1980); Alan Lupo, Frank Colcord, and Edmund P. Fowler, *Rites of Way: The Politics of Transportation in Boston and the U.S.*

City (Boston: Little, Brown, 1971); Michael P. Conzen and George K. Lewis, *Boston: A Geographical Portrait* (Cambridge, Mass.: Ballinger, 1976); and Matthew Edel, Elliott D. Sclar, and Daniel Luria, *Shaky Palaces: Homeownership and Social Mobility in Boston's Suburbanization* (New York: Columbia University Press, 1984).

6. The New Income Security

Theda Skocpol, *Protecting Soldiers and Mothers,* cited previously, is a superb study of income-assistance policy in the transition era. Other analyses of the subject before 1935 include William Graebner, *A History of Retirement: The Meaning and Function of an American Institution, 1885–1978* (New Haven, Conn.: Yale University Press, 1980) and Roy Lubove, *The Struggle for Social Security, 1900–1935* (Cambridge, Mass.: Harvard University Press, 1968). Robert H. Bremner, "The New Deal and Social Welfare," in *Fifty Years Later: The New Deal Evaluated,* ed. H. Sitkoff (New York: Knopf, 1985), surveys Federal policy in the 1930s; Donald S. Howard, *The WPA and Federal Relief Policy* (New York, Russell Sage Foundation,1943), describes America's most significant jobs program.

Some of the best writing about policy history has analyzed the Social Security old-age pension program. Two superb studies are Martha Derthick, *Policymaking for Social Security* (Washington, D.C.: Brookings Institution, 1979), and Carolyn Weaver, *The Crisis in Social Security: Economic and Political Origins* (Durham, N.C.: Duke University Press, 1982). Also useful but limited to the 1983 reforms is Paul Light, *Artful Work: The Politics of Social Security Reform* (New York: Random House, 1985). Also see John P. Bradly, "Party Platforms and Party Performance concerning Social Security," *Polity* 1 (1969): 337–58. James T. Patterson, *America's Struggle against Poverty, 1900–1994* (Cambridge, Mass.: Harvard University Press, 2000), is an excellent synthesis of the evolution of attitudes and policy concerning the poor in the twentieth century. An important interpretation on welfare policy is Frances F. Piven and Richard A. Cloward, *Regulating the Poor: The Functions of Public Welfare* (New York: Vintage Books, 1971). Advisory Commission on Intergovernmental Relations, *Public Assistance: The Growth of a Federal Function* (Washington, D.C.: ACIR, 1980) is succinct and full of data. Although Paul Starr, *The Social Transformation of American Medicine* (New York: Basic Books, 1982) primarily concerns the medical profession, the book also develops the contextual background for Medicaid and Medicare.

The growth of income-assistance policy in postwar America has stimulated an outpouring of writing. Three fine essays review the subject: William P. O'Hare, "Poverty in America: Trends and New Patterns," *Population Bulletin* 40, no. 3 (Washington, D.C.: Population Reference Bureau, 1985); Rudolph G. Penner, "Federal Government Growth: Leviathan or Protector of the Elderly?" *National Tax Journal* 44 (1991): 437–50; and Christopher Howard, "The Hidden Side of the American Welfare State," *Political Science Quarterly* 198 (1993): 403–36. On the contemporary debate over income support policy, see Charles Murray, *Losing Ground: American Social Policy, 1950–1980* (New York: Basic Books, 1984); William T. Wilson, *The Truly Disadvantaged: The Inner City, the Underclass, and Public Policy* (Chicago: University of Chicago Press, 1987, 2010); and Peter J. Peterson, *On Borrowed Time: How the Growth of Entitlement Spending Threatens America's Future* (San Francisco: ICP Press, 1988). On the role of gender in Social Security, see Gail B. King, "Women and Social Security," *Social Science History* 6 (1982): 227–32, and Howard M. Iwams, "Working Wives and Social Security," *Population Today* 21 (November 1993): 6–7, 9.

7. The New Equality

The background of the civil rights revolution can be followed in Nicholas Lemann, *Promised Land: The Great Black Migration and How It Changed America* (New York: Knopf, 1991); John

Modell, M. Goulden, and S. Magnusson, "World War II in the Lives of Black Americans: Some Findings and an Interpretation," *Journal of American History* 76 (1989): 838–48; Jules Tygiel, *Baseball's Great Experiment: Jackie Robinson and His Legacy* (New York: Oxford University Press, 1983); Todd Gitlin, *The Sixties: Years of Hope, Days of Rage* (Toronto: Bantam Books, 1987), especially for the impact of black music on the white radical movements of the 1960s; and William H. Harris, *The Harder We Run: Black Workers since the Civil War* (New York: Oxford University Press, 1982).

The civil rights movement and the adoption of nondiscrimination legislation in the 1960s is reviewed by Robert Weisbrot, *Freedom Bound: A History of the Civil Rights Movement* (New York: W. W. Norton, 1990); David J. Garrow, *Bearing the Cross: Martin Luther King, Jr., and the Southern Christian Leadership Conference* (New York: William Morrow, 1986); Hugh Davis Graham, *The Civil Rights Era: Origins and Development of the National Policy, 1960–1972* (New York: Oxford University Press, 1990); and Charles and Barbara Whalen, *The Longest Debate: A Legislative History of the 1964 Civil Rights Act* (New York: New American Library, 1985). Racial equality and education are considered by Diane Ravitch, *The Troubled Crusade: American Education, 1945–1908* (New York: Basic Books, 1983). The implementation of nondiscrimination policy is analyzed in Charles S. Bullock III and Charles M. Lamb, *Implementation of Civil Rights Policy* (Monterey, Calif.: Brooks/Cole, 1984); Norman C. Amaker, *Civil Rights and the Reagan Administration* (Washington, D.C.: Urban Institute, 1988); Abigail M. Thernstrom, *Whose Votes Count? Affirmative Action and Minority Voting Rights* (Cambridge, Mass.: Harvard University Press, 1987); Gary Bryner, "Congress, Courts, and Agencies: Equal Employment and the Limits of Policy Implementation," *Political Science Quarterly* 96 (1981): 411–30; and David Rosenbloom, "The Federal Affirmative-Action Policy," in *The Practice of Policy Evaluation,* ed. David Nachmias (New York: St. Martin's Press, 1980).

Gender issues are analyzed in Joan Hoff, *Law, Gender, and Injustice: A Legal History of U.S. Women* (New York: New York University Press, 1991); Deborah L. Rhode, *Justice and Gender: Sex Discrimination and the Law* (Cambridge, Mass.: Harvard University Press, 1989); Sara M. Evans and Barbara N. Nelson, *Wage Justice: Comparable Worth and the Paradox of Technocratic Reform* (Chicago: University of Chicago Press, 1990). Important studies of women and the economy during the Second World War include D'Ann Campbell, *Women at War with America: Private Lives in a Patriotic Era* (Cambridge, Mass.: Harvard University Press, 1984), and Karen Anderson, *Wartime Women: Sex Roles, Family Relations and the Status of Women during World War II* (Westport, Conn.: Greenwood Press, 1981). Generally, see Claudia Goldin, *Understanding the Gender Gap: An Economic History of American Women* (New York: Oxford University Press, 1990).

8. Paying for Modern Government

Studenski and Krooss, *Financial History,* cited earlier, is the closest approximation to a comprehensive history of American public finance, but it is outdated and also skimps on state and local government coverage. Ch. 4, "Financing Federal Growth," in Advisory Commission on Intergovernmental Relations, *The Condition of Contemporary Federalism* (Washington, D.C., 1981), is useful as an overview of fiscal trends. John F. Witte, *The Politics and Development of the Federal Income Tax* (Madison: University of Wisconsin Press, 1985), is a model of integrating policy history with policy analysis. A useful compilation of policy changes is Joseph A. Pechman, *Federal Tax Policy,* rev. ed. (New York: W. W. Norton, 1971), and subsequent editions; also Jon Bakija and Eugene Steuerle, "Individual Income Taxation since 1948," *National Tax Journal* 44 (1991): 451–75. Studies of tax policy making include Mark H. Leff, *The Limits of Symbolic Reform: The New Deal and Taxation, 1933–1939* (New York: Cambridge University Press, 1984); John Manley, *The Politics of Finance: The House Committee on Ways and Means* (Boston: Little, Brown, 1970); Susan B. Hansen, *The Politics of Taxation: Revenue without Representation* (New York: Praeger, 1983); and R. Douglas Arnold, *The Logic of Congressional Action* (New Haven, Conn.: Yale University Press, 1990), esp. ch. 8, "Tax Policy." The dynamics of financing Social Security is analyzed by Carolyn Weaver, *The Crisis in Social Security*. Herman B. Leonard, *Checks Unbalanced: The Quiet Side of Public Spending* (New York: Basic Books, 1986), and Robert Heilbroner and Peter Bernstein, *The Debt and the Deficit: False Alarms, Real Possibilities* (New York: W. W. Norton, 1989), dispel some misconceptions about the volatile topic of their books.

Federalism had a major impact on the history of American public finance. The works by Graves (1964), Elazar (1972), Scheiber (1978), Kincaid (1993), and Campbell (1992, 1994), cited earlier review historical dimensions of intergovernmental fiscal patterns. Excellent coverage of developments in the second half of the twentieth century are David B. Walker, *Toward a Functioning Federalism* (Cambridge, Mass.: Winthrop, 1981); Deil S. Wright, *Understanding Intergovernmental Relations* (North Scituate, Mass.: Duxbury Press, 1982); and Thomas J. Anton, *American Federalism and Public Policy: How the System Works* (New York: Random House, 1989). The Advisory Commission on Intergovernmental Relations has sponsored numerous studies of the federal grant system; one of their best is *Categorical Grants: Their Role and Design* (Washington, D.C, 1978). On this subject, see also Donald H. Haider, *When Governments Come to Washington: Governors, Mayors, and Intergovernmental Lobbying* (New York: Free Press, 1974); George E. Hale and Marian L. Palley, *The Politics of Federal Grants* (Washington, D.C., Congressional Quarterly Press, 1981); and Timothy J. Conlan, "The Politics of Federal Block Grants," *Political Science Quarterly* 99 (1984): 247–70. The growth of Federal rules that had been imposed on other governments is examined in ACIR, *Regulatory Federalism: Policy, Process, Impact, and Reform* (Washington, D.C., 1984), and Donald F. Kettl, *The Regulation of American Federalism* (Baltimore: Johns Hopkins University Press, 1988). A fine assessment of recent interpretations of federalism is Thomas J. Anton, "Intergovernmental Change in the United States: An Assessment of the Literature," in *Public Sector Performance*, ed. Trudi Miller (Baltimore: Johns Hopkins University Press, 1984), 15–64.

On state finances, see James A. Maxwell, *Financing State and Local Governments*, 3rd ed. (Washington, D.C.: Brookings Institution, 1977; 1946 for the 1st ed.); Ira Sharkansky, *The Politics of Taxing and Spending* (Indianapolis: Bobbs-Merrill, 1969); and Ross Stephens, "State Centralization and the Erosion of Local Autonomy," *Journal of Politics* 36 (1974): 44–76. The impact of Federal grants and their conditional rules on state government and finances is discussed in Theodore J. Lowi and Alan Stone, eds., *Nationalizing Government: Public Policies in America* (Beverly Hills, Calif.: Sage Publications, 1978); and Jerome Hanus, *The Nationalization of State Government* (Lexington, Mass.: D. C. Heath, 1981). I relied heavily on various editions of the ACIR's *Significant Features of Fiscal Federalism* to follow contemporary developments in state and local finances.

9. The New Faces of Power

A place to begin a review of American policy makers is with essays that synthesize recent political trends. One of the best collections is Anthony King, ed., *The New American Political System* (Washington, D.C.: American Enterprise Institute, 1978), which contains chapters on the president (Greenstein), Congress (Patterson), the executive establishment (Heclo), the Supreme Court (Shapiro), and the evolution of ideology (Beer). Insightful essays on state government, especially by Samuel C. Patterson on legislatures and Sarah M. Morehouse on governors, appear in Herbert Jacob and Kenneth N. Vines, eds., *Politics in the American States: A Comparative Analysis* (Boston: Little, Brown, 1976). James Q. Wilson, ed., *The Poli-*

tics of Regulation (New York: Basic Books, 1980), is an anthology on modern administration. Selections in Louis Galambos, ed., *The New American State: Bureaucracies and Policies since World War II* (Baltimore: Johns Hopkins University Press, 1987) survey the evolution of administrative behavior.

In addition to the articles by Price (1971) and Polsby (1968) on congressional careers cited in the notes to this chapter, see H. Douglas Price, "Congress and the Evolution of Legislative 'Professionalism,'" in *Congress in Change: Evolution and Reform,* ed. Norman J. Ornstein (New York: Praeger, 1975); Joseph Cooper and David W. Brady, "Institutional Context and Leadership Style: The House from Cannon to Rayburn," *American Political Science Review* 75 (1981): 411–25; and Ronald M. Peters Jr., *The American Speakership: The Office in Historical Perspective* (Baltimore: Johns Hopkins University Press, 1990). The important interpretations of congressional motivation and performance are David R. Mayhew, *Congress: The Electoral Connection* (New Haven, Conn.: Yale University Press, 1974), and Morris P. Fiorina, *Congress: Keystone of the Washington Establishment* (New Haven, Conn.: Yale University Press, 1977). Patterns of behavior in modern Congresses are ably analyzed by James L. Sundquist, *The Decline and Resurgence of Congress* (Washington, D.C.: Brookings Institution, 1981); Allen Schick, "The Distributive Congress," in *Making Economic Policy in Congress,* ed. Allen Schick (Washington, D.C.: American Enterprise Institute, 1983); and D. Douglas Arnold, *The Logic of Congressional Action* (New Haven, Conn.: Yale University Press, 1990). Arnold has provided a closely reasoned analysis of how members of Congress used the prerogatives of power, especially for their own self-interest.

Roll-call votes are valuable data for analyzing legislative policy making, especially in historical settings when modern research techniques cannot be used. A modern classic in this genre is Aage R. Clausen, *How Congressmen Decide: A Policy Focus* (New York: St. Martin's Press, 1973), which argues that subject matter bears fundamentally on how lawmakers vote. Important examinations of historical and longitudinal voting are David W. Brady, *Congressional Voting in a Partisan Era: A Study of the McKinley Houses and a Comparison to the Modern House of Representatives* (Lawrence: University Press of Kansas, 1973); Richard Franklin Bensel, *Sectionalism and American Political Development, 1880–1980* (Madison: University of Wisconsin Press, 1984); Eileen Lorenzi McDonagh, "Representative Democracy and State Building in the Progressive Era," *American Political Science Review* 86 (1992): 938–50; Barbara Sinclair, *Congressional Realignment, 1925–1978* (Austin: University of Texas Press, 1982); and Jerome M. Clubb and Santa A. Traugott, "Partisan Cleavage and Cohesion in the House of Representatives, 1861–1974," *Journal of Interdisciplinary History* 7 (1977): 375–401. A convenient review of the scholarship on legislative voting and other aspects of legislative policy making is Gerhard Loewenberg and others, eds., *Handbook of Legislative Research* (Cambridge, Mass.: Harvard University Press, 1985). Informative essays on a wide variety of legislative topics, including legislative history, are contained in Joel H. Silbey, ed., *Encyclopedia of the American Legislative System,* 3 vols. (New York: Scribner, 1994).

The performance of state lawmakers is the subject of L. Harmon Zeigler and Michael A. Baer, *Lobbying: Interaction and Influence in American State Legislatures* (Belmont, Calif.: Wadsworth, 1969); Malcolm E. Jewell, *The State Legislature: Politics and Practice* (New York: Random House, 1962); and Alan Rosenthal, *Legislative Life: Process and Performance in the States* (New York: Harper and Row, 1981). Susan Welch and John G. Peters, eds., *Legislative Reform and Public Policy* (New York: Praeger, 1977), also includes essays on Congress.

Arthur M. Schlesinger Jr., *The Imperial Presidency* (Boston: Houghton Mifflin, 1973), offers the closest approximation of a modern history of the presidency. Schlesinger argues that foreign policy has been the primary lever for growth in presidential power. A readable up-to-date survey of foreign affairs is Thomas C. Patterson and others, *American Foreign Policy: A History since 1900* (Lexington, Mass.: D. C. Heath, 1991 and later editions). Other studies of change in the presidency are Peri E. Arnold, *Making the Managerial Presidency: Comprehensive Reorganization Planning, 1905–1980* (Princeton, N.J.: Princeton University Press, 1986); Barry D. Karl, *Executive Reorganization and Reform in the New Deal: The Genesis of Administrative Management, 1900–1939* (Cambridge, Mass.: Harvard University Press, 1979); and William E. Leuchtenburg, *In the Shadow of FDR: From Harry Truman to Ronald Reagan* (Ithaca, N.Y.: Cornell University Press, 1983). Overviews of the modern presidency are Thomas E. Cronin, *The State of the Presidency* (Boston: Little, Brown, 1980), and Richard Pious, *The American Presidency* (New York: Basic Books, 1979). Theodore J. Lowi, *The Personal President: Power Invested, Promise Unfulfilled* (Ithaca, N.Y.: Cornell University Press, 1985) is a perceptive essay that draws on history to trace the contradictory pressures that confront modern presidents. Larry Sabato, *Goodbye to Good-Time Charlie: The American Governor Transformed, 1950–1975* (Lexington, Mass.: Lexington Books, 1978), and Robert H. Connery and Gerald Benjamin, *Rockefeller of New York: Executive Power in the State* (Ithaca, N.Y.: Cornell University Press, 1979), review the condition of modern governors.

James Q. Wilson, "The Rise of the Bureaucratic State," *Public Interest* 41 (1975): 77–103, is a historically based essay. A longer survey of the topic is Lawrence C. Dodd and Richard L. Schott, *Congress and the Administrative State* (New York: Wiley, 1979), which also has some historical perspective. Instructive examinations of administrative behavior are Eugene Lewis, *Public Entrepreneurship: Toward a Theory of Bureaucratic Power* (Bloomington: Indiana University Press, 1984); Aaron Wildavsky, *Speaking Truth to Power* (New York: Wiley, 1979); Martha W. Weinberg, *Managing the State* (Cambridge, Mass.: MIT Press, 1977), on Massachusetts; and David H. Rosenbloom, *Public Administration* (New York: Random House, 1986).

The examination of individual careers is a fruitful way of tracing the rise of bureaucratic power. The intoxicating appeal of power comes across clearly in Robert Caro's study of *The Power Broker: Robert Moses and the Fall of New York* (New York: Knopf, 1974), and in Richard Gid Powers, *Secrecy and Power: The Life of J. Edgar Hoover* (New York: Free Press, 1987), two outstanding biographies. On Hoover also see Athan Theoharis and John S. Cox, *The Boss: J. Edgar Hoover and the Great American Inquisition* (Philadelphia: Temple University Press, 1988). Other revealing examinations of administrators and their agencies are Thomas K. McCraw, *Prophets of Regulation* (Cambridge, Mass.: Harvard University Press, 1984); Bruce E. Seely, *Building the American Highway System: Engineers as Policy Makers* (Philadelphia: Temple University Press, 1987); and David Burnham, *A Law unto Itself: Power, Politics, and the I.R.S.* (New York: Random House, 1989). Joseph A. Califano Jr., *Governing American: An Insider's Report from the White House and the Cabinet* (New York: Simon and Schuster, 1981) contains a wealth of information about programs under HEW's charge and the pressures the secretary faced in administering them.

10. The Reagan Era and the Restrained Polity

Because many of the topics reviewed in this chapter overlap with subjects discussed previously, the reader is invited to consult the listings for chapters 5 (economic policy), 6 (income-assistance policy), 7 (civil rights), 8 (taxation and grants), and 9 (public officials). Theodore Caplow, *American Social Trends* (Fort Worth: Harcourt Brace Jovanovich, 1991), provides a tightly written overview of recent social, economic, and political trends. More detailed analyses of income patterns appear in Sheldon Danizer and Peter Gottschalk, eds., *Uneven Tides: Rising Inequality in America* (New York: Russell Sage Foundation, 1993). The dilemmas of contemporary governance are discussed in Samuel H. Beer, "Political Overload and Federalism," *Polity* 10 (1977): 5–17; Advisory Commission on Intergovernmental Relations, *A Crisis of Confidence and Competence* (Washington, D.C.: ACIR, 1980); Charles O. Jones, *The Trusteeship Presidency: Jimmy Carter and the U.S. Congress* (Baton Rouge: Louisiana State University Press, 1988); and Linda L. M. Bennett and Stephen E. Bennett, *Living with Leviathan: Americans Coming to Terms with Big Government* (Lawrence: University Press of Kansas, 1990).

An interesting essay on Reagan's background is Gary Wills, *Reagan's America* (New York: Penguin Books, 1988). National elections in the Reagan era are analyzed in Gerald Pomper and others, *The Election of 1980: Reports and Interpretations* (Chatham, N.J.: Chatham House, 1981); Pomper and others, *The Election of 1988* (Chatham, N.J.: Chatham House, 1989); and Everett Carl Ladd, "The 1988 Elections: Continuation of the Post–New Deal System," *Political Science Quarterly* 104 (1989): 1–18. Analyses of policy development during the restrained polity are Michael A. Bernstein, "The Contemporary American Banking Crisis in Historical Perspective," *Journal of American History* 80 (1994): 1382–96; Martha Derthick and Paul J. Quirk, *The Politics of Deregulation* (Washington, D.C.: Brookings Institution, 1985); D. Lee Bawden and John L. Palmer, eds., *The Reagan Record* (Cambridge, Mass.: Ballinger, 1984); Roger G. Noll, ed., *Regulatory Policy and the Social Sciences* (Berkeley: University of California Press, 1985); S. H. Danziger and K. E. Portnoy, eds., *The Distributional Aspects of Public Policy* (New York: St. Martin's Press, 1988); R. Kent Weaver, *Automatic Government: The Politics of Indexation* (Washington, D.C.: Brookings Institution, 1988); and Raymond Tatalovich and Byron Daynes, eds., *Social Regulatory Policy: Moral Controversies in American Politics* (Boulder, Colo.: Westview Press, 1988).

Two critiques of Reagan policies, the first from a liberal perspective and the second from conservative leanings, are John E. Schwarz, *America's Hidden Success: A Reassessment of Public Policy from Kennedy to Reagan: Revised* (New York: W. W. Norton, 1988), *esp.* ch. 6, and Kevin Phillips, *Boiling Point: Democrats, Republicans, and the Decline of Middle-Class Prosperity* (New York: Random House, 1993). Demetrios Caraley, "Washington Abandons the Cities," *Political Science Quarterly* 107 (1992): 1–30, implicitly faults the priorities of Reagan fiscal policy. Jeffrey R. Henig, "Privatization in the United States: Theory and Practice," *Political Science Quarterly* 104 (1989–1990): 649–70, reviews the intellectual origins and outcome of downsizing proposals during the Reagan years.

A splendid study of congressional policy making in the postwar era is David R. Mayhew, *Divided We Govern: Party Control, Lawmaking, and Investigations, 1946–1990* (New Haven, Conn.: Yale University Press, 1991). Dimensions of modern congressional behavior are illuminated in Kenneth A. Shepsle, "Representation and Governance: The Great Legislative Trade-off," *Political Science Quarterly* 103 (1988): 461–84; Gary C. Jacobson, "Deficit Cutting Politics and Congressional Elections," *Political Science Quarterly* 108 (1993): 375–402; and Christopher Howard, "The Hidden Side of the American Welfare State," *Political Science Quarterly* 108 (1993): 403–36. Paul E. Peterson, in "The Rise and Fall of Special Interest Politics," *Political Science Quarterly* 105 (1990–1991): 539–56, argues that Reagan budget cuts reduced special-interest group influence in Congress.

Like all Republican presidents since Coolidge, Reagan linked the limitation of Federal growth to greater decentralization of governance. On intergovernmental relations and political institutions in the period, see Timothy Conlan, *New Federalism: Intergovernmental Reform from Nixon to Reagan* (Washington, D.C.: Brookings Institution, 1988); Joseph F. Zimmerman, *Federal Preemption: The Silent Revolution* (Ames: Iowa State University Press, 1991); Advisory Commission on Intergovernmental Relations, *Readings in Federalism: Perspectives on a Decade of Change* (Washington, D.C.: ACIR, 1989); and Gerald Rosenberg, *The Hollow Hope: Can Courts Bring about Social Change?* (Chicago: University of Chicago Press, 1991). Three excellent analyses of how the states coped with modern demands on them are Advisory Commission on Intergovernmental Relations, *The Question of State Governmental Capability* (Washington, D.C.: ACIR, 1985); Richard P. Nathan, Fred C. Doolittle, and Associates, *Reagan and the States* (Princeton, N.J.: Princeton University Press, 1987); and Thomas R. Swartz and John E. Peck, eds., *The Changing Face of Fiscal Federalism* (Armonk, N.Y.: ˙ M. E. Sharpe, 1990). Also see the bibliography for chapter 11, below.

11. The Debate over "Big" Government

Conservatism and Liberalism in America

An overview of the evolution of conservatism since the 1930s is traced in Godfrey Hodgson, *The World Turned Right Side Up: A History of the Conservative Ascendancy in America* (Boston: Houghton Mifflin, 1996) and Donald T. Critchlow, *The Conservative Ascendancy: How the GOP Made Political History* (Cambridge, Mass.: Harvard University Press, 2011). The roots of the conservative revival is examined in Alan Brinkley, *The End of Reform: New Deal Liberalism in Recession and War* (New York: Knopf, 1995); Kim Phillips-Fein, *Invisible Hands: The Businessmen's Crusade Against the New Deal* (New York: W.W. Norton, 2009); and Mary C. Brennan, *Turning Right in the Sixties: The Conservative Capture of the GOP* (Chapel Hill: University of North Carolina Press, 1995).

Older surveys of conservatism in the United States that remain useful are Arthur A. Ekrich, *The Decline of American Liberalism* (New York: Atheneum, 1955); Clinton Rossiter, *Conservatism in America: The Thankless Persuasion* (New York: Vintage, 1962); and Ronald Lora, *Conservative Minds in America* (Chicago: Rand McNally, 1971). A classic statement on American political values is Louis Hartz, *The Liberal Tradition in America: An Interpretation of American Political Thought since the Revolution* (New York: Harcourt Brace, 1955). Michael Kammen, *A Machine That Would Go of Itself: The Constitution in American Culture* (New York, Knopf, 1986), offers a cultural analysis of constitutionalism. Price Fishback et al., eds., *Government and the American Economy: A New History* (Chicago: University of Chicago Press, 2007) interprets its subject from conservative perspectives.

The conservative perspective is expressed by some well-known spokespersons: Herbert Hoover, *Challenge to Liberty* (New York: Scribner, 1934); Friedrich A. Hayek, *The Road to Serfdom* (Chicago: University of Chicago Press, 1944); Barry Goldwater, *The Conscience of a Conservative* (Shepherdsville, Ky.: Victor Publishing, 1960); and Milton Friedman and Rose Friedman, *Free to Choose: A Personal Statement* (New York: Avon, 1980), a book that accompanied their TV series on PBS. Michael K. Deaver, ed., *Why I Am a Reagan Republican* (New York: William Morrow, 2005), contains short testimonials from fifty-five modern conservatives. Donald T. Critchlow and Nancy Maclean, *Debating the American Conservative Movement: 1945 to the Present* (Lanham, Md.: Rowman and Littlefield, 2009) contains selections from conservative authors. Charlotte A. Twight, *Dependent on D.C.: The Rise of Federal Control over the Lives of Ordinary Americans* (New York: Palgrave, 2002), dissects domestic policies from a libertarian perspective.

The liberal perspective: Steven Conn, ed., *To Promote the General Welfare: The Case for Big Government* (New York: Oxford University Press, 2012); E. J. Dionne, *Our Divided Political Heart: The Battle for the American Idea in an Age of Discontent* (New York: Bloomsbury, 2012); Paul Krugman, *The Accidental Theorist, and Other Dispatches from the Dismal Science* (New York: Norton, 1998). A handy summary of political ideologies is Vernon Van Dyke, *Ideology and Po-*

litical Choice (Chatham, N.J.: Chatham House Publishers, Inc., 1995). Also see the critiques of business policy, below.

Jules Tygiel, *Ronald Reagan and the Triumph of American Conservatism* (New York: Pearson Longman, 2006) offers a short yet perceptive interpretation of this seminal figure in modern conservatism. On George H. W. Bush, see Herbert S. Parmet, *George Bush: The Life of a Lone Star Yankee* (New York: Transaction, 1997). Kevin Phillips, *American Dynasty: Aristocracy, Fortune, and the Politics of Deceit in the House of Bush* (New York: Viking, 2004), offers an un-complimentary view of the two Bush presidents. On Clinton, see William C. Berman, *From the Center to the Edge: The Politics and Policies of the Clinton Presidency* (Lanham, Md.: Row-man and Littlefield, 2001). A short survey of the modern Republican party is Michael Schaller and George Rising, *The Republican Ascendancy: American Politics, 1968–2001* (Wheeling, Ill.: Harlan Davidson, 2002). A fine analysis of the rise of fierce partisanship is Ronald Brown-stein, *The Second Civil War: How Extreme Partisanship Paralyzed Washington and Polarized America* (New York: Penguin Press, 2007), as is Benjamin Ginsberg and Martin Shefter, *Politics by Other Means: Politicians, Prosecutors, and the Press from Watergate to White Water*, 3rd ed. (New York: Norton, 2002). Harold W. Stanley and Richard G. Niemi, *Vital Statistics on American Politics* (Washington, D.C.: Congressional Quarterly, biennial) is an invaluable source of political information.

Economic and Social Trends

On the slump in incomes, see Wallace C. Peterson, *Silent Depression: Twenty-five Years of Wage-Squeeze and Middle-Class Decline* (New York: W. W. Norton, 1994); Barry Bluestone and Bennett Harrison, *Growing Prosperity* (Berkeley: University of California Press, 2000). Hendrick Smith, *Who Stole the American Dream?* (New York: Random House, 2012), blames business, Wall Street, and the Radical Right for undermining the economic stability of the middle class. On corporate practices, see David M. Gordon, *Fat and Mean: The Corporate Squeeze of Working Americans and the Myth of "Managerial Downsizing"* (New York: Free Press, 1996) and Alan S. Binder, *After the Music Stopped: The Financial Crisis, the Recession, and the Work Ahead* (New York: Penguin, 2013). For an overview of trends in the twentieth-century economy, see Stanley L. Engerman and Robert E. Gallman, *The Cambridge Economic History of the United States*, vol. 3 (New York: Cambridge University Press, 2000), especially ch. 17, W. Elliot Brownlee, "The Public Sector." Michael A. Bernstein, *A Perilous Progress: Economists and Public Purpose in Twentieth-Century America* (Princeton, N.J.: Princeton University Press, 2001) charts the influence of Keynesianism from its triumph to irrelevance.

Public Policy

Valuable references for policy developments are Congressional Quarterly Press, *Congress and the Nation* (quadrennial volumes coordinated with presidential administrations), CQ's on-line suite of reports on political and national policy activities, and *Vital Statistics on American Politics, 2011–2012*, online, and earlier editions, which covers many subjects; the Coun-cil of State Governments, *The Book of the States* (biennial); U.S. Census Bureau, *Statistical Abstract of the United States* (annual through 2012). For trends in federal finances, see *Budget of the U.S. Government: Historical Tables* (annual). Informative studies of public finance in-clude Iwan Morgan, *The Age of Deficits: Presidents and Unbalanced Budgets from Jimmy Carter to George W. Bush* (Lawrence: University Press of Kansas, 2009), and Michael Nelson and John L. Mason, *Governing Gambling: Politics and Policy in State, Tribe, and Nation* (New York: Century Foundation Press, 2001). On the judiciary, see Melvin I. Urofsky and Paul Finkel-man, *A March of Liberty*, vol. 2 (New York: Oxford University Press, 2011), and John A. Ferejohn and Barry R. Weingast, eds., *The New Federalism: Can the States Be Trusted?* (Stanford, Calif.: Hoover Institute Press, 1997).

Critiques of policy toward business, labor, and the economy include Robert Kuttner, *Everything for Sale: The Virtues and Limits of Markets* (New York: Knopf, 1998); David Cay Johnston, *Free Lunch: How the Wealthiest Americans Enrich Themselves at Government Expense* (New York: Portfolio, 2007); Smith, *American Dream;* and Clyde Prestowitz, *The Betrayal of American Prosperity* (New York: Free Press, 2010). Louis Uchitelle, *The Disposable American: Layoffs and Their Consequences* (New York: Vintage Books, 2007), looks at the personal side of corporate downsizing. On social policy, see Theda Skocpol, *Boomerang: Health Care Reform and the Turn against Government* (New York: Norton, 1997); Martha A. Derthick, *Up in Smoke: From Legislation to Litigation in Tobacco Politics* (Washington, D.C.: CQ Press, 2012). On defense and national security, see Jeremy Scahill, *Blackwater: The Rise of the World's Most Powerful Mercenary Army* (New York: Nation Books, 2007); Richard A Clarke, *Against All Enemies: Inside America's War on Terror* (New York: Free Press, 2004); Julian E. Zelizer, *Arsenal of Democracy: The Politics of National Security–From World War II to the War on Terror* (New York: Basic Books, 2010).

Supplement to the Revised and Updated Edition, Chapters 1–10.

American Political Development

Balogh, Brian. *A Government Out of Sight: The Mystery of National Authority in Nineteenth Century America.* New York: Cambridge University Press, 2009.

Flanagan, Maureen. *Seeing with their Hearts: Chicago Women and the Vision of the Good City, 1871–1933.* Princeton, N.J.: Princeton University Press, 2002.

Keller, Morton. *America's Three Regimes: A New Political History.* New York: Oxford University Press, 2007.

Maier, Charles. *Among Empires: American Ascendancy and Its Predecessors.* Cambridge, Mass.: Harvard University Press, 2006.

Novak, William J. "The Myth of the 'Weak' American State." *American Historical Review* 113, no. 3 (June 2008): 752–772.

Orren, Karen, and Stephen Skowronek. *The Search for American Political Development.* New York: Cambridge University Press, 2004.

Porter, Bruce D. *War and the Rise of the State.* New York: Free Press, 1994.

Sklar, Kathrun Kish. *Florence Kelley and the Nation's Work: The Rise of Women's Political Culture, 1930–1900.* New Haven, Conn.: Yale University Press, 1995.

Sylla, Richard, et al., eds. *The State, the Financial System, and Economic Modernization.* New York: Cambridge University Press, 1999.

Urofsky, Melvin I., and Paul Finkelman. *A March of Liberty: A Constitutional History of the United States.* New York: Oxford University Press, 2011.

Wiebe, Robert. *Who We Are: A History of Popular Nationalism.* Princeton, N.J.: Princeton University Press, 2001.

———. *Self-Rule: A Cultural History of American Democracy.* Chicago: University of Chicago Press, 1995.

The Federal Government, the States, and Federalism

Carpenter, Daniel P. *The Forging of Bureaucratic Autonomy: Networks and Policy Innovation in Executive Agencies, 1862–1928.* Princeton, N.J.: Princeton University Press, 2001.

Harrison, Robert. *Congress, Progressive Reform, and the New American State.* New York: Cambridge University Press, 2004.

Mayhew, David R. *America's Congress: Actions in the Public Sphere, James Madison through Newt Gingrich.* New Haven, Conn.: Yale University Press, 2000.

Robertson, David Brian. *Federalism and the Making of America.* New York: Routledge, 2012.

Sanders, Elizabeth. *Roots of Reform: Farmers, Workers, and the American State, 1877–1917.* Chicago: University of Chicago Press, 1999.

Teaford, Jon C. *The Rise of the States: Evolution of American State Government.* Baltimore: Johns Hopkins University Press, 2002.

Unger, Nancy C. *Fighting Bob La Follette: The Righteous Reformer.* Chapel Hill: University of North Carolina Press, 2000.

Policy Studies

Campbell, Ballard C. *American Wars.* New York: Facts On File, 2012.

Koistinen, Paul A. C. *Mobilizing for Modern War: The Political Economy of American Warfare, 1865–1919.* Lawrence: University Press of Kansas, 1997.

Melosi, Martin. *The Sanitary City: Urban Infrastructure from Colonial Times to the Present.* Baltimore: Johns Hopkins University Press, 2000.

O'Connor, Alice. *Poverty Knowledge: Social Science, Social Policy, and the Poor in Twentieth-Century U. S. History.* Princeton, N.J.: Princeton University Press, 2002.

Rodgers, Daniel T. *Atlantic Crossings: Social Politics in a Progressive Age.* Cambridge, Mass.: Harvard University Press, 1998.

The Law

Friedman, Lawrence M. *American Law in the 20th Century.* New Haven, Conn.: Yale University Press, 2002.

Freyer, Tony. *Hugo Black and the Dilemma of American Liberalism.* New York: Longman, 2008.

Hall, Kermit L. *The Magic Mirror: Law in American History.* New York: Oxford University Press, 1989.

Kammen, Michael. *A Machine That Would Go of Itself: The Constitution in American Culture.* New York: Knopf, 1986.

Novak, William J. *The People's Welfare: Law and Regulation in Nineteenth-Century America.* Chapel Hill: University of North Carolina Press, 1996.

Powe, Lucas A., Jr. *The Warren Court and American Politics.* Cambridge, Mass.: Harvard University Press, 2000.

INDEX

abortion ruling *(Roe v. Wade)*, 198, 268
Adair v. U.S., 31
Adams, John, 22, 287
administration: emergence of professional, 25, 72–74, 76, 78, 81, 84; in government appointments, 71–73, 249, 254–55; and public-sector expansion, 60
administrative complexity: of grants-in-aid, 154, 156 57, 216, 223 26, 269, 274; as measure of growth, 40, 42–43, 114, 118, 136, 157; of social security, 171, 263
affirmative action, 70, 202–203, 266, 270
African Americans: discrimination against, 30, 32; failure of integration into mainstream, 114, 183–85, 190–91; outmigration from rural South, 53, 178, 190–92; and public-sector expansion, 60, 183–85. *See also* civil rights
Afghanistan, 251, 268, 303, 307, 310, 316
Agricultural Act of 1933, 39, 116–17
Agricultural Experiment Station Act (Hatch Act), 4, 56–57, 61, 91, 99, 115, 223
Agriculture, aid to, 105, 114–19, 150–51. *See also* Agricultural Act of 1933; Agricultural Experiment Station Act (Hatch Act); Department of Agriculture (USDA)
Aid to Families with Dependent Children (AFDC), 164, 173–78, 176 (table), 181–82, 211, 301, 313

American Association of Retired Persons (AARP), 58, 181, 278
American Farm Bureau Federation, 58, 116
American Medical Association, 58, 73, 84, 277
American Trucking Association, 120
antistatism, 5, 66–68; modern antigovernment movement, 266, 285–93, 297, 317. *See also* republicanism
Arlington, MA, 12, 21, 24, 26 27, 77, 79 81, 83, 99, 142, 145, 148–49, 266, 283
authorities, public, 232–33, 259. *See also* Moses, Robert

Baby boomers, 142, 219, 231, 267, 311
ballot reform, 71–72
banking reform, 82, 90, 105, 107–108, 256, 269, 279, 314; Wall Street Reform and Consumer Protection Act (2010), 314
Beard, Charles, 36
Bellamy, Edward, 65–66
big business, 23, 35, 67, 71, 128, 138, 140–41, 149–51, 236, 298; Chamber of Commerce, 58, 298; Corporate Fraud Act (2002), 314; and debate on private power, 65–66, 69; and monopolies, 89–90. *See also* chapter 5; New Deal; railroad regulation
Birmingham, AL, 13, 52, 81, 85, 189, 202
boards and commissions (in states), establishment of, 24–25, 73, 74, 82, 84–85

BALLARD C. CAMPBELL is professor of history and public policy at Northeastern University in Boston. He holds a BS in political science from Northwestern University (Evanston, Illinois), an MA in History from Northeastern University, and a PhD in history from the University of Wisconsin, Madison. He has written or edited six books, including *American Wars* (2012); *American Disasters: 201 Calamities That Shook the Nation* (2008); and *Representative Democracy: Public Policy and Midwestern Legislatures in the Late Nineteenth Century* (1980), as well as numerous articles and book chapters. Professor Campbell is past president of the Society for Historians of the Gilded Age and Progressive Era (2002–2004) and the New England Historical Association (2008–2009), and has served as a Distinguished Lecturer for the Organization of American Historians. Professor Campbell lives in Portland, Maine.